THE ZEITGEIST MOVEMENT
DEFINED

REALIZING A NEW TRAIN OF THOUGHT

"The tremendous and still accelerating development of science and technology has not been accompanied by an equal development in social, economic, and political patterns...We are now...only beginning to explore the potentialities which it offers for developments in our culture outside technology, particularly in the social, political and economic fields. It is safe to predict that...such social inventions as modern-type Capitalism, Fascism, and Communism will be regarded as primitive experiments directed toward the adjustment of modern society to modern technology"
- Dr. Ralph Linton

www.thezeitgeistmovement.com

The Zeitgeist Movement Defined
Realizing a New Train of Thought
1st Edition, January, 2014

Acknowledgments:
The material authored here is a product of many forms of contribution,
specifically the research of The Zeitgeist Movement's expanding lecture team.
While not all figures relevant could be credited below (alphabetical order), an
enormous thanks extends to all others not listed who have contributed news,
sources, tips and other research.

Compiled & Edited by
Ben McLeish
Matt Berkowitz
Peter Joseph

Thanks to:

Andrés Delgado
Bakari Pace
Brandon Kristy
Brandy Hume
Douglas Mallette
Eva Omori
Federico Pistono

Gilbert Ismail
James Phillips
Jason Lord
Jen Wilding
Miguel Oliveira
Sharleen Bazeghi
Tom Williams

If you would like to help in translating this text,
please contact TZM's linguistics team:
LinguisticTeam@gmail.com

ISBN-13:
978-1495303197

ISBN-10:
1495303195

Contents

-PREFACE-

*The outcome of any serious research can only be to make two
questions grow where only one grew before.*[1]
-Thorstein Veblen

Origin of the name

"The Zeitgeist Movement" (TZM) is the identifier for the social
movement described in the following essays. The name has no
relevant historical reference to anything culturally specific and is not to
be confused or associated with anything else known before with a
similar title. Rather, the title is based upon the semantic meaning of
the very terms, explicitly.

The term "zeitgeist" is defined as the "general intellectual,
moral and cultural climate of an era." The term "movement" simply
implies "motion" or change. Therefore, *The Zeitgeist Movement* is an
organization that urges change in the dominant intellectual, moral and
cultural climate of the time.

Document Structure

The following text has been prepared to be as concise and yet
comprehensive as possible. In form, it is a series of essays, ordered by
subject in a manner that works to support a broader *context*. While
each essay is designed to be taken on its own merit in evaluation, the
true context resides in how each issue works to support a larger *train
of thought* with respect to the most efficient organization of human
society.

It will be noticed by those who read through these essays in a
linear fashion that a fair amount of overlap exists with certain ideas or
subjects. This is deliberate as such repetition and emphasis is
considered helpful given how foreign some of the concepts might seem
to those with no prior exposure to such material.

Also, since only so much detail can be afforded to maintain
comprehension given the gravity of each subject and how they
interrelate, great effort has been made to source relevant third party
research throughout each essay via footnotes, allowing the reader to
follow through with further study as the interest arises.

The Organism of Knowledge

As with any form of presented research we are dealing with *serially
generated data composites*. Observation, its assessment,
documentation and integration with other knowledge, existing or
pending, is the manner by which all distinguishable ideas come to
evolve.

This continuum is important to understand with respect to the
way we think about what we believe and why, for information is always
separate in its merit from the person or institution communicating or

---

1   *The Evolution of the Scientific Point of View,* Thorstein Veblen, University of
California Chronicle, 1908

representing. Information can only be evaluated correctly through a systematic process of comparison to other *physically verifiable* evidence as to its proof or lack thereof.

Likewise, this continuum also implies that there can be no empirical "origin" of ideas. From an epistemological perspective, knowledge is mostly culminated, processed and expanded through communication amongst our species. The individual, with his or her inherently different life experience and propensities, serves as a custom-processing *filter* by which a given idea can be morphed. Collectively, we individuals comprise what could be called a *group mind*, which is the larger order social processor by which the efforts of individuals ideally coalesce. The traditional method of data transfer through literature, sharing books from generation to generation, has been a notable path of this group mind interaction, for example.[2]

Isaac Newton perhaps put this reality best with the statement: "If I have seen further than others, it is by standing upon the shoulders of giants."[3] This is brought up here in order to focus the reader on the critical consideration of data, not a supposed "source", as there actually is no such thing in an empirical sense. It is only in the temporal, traditional patterns of culture, such as with literary credits in a textbook for future research reference, is such a recognition technically relevant.

There is no statement more erroneous than the declaration that "this is my idea". Such notions are byproducts of a material culture that has been reinforced in seeking physical rewards, usually via money, in exchange for the illusion of their "proprietary" creations. Very often an ego association is culminated as well where an individual claims prestige about their "credit" for an idea or invention.

Yet, that is not to exclude gratitude and respect for those figures or institutions that have shown dedication and perseverance towards the expansion of knowledge itself, nor to diminish the necessity of importance of those who have achieved a skilled, specialized "expert" status in a particular field. The contributions of brilliant thinkers and engineers such as R. Buckminster Fuller, Jacque Fresco, Jeremy Rifkin, Ray Kurzweil, Robert Sapolsky, Thorstein Veblen, Richard Wilkinson, James Gilligan, Carl Sagan, Nikola Tesla, Stephen Hawking and many, many more researchers, past and present, are quoted and sourced in this text and serve as part of the larger *data composite* you are about to read. Great gratitude is also expressed here towards all dedicated minds that are working to contribute to an improving world.

---

2   In Carl Sagan's work "Cosmos", he stated with respect to the destruction of the Library of Alexandria, noted as the largest and most significant library of the ancient world: "It was as if the entire civilization had undergone some self-inflicted brain surgery, and most of its memories, discoveries, ideas and passions were extinguished irrevocably." *Cosmos,* Carl Sagan, Ballantine Books, New York, 1980, Chapter XIII, p279
3   *The Correspondence of Isaac Newton,* Volume 1, edited by HW Turnbull, 1959, p416

That understood, "The Zeitgeist Movement" claims no origination of any idea it promotes and is best categorized as an activist/educational institution that works to amplify a *context* upon which existing/emerging scientific findings may find a concerted social imperative.

Websites and Resources

The following 10 websites are officially related to The Zeitgeist Movement's global operations:

-Main Global Hub:
http://www.thezeitgeistmovement.com

This is the main website and hub for TZM related actions/events/updates.

-Global Chapters Hub:
http://www.tzmchapters.net/

This is the main global hub for chapter information and materials. It includes maps, a chapter's tool kit and more.

-Global Blog:
http://blog.thezeitgeistmovement.com/

This is the official blog which allows submissions of editorial style essays.

-Global Forum:
http://www.thezeitgeistmovementforum.org/

This is the official forum for members to discuss projects and share ideas from across the world.

-Zeitgeist Media Project:
http://zeitgeistmediaproject.com/

The Media Project website hosts and links to various audio/visual/literary expressions create by TZM members. Users donate their work for posting and it is often used as a resource *toolkit* for flyer graphics, video presentations, logo animations and the like.

-ZeitNews:
http://www.zeitnews.org/

ZeitNews is a news style service that contains articles relating to socially relevant advancements in science and Technology.

-Zeitgeist Day ("ZDay") Global:

http://zdayglobal.org/

This site becomes active annually to facilitate our "Zday" global event, which occurs in March of each year.

-Zeitgeist Media Festival:
http://zeitgeistmediafestival.org/

This site becomes active annually to facilitate our "Zeitgeist Media Festival", which occurs in autumn of each year.

-Global Redesign Institute:
http://www.globalredesigninstitute.org/

The Global Redesign Institute is a virtual graphic interface "think tank" project which uses map/data models to express direct technical changes in line with TZM's train of thought in various regions.

General Social Networks
TZM Global on Twitter:
http://twitter.com/#!/tzmglobal

TZM Global on Facebook:
http://www.facebook.com/tzmglobal

TZM Global Youtube:
http://www.youtube.com/user/TZMOfficialChannel

PART I: INTRODUCTION

-OVERVIEW-

Neither the great political and financial power structures of the world, nor the specialization-blinded professionals, nor the population in general realize that...it is now highly feasible to take care of everybody on earth at a "higher standard of living than any have ever known". It no longer has to be you or me. Selfishness is unnecessary and henceforth unrationalizable as mandated by survival. War is obsolete.[4]
-R. Buckminster Fuller

About
Founded in 2008, The Zeitgeist Movement (TZM) is a sustainability advocacy group that operates through a network of regional chapters, project teams, public events, media expressions and charity operations. TZM's activism is explicitly based on *non-violent* methods of communication with the core focus on *educating* the public about the true *root sources* of many common personal, social and ecological problems today, coupled with the vast *problem solving* and *humanity improving potential* science and technology has now enabled, but yet goes unapplied due to barriers inherent in the current, established social system.

While the term "activism" is correct by its exact meaning, TZM's awareness work should not be misconstrued as relating to culturally common, traditional "activist protest" actions such as we have seen historically. Rather, TZM expresses itself through targeted, rational educational projects that work not to impose, dictate or blindly persuade, but to set in motion a *train of thought* that is *logically self-realizing* when the causal considerations of "sustainability"[5] and "public health"[6] are referenced from a scientific perspective.

However, TZM's pursuit is still very similar to traditional civil rights movements of the past in that the observations reveal the truly

---

4   Source: *Critical Path,* R. Buckminster Fuller, St. Martin's Press, 1981, Introduction, xxv

5   The term "sustainability", generally defined "as the ability to be sustained, supported, upheld, or confirmed" (http://dictionary.reference.com/browse/sustainability) is often today commonly referenced/understood within an environmental science context. TZM's context extends farther, however, including the notion of cultural or behavioral sustainability, which considers the merit of belief systems in general, and their less obvious causal consequences.

6   The term "public health", generally defined as "the science and practice of protecting and improving the health of a community, as by preventive medicine, health education, control of communicable diseases, application of sanitary measures, and monitoring of environmental hazards" (http://dictionary.reference.com/browse/public+health?s=t) is used in this text as a basis of measure for the physical, psychological and hence sociological well-being of a societies' people over time. This is to be considered the ultimate barometer of the success or failure of an applied social system.

unnecessary *oppression* inherent in our current social order, which structurally and sociologically restricts human well-being and potential for the vast majority of the world's population, not to mention stifles broad improvement in general due to its established methods.

For instance, the current social model, while perpetuating enormous levels of corrosive economic inefficiency in general, as will be described in further essays, also intrinsically supports one economic group or "class" of people over another, perpetuating technically unnecessary imbalance and high relative deprivation. This could be called "economic bigotry" in its effect and it is no less insidious than discrimination rooted in gender, ethnicity, religion, creed or the like.

However, this inherent bigotry is really only a part of a larger condition that could be termed "structural violence",[7] illuminating a broad spectrum of *built in* suffering, inhumanity and deprivation that is simply accepted as normality today by an uninformed majority. This context of violence stretches much farther and deeper than many tend to consider. The scope of how our socioeconomic system unnecessarily diminishes our public health and inhibits our progress today can only be recognized clearly when we take a more detached technical or *scientific* perspective of social affairs, bypassing our traditional, often blinding familiarities.

The relative nature of our awareness often falls victim to assumptions of *perceived normality* where, say, the ongoing deprivation and poverty of over 3 billion people[8] might be seen as a "natural", inalterable social state to those who are not aware of, for example, the amount of food actually produced in the world, where it goes, how it is wasted or the technical nature of efficient and abundant food production possibilities in the modern day.

This *unseen violence* can be extended to cultural memes[9] as well where social traditions and their psychology can, without direct malicious intent, create resulting consequences that are damaging to a human being. For instance, there are religious cultures in the world

---

7   The term "structural violence" is commonly ascribed to Johan Galtung, which he introduced in the article "Violence, Peace, and Peace Research" (*Journal of Peace Research*, Vol. 6, No. 3, 1969, pp. 167-191) It refers to a form of violence where some social structure or social institution harms people by preventing them from meeting their basic needs. It was expanded upon by other researchers, such as criminal psychiatrist Dr. James Gilligan, who makes the following distinction between "behavioral" and "structural" violence: "The lethal effects of structural violence operate continuously, rather than sporadically, whereas murders, suicides...wars and other forms of behavioral violence occur one at a time." (*Violence,* James Gilligan, G.P. Putnam, 1996, p192)

8   Source: *Poverty Facts and Stats,* Global Issues / 2008 World Bank Development Indicators (http://www.globalissues.org/article/26/poverty-facts-and-stats)

9   A "meme" is an idea, behavior, style, or usage that spreads from person to person within a culture (http://www.merriam-webster.com/dictionary/meme)

that opt out of any form of common medical treatment.[10] While many might argue the moral or ethical parameters of what it means for a child in such a culture to die of a common illness that could have been resolved if modern scientific applications were allowed, we can at least agree that the death of such a child is really being caused not by the disease at that point, but by the sociological condition that disallowed the application of the solution.

As a broader example, a great deal of social study has now been done on the subject of "social inequality" and its effects on public health. As will be discussed more so in further essays, there is a vast array of physical and mental health problems that appear to be born out of this condition, including propensities towards physical violence, heart disease, depression, educational deficiency and many, many other detriments that have a truly *social consequence* which can affect us all.[11]

The bottom line here is that when we step back and consider newly realized understandings of causality that are clearly having negative effects on the human condition, but go unabated unnecessarily due the pre-existing traditions established by culture, we inevitably end up in the context of *civil rights* and hence *social sustainability*. This new civil rights movement is about the sharing of human knowledge and our technical ability to not only solve problems, but to facilitate a scientifically derived social system that actually optimizes our potential and well-being. Anything less will create unnecessary imbalance and social destabilization and constitute what could be considered a *hidden form of oppression.*

So, returning to the broad point, TZM works not only to create awareness of such problems and their true root causes (and hence logic for resolution), it also works to express the incredible potential we have, beyond such direct problem solving, to greatly improve the human condition in general, solving problems which, in fact, have not yet even been realized.[12] This is initiated by embracing the very nature of *scientific reasoning* where the establishment of a near empirical *train of thought* takes precedence over everything else in importance. A train of thought by which societal organization as a whole can find a more accurate context for *sustainability* and *efficiency* on a scale never before seen, through an active recognition (and application) of the scientific method.

---

10 Reference: *Very religious parents causing suffering to sick kids, says report* (http://uk.lifestyle.yahoo.com/religious-parents-causing-suffering-sick-kids-says-report-115021612.html)
11 Reference: *The Spirit Level,* Richard Wilkinson and Kate Pickett, Penguin, March 2009
12 More on this issue will be presented in a following essay titled *Sourcing Solutions*

Focus

TZM's broad actions could be summarized as to *diagnose, educate and create.*

Diagnose:
Diagnosis is "the identification of the nature and cause of anything." To properly diagnose the causal condition of the vast social and ecological problems common to modern culture is not merely to complain about them or criticize the actions of people or particular institutions, as is frequent today. A true diagnosis *must seek out the lowest causal denominator possible and work at that level for resolution.*

The central problem is that there is often what could be called a *truncated frame of reference,* where shortsighted, misdiagnosis of given consequences persist. For instance, the traditional, established solution to the reformation of human behavior for many so-called "criminal acts" is often punitive incarceration. Yet, this says nothing about the deeper motivation of the "criminal" and why their psychology led to such acts to begin with.

At that level, such a resolution becomes more complex and reliant upon the *synergetic* relationship of their physical and cultural culmination over time.[13] This is no different than when a person dies of cancer, as it isn't really the cancer that kills them in the literal sense, as the cancer itself is the product of *other forces.*

Educate:
As an educational movement that operates under the assumption that knowledge is the most powerful tool we have to create lasting, relevant social change in the global community, there is hence nothing more critical than the quality of one's personal education and their ability to *communicate* such ideas effectively and constructively to others.

TZM is not about following a rigid text of static ideas. Such confined, narrow associations are typical of religious and political cults, not the recognition of *emergence* that underscores the "anti-establishment"[14] nature of TZM. TZM does not impose in this sense. Rather, it works to make an open-ended *train of thought* become realized by the individual, hopefully empowering their independent ability to understand its relevance on their own terms, at their own pace.

---

13 The correlation between human behavior (in this context behavior of a socially offensive nature as determined by the laws of society) and the environmental influence of a person's upbringing/life experience is now without debate. A related term to note is the "bio-psycho-social" nature of the human organism.

14 The term "anti-establishment" is usually used in a context implying opposition to an existing, established group. Used here, the context is more literal in that TZM itself works to not "institutionalize" itself as a rigid entity but rather be understood as more of a gesture; a symbol of a new manner of thought or worldview that simply has no boundaries.

Furthermore, education is not only an imperative for those unfamiliar with this *train of thought* and the *application set*[15] related, but also for those who already subscribe to it. Just as there is no "utopia", there is no final state of understanding.

Create:
While certainly related to the need to adjust *human values* through education so the world's people understand the need for such social changes, TZM also works to consider how a new social system, based on *optimum economic efficiency,*[16] would appear and operate in detail, given our current state of technical ability.

Programs such as the Global Redesign Institute,[17] which is a digital think tank that works to express how the core societal infrastructure could unfold based on our current state of technology, working to combine that *technical capacity* with the *scientific train of thought* so as to calculate the most efficient technical infrastructure possible for any given region of the world, is one example.

It is worth briefly noting that TZM's advocated "governance" approach, which has little semblance to the current manner of governance known today or historically, originates out of a multi-disciplinary bridging of various proven methods for maximized optimization, unified through a counter-balancing *systems* approach that is designed to be as adaptive as possible to new, emerging improvements over time.[18]

As will be discussed at length, the only possible reference that could be considered "most complete" at any given time is one that takes into account the largest interacting observations (system) tangibly relevant. This is the nature of the cause and effect synergy that underscores the technical basis for a truly sustainable economy.

Natural Law/Resource-Based Economy
Today, various terms exists to express the general logical basis for a more scientifically oriented social system in different circles, including the titles "Resource-Based Economy" or "Natural Law Economy." While these titles are historically referential and somewhat arbitrary overall, the title "Natural Law/Resource-Based Economy" (NLRBE) will be utilized here since it has the most concrete semantic basis.[19]

---

15 The phrases "train of thought" and "application set" are paired. The former refers to the scientific reasoning (sustainability and efficiency principles) which arrive at a given conclusion, while the latter refers to temporal methods of action, such as technological tools, which invariably change over time.

16 This will be expanded upon more so in part III.

17 Reference: Official website: http://www.globalredesigninstitute.org

18 See part III for more on the subject of "government"

19 The term "Resource-Based Economy" can be literally interpreted as 'an economy based on resources'. This has historically drawn confusion in that one could argue that all "economies", by definition, are "based" on "resources". The term itself also has a strong association to an organization called The Venus Project which claims to have originated the term & idea,

A *Natural Law/Resource-Based Economy* is defined as "an adaptive socioeconomic system actively derived from direct physical reference to the governing scientific laws of nature."

Overall, the observation is that through the use of socially targeted research and tested understandings in science and technology, we are now able to *logically arrive* at societal approaches which could be profoundly more effective in meeting the needs of the human population. We are now able to dramatically increase public health, better preserve the habitat, create a general material abundance, while also strategically reduce or eliminate many common social problems present today which are sadly considered inalterable by many due to their cultural persistence.

Train of Thought

Many figures or groups have worked to create temporally advanced technological applications, working to apply current possibilities to this *train of thought* in order to enable new efficiencies and problem solving, such as Jacque Fresco's "City Systems"[20] or R. Buckminster Fuller's Dymaxion House.[21]

Yet, as obviously important as this applied engineering is, it is still critical to remember that all specific technological applications can *only be transient* when the evolution of scientific knowledge and its emerging technological applications are taken into account. In other words, all current applications of technology tend to become obsolete over time.

Therefore, what is left can only be a *train of thought* with respect to the underlying causal scientific principles. TZM is hence loyal to this *train of thought*, not figures, institutions or temporal technological advancements. Rather than follow a person or design, TZM follows this *self-generating premise of understanding* and it hence operates in a non-centralized, holographic manner, with this *train of thought* as the origin of influence for action.

Superstition to Science

A notable pattern worth mentioning is how the evolution of mankind's understanding of itself and its habitat also continues to expand away from older ideas and perspectives which are no longer supported due to the constant introduction of new, schema altering information. A

---

seeking at one time to trademark the name (http://tdr.uspto.gov/search.action?sn=77829193). The term "Natural Law/Resource-Based Economy" is considered more complete here not only to avoid such possible associative confusion but also because of the more semantic accuracy of the term itself, since it more clearly references nature's physical law system and processes rather than just planetary resources.

20 Reference: *The Best That Money Can't Buy,* Jacque Fresco, Global Cybervisions, 2002, Chapter 15
21 Reference: Dymaxion House information: http://en.wikipedia.org/wiki/Dymaxion_house

worthy notion to note here is *superstition*, which, in many circumstances, can be viewed as a category of belief that once appeared to be adequately supported by experience/perception but can no longer be held as viable due to new, conflicting data.

For example, while traditional religious thought might seem increasingly implausible to more people today than ever in the West, due to the rapid growth in information and general literacy,[22] the *roots* of religious thought can be traced to periods where humans could justify the validity and accuracy of such beliefs given the limited understanding they had of their environment in those early times.

This pattern is apparent in all areas of understanding, including modern "academia". Even so-called "scientific" conclusions that, again, with the advent of new information and updated tests, often cannot be held as valid anymore,[23] are still commonly defended due to their mere inclusion in the current cultural tradition.

Such "established institutions", as they could be called, often wish to maintain permanence due to reasons of ego, power, market income or general psychological comfort. This problem is, in many ways, at the core of our social paralysis.[24] So, it is important to recognize this pattern of transition and realize how critical being vulnerable really is when it comes to belief systems, not to mention coming to terms with the rather dangerous phenomenon of "established institutions" which are culturally programmed and reinforced to seek *self-preservation* rather than evolve and change.

---

22 The inverse relationship of literacy/knowledge accumulation to superstitious belief is clear. According to the United Nations' Arab Human Development Reports, less than 2% of Arabs have access to the Internet. Arabs represent 5% of the world's population and yet produce only 1% of the world's books, most of them religious. According to researcher Sam Harris: "Spain translates more books into Spanish each year than the entire Arab world has translated into Arabic since the ninth century." It is axiomatic to assume that the growth of the Islamic Religion in Arab Nations is secured by a relative lack of outside information in those societies.

23 A Nobel Prize for what is known as "lobotomy" was awarded to Portuguese neurologist Egas Moniz in 1949. Today, it is considered a barbaric and ineffective procedure. (http://www.npr.org/templates/story/story.php?storyId=4794007)

24 The financial support inherently needed in the perpetuation of a given business, "for profit" or even so-called "not for profit", sets up a dissonance between the business's sold product or service and the actual necessity or viability of that product or service over time. In fact, the obsolescence of any given product/service, which implies often the obsolescence of the producing business or corporation, appears inevitable as new technical advancements emerge. The consequence is a perpetual tendency to stifle new ideas and inventions that would disturb or override pre-existing ventures of established institutions, resulting in a loss of income. A cursory glance at the state of technological possibility today, whilst also considering the question as to why those improvements have not been immediately made, illuminates the paralyzing nature of income requiring institutions.

11

Tradition to Emergence

The perceptual clash between our *cultural traditions* and our ever growing database of *emergent knowledge* is at the core of what defines the "zeitgeist" as we know it and a long-term review of history shows a slow grind out of superstitious cultural traditions and assumptions of reality as they heed to our newly realized benchmark of emergent, *scientific causality*. This is what TZM represents in its broadest philosophical context: A movement of the cultural zeitgeist itself into new, verifiable and more optimized understandings and applications.

Hence, while society certainly has witnessed vast and accelerating changes in different areas of awareness and practice, such as with our vast material technology today, it appears our *social system* is still long behind. Political persuasion, market economics, labor-for-income, perpetual inequality, nation states, legal assumptions and many other staples of our current social order continue to be largely accepted as normality by the current culture, with little more than their persistence through time as evidence of their value and empirical permanence.

It is in this context that TZM finds its most broad imperative: changing the social system. Again, there are many problem solving technical possibilities for personal and social progress today that continue to go unnoticed or misunderstood.[25] The ending of war, the resolution of poverty, the creation of a material abundance unseen in history to meet human needs, the removal of most crime as we know it, the empowerment of *true personal freedom* through the removal of pointless and/or monotonous labor, and the resolution of many environmental threats, are but a few of the calculated possibilities we have when we take our *technical reality* into account.

However, again, these possibilities are not only largely unrecognized, they are also literally *restricted* by the current social order for the implementation of such problem solving efficiency and prosperity stands in direct opposition to the very mechanics of how our current social system is operating at the core level.[26]

Therefore, until the socioeconomic tradition and its resulting *social values* are challenged and updated to present day understandings; until the majority of the human population understands the basic, underlying *train of thought* technically needed to support human sustainability and public health, as derived from the rigor of objective scientific investigation and validation; until much of the baggage of prior false assumptions, superstition, divisive loyalties and other socially unsustainable, conflict generating, cultural hindrances are overcome - all the life improving and problem resolving possibilities we now have at hand will remain largely dormant.

The real revolution is the *revolution of values*. Human society appears centuries behind in the way it operates and hence what it

---

25 Reference: "Zeitnews", a science and technology website related to TZM, is recommended (http://www.zeitnews.org/)

26 See part II for supporting details regarding this statement.

values. If we wish to progress and solve the mounting problems at hand and, in effect, reverse what is an accelerating decline of our civilization in many ways, we need to change the way we think about ourselves and hence the world we inhabit. The Zeitgeist Movement's central task is to work to bring this value shift to light, unifying the human family with the basic perspective that we all share this small planet and we are all bound by the same natural order laws, as realized by the method of science.

This *common ground* understanding extends much farther than many have understood in the past. The symbiosis of the human species and the synergistic relationship of our place in the physical world confirm that we are not separate entities in any respect. The new societal awakening must show a working social model that is *arrived at* from this inherent logic if we expect to survive and prosper in the long term. We can align or we can suffer. It is up to us.

-THE SCIENTIFIC WORLDVIEW-

Almost every major systematic error which has deluded men for thousands of years relied on practical experience. Horoscopes, incantations, oracles, magic, witchcraft, the cures of witch doctors and of medical practitioners before the advent of modern medicine, were all firmly established through the centuries in the eyes of the public by their supposed practical successes. The scientific method was devised precisely for the purpose of elucidating the nature of things under more carefully controlled conditions and by more rigorous criteria than are present in the situations created by practical problems.[27]
-Michael Polanyi

Generally speaking, the evolution of human understanding can be seen as a move from *surface observations,* processed by our limited five physical senses, "intuitively" filtered through the educational framework & value characteristics of that period of time, to the technique of objective measuring and self-advancing methods of analysis which work to *arrive at* (or calculate) conclusions through testing and retesting proofs, seeking validation through the *benchmark* of *scientific causality* – a causality that appears to comprise the physical characteristics of what we call "nature" itself.

The "natural laws" of our world exist whether we choose to recognize them or not. These inherent rules of our universe were around long before human beings evolved a comprehension to recognize them and while we can debate as to exactly how accurate our interpretation of these laws really is at this stage of our intellectual evolution, there is enough reinforcing evidence to show that we are, indeed, bound by static forces that have an inherent, measurable, determining logic.

The vast developments and predictive integrity found in mathematics, physics, biology and other scientific disciplines proves that we as a species are slowly understanding the processes of nature and our growing, inventive capacity to emulate, accentuate or repress such natural processes confirms our progress in understanding it. The world around us today, overflowing with material technology and life-altering inventions, is a testament as to the integrity of the scientific process and what it is capable of.

Unlike historical traditions, where a certain stasis exists with what people believe, as is still common in religious type dogma today, this recognition of "natural law" includes characteristics which deeply challenge the assumed stability of beliefs which many hold sacred. As will be expanded upon later in this essay in the context of "emergence", the fact is, there simply cannot exist a singular or static intellectual conclusion with respect to our perception and knowledge except, paradoxically, with regard to that very underlying *pattern of uncertainty* regarding such change and adaptation itself.

This is part of what could be called a *scientific worldview.* It is

---

27 Source: *Personal Knowledge: Towards a Post-Critical Philosophy,* Michael Polanyi, University of Chicago Press, p.183

one thing to isolate the techniques of scientific evaluation for select interests, such as the logic we might use in assessing and testing the structural integrity of a house design we might build, and another when the universal integrity of such physically rooted, causal reasoning and validation methods are applied to all aspects of our lives. Albert Einstein once said "the further the spiritual evolution of mankind advances, the more certain it seems to me that the path to genuine religiosity does not lie through the fear of life, and the fear of death, and blind faith, but through striving after rational knowledge".[28]

While cynics of Science often work to reduce its integrity to yet another form of "religious faith", demean its accuracy as "cold" or "without spirituality" or even highlight consequences of applied technology for the worst, such as with the creation of the atomic bomb (which, in actuality, is an indication of a distortion of *human values* rather than engineering), there is no ignoring the incredible power this approach to understanding and harnessing reality has afforded the human race. No other "ideology" can come close in matching the predictive and utilitarian benefits this method of reasoning has provided.

However, that is not to say active cultural denial of this relevance is not still widespread in the world today. For example, when it comes to theistic belief, there is often a divisive tendency that wishes to elevate the human being above such "mere mechanics" of the physical reality. The implied assumption here is usually that we humans are "special" for some reason and perhaps there are forces, such as an intervening "God", that can override natural laws at will, making them less important than, say, ongoing obedience to God's wishes, etc. Sadly, there still exists a great human conceit in the culture which assumes, with no verifiable evidence, that humans are separate from all other phenomena and to consider ourselves connected or even a product of natural, scientific forces is to demean human life.

Concurrently, there is also a tendency for what some call "metamagical"[29] thinking which could be considered a *schizotypal* kind of personality disorder where fantasy and mild delusion helps reinforce false assumptions of causality on the world, never harnessing the full rigor of the scientific method. Science requires testing and replication of a result for it to be validated and many beliefs of seemingly "normal" people today exist far outside this requirement.

Apart from traditional religions, the cultural concept of "new age"[30] is also commonly associated with this type of superstitious

---

28 Source: As quoted in *All the Questions You Ever Wanted to Ask American Atheists*, by Madalyn Murray O'Hair, Amer Atheist Press, 1986

29 Stanford University Behavioral Biology Professor, Dr. Robert Sapolsky is likely most notable with his use of the term "MetaMagical". His work is recommended: http://benatlas.com/2009/12/robert-sapolsky-on-metamagical-schizotypal-thinking/

30 The term *New Age* is generally defined as "A broad movement characterized by alternative approaches to traditional Western culture, with an interest in

thought. While it is extremely important that we as a society are aware of the uncertainty of our conclusions in general and hence must keep a creative, vulnerable state of mind to all postulations, the validation of those postulations can only come through measurable consistency, not wishful thinking or esoteric fascination.

Such un-validated ideas and assumptions pose a frame of reference that is often secured by "faith"[31] not *reason*, and it is difficult to argue the merit of faith with anyone since the rules of faith inherently refuse argument itself. This is part of the quandary within which human society exists today: do we simply believe what we have been traditionally taught by our culture or do we question and test those beliefs against the physical reality around us to see if they hold true?

Science is clearly concerned with the latter and holds nothing sacred, always ready to correct prior false conclusions when new information arises. To take such an inherently uncertain, yet still extremely viable and productive approach to one's day to day view of the world, requires a very different sensitivity – one that embodies *vulnerability*, not certainty.

In the words of Prof. Frank L. H. Wolfs (Department of Physics and Astronomy, University of Rochester, NY): "It is often said in science that theories can never be proved, only disproved. There is always the possibility that a new observation or a new experiment will conflict with a long-standing theory."[32]

Emergence

So, at the heart of the scientific method is skepticism and vulnerability. Science is interested in the *closest approximation to the truth* it can find and if there is anything science recognizes explicitly, it is that virtually everything we know will be revised over time as new information arises.

Likewise, what might seem far-fetched, impossible or even "superstitious" upon its first culmination might very well prove to be a useful, viable understanding in the future once validated for integrity. The implication of this constitutes an *emergence of thought,* or even an emergence of "truth", if you will. A cursory examination of history shows an ever-changing range of behaviors and practices based upon ever updating knowledge and this humbling recognition is critical for human progress.

---

spirituality, mysticism..."

31 Carl Sagan was notable for confirming the definition of faith as "belief without evidence" .
32 Source: *Introduction to the Scientific Method,* Frank L. H. Wolfs (http://teacher.nsrl.rochester.edu:8080/phy_labs/AppendixE/AppendixE.htm l)

Symbiosis

A second point deeply characteristic of the *scientific worldview* worth bringing up in this regard has to do with the *symbiotic* nature of things, as we know them. Largely dismissed as common sense today by many, this understanding holds profound revelations for the way we think about our world, our beliefs, our conduct and ourselves.

The term "symbiotic" is typically used in the context of interdependent relationships between biological species.[33] However our context of the word is broader, relating to the *interdependent relationship of everything*. While early, intuitive views of natural phenomena might have looked upon, say, the manifestation of a "tree" as an independent entity, seemingly self-contained in its illusion of separation, the truth of the matter is that a tree's life is entirely dependent on seemingly "external" input forces for its very culmination and existence.[34]

The water, sunlight, nutrients and other needed interactive "external" attributes to facilitate the development of a tree is an example of a *symbiotic or synergetic* relationship. However, the scope of this symbiosis has become much more revealing than we have ever known in the past and it appears the more we learn about the dynamics of our universe, the more immutable its interdependence.

The best concept to embody this notion is that of a "system".[35] The term "tree" is really a reference to a *perceived system*. The "root", "trunk", "branches", "leaves" and other such attributes of that tree could be called "sub-systems". Yet, the "tree" itself is *also* a sub-system, it could be said, of, perhaps, a "forest", which itself is a sub-system of other larger, encompassing phenomena such as an "ecosystem". Such distinctions might seem trivial to many but the fact is, a great failure in human awareness has been not to fully respect the scope of the "Earth system" and how each sub-system plays a relevant role.

The term "categorical systems"[36] could even be used here to describe *all systems*, seemingly small or large, because such language distinctions are ultimately arbitrary. These perceived systems and the words used to reference them are simply human conveniences for communication. The fact is, there appears to be only *one* possible system, as organized by natural law, which can be legitimately referenced since *all* the systems we perceive and categorize today can

---

33 Source: Dictionary.com (http://dictionary.reference.com/browse/symbiotic)
34 The term "external" in this context is framed as relative to a perceived object. The broader point here is that there is no such thing as "external" or "internal" in the context of larger order systems.
35 A "system" is defined as: "a set of things working together as parts of a mechanism or an interconnecting network." It is worth noting up front the importance of this concept as the relevance of the "system" or "systems theory" will be a returning theme with respect to what frame of reference actually supports true human sustainability in our habitat.
36 This term is a variation on the more common notion of "categorical thinking" which is thinking by assigning people or things to categories and then using the categories as though they represented something in the real world.

only be *sub-systems*. We simply cannot find a truly closed system anywhere. Even the "Earth system", which intuitively appears autonomous, with the Earth floating about the void of space, is entirely reliant on the sun, the moon and likely many, many other symbiotic/synergistic factors we have yet to even understand for its defining characteristics.

In other words, when we consider the interactions that link these perceived "categorical systems" together, we find a *connection of everything* and, on a societal level, this system interaction understanding is at the foundation of likely the most viable perspective for true human sustainability.[37] The human being, like a tree or the Earth, again intuitively *appears* self-contained. Yet, without, for example, oxygen to breathe, one will not survive. This means the *human system* requires interaction with an *atmospheric system* and hence a system of oxygen production and since the process of photosynthesis accounts for the majority of the atmospheric oxygen we breathe, it is to our advantage to be aware of what affects this particular system, and work to harmonize our social practices with it.

When we witness, say, pollution of the oceans or the rapid deforestation of Earth, we often forget how important such phenomena really are to the integrity of the *human system*. In fact, there are so many examples of environmental disturbances perpetuated by our species today due to a truncated awareness of this symbiotic cause and effect that links all known categorical systems, volumes could be dedicated to the crisis. At any rate, the failure to recognize this *connectedness* is a fundamental problem and once this *principle of interacting systems* is fully understood, many of our most common practices today will likely appear grossly ignorant and dangerous in future hindsight.

Sustainable Beliefs

This brings us to the level of *thought and understanding* itself. As noted prior, the very language system we use isolates and organizes elements of our world for general comprehension. Language itself is a system based upon categorical distinctions, which we associate to our perceived reality. However, as needed as such a mode of identification and organization is to the human mind, it also inherently implies false division.

Given that foundation, it is easy to speculate as to how we have grown so accustomed to thinking and acting in inherently divisive ways and why the history of human society has been a history of imbalance and conflict.[38] It is on this level that such physical systems

---

37 This will be expanded upon in greater detail in part III of this text.
38 The Neolithic Revolution is a notable marker for a dramatic change in social operation and human relationships as civilization went from foraging and hunting – living in subservience to natural processes – to a profound ability to control agriculture for food and create tools/machines to ease human labor. It could be argued that human society has not been mature enough to handle this ability and the perpetuation of fear and scarcity led to hoarding,

we have discussed come into relevance with *belief and thought systems.*[39]

While the notion of "sustainability" might be typically associated with technical processes, eco-theory and engineering today, we often forget that our *values and beliefs* precede all such technical applications. Therefore, we need our cultural orientation to be sustainable to begin with and that awareness can only come from a valid recognition of the laws of nature to which we are bound.

Can we measure the integrity of a belief system? Yes. We can measure it by how well its principles align with scientific causality, based upon the *feedback* resulting. If we were to compare outcomes of differing belief systems seeking a common end,[40] how well those perspectives accomplish this end can be measured and hence these systems can then be qualified and ranked against each other as to their merit or lack thereof.

As will be explored in detail later in this work, the central belief system comparison here is between the "market economy" and the aforementioned "Natural Law/Resource-Based Economy." At the core of these systems is essentially a conflicting belief about causality and possibility and the reader is challenged to make objective judgments about how well each perspective may accomplish certain common end human goals.

That noted and in the context of this essay, specifically the points about emergence & symbiosis, it could be generalized that any belief system that (a) does not have built into it the allowance for that entire belief system itself to be altered or even made completely obsolete due to new information, is an unsustainable belief system; and (b) any belief system that supports isolation and division, supporting the integrity of one segment or group over another is also an unsustainable belief system.

Sociologically, having a *scientific worldview* means being

---

privatization, nation "gangs" and other divisive tendencies for group self-preservation on various levels.

39 For philosophical clarity, it could be argued that all outcomes of human perceptions are projected – even the laws of nature themselves. However, this doesn't change the efficacy that has been seen with respect to the immense control and understanding we have through the method of science.

40 The notion of the "common end" or "common ground" will be repeated in this text and it is a critical awareness to average the needs, intents and consequences of the human being. A central premise of what TZM is advocating is that human beings are more alike than they are different as we share the same basic quantifiable needs and reactions. In many ways this is the unifying attribute that could comprise what is called "human nature" and, as will be described more so in later essays, human beings indeed have shared, predictable, common reactions to positive and negative influences both psychological and physiological. Therefore, the intelligent, humane organization of a society is required to take this into account directly for the sake of public health – something the current monetary-market system does not do.

19

willing and able to adapt both as an individual and as a civilization when new understandings and approaches emerge that can better solve problems and further prosperity. This worldview likely marks the greatest shift in human comprehension in history. Every modern convenience we take for granted is a result of this method whether recognized or not, as the inherent, self-generating, mechanistic logic appears to be universally applicable to all known phenomena.

While many in the world still attribute causality to gods, demons, spirits and other non-measurable "faith" based views, a new period of *reason* appears to be on the horizon where the emerging scientific understanding of ourselves and our habitat is challenging the traditional, established frameworks we have inherited from our less informed ancestors. No longer is the "technical"[41] orientation of science demeaned to mere gadgets and tools. The true message of this worldview is about the very philosophy by which we *need* orient our lives, values and social institutions.

So, as will be argued in further essays, the social system, its economic premise, along with its legal and political structure, has become arguably linked to a condition of *faith* in the manner it is now perpetuated. The market and monetary-driven system of economy, for example, is argued to be based on little more than a set of now outdated, increasingly inefficient assumptions, no different than how early humans falsely assumed the world was flat, demons caused sickness, or that the constellations in the sky were fixed, static, two-dimensional, tapestry-like constructs. There are enormous parallels to be found with traditional religious faith and the established, cultural institutions we assume to be valid and "normal" today.

Just as the church in the Middle Ages held absolute power in Europe, promoting loyalties and rituals which most would find absurd or even insane today, those a number of generations from now will likely look back at the established practices of our current time and think the exact same thing.

---

41 As will be prolific in this text, the term "technical", while virtually synonymous with "scientific", is employed to better express the *causal nature* of all existing phenomena – even including human behavior and psychology/sociology itself. Another central premise of what TZM is advocating is that problem resolution and the manifestation of potential is a "technical" evaluation and this approach, being applied to all societal attributes, is at the core of the new social model advocated.

-SOURCING SOLUTIONS-

A new type of thinking is essential if mankind is to survive
and move toward higher levels.[42]
– Albert Einstein

A central consideration inherent to TZM's perspective on societal change for the better regards understanding "progress" itself. There appear to be two basic angles to consider when it comes to personal or social progress: *manifesting potential and problem resolution.*

Potential & Resolution
Manifesting potential is simply the improvement of a condition that was not considered prior to be in a problematic state. An example would be the ability to improve human athletic performance in a particular field through targeted strengthening, diet, refining techniques and other means that were simply not known before.

Problem resolution, on the other hand, is the overcoming of an issue that has currently recognized detrimental consequences and/or limitations to a given affair. A general example would be the discovery of a medical cure for an existing, debilitating disease so that said disease no longer poses harm.

However, taken in the broad view, there is a distinct overlap with these two notions when the nature of knowledge development is taken into account. For example, an "improvement" to a given condition, a practice that then becomes normalized and common in the culture, can also potentially be part of a "problem" in a familiar or different context, which requires resolution in the event new information as to its inefficiency is found or new advancements make it obsolete by comparison.

For example, human air transportation, which is fairly new in society, expanded transport efficiency greatly upon its application. However, at what point will modern air transport be seen more as a "problem" due to its inefficiency by comparison to another method?[43] So, efficiency is *relative* in this sense as only when there is an expansion of knowledge that what was once considered the "best" approach becomes "inferior".

This seemingly abstract point is brought up to communicate the simple fact that every single practice we consider normal today has *built into it* an inevitable inefficiency which, upon new developments in science and technology, will likely produce a "problem" at some point in the future when compared to newer, emerging potentials. This is the nature of change and if the scientific patterns of history reflect anything, it is that knowledge and its applications continue to evolve

---

42 Source: *Atomic Education Urged by Einstein*, New York Times, May 25th 1946
43 A notable modern example is new transport technology such as "Maglev" transport that uses less energy and moves substantially faster than commercial airlines http://www.et3.com/

and improve, generally speaking. So, back to the seemingly separate issues of *manifesting potential* and *problem resolution,* it can hence be deduced that all problem resolutions are *also* acts of manifesting potential and vice versa.

This also means that the actual *tools* used by society for a given purpose are always transient. Whether it is a medium of transportation, medical practices, energy production, the social system itself, etc.[44] These practices are all manifest/resolutions with respect to human necessity and efficiency, based upon the ever-changing state of understanding we have/had at the time of their creation/evolution.

Root Purpose & Root Cause
Therefore, when it comes to thinking about any act of invention or problem solving, we must get as close to the *root purpose (manifest)* or the *root cause (problem)* as possible, respectively, to make the most accurate assessment for action. Just as tools and techniques for potential are only as viable as the understanding of their foundational purpose, actions toward problem resolution are only as good as the understanding of the root cause. This might seem obvious, but this awareness is often missing in many areas of thought in the world today, *especially when it comes to society.* Rather than pursuing such a focus, most social decisions are based around *traditional customs* that have inherent limits.

A simple example of this is the current method of human incarceration for so called "criminal behavior". For many, the solution to offensive forms of human behavior is to simply remove the individual from society and *punish* them. This is based on a series of assumptions that stretch back millennia.[45]

Yet, the science behind human behavior has changed tremendously with respect to understanding causality. It is now common knowledge in the social sciences that most acts of "crime" would likely not occur if certain basic, supportive environmental conditions were set for the human being.[46] Putting people in prisons is not actually resolving anything with respect to the causal problem. It is more of a mere "patch", if you will, which only temporarily stifles some effects of the larger problem.[47]

---

44 Again, this reality is embodied by the term "application set".
45 Reference: *Violence: Our Deadly Epidemic and Its Causes,* Dr. James Gilligan, 1996
46 The 'Merva-Fowles' study, done at the University of Utah in the 1990s, found powerful connections between unemployment and crime. They based their research on 30 major metropolitan areas with a total population of over 80 million. Their findings found that a 1% rise in unemployment resulted in: a 6.7% increase in Homicides; a 3.4% increase in violent crimes; a 2.4% increase in property crime. During the period from 1990 to 1992, this translated into: 1,459 additional Homicides; 62,607 additional violent crimes; 223,500 additional property crimes. (Merva & Fowles, *Effects of Diminished Economic Opportunities on Social Stress,* Economic Policy Institute, 1992)
47 Reference: Ben McLeish lecture: "Out of the Box: Prisons"

Another example, while seemingly different than the prior but equally as "technical", is the manner by which most think about solutions to common domestic problems, such as traffic accidents. What is the solution to a situation where a driver makes a mistake and haphazardly changes lanes, only to impact the vehicle next to it, causing an accident? Should there be a huge wall between them? Should there be better training? Should the person simply have his or her driver's license revoked so they cannot drive again? It is here, again, where the notion of *root cause* is often lost in the narrow frames of reference commonly understood by culture.

The root cause of the accident can only partially be the question of integrity of the driver with the more important issue being the lack of integrity of the technology and infrastructure being used. Why? - Because, in part, human fallibility is historically acknowledged and immutable.[48] So, just as early vehicles did not have driver and/or passenger side "airbags" common today, which now reduce a large number of injuries that existed in the past,[49] the same logic should be applied to the system of vehicle interaction itself, taking into account new technical possibilities for increased safety, to compensate for inevitable human error.

Just as the airbag was developed years ago as the evolution of knowledge unfolded, today there is technology that enables automated, *driverless* vehicles which can not only detect every necessary element of the street needed to operate with accuracy, the vehicles themselves can detect each other, making collision almost impossible.[50] This is the current state of such a solution when we consider the root cause and root purpose, overall.

Yet, as advanced as that solution may seem, especially given the roughly 1.2 million people who unnecessarily die in automobile accidents each year,[51] this thought exercise may still be incomplete if we continue to extend the context with respect to the core goals. Perhaps there are other inefficiencies that relate to the transport infrastructure and beyond that need to be taken into account and overcome. Perhaps, for example, the use of individual automobiles, regardless of their safety, has other inherent problems that can only be logically resolved by the removal of the automobile application itself. Perhaps in a city, with an expanding mobile population, such independent vehicle transport becomes unnecessarily cumbersome,

---

(www.thezeitgeistmovement.com)

48 Reference: *Human error: models and management*, James Reason, 2000 (http://www.ncbi.nlm.nih.gov/pmc/articles/pmc1117770/)

49 A 1996 NHTSA study found the fatality reduction benefit of airbags for all drivers at an estimated 11 percent.
(http://www.nhtsa.gov/cars/rules/regrev/evaluate/808470.html)

50 Source: *Google Engineer Claims Its Driverless Cars Could Save A Million Lives Every Year*, Blake Z. Rong (http://www.autoguide.com/auto-news/2011/04/google-engineer-claims-its-driverless-cars-could-save-a-million-lives-every-year.html)

51 Source: *Car Accident Statistics* (http://www.car-accidents.com/pages/stats.html)

slow and generally inefficient.[52]

The more viable solution in this circumstance might become the need for a unified, integrated mass transit system that can increase speed, reduce energy use, reduce resource use, and reduce pollution along with many other related issues to the effect that using automobiles in such a condition then becomes part of an emerging *problem*. If the goal of a society is to do the "correct" and hence sustainable thing, reducing threats to humans and the habitat, ever increasing efficiency, a dynamic, self-generating logic unfolds with respect to our technical possibility and design approaches.

Our Technical Reality

Of course, the application of this type of problem solving is far from limited to such physical examples. Is politics as we know it the best means to address our social woes? Does it address root causes by its very design? Is money and the market system the most optimized method for sustainable progress, problem resolution and the manifesting of economic potential? What does our modern state of science and technology have to contribute in the realm of understanding cause and purpose on the societal level?

As further essays will denote in great detail, these understandings create a natural, clear train of thought with respect to how much better our world could be if we simply follow the logic created via *the scientific method* of thought to fulfill our *common goal* of human sustainability. The one billion people starving on this planet are not doing so because of some immutable natural consequence of our physical reality. There is plenty of food to go around.[53] It is the social system, which has its own outdated, contrived logic, that perpetuates this social atrocity, along with countless others.

It is important to point out that TZM is not concerned with promoting "patches" as its ultimate goal, which, sad to say, is what the vast majority of activist institutions on the planet are currently doing.[54]

---

52 A slow, general shift, even in modern commercial society, from "ownership" to "access" is beginning to find favor today.
(http://gigaom.com/2011/11/10/airbnb-roadmap-2011/)

53 Major international organizations have stated statistically that there is enough food for everyone and that starvation is not caused by a lack of resources. (http://www.wfp.org/hunger/causes) In combination with efficiency improvements which will be noted more so in Part III, the possibly for absolute global food abundance of the highest nutrient quality is also possibly today.

54 This comment is not meant to demean any well-meaning social institution working to help within the bounds of the current socioeconomic method. However, as will be described more so in Part II, the current social model inherently restricts a vast amount of possible prosperity/problem solving due to its very design and hence activist and social institutions which avoid this reality and can only be working to help "patch" problems, not fix them, since they originate from the social system itself. A common example is charity organizations that wish to provide food to the poor. These organizations are not usually addressing *why* those people are poor to begin

We want to promote the largest order, highest efficiency set of solutions available at a given time, aligned with natural processes, to improve the lives of all, while securing the integrity of our habitat. We want everyone to understand this "train of thought" clearly and develop a *value* identification with it. In the end, there is no single solution – only the near empirical natural law reasoning that arrives at solutions and purpose.

---

with and hence are not truly working to resolve the root problem(s).

-LOGIC vs. PSYCHOLOGY-

We do not act rightly because we have virtue or excellence, but we
rather have those because we have acted rightly.[55]
-Aristotle

A powerful yet often overlooked consequence of our environmental
vulnerability to adapt to the existing culture is that our very identity
and personality is often linked to the institutions, practices, trends and
hence values we are born into and exist in. This psychological
adaptation and inevitable familiarity creates a *comfort zone* which,
over time, can be painful to disrupt, regardless of how well reasoned
the data standing to the contrary of what we believe may be.

In fact, the vast majority of objections currently found against
The Zeitgeist Movement, specifically points made with respect to
solutions and hence change, appear to be driven by narrow frames of
reference and emotional bias more than intellectual assessment.
Common reactions of this kind are often singular propositions that,
rather than critically addressing the actual premises articulated by an
argument, serve to dismiss them outright via haphazard associations.
The most common classification of such arguments are "projections"[56]
and it becomes clear very often that such opponents are actually more
concerned with *defending their psychological identity* rather than
objectively considering a new perspective.[57]

Mind Lock
In a classic work by authors Cohen and Nagel titled "An Introduction to
Logic and The Scientific Method", this point is well made with respect
to the process of logical evaluation and its independence from human
psychology.

"The weight of evidence is not itself a temporal event, but a
relation of implication between certain classes or types of
propositions...Of course, thought is necessary to apprehend such

---

55 Source: *The Story of Philosophy: The Lives and Opinions of the World's
Greatest Philosophers*, Will Durant, 1926
56 Sigmund Freud was first to make famous the idea of Psychological
Projection, defined as 'a psychological defense mechanism where a person
subconsciously denies his or her own attributes, thoughts, and emotions,
which are then ascribed to the outside world, usually to other people.'
However, the use of the term is more general in this context, reflecting the
simple notion of assuming to understand an idea based on a false or
superficial relationship to prior understandings - usually in a defensive
posture for dismissal of validity.
57 The term "cognitive pathology" is a suggested descriptor of this
phenomenon. A common characteristic is 'circular reasoning' where a belief
is justified by merely re-referencing the belief itself. For example, to ask a
Theist why they believe in God, a common answer might be "Faith". To ask
why they have "Faith" often results in a response like "because God rewards
those who have Faith". The causality orientation is truncated and self-
referring.

implications...however [that] does not make physics a branch of psychology. The realization that logic cannot be restricted to psychological phenomenon will help us to discriminate between our science and rhetoric - conceiving the latter as the art of persuasion or of arguing so as to produce the feeling of certainty. Our emotional dispositions make it very difficult for us to accept certain propositions, no matter how strong the evidence in their favor. And since all proof depends upon the acceptance of certain propositions as true, no proposition can be proved to be true to one who is sufficiently determined not to believe it."[58]

The term "mind lock" has been coined by some philosophers[59] with respect to this phenomenon, defined as 'the condition where one's perspective becomes self-referring, in a closed loop of reasoning'. Seemingly empirical presuppositions frame and secure one's worldview and anything contradictory coming from the outside can be blocked or rejected, often even subconsciously. This reaction could be likened to the common physical reflex to protect oneself from a foreign object moving towards your person – only in this circumstance the "reflex" is to defend one's *beliefs*, not body.

While such phrases as "thinking outside the box" might be common rhetoric today in the activist community, seldom are the foundations of *our way of thinking* and the integrity of our most *established institutions* challenged. They are, more often than not, considered to be "givens" and assumed inalterable.

For example, in the so-called democracies of the world, a "president", or the equivalent, is a common point of focus with respect to the quality of a country's governance. A large amount of attention is spent toward such a figure, his perspectives and actions. Yet, seldom does one step back and ask: "Why do we have a president to begin with?" "How is his/her power as an institutional figure justified as an optimized manner of social governance?" "Is it not a contradiction of terms to claim a democratic society when the public has virtually no *real* say with respect to the actions of the president once he or she is elected?"

Such questions are seldom considered as people tend, again, to adapt to their culture without objection, assuming it is "just the way it is". Such static orientations are almost universally a result of *cultural tradition* and, as Cohen and Nagel point out, it is very difficult to communicate a new, challenging idea to those who are *"sufficiently determined not to believe it"*.

Such traditional presuppositions, held as empirical, are likely a root source of personal and social retardation in the world today. This phenomenon, coupled with an educational system that constantly reinforces such established notions through its institutions of "academia", further seals this cultural inhibition and compounds the

---

58 *Logic and The Scientific Method*, Cohen and Nagel, Harcourt, 1934, p.19
59 Reference: *The Cancer Stage of Capitalism*, John McMurtry, Pluto Press, 1999, Chapter 1

hindrance to relevant change.[60]

While the scope of this tendency is wide with respect to debate, there are two common *argumentative fallacies* worth noting here as they constantly come up with respect to the *application-set* and *train of thought* promoted by TZM. Put in colorful terms, these tactics comprise what could be called a "value war"[61] which is waged, consciously or not, by those who have vested emotional/material interest in keeping things the same, opposing change.

The "Prima Facie" Fallacy

The first is the "prima facie" association. This simply means "upon first appearance"; "before investigation".[62] This is by far the most common type of objection. A classical case study is the common claim that the observations and solutions presented by TZM are simply rehashed "Marxist communism".

Let's briefly explore this as an example. Referencing "The Communist Manifesto"[63] Marx and Engels present various observations with respect to the evolution of society, specifically "class war", inherent structural relationships regarding "capital", along with a general logic as to how the social order will transition through "revolution" to a stateless, classless system, in part, while also noting a series of direct social changes, such as the "centralization of the means of communication and transport in the hands of the state", "equal liability of all to labor." and other specifics. Marx creates players in the schema he suggests like the ongoing battle between the "bourgeoisie and proletarians", expressing contempt for the inherent exploitation, which he says is essentially rooted in the idea of "private property". In the end, the accumulated goal in general is in seeking a "stateless and classless society".

On the surface, reformations proposed in TZM's promoted solutions might *appear* to mirror attributes of "Marxism" if one was to completely ignore the underlying reasoning. The idea of a society "without classes", "without universal property", and the complete

---

60 Criticism here of "academia" is not to be confused with its standard definition, meaning a 'community of students and scholars engaged in higher education and research.' The context here is the inhibiting nature of "schools" of thought which all too often evolve to create an ego unto itself where conflicting data is ignored or haphazardly dismissed. Also, there is a risk common to this mode of thought where "theory" and "tradition" take prominence over "experience" and "experiment" very often, perpetuating false conclusions.

61 Reference: *Value Wars: The Global Market Versus the Life Economy: Moral Philosophy and Humanity,* John McMurtry, Pluto Press, 2002

62 Source: Dictionary.com
(http://dictionary.reference.com/browse/prima+facie)

63 Written by Karl Marx and Friedrich Engels in 1848 this text is widely considered the definitive ideological expression of Marxist communism. "Communism" is said to be the practical implementation of "Marxism". View Online: (http://www.marxists.org/archive/marx/works/1848/communist-manifesto/index.htm)

redefinition of what comprises the "state" might, on the surface, show confluence by the mere gestures themselves, especially since western academia commonly promotes a "duality" between "communism" and "capitalism" with the aforementioned character points noted as the core differences. However, the actual *train of thought* to support these *seemingly* similar conclusions is quite different.

TZM's advocated benchmark for decision-making is not a *Moral Philosophy*,[64] which, when examined at its root, is essentially what Marxist philosophy was a manifestation of. TZM is not interested in the poetic, subjective and arbitrary notions of "a fair society", "guaranteed freedom", "world peace", or "making a better world" simply because it sounds "right", "humane" or "good". Without a *technical framework* that has a direct physical referent to such terms, such moral relativism serves little to no long-term purpose.

Rather, TZM is interested in *scientific application*, as applied to *societal sustainability*, both *physical* and *cultural*.[65] As will be expressed in greater detail in further essays, the method of science is not restricted in its application within the "physical world"[66] and hence the social system, infrastructure, educational relevance and even understanding human behavior itself, all exist within the confines of scientific causality. In turn, there is a natural feedback system built into physical reality which will express itself very clearly in the context of what "works" and what doesn't over time,[67] guiding our conscious adaptation.

---

64 Defined as 'the branch of philosophy dealing with both argument about the content of morality and meta-ethical discussion of the nature of moral judgment, language, argument, and value.'
(http://www.thefreedictionary.com/moral+philosophy)

65 The argument that science is not a philosophy is certainly open to semantics and interpretation but the point being made here is that notions of "right and wrong" and other "ethical" distinctions common to philosophy take on a very different light in the scientific context as it has more to do with utility and balance than mere concepts of "morality" as it is classically defined. In the view of Science, human behavior is best aligned with the inherent causality discovered in the natural world, validated by testing, building inference and logical associations to justify human actions as "appropriate" to a given purpose. Again, this is always ambiguous on some level and likely the most accurate context of philosophy as related to science is as a precursor to validation during investigation and experimentation.

66 The term "physical world" is often used to differentiate between the "mental" processes of the human mind or sociological type phenomena, and the physical environment that exists outside of the cognitive processes of human perception. In reality there is nothing outside the "physical world" as we know it, as there is to be found no concrete example where causal relationships are simply voided.

67 Feedback from the Environment could be said to be the "correction mechanism" of nature as it relates to human decisions. A simple example would be the industrial production of chemicals that produce negative retroactions when released into the environment, showing incompatibility with environmental needs for life-support - such as was the case with CFCs and their effect on Ozone Depletion.

Marxism is not based on this "calculated" worldview at all, even though there might be some scientifically based characteristics inherent. For example, the Marxist notion of a "classless society" was to overcome the capitalist originating "inhumanity" imposed on the working class or "proletariat".

TZM's advocated train of thought, on the other hand, sources advancements in human studies. It finds, for example, that *social stratification*, which is inherent to the capitalist/market model, to actually be a form of *indirect violence* against the vast majority as a result of the evolutionary psychology we humans naturally posses.[68] It generates an unnecessary form of human suffering on many levels, which is *destabilizing* and, by implication, *technically unsustainable*.

Another example is TZM's interest in removing *universal property*[69] and setting up a system of "shared access". This is often quickly condemned to the Marxist idea of "abolishing private property". However, generally speaking, the Marxist logic relates the existence of private property to the perpetuation of the "bourgeois" and their ongoing exploitation of the "proletariat". He states in the Manifesto: "The distinguishing feature of Communism is not the abolition of property generally, but the abolition of bourgeois property."

TZM's advocated logic, on the other hand, relates the fact that the practice of universal, individual ownership of goods is *environmentally inefficient, wasteful and ultimately unsustainable* as a practice. This supports a restrictive system behavior and a great deal of unnecessary deprivation, and hence crime is common in societies with an unequal distribution of resources.

At any rate, such "prima facie" allegations are very common and many more could be expressed. However, it is not the scope of this section to discuss all alleged connections between Marxism and TZM's advocated *train of thought.* In the end, the debate is essentially *pointless* as to argue such a correlation is to simply ignore the true *purpose* and *merit* of the societal conception itself.

The "Straw-Man" Fallacy
The second argumentative fallacy has to do with the *misrepresentation of a position*, deliberate or projected, commonly referred to as a "straw-man".[70] When it comes to TZM, this usually has to do with

---

68 Reference: *The Spirit Level*, Kate Pickett & Richard Wilkinson, Bloomsbury Press, 2011
69 This concept will be explored more in part III but it is worth noting that the type of "access" enabled by the suggested social system (NLRBE) does not rule out legal relationships to secure the use of goods. The idea of reducing the current property system to one of 'protected access' where, for example, a camera obtained from a distribution center is given legal status upon it rental to that person, is not to be confused with the capitalist notion of property, which is a universal distinction and a great source of industrial inefficiency and imbalance.
70 Likely the best description of this is to imagine a fight in which one of the opponents sets up a man made of straw, attacks it, then proclaims victory. All the while, the real opponent stands by untouched.

imposed interpretations that are without legitimate evidence to be considered relevant to a point in question.

For example, when discussing the organization of a new social system, people often project their current values and concerns into the new model without considering the vast change of context inherent which would likely nullify such concerns immediately. A common straw-man projection in this context would be that in a society where material production were based upon technological application directly and not an exchange system requiring paid human labor, people would have *no incentive* to do anything and therefore the model would fail as nothing would get done.

This kind of argument is without testable validity with respect to the human sciences and is really an *intuitive assumption* originating from the current cultural climate where the economic system coerces all humans into labor roles for survival (income/profit). This often occurs regardless of one's personal interest or social utility, often generating a psychological distortion with respect to motivation.

In the words of Margaret Mead: "If you look closely you will see that almost anything that really matters to us, anything that embodies our deepest commitment to the way human life should be lived and cared for, depends on some form of volunteerism."[71] In a 1992 Gallup Poll, more than 50% of American adults (94 million Americans) volunteered time for social causes, at an average of 4.2 hours a week, for a total of 20.5 billion hours a year.[72]

It has also been found in studies that repetitive, mundane jobs lend themselves more to traditional rewards such as money, whereas money doesn't seem to motivate innovation and creativity.[73] In later essays, the idea of *mechanization/automation* applied to mundane labor to free the human being will be discussed, expressing how the labor-for-income system is outdated and restrictive of not only industrial potential and efficiency, but also human potential and creativity overall.

Another common, contextual example of a "straw-man" is the claim that if the transition to a new social system was acted upon, the property of others must be *forcefully confiscated* by a "ruling power" and violence would be the result. This, once again, is a value projection/fear, imposed upon TZM's advocated logic without validation.

TZM sees the materialization of a new socioeconomic model happening with the *needed consensus* of the population. Its very understanding, along with the "bio-social pressures" occurring as the current system worsens, is the basis of influence. The logic does not support a "dictatorial" disposition because that approach, apart from

---

71 Source: *"Have you noticed..."*, Vital Speeches of the Day, Robert Krikorian, 1985, p.301
72 Source: *Giving and Volunteering in the United States: Findings from a National Survey*, Hodgkinson & Weitzman, 1992, p.2
73 Reference: *Drive: The Surprising Truth About What Motivates Us*, Daniel Pink, Riverhead, 2011

being inhumane, wouldn't work.

In order for such a system to work, it needs to be accepted without active state coercion. Therefore, it is an issue of investigation, education, and broad personal acceptance in the community. In fact, the very specifics of social interaction and lifestyle actually *demand* a vast majority acceptance of the system's mechanics and values.

Similarly, and final example here of the "straw-man", is the confusion about how a *transition* to a new system could happen at all. In fact, many tend to dismiss TZM's proposals on that basis alone, simply because they don't understand how it can happen. This argument, in principle, is the same reasoning as the example of a sick man who is seeking treatment for his illness but does not know where he can get such treatment, when it would be available, or what the treatment is. Does his lack of knowing how and when stop his need to seek? No - not if he wants to be healthy. Given the dire state of affairs on this planet, humanity must also keep seeking and a path will inevitably come clear.[74]

In the end, it is worth reiterating that the battle between *logic* and *psychology* is really a central conflict in the arena of societal change. There is no context more personal and sensitive than the way we organize our lives in society and an important objective of TZM, in many ways, is to find techniques that can educate the public as to the merit of this logical *train of thought*, overcoming the baggage of outdated psychological comforts which serve no progressive, viable value role in the modern world.

---

74 More on the subject of *transition* in part IV.

-THE CASE FOR HUMAN UNITY-

My country is the world, and my religion is to do good.[75]
-Thomas Paine

A critical conclusion present in the logic that defines TZM's intention is that human society needs to unify its economic operations and work to *align with the natural dynamics of the physical world as a single species sharing one habitat* if we intend to resolve existing problems, increase safety, increase efficiency and further prosperity. The world economic divisions we see today are not only a clear source of conflict, destabilization and exploitation, the very manner of conduct and interaction itself is also grossly inefficient in a pure economic sense, severely limiting our societal potential.[76]

While the nation-state, competition-based structure is easy to justify as a natural outgrowth of our cultural evolution given the resource scarcity inherent historically and the long history of warfare in general, it is also natural to consider that human society could very well find purpose in moving away from these modes of operation if we were to realize that it is truly to our advantage as a whole group.

As will be argued here, the detriments and inefficiencies of the current model, when compared to the benefits and solutions possible, are simply *unacceptable.* The efficiency and abundance possibilities, extrapolated within TZM's intention to install a new socioeconomic system, rest, in part, on a concerted effort by the human population to *work together* and *share resources intelligently*, not restrict and fight as we do today.

Moreover, the social pressures and risks now emerging today around technological warfare, pollution, environmental destabilization and other problems not only express a deeply needed gravitation for true global organization, they show a rational necessity. The xenophobic and mafia-like mentality indigenous to the nation-state today, often in the form of "patriotism", is a source of severe destabilization and inhumanity in general, not to mention, again, a substantial loss of technical efficiency.

False Divisions
As noted in prior essays, the core basis of our survival and quality of life as individuals and as a species on the Earth revolves around our

---

75 Source: *Rights of Man*, Thomas Paine, 1791, p.162
76 One example of this would be the patriotic economic bias that often influences the actions of regional industry. In physical reality, there is technically only one economy when working with the planet earth's resources and natural laws. The idea of "Made in America", for instance, generates an immediate technical inefficiency, for proper goods production is a global affair on all levels, including the usufruct of world knowledge. To intentionally restrict labor and materials use/acquisition to only within the borders of a given country is economically counterproductive in the truest sense of the word "economy".

understanding of *natural law* and how it relates to our method of economy. This premise is a simple referential understanding where the physical laws of nature are considered in the context of economic efficiency, both on the human and habitat levels. It is only logical that any species present in and reliant on the habitat in which it exists should conform all conduct to *align* with the natural orders inherent to that habitat, as best they can be understood at the time. Any other orientation is simply irrational and can only lead to problems.

Understanding that Earth is a symbiotic/synergistic "system" with resources existing in all areas, coupled with the provably inherent, underlying causal scientific order that exists, in many ways, as a logical "guide" for the human species to align with for the greatest societal efficacy, we find that our larger context as a *global society* transcends all notions of traditional/cultural division, including having no *loyalty* to a country, corporation or even "political" tradition.

If an "economy" is about *increasing efficiency in meeting the needs of the human population while working to further sustainability and prosperity*, then our economic operations must take this into account and align with the largest relevant "system" that we can understand. So again, from this perspective, the nation-state entities are clearly false, arbitrary divisions perpetuated by cultural tradition, not logical, technical efficiency.

Values

The broad organization of society today is based on multi-level human competition. Nation-states compete against each other for economic/physical resources; corporate market entities compete for profit/market-share; and average workers compete for wage providing occupations/income and hence personal survival itself.

Within this competitive ethic is a basic psychological propensity to disregard the wellbeing of others and the habitat. The very nature of competition is about having *advantage* over others for personal gain and hence, needless to say, division and exploitation are common attributes of the current social order. Interestingly, virtually all so-called "corruption" which we may define as "crime" in the world today is based upon the very same mentality assumed to guide "progress" in the world through the competitive interest.

It is no wonder, in fact, given this framework, that various other detrimental, superficial social divisions are still pervasive such as race, religion, creed, class or xenophobic bias. This divisive baggage from early, fear-oriented stages of our cultural evolution simply has no working basis in the physical reality and serves now only to hinder progress, safety and sustainability.

Today, as will be described in later essays, the possible efficiency and abundance-producing methods that could remove most all human deprivation, increase the average standard of living enormously and perfect public health and ecological sustainability greatly – go *unembraced* due to the older social traditions in place, including the nation-state idea. The fact is, there is technically only one race - the human race;[77] there is only one basic habitat - Earth; and there is only one working manner of operational thought – scientific.

Origins and Influence

Let's quickly consider the root origins of the competitive/divisive model. Without going into too much detail, it is clear that the evolution of society has included a vast history of conflict, scarcity and imbalance. While there is debate as to the nature of society during the period of time preceding the Neolithic Revolution,[78] the Earth since that time has been a battlefield where countless lives have been taken for the sake of competition, whether material or ideological.[79]

This recognized pattern is so pervasive in fact that many today attribute the propensity for conflict and domination to an irreconcilable, impulsive characteristic of our *human nature* with the conclusion that the human being is simply unable to operate in a social system that is not based upon this competitive framework and any such attempt will create vulnerability that will be exploited by power abuse, expressing this apparent competitive/dominance trait.[80]

While the subject of human nature itself is not the direct focus of this essay,[81] let it be stated that the "empirical power abuse" assumption has been a large part of the defense of the competitive/divisive model, using a general broad view of history as its basis for validity. However, the specifics of the *conditions* in those periods, coupled with the known flexibility of the human being are often disregarded or ignored in these assessments.[82]

---

77 In the field of human genetics, "Mitochondrial Eve" refers to the matrilineally most recent common ancestor (MRCA) of modern humans. In other words, she was the most recent woman from whom all living humans today descend, on their mother's side. We are one family. Also, all characteristics of race difference (facial features/skin color) have been found to be linked to the environmental conditions where such sub-groups of humans lived/evolved. Hence it is a false distinction as a means for superficial discrimination.

78 Sometimes also called the Agricultural Revolution, it was the world's first historically verifiable revolution in agriculture. It was the wide-scale transition of many human cultures from a lifestyle of hunting and gathering to one of agriculture and settlement that supported an increasingly large population and the basis for modern social patterns today.

79 In the 20th century alone, statisticians put the human death toll from war between 180 to 220 million, with some challenging those numbers by claiming evidence puts the toll 3 times higher in many regional cases: (http://www.sciencedaily.com/releases/2008/06/080619194142.htm)

80 A classic text that employed this basic fear was Hayek's *The Road to Serfdom*. "Human Nature" had a very clear implication, justified fundamentally by historical trends of totalitarianism suggested to be linked to collaborative/planned economies.

81 This is expanded upon in the essay *The Final Argument: Human Nature.*

82 The Nature/Nurture Debate has been well established as a false duality in behavioral biology/evolutionary psychology fields of study. The reality is that of a perpetual interaction with the gravity of relevance shifting on a per case

The historical pattern of conflict cannot be considered in mere isolation. Detailed reference to the conditions and *circumstances* are needed. In fact, it's likely accurate to say that the dominance/conflict propensity which is clearly a possible *reaction* for nearly all humans in our need for self-preservation and survival in general[83] is being *provoked* by pressures rather than being the source of any negative reaction. When we wonder how the massive Nazi army were able to morally justify their actions in World War II, we often forget the enormous propaganda campaign put out by that regime which worked to exploit this essentially biological vulnerability.[84]

True "Self-Interest"

The notion of "self-interest" is clearly inherent to the human being's common urge to survive. This is obvious enough and it is easy to see historically how the raw necessity of personal survival, often extending to family and then the "tribe" (community), set the stage for the divisive, protectionist paradigm we exist in today. It should have been expected from the standpoint of history that vast economic theories would also be based upon the notion of competition and inequality, such as in the work of Adam Smith. Considered the father of the "free market", he made popular the assumption that if everyone had the ethic to look out for themselves only, the world would progress as a community.[85]

This "invisible hand" notion of human progress arising from narrow personal self-interest alone might have been a semi-workable

---

basis. However, what is relevant here is the study of the human being's "range of behavior" and exactly how adaptable and flexible we are. Reference: *Why Zebras Don't Get Ulcers*, Robert Sapolsky, W. H. Freeman, 1998

83 Commonly termed: "The fight-or-flight response" (or the acute stress response) and was first described by American physiologist Walter Bradford Cannon.

84 "Why of course the people don't want war. Why should some poor slob on a farm want to risk his life in a war when the best he can get out of it is to come back to his farm in one piece? Naturally the common people don't want war neither in Russia, nor in England, nor for that matter in Germany. That is understood. But, after all, it is the leaders of the country who determine the policy and it is always a simple matter to drag the people along, whether it is a democracy, or a fascist dictatorship, or a parliament, or a communist dictatorship. Voice or no voice, the people can always be brought to the bidding of the leaders. That is easy. All you have to do is tell them they are being attacked, and denounce the peacemakers for lack of patriotism and exposing the country to danger. It works the same in any country." -Hermann Göring (A leading member of the Nazi Party; From an interview with Gilbert in Göring's jail cell during the Nuremberg War Crimes Trials, 18 April 1946)

85 "It is not from the benevolence of the butcher, the brewer, or the baker that we expect our dinner, but from their regard to their own self-interest. We address ourselves not to their humanity but to their self-love, and never talk to them of our own necessities, but of their advantages". (*An Inquiry into the Nature & Causes of the Wealth of Nations*, Adam Smith, Vol. 1)

philosophy many years ago when the simplicity of the society itself was based on everyone being something of a producer.[86] However, the nature of society has changed greatly over time, with population increases, entirely different role structures and exponentially advancing technology. The risks associated with this manner of thought are now proving to be more dangerous than beneficial, and the *true* definition of "self-interest" is taking a *larger context* than ever before.

Is it not in your self-interest to protect and nourish the habitat that supports you? Is it not in your self-interest to take care of society as a *whole*, providing for its members, so that the consequences of deprivation, such as "crime" are reduced as much as possible to ensure your safety? Is it not self-interest to consider the consequences of imperialist wars that can breed fierce jingoistic hatred on one side of the planet, only to have, say, a suitcase bomb explode behind you at a restaurant as a desperate "blow-back" act of retribution?

Is it not self-interest to assure all of societies' children have the best upbringing and education so that your future and the future of your children can exist in a responsible, educated, and increasingly productive world? Is it not in your self-interest to make sure industry is as organized, optimized and scientifically accurate as possible, so that we do not produce shoddy, cheap technology that might perhaps cause a problem in the future if it fails?

The bottom line is that things have changed in the world today and *your self-interest is now only as good as your societal interest.* Being competitive and going out for yourself, "beating" others only has a negative consequence in the long-term, for it is denying awareness of the synergistic system we are bound within. A cheaply made nuclear power plant in Japan might not mean much to people in America. However, if that plant was to have a large scale technical failure, the fallout and pollution might make its way over to American homes, proving that *you are never safe in the long run unless you have a global consciousness.*

In the end, only an Earth-humankind conscious view can assure a person's true self-interest and hence, in many ways, also

---

86 Sociologist Thorstein Veblen, writing in 1917, made this acute observation with respect to the changes in society and how they reflect the original premise of the market economy. "The standard theories of economic science have assumed the rights of property and contract as axiomatic premises and ultimate terms of analysis; and their theories are commonly drawn in such a form as would fit the circumstances of the handicraft industry and the petty trade... these theories ...appear tenable, on the whole, when taken to apply to the economic situation of that earlier time... It is when these standard theories are sought to be applied to the later situation, which has outgrown the conditions of handicraft, that they appears nugatory or meretricious." (*An Inquiry Into The Nature Of Peace And The Terms Of Its Perpetuation*) He also foreshadowed the rise of the "investment class" as today non-producing financial institution like banks & the stocks market have become more rewarding profit-wise than the actual manufacturing of true goods.

assure our society's "evolutionary fitness".[87] The very idea of wishing to support "your country" and ignoring or even enjoying the failure of others, is a destabilizing value system.

Warfare

The days of practical warfare are long over. New technology on the horizon has the ability to create weapons that will make the atom bomb look like a roman catapult in destructive power.[88] Centuries ago, warfare could at least be minimized to the warring parties overall. Today, the entire world is threatened. There are over 23,000 Nuclear Weapons today, which could wipe out the human population many times over.[89]

In many ways, our very *social maturity* is being questioned at this time. Battles with only sticks and stones as weapons could tolerate a great deal of human distortion and malicious intent. However, in a world of nano-tech weapons that could be constructed in a small lab with enormous destructive power, our *expanded self-interest* needs to take hold and the institution of war needs to be systematically shutdown. In order to do this, nations must technically unify and share their resources and ideas, not hoard them for competitive self-betterment, which is the norm today.

Institutions like the United Nations have become complete failures in this regard because they naturally become tools of empire building due to the underlying nature of country divisions and the socioeconomic dominance of the property/monetary/competition-based system orientation. It is not enough to simply gather global "leaders" at a table to discuss their problems. The structure itself needs to change to support a *different type of interaction* between these regional "groups" where the perpetual "threat" inherent between nation-states is removed.

In the end, there is no empirical ownership of resources or ideas. Just as all ideas are serially developed across culture through the *group mind,* the resources of the planet are equally as transient in their function and scientifically defined as to their possible purposes. The Earth is a single system, along with the laws of nature that govern it. Either human society recognizes and begins to act and organize on this inherent logic, or we suffer in the long run.

---

87 Evolutionary Fitness is a biological term generally defined as "The probability that the line of descent from an individual with a specific trait will not die out." In this context we are linking human actions, socially, to the idea of species survival.

88 Reference: *Applications for Warfare* (http://crnano.typepad.com/crnblog/2005/05/applications_fo.html)

89 Source: *Nuclear Weapons: 20 Facts They Don't Want You to Think About,* Jim McCluskey, 2011 (http://www.wagingpeace.org/articles/db_article.php?article_id=253

-THE FINAL ARGUMENT: HUMAN NATURE-

Man acquires at birth, through heredity, a biological constitution which we must consider fixed and unalterable, including the natural urges which are characteristic of the human species. In addition, during his lifetime, he acquires a cultural constitution which he adopts from society through communication and through many other types of influences. It is this cultural constitution which, with the passage of time, is subject to change and which determines to a very large extent the relationship between the individual and society.[90]
-A. Einstein

The Only Argument Remaining

The "train of thought" and "application-set"[91] presented in TZM's materials are *technical* by nature, expressing the interest of applying the method and merit of *scientific causality* to the social system as a whole.

The benefits of this approach are not only to be taken on their own merit but should also be considered in contrast to today's established, traditional methods and their consequences. It will likely then be noticed that our current societal methods are not only grossly outdated and inefficient by comparison - they are increasingly dangerous and inhumane - with the necessity for large scale social change becoming ever more important. This isn't about "utopia". It is about truly practical improvements.

The overall basis of the market concept has to do fundamentally with assumptions related to *human behavior, traditional values* and an *intuitive* view of history - not emergent reasoning, actual public health measures, technical capacity or ecological responsibility. It is a non-technical, philosophical approach, which merely assumes that human decisions made through its internal logic (and incentive system), will produce a responsible, sustainable and humane outcome, driven by the illusive notion of "freedom of choice" which, on the scale of societal functionality, appears tantamount to organizational anarchy.[92]

---

90 *Why Socialism?*, Albert Einstein, 1949
(http://monthlyreview.org/2009/05/01/why-socialism)
91 The "train of thought" has to do with the underlying reasoning that arrives at the conclusions of TZM's advocation - while the "application-set" is simply the current state of applied technology today. The difference between the two is that the former is near empirical while the latter is transient since technological tools are always undergoing change.
92 Much can be said on the subject of economic organization and mechanisms for industrial production and more will be described in part III. However, let it be stated here that the "price mechanism", which is the central catalyst for economic unfolding today, is inherently anarchistic due to the lack of efficient system relationships within macro-industrial practices. Production, distribution and resource allocation is not "strategic" in a technical, physical sense by any stretch of the imagination – the only strategy employed, which is the defining context of "efficiency" in the market economy, has to do with the profit and loss/labor cost/expense type monetary parameters which have no relationship to physical efficiency at all.

This is why the monetary-market model of economics is often considered *religious* by nature in TZM materials as the causal mechanism is really based on virtually superstitious assumptions of the human condition with little linkage to emerging scientific understandings about ourselves and the rigid symbiotic/synergistic relationship of our habitat and its governing natural laws.

When presenting TZM's solution-oriented *train of thought* to those unfamiliar, it is usually just a matter of time before, at a minimum, the basic scientific premise is understood and accepted in abstraction. For example, the isolated technical reality that we have the resources and industrial methods to easily feed everyone on the planet earth, so no one has to starve,[93] rarely finds argument in and of itself. If you were to ask an average person today if they would like to see an end to the over one billion people in currently in chronic starvation on the planet,[94] they would most likely agree.

However, it is when the logic runs its course and starts to depict the type of large-scale social and economic *reformations needed* to facilitate true system support for those 1+ billion people that many find contempt and objection. Apart from stubborn, temporal "value" associations, where people essentially refuse to change anything they have become used to in their lives, even if that change clearly supports a better outcome in the long term, there is one argument so common that it warrants a preliminary discussion in and of itself.

That is the argument of "human nature". This argument might also be said to be the *only real objection left,* if you think about it, outside again of the near arbitrary cultural lifestyle practices people are afraid to change due to their identity associations and conditioned comforts. Are humans compatible with a truly sustainable, scientific socioeconomic system or are we doomed to the world we have now due to our genetics?

Everything is Technical

The case for a new social system based directly on a *scientific* view for understanding and maximizing sustainability and prosperity, technically, really cannot be contradicted by another approach, as bold as such a statement may seem. Why? Because there simply isn't one when the unifying, natural law logic of the scientific method is accepted as the root mechanism of physical causality and interrelationship.

For example, great surface variation (ornament) might exist with the design of an airplane, but the mechanics which enable flight are bound by physical laws and hence so must the overall *physical*

---

93 The United Nations Food and Agriculture Organization and the World Food Programme have confirmed this. This site is recommend for reference: (http://overpopulationisamyth.com/food-theres-lots-it#header-1)
94 Source: *1.02 billion starving people worldwide, U.N. Says* (http://www.news-medical.net/news/20090623/102-billion-starving-people-worldwide-UN-says.aspx)

design of the airplane in order to function properly. Constructing such a machine to perform a job with the goal of optimized performance, safety and efficiency is not a matter of opinion, just as no matter how many ornaments we may place around our homes, the physical structure of the building must adhere to the rigid laws of physics and natural dynamics of the habitat for safety and endurance and hence can have little respective variation in a technical sense.

The *organization of human society* can be no different if the intention is integrity and optimization. To think of the functional nature of a working society is to think about a *mechanistic schematic*, if you will. Just as we would design an airplane to work in the best way possible, technically, so should our approach be to the social system, which is equally as technical in its needed functionality. Unfortunately, this general perspective has never been given a real chance in history and today our world is still run in an incongruous manner where the principal incentive is more about detached, immediate, shortsighted personal gain and differential advantage than it is about proper, strategic industrial methods, ecological alignment, social stability, public health considerations and generational sustainability.

This is all pointed out, again, because the "human nature" argument against such an approach is really the only *seemingly* technical argument that can possibly defend the old system we have today; it is really the only argument left when people who wish to uphold this system realize that nothing else they logically argue can possibly be viable given the irrationality inherent to every other claim against a *natural law based social model*.

Irrationally Bound?

Boiling it down, this challenge can be considered in one question: "Is the human species able to adapt and thrive in a technically organized system, where our values and practices align with the known laws of nature in practice, or are we confined by our genes, biology and evolutionary psychology to operate in only the way we know today?"

While many today argue the specifics of the *nature vs. nurture* debate - from "blank slate" behaviorism[95] to genetic determinism[96] - it has become clear, at a minimum, that our biology, our psychology and

---

95 The notion of the "Blank Slate" was made popular by Thomas Hobbes but can be linked back to the writings of Aristotle. This is the idea that, in short, individuals are born without built-in mental orientation and everything is learned. Now largely debunked as a broad view due to proven "programmed learning" and humans' inherent "evolutionary psychology", the idea still persists in general.

96 The view that human beings are substantially more affected by Genes and Biology than environmental conditioning with respect to human behavior is still a heated debate, not to mention a frequent intuitive reaction by many to certain human patterns. The phrase "it's just human nature" is all too often tossed out by the layman. Authors such as Steven Pinker are notable for promoting the dominance of evolutionary psychology over environmental conditioning.

our sociological condition are inexorably linked to the environment we inhabit, both from the standpoint of generational evolutionary adaptation (biological evolution), to short-term biases and values we absorb from our environment (cultural evolution).

So, before we go into detail on this issue, it is well worth noting that our *very definition* as human beings in the long and short-term view is based upon a process of *adaptation* to existing conditions, including the genes themselves.[97] This is not to discount the per-case genetic relevance itself but to highlight the *process* to which we are a part, for the gene-environment relationship can only be considered as an ongoing interaction, with the outcomes largely a result of the environmental conditions in the long and short term. If this wasn't the case, there is little doubt the human species would have likely perished long ago due to a failure to adapt.

Moreover, while it is clear we humans still appear to maintain "hardwired", predictable reactions for raw, personal survival,[98] we have also proven the ability to evolve our behaviors through thought, awareness and education,[99] allowing us to, in fact, control/overcome those impulsive, primitive reactions, if the conditions for such are supported and reinforced. This is an extremely important distinction

---

97 An "adaptation" in biology is a trait with a current functional role in the life history of an organism that is maintained and evolved by means of 'natural selection'. In short, this occurs due to pressures existing on the organism in the environment. Likewise, "epigenetics" is a fairly new awareness and study of heritable changes in gene expression or cellular phenotype caused by mechanisms *other* than changes in the underlying DNA sequence. In short, it is a shorter-term "expression" adaptation influenced by the environment as well. As far as culture, this is simpler to understand. For instance, the language you speak is an adaptation to the existing cultural group, just like the religion you might be taught and hence many of the values you hold are directly a result of the cultural conditions you are within.

98 The notion of an "instinctual reaction" could be applied here. However, the differentiation of what is or isn't instinctual has become increasingly ambiguous in the study of human behavior. Yet, it is clear in a fundamental sense that there are very specific patterns in common regarding the human species, especially in the context of survival and stress influence. Faced with pressing danger, very common biological/endocrinological reactions occur almost universally and these often generate behavioral propensities which are also predictable consistently across the species as a whole.

99 The term "behavioral plasticity" can be applied here as an extension of "neuroplasticity" which refers to active changes in neural pathways and synapses. Just as the brain used to be considered a static organ, human behavior – the expression of brain activity – clearly also undergoes change. As complex a subject as "free-will" and decision processes are to the psychological sciences, the nature of the human mind shows clear adaptability and vulnerability to input conditions. Unlike our primate ancestors, our advanced Neocortex appears to be a center for conscious thought and in the words of Dr. Robert Sapolsky, Neuroscientist from Stanford University: "On a certain level, the nature of our nature is not to be particularly constrained by our nature." (from 2011 film *Zeitgeist: Moving Forward*, Peter Joseph)

and is what separates the variance of human beings from their lesser-evolved primate family in many ways.[100]

A quick glance at the diversity in historical human conduct we see throughout time, contrasted with the relatively slow pace of larger structural changes of our brains and DNA[101] over the past couple of thousand years, shows that our adaptive capacity (via thought/education) is *enormous* on the cultural level. It appears that we are capable of many possible behaviors and that a fixed "human nature", as an unalterable, universal set of behavioral traits/reactions shared by all humans without exception cannot be held as valid. Rather, there appears to be a spectrum of possible behaviors and predictable reactions, all more or less contingent upon the type of development, education, stimuli & conditions we experience.

The *social imperative* in this respect cannot be emphasized enough for environmental influence is a massive factor that grooms not only our decision-making preferences in both the long and short term, but the overall environmental interaction with our biology in general also has powerful effects on personal well-being and hence broad public health in many specific ways.

It has been found that environmental conditions, including factors such as nutritional input,[102] emotional security,[103] social association,[104] and all forms of stress in general can influence the

---

100 Reference: *Evolution of the neocortex: a perspective from developmental biology*, Nature Review, 2009
(http://www.nature.com/nrn/journal/v10/n10/abs/nrn2719.html)

101 DNA mutation rates vary from species to species and have historically been very difficult to estimate. Today, with *Direct Sequencing* it is now possible to isolate exact changes. In a study performed in 2009, two distant male-line relatives - separated by thirteen generations - whose common ancestor lived two hundred years ago, were sequenced, finding only 12 differences among all the DNA letters examined. "The two Y chromosomes were still identical at 10,149,073 of the 10,149,085 letters examined. Of the 12 differences...only four were true mutations that had occurred naturally through the generations."
(http://www.sciencedaily.com/releases/2009/08/090827123210.htm) As far as the human genome, it is estimated that the genome might undergo only a few 100 changes over tens of thousands of years.

102 A classical example is the "Dutch Hunger Winter". A study tracking people who suffered severe malnutrition as fetuses during World War II found that in their adult life they suffered from various metabolic syndromes and metabolism problems due to the "programming" which occurred during that In Utero period. Reference: *Famine and Human development: The Dutch hunger winter of 1944-1945*. New York, NY, US: Oxford University Press.

103 Dr. Gabor Maté in his work "*In the Realm of Hungry Ghosts*" (North Atlantic Books, 2012) presents an enormous amount of research regarding how 'emotional loss' occurring at young ages affects behavior in later life, specifically the propensity for addictions.

104 The relevance of the nature of social interaction is more profound than once thought. The correlation between different macro-societal factors and public health issues such as life expectancy, mental disorder, obesity, heart disease, violence and many other sociological issues were well summarized in the book *The Spirit Level* by Richard Wilkinson and Kate Pickett, Penguin,

human being in many more ways than previously thought. This process begins *in utero*, through the sensitive post-natal and childhood "planned learning" adaption periods,[105] and carries on throughout life on all physiological and psychological levels.

For example, while there is evidence that depression as a psychological disorder can have a genetic predisposition, it is the *environment* that really triggers it or not.[106] Again, this is not to downplay the influence of biology on our personalities but to show the critical importance of understanding these realities and *adapting our social system and macro influences to support the most positive outcome we can.*

Changing The Condition

The idea of changing society's influences/pressures to bring out the best of the human condition rather than the worst is at the core of the social imperative of TZM and this idea is sadly lost in the culture's social considerations today. Enormous evidence exists to support how the influence of our environment is what essentially creates our *values and biases* and while genetic and physiological influences can set propensities and accentuations for certain behaviors, the most active influence regarding our *variability* is the life experience and condition of the human being, hence the manner of interaction between the "internal" (physiological) and "external" (environmental).

In the end, the most relevant issue is *stress.* Our genes, biology and evolutionary psychology might have some hang-ups, but they are nothing compared to the environmental disorder we have created in our culture. The enormity of now unnecessary stress in the world today – debt, job insecurity, increasing health risks both mental and physiological - and many other issues have created a climate of unease that has been increasingly making people sick and upset. If we were faced with an option to adapt our society in a way that could provably better public health, increase social stability, generate abundance and help sustainability, would we not just do it? To think human beings are simply *incompatible* with methods that can increase their standard of living and health is extremely unlikely.

So, in conclusion to this section, let it be stated that the subject of "human nature" is one of the most complex issues there is when it comes to specifics. However, the broad and viable awareness with respect to basic public health improvement via reducing stress, increasing quality nutrition and stabilizing society by working toward

---

March 2009.

105 A unique study of premature infants in incubators found that by simply stimulating them during that time (or showing "affection" by simple touch) their longer term physiological health was greatly improved compared to those untouched. Reference: *Tactile/kinesthetic stimulation effects on preterm neonates*, Pediatrics, 1986

106 Reference: *The Structure of Genetic and Environmental Risk Factors for Common Psychiatric and Substance Use Disorders in Men and Women*, Arch Gen Psychiatry. 2003;60

abundance and ease rather than strife and complexity – is not susceptible to much debate.

We now have some refined truths about the human condition that give enough evidence to see that we are not only generating poor reactions and habits due to the influence of the current socioeconomic order, we are also greatly disrespecting the habitat as well, creating not only a lack of sustainability in an ecological sense, but, again, in a cultural sense as well. Once again, to think humans are simply incompatible with these resolutions, even if it means changing our world greatly, defies the long history of adaptation we have proven to be capable of.

PART II: SOCIAL PATHOLOGY

-DEFINING PUBLIC HEALTH-

We are all responsible for all.[107]
-Dostoyevsky

Overview

What is the true measure of *success* for a society? What is it that makes us happy, healthy, stable and in balance with the world around us? Is not our success *really* our ability to understand and adapt to the realities of our world for the best outcome possible for any given circumstance? What if we were to find that the very nature of our social system was actually *reducing our quality of life in the long term?*

As will be argued in this essay, modern social structures, values and practices have deviated away from, or are largely ignorant of, what true societal health means. What our social institutions today give priority to or discount by design, coupled with the goals and motivations associated with personal "success", which are all too often clearly "decoupled" from what true *life support and advancement* means,[108] is a subject given little thoughtful consideration in the world today. In fact, most "prosperity" and "integrity" measures for the human condition are now haphazardly equated to mere economic baselines such as GDP, PPI or employment figures. Sadly, these measures tell us virtually nothing about *true* human wellbeing and prosperity.[109]

The term *public health* is a medical classification, essentially defined as: "the approach to medicine that is concerned with the health of the community as a whole."[110] While often narrowly used in relationship to transmittable disease and broad social conditions, the context here will extend into all aspects of our lives, including not only physiological health but mental health as well. If the value of a social system is measured by the health of its citizenry over time, assessing and comparing conditions and consequences through simple trend analysis and factor accounting should give insight into what can be

---

107 Source: Paraphrased, from *Karamazov Brothers*, Fyodor Dostoyevsky, 1880, p316

108 The point here relates to how modern society rewards and reinforces certain behaviors over others. For instance, in the Western World more financial reward comes to non-producing financial institutions than from true good and service production. This has generated an incentive problem, which also includes environmental disregard and the ignoring of public health in general. As will be alluded to later in this text, the psychology of the market economy actually *opposes* life support.

109 In recent years other attempts have been made to quantify "happiness" and well-being, such as the *Gross National Happiness Indicator* (GNH) which conducts measures via periodic surveys (http://www.grossnationalhappiness.com/)

110 Public Health defined: (http://www.medterms.com/script/main/art.asp?articlekey=5120)

changed or improved on the social level.

The central context here is how the social condition itself - the socioeconomic system - is affecting human health on the whole. In the words of physician Rudolph Virchow: "Medicine is a social science and politics nothing but medicine on a large scale."[111] Virchow recognized that any public health issue is invariably related to *society* as a whole. Its structure, characteristics and value reinforcements have a profound influence on the health and behavior of a society and arguments regarding the merit of new social ideas inevitably come down to a rational assessment of quality through comparison.

Since each respective component of public health has its own characteristics and causality, we can also work to consider alternative approaches to a given problem resolution or improvement that might not be currently in practice, but clearly should be. An analysis of current public health components to understand what is happening over time and in different circumstances, coupled with a per case evaluation of each issue with an inferential consideration of what could "fix" or "improve" these results on the largest possible scale, is the basis of the *train of thought* expressed here.

It is the conviction of TZM that the existing social model is a cause of "social pathology", with a perpetuation of imbalance that is unnecessarily generating both physiological and psychological disorders across the population, not to mention systemically limiting human potential and problem resolution in many ways. Of course, this context also naturally extends into *environmental health*, meaning the state of the planet, as such ecological problems/pressures/alleviations always have an effect on our public health in the long-term. However, that will not be a focus in this essay.

This analysis will separate the subject of public health into two general categories - physiological and psychological[112] - with each category broken into categorizes that represent dominant problems seen in a relevant percentage of the overall population. However, let it be well understood that physiological and psychological outcomes rarely, if ever, have singular causes. There is a *bio-psycho-social*[113] relationship to virtually all human phenomena, illuminating, once again, the multi-level symbiosis characteristic of the human being. In

---

111 Source: *The Evolution of Social Medicine*, Rudolph Virchow: Rosen G., from the *Handbook of Medical Sociology*, Prentice-Hall, 1972

112 Sociological phenomena will be grouped in the Psychological category here for the sake of simplicity, as the result of a sociological condition is the aggregate psychological states of individuals.

113 *Bio-Psycho-Social* means the interaction of biological, psychological and sociological influence on a given consequence. For example, Obesity, on the surface, simply relates to eating. If a person eats too much, they gain weight. However, there is a large degree of evidence now (as will be presented later in this essay) that shows how a person's psychology can be effected to crave the *comfort* of consuming due to *external* factors – such as a deprived emotional history or poor bodily adaption where bad habits are formed and expected. These latter notions, which influence one's psychology, are a result of the *sociological* condition.

other words, while the problem being focused on might be considered "physiological" on the surface, the *underlying cause* of that outcome might very well be "psychological" or "sociological", for example.

The Economic Factor

As noted, the main thesis of this essay is to show the deep effect our global socioeconomic system has on public health, with a specific focus on the power of *poverty, stress* and *inequality*. If one was to take a quick glance at the major causes of death globally, as put forward by the World Health Organization,[114] clear differences based on the economic state of a region, such as the fact that cancers are more common in high income societies while diarrhoeal diseases are more common in low income societies, gives insight as to how the broad context of socioeconomic position can affect public health.

Mahatma Gandhi once said "Poverty is the worst form of violence."[115] His context relates to the unnecessary deaths caused by poverty in the sense of the broad limitations such severe financial restrictions have on health. This idea was later encompassed in the term *structural violence,*[116] defined by Dr. James Gilligan as "...the increased rates of death and disability suffered by those who occupy the bottom rungs of society." He differentiates structural violence from *behavioral violence*, where the former "operates continuously rather than sporadically".[117]

Please note that the term "violence" in this context is not limited to the usual classification of physical harm, such as person-to-person combat or abuse. The context extends to include the often unseen *social oppression* that, through the chain of causality characteristics inherent to our social system, leads to the unnecessary harm of people, both physical, psychological or both. Examples of this can range from obvious to complex in the chain of cause and effect.

A simple "macro" example would be the prevalence of *diarrhoeal* diseases in poverty-stricken societies. These diseases kill about 1.5 million children each year.[118] It is completely preventable and treatable and while the infection itself is spread through contaminated food and drinking-water, or from person-to-person as a result of poor hygiene, its very preventability and rarity in first world nations by comparison shows that the *real cause* is now not the disease itself, but *the poverty condition* that enables it to flourish.

---

114 Source: *The top 10 causes of death*, WHO, 2013
   (http://www.who.int/mediacentre/factsheets/fs310/en/index.html)
115 Source: Quoted in *A Just Peace through Transformation: Cultural, Economic, and Political Foundations for Change,* International Peace Association, 1988
116 Reference: *An Empirical Table of Structural Violence*, Gernot Kohler and Norman Alcock, 1976
   http://jpr.sagepub.com/content/13/4/343.extract
117 Source: *Violence*, James Gilligan, Grosset/Putnam, New York, 1992, p.192
118 Source: *Diarrhoeal disease*, WHO, 2013
   (http://www.who.int/mediacentre/factsheets/fs330/en/index.html)

However, the causality doesn't stop there. We then need to ask the question: "what is causing the poverty?"

A more abstract "micro" example would be human development problems when adverse pressures in family or community structures occur. Imagine a single mother who, due to the financial need to raise her child, must work for income a great deal in order to make ends meet, limiting her availability for the child personally. The pressures not only reduce needed support and guidance for the child's development, she also develops tendencies for depression and anxiety due to the ongoing stress of debt, bills and the like, and frustration-driven abuse begins to materialize in the family. This then causes severe *emotional loss*[119] in the child and the development of neurotic and unhealthy mental states emerge, such as a propensity for drug addiction.[120] Years later, still suffering from the pain felt in those early periods, the now adult child dies in a heroin overdose. Question: what caused the overdose? The heroin? The mother's influence? Or the economic circumstance the mother found herself which disallowed balance and thoughtful care of her child?[121]

Clearly, there is no utopia for the human condition and to think we can adjust the socioeconomic system to thwart all such "structurally" related issues, macro and micro, 100% of the time, is absurd. However, what *is possible* is a dramatic improvement of such public health problems by shifting the nature of the socioeconomic condition in the most strategic manner we can. As we proceed with the per case analysis of major mental and physical disorders in the world, it will be found that the true imperative for public health improvement rests almost entirely on this socioeconomic premise of causality.[122]

According to Gernot Kohler and Norman Alcock in their 1976 work *An Empirical Table of Structural Violence*, a dramatic 18 million

---

119 The term *emotional loss* relates to severe emotional trauma experienced, mostly as a child, that persist in effect. In the words of Dr. Gabor Maté "The greatest damage done by neglect, trauma or *emotional loss* is not the immediate pain they inflict but the long-term distortions they induce in the way a developing child will continue to interpret the world and her situation in it." *In the Realm of Hungry Ghosts"*, North Atlantic Books, 2012, p.512

120 As noted prior, the work of Gabor Maté is highly recommended on the subject of addiction resulting from emotional loss in childhood and feelings of insecurity. "*In the Realm of Hungry Ghosts"*, North Atlantic Books, 2012

121 The work *Mental Illness and the Economy,* by M.H. Brenner is recommended. Abstract: "By correlating extensive economic and institutional data from New York State for the period from 1841 to 1967, Harvey Brenner concludes that instabilities in the national economy are the single most important source of fluctuations in mental-hospital admissions or admission rates."

122 A study for reference in the same basic context is *The Effect of Known Risk Factors on the Excess Mortality of Black Adults in the United States,* Journal of the American Medical Association, 263(6):845-850, 1990. This epidemiological study found that two-thirds of African-American deaths noted in context could only be accounted for due to *low socioeconomic status itself* and its direct/indirect consequences.

deaths were found to occur *each year* due to structural violence[123] and that study was over 30 years ago. Since that time the global gap between rich and poor has more than doubled, suggesting now that the death toll is even much higher today. In effect, structural violence is the most deadly killer on the planet. The following chart shows rates of death of a specific demographic, revealing the more broad correlation of low-income and increased mortality.

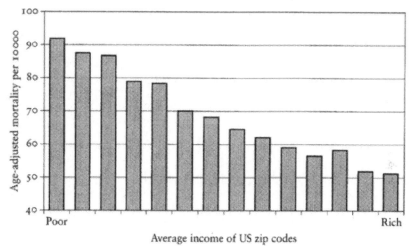

Average income of US zip codes

(Above) G. D. Smith, J. D. Neaton, D. Wentworth, R. Stamler and J. Stamler, 'Socioeconomic differentials in mortality risk among men screened for the Multiple Risk Factor Intervention Trial: I. White men', *American Journal of Public Health* (1996) 86 (4): 486-96.

Physiological Health
The core physiological problems of the human population today include *major* mortality producing epidemics such as cancer, heart disease, stroke, etc. Relatively *minor* problems that not only reduce quality of life, but also often precede those major illnesses include high blood pressure, obesity and other issues that, while less critical by comparison, are still usually a part of the process that can lead to major illnesses and death over time.[124]

Again, it is important to remember that the causality of these "physical" diseases is not strictly "physical" in the narrow sense of the word as modern study has found deep *psychosocial*[125] stress

---

123 Source: *An Empirical Table of Structural Violence*, Gernot Kohler and Norman Alcock, 1976
124 Reference: *As obesity rates rise, chief heart surgeon sees more high-risk patients in operating room,* Caitlin Heaney, 2012 (http://thetimes-tribune.com/lifestyles-people/as-obesity-rates-rise-chief-heart-surgeon-sees-more-high-risk-patients-in-operating-room-1.1379223)
125 *Psychosocial* defined: Involving aspects of both social and psychological behavior; Interrelationship (http://medical-dictionary.thefreedictionary.com/psychosocial)

relationships to seemingly detached physiological issues. According to the World Health Organization, the most common shared major causes of death in low, middle and high-income countries are heart disease, lower respiratory infections, stroke and cancer.[126] While each of these illnesses (and many more) can be found related to the causal points that follow, for simplicities sake heart disease will be a focus here.

Case Study: Heart Disease

While the treatment of heart disease has led to a recent mild global decline in heart attacks and deaths overall,[127] the diagnosis of heart disease has not subsided and by some regional studies is on the rise,[128] or on pace to increasing substantially.[129] Coronary heart disease is still considered by the WHO as the "leading cause of death" globally[130] and it has been found that while there are genetic factors in play, 90% of those dying "have risk factors influenced by lifestyle"[131] and overall the disease is widely considered *preventable* if lifestyle adjustments are made.

In short, well established relationships to high fat diets, smoking, alcohol, obesity, high cholesterol, diabetes and other risk factors allow us to extend the causality of heart disease and when we follow the influences, the most profound broad influence found has to do not only with *absolute income,* but *relative socioeconomic* status.

The WHO makes it generally clear that on the global scale, lower socioeconomic status breeds more heart disease and naturally more of the risk factors that lead to it.[132] This, on one side, depicts a *direct economic relationship* to the occurrence of disease. There is no evidence to show that genetic differences between regional groups could be responsible for these variations and it is obvious to see how a lack of purchasing power leads people into lifestyles that include many such risk factors.

A 2009 study in the American Journal of Epidemiology called "Life-Course Socioeconomic Position and Incidence of Coronary Heart Disease" found that the longer a person remains in poverty, the more

---

126 *The top ten causes of death,* WHO, 2013
(http://www.who.int/mediacentre/factsheets/fs310/en/index.html)
127 *U.S. Trends in Heart Disease, Cancer, and Stroke,* Population Reference Bureau,
(http://www.prb.org/Articles/2002/USTrendsinHeartDiseaseCancerandStrok e.aspx)
128 *Heart disease to rise 25% by 2020,* Belfast Telegraph, 2012
(http://www.belfasttelegraph.co.uk/news/local-national/northern-ireland/heart-disease-to-rise-25-by-2020-16177410.html)
129 *New European Statistics Released On Heart Disease and Stroke,* Science Daily, 2012
(http://www.sciencedaily.com/releases/2012/09/120929140236.htm)
130 *The Atlas of Heart Disease and Stroke,* WHO & CDC, Part 3, *Global Burden of Coronary Heart Disease*
131 Ibid.
132 Ibid., Chapter 11, *Socioeconomic Status*

likely he or she is to develop heart disease.[133] People who were economically disadvantaged throughout life were more likely to smoke, be obese, and have poor diets and the like. In an earlier study by epidemiologist Dr. Ralph R. Frerichs, focusing specifically on the socioeconomic divide in the city of Los Angeles, CA, found that the death rate from heart disease was *40 percent higher* for poor men over all than for wealthier ones.[134]

Given our original thesis to consider a link from the social system itself to the prevalence of disease and their associated risk factors, we need to consider the direct relationship of *stress* & *purchasing power.* Beginning with the latter, which is more simple, clearly poor health habits occur in lower income environments due to the lack of funds for better nutrition,[135] medical attention[136] and education.[137] For example, many of the high fat, high sodium risk factor foods leading to heart disease tend to be the most inexpensive food found in stores.

It is worth noting that our socioeconomic model produces goods based upon the purchasing power of targeted demographics. The decision to produce poor quality food goods is made for the interest of *profit* and since the vast majority of the planet is relatively poor, it is no surprise that in order to meet that market, quality must be reduced to allow for competitive buying.

In other words, there is a market for each social class and naturally the lower the class, the lower the quality. This reality is an example of a *direct social system link to causality for heart disease.* While education about the difference between quality food products could help the decision process of a poor person to eat better, the financial restrictions inherent to their condition could easily make that decision difficult if not impossible as, again, such goods are more expensive on average.

In an age where food production and human nutrition is a well

---

133 *Life-Course Socioeconomic Position and Incidence of Coronary Heart Disease*, American Journal of Epidemiology, April 1, 2009.
(http://aje.oxfordjournals.org/content/early/2009/01/29/aje.kwn403)
134 *Heart Disease Tied to Poverty, New York Times, 1985*
(http://www.nytimes.com/1985/02/24/us/heart-disease-tied-to-poverty.html)
135 Quote from the study *Can Low-Income Americans Afford a Healthy Diet?:* "Many nutritional professionals believe that all Americans, regardless of income, have access to a nutritious diet of whole grains, lean meats, and fresh vegetables and fruit. In reality, food prices pose a significant barrier for many consumers who are trying to balance good nutrition with affordability." (http://www.ncbi.nlm.nih.gov/pmc/articles/PMC2847733/)
136 Reference: *Medical costs push millions of people into poverty across the globe*, WHO
(http://www.who.int/mediacentre/news/releases/2005/pr65/en/index.html)
137 Reference: *Education Gap Grows Between Rich and Poor, Studies Say,* New York Times, 2012
(http://www.nytimes.com/2012/02/10/education/education-gap-grows-between-rich-and-poor-studies-show.html?pagewanted=all)

understood scientific phenomenon as far as what works and what doesn't - what is healthy and what isn't on the whole - we have to wonder why the abundance of deliberately unhealthy foods and detrimental industrial methods exist at all. The reasoning is that human health is *not* the pursuit of industrial food production and never has been due to the isolated interest to generate income. More on this *incentive disorder* inherent to the market economy in later essays.

The Stress Factor

Let's now consider the role of *stress*. Stress has more of an effect on heart disease than previously thought and this isn't just referring to the statistical fact that lower income peoples tend to have a propensity to cope by smoking and/or drinking, manifesting high blood pressure and hence disregard their bodies and well-being due to the ongoing struggle for income and survival. While those factors are clearly evident and, again, found tied to the inevitable stratification found in the market economy,[138] the most detrimental form of stress comes in the form of *psychosocial* stress, meaning stress related to one's psychological connection with the social environment.

Professor Michael Marmot of the Department of Epidemiology and Public Health at the University College of London directed two important studies relating social status to health.[139] Using the British civil service system as the subject group, they found that the gradient of health quality in industrialized societies is not simply just a matter of poor health for the financially disadvantaged and good health for everyone else. They found that there was also a *social distribution of disease* as you went from the top of the socioeconomic ladder, to the bottom and the types of diseases people would get would change on average.

For example the lowest rungs of the hierarchy had a *fourfold increase* of heart disease based mortality, compared to the highest rungs. Even in a country with universal health care, the worse a person's financial status and position in the hierarchy, the worse their health is going to be on average. The reason is essentially psychological as it has been found that the more stratified a given society, the worse public health is in general, *specifically* for the lower

138 Class stratification is an immutable part of the current socioeconomic model due to both the incentive system generated that disproportionately distributes income, strategically favoring the upper tiers of the hierarchy – such as in 2007, Chief executives of the largest 365 US companies received well over *500 times* the pay of the average employee. This can be coupled with practices of macroeconomic monetary policy that structurally reward the wealthy and punish the poor through the *interest system*. (The wealthy gain interest income off investment while the poor, lacking investment capital, take loans for the majority of large purchases, paying interest. Put in abstraction, the poor are forced to give the rich their money through this mechanism.)

139 Whitehall Study I & II, (http://www.ucl.ac.uk/whitehallII/) Also see: *Epidemiology of socioeconomic status and health,* M. Marmot (http://www.ncbi.nlm.nih.gov/pubmed/10681885)

classes.[140]

This pattern has been corroborated by many other studies over the years, including a deep collection of research organized by Richard Wilkinson and Kate Pickett. In their work, *The Spirit Level – Why Equality is Better for Everyone*, they source hundreds of epidemiological studies on the issue, outlining how more unequal societies perpetuate a vast array of public health problems, both physiological and psychological.

Heart disease aside, some cancers, chronic lung disease, gastrointestinal disease, back pain, obesity, high blood pressure, low life expectancy and many other problems are also now found to be linked to socioeconomic status in the broad view, not just singular risk factors.[141] There is a *social gradient* in health quality across society and where we are placed in relation to other people has a powerful *psychosocial* effect. Those above us have better health on average while those below us have worse health on average.[142]

In fact, a statistical comparison of public health between countries with high levels of income inequality (such as the United States) and those with lower levels of income inequality (such as Japan) reveals these truths quite obviously.[143] However, such generally deemed "physical" illnesses are only part of the *public health crisis* generated by inequality that, again, is yet a consequence unto itself originating out of the direct, *immutable* stratification inherent to our global social system.

Psychological Health

Perhaps more profound in its public health implication is the result of social inequality on our mental or psychological health. This extends into behavioral reactions and tendencies such as acts of violence or abuse, along with emotional issues like depression, anxiety and personality disorders.

A general trend assessment of depression and anxiety in developed countries, countries that many intuitively would think would have more joy and ease due to the material wealth available, reveals a much different reality.[144] [145] A British study examining depression

---

140 Ibid.
141 A qualifier here to note is that this phenomenon relates more so to relatively wealthy societies in general than it does to inherently poverty stricken societies.
142 Reference: *Social Determinants of Health: The Solid Facts*, R.G. Wilkinson & M. Marmot, World Health Organization, 2006
143 A summary PDF of regression line charts extracted from the work of R. Wilkinson and K. Pickett can be found here for reference: http://www.tantor.com/Extras/B0505_SpiritLevel/B0505_SpiritLevel_PDF_1.pdf
144 Reference: *The Dramatic Rise of Anxiety and Depression in Children and Adolescents*, Peter Gray, 2012 (http://www.psychologytoday.com/blog/freedom-learn/201001/the-dramatic-rise-anxiety-and-depression-in-children-and-adolescents-is-it)
145 *Anxiety Disorders Are Sharply on the Rise,* Timi Gustafson R.D

among people in their 20s found that it was twice as common in 1970 than it was in 1958.[146] An American study of about 63,700 college students found that five times as many young adults are dealing with higher levels of anxiety than in the late 1930s.[147] A 2011 study presented at the American Psychological Association showed that mental illness was more common among college students than it was a decade ago.[148]

Psychologist Jean Twenge of San Diego University located 269 related studies measuring anxiety in the United States sourced between 1952 and 1993 and the aggregate assessment shows a dramatically clear trend in the rise of anxiety over this period, with, for example, the conclusion that by the late 1980s the *average* American child was more anxious than child *psychiatric patients* in the 1950s.[149]

A 2011 NCHS report revealed that the rate of antidepressant use in America among teens and adults (people ages 12 and older) increased by almost 400% between 1988–1994 and 2005–2008. Antidepressants were the third most common prescription medication taken by Americans in 2005–2008.[150]

While a genetic component for depression may have relevance, the trend rate clearly shows an environmental causality as the driving force. In the words of Richard Wilkinson: "[A]lthough people with mental illness sometimes have changes in the levels of certain chemicals in the brain, nobody has shown that these are *causes* of depression, rather than *changes* caused by depression...although some genetic vulnerability may underlie some mental illness, this can't by itself explain the huge rises in illness in recent decades - our genes can not change that fast."[151]

It appears our relative social status has a profound effect on our mental wellbeing and this tendency can also be found in what could be declared as the *evolutionary psychology* of similar primates as well. A 2002 study performed with macaque monkeys found that those who were subordinate/lower in a given social hierarchy had less dopamine activity than the dominant ones and this relationship would

---

(http://timigustafson.com/2011/anxiety-disorders-are-sharply-on-the-rise/)

146 *Time Trends in child and adolescent mental health*, Maughan, Collishaw, Goodman & Pickles, Journal of Child Psychology and Psychiatry, 2004

147 Sourcing the *Anxiety Disorders Association of America*, this article is a recommend summation:
http://www.msnbc.msn.com/id/39335628/ns/health-mental_health/t/why-are-anxiety-disorders-among-women-rise/#.UI9PRoUpzZg

148 *Depression On The Rise In College Students*, NPR, 2011
(http://www.npr.org/2011/01/17/132934543/depression-on-the-rise-in-college-students)

149 *The age of anxiety? Birth cohort change in anxiety and neuroticism*, J.M. Twenge, Journal of Personality and Social Psychology, 2007

150 *Antidepressant Use in Persons Aged 12 and Over: United States, 2005–2008*, Laura A. Pratt, NCHS, Oct 2011
(http://www.cdc.gov/nchs/data/databriefs/db76.htm)

151 *The Spirit Level* by Richard Wilkinson and Kate Pickett, Penguin, March 2009, p.65

change as different sets were regrouped. In other words, it had nothing to do with their specific biology – only the social arrangement that reduced or elevated their dopamine levels. It also found that lower hierarchy monkeys would use more cocaine to compensate. This is revealing as low dopamine levels in primates (including humans) are found to have a *direct correlation to depression.*[152]

The pattern has become very clear and while direct stressors such as job security, debt and other largely economic factors inherent to the social system may play a major role,[153] the relevance of socioeconomic status itself is still dominant. The following chart is a comparison of overall mental health and drug use by country.[154] It includes nine countries, sourcing data from WHO surveys, including anxiety disorders, mood disorders, impulsive disorders, addictions and others. One can clearly see that the United States, which also has the highest level of inequality, has an enormous level of mental health and drug disorders as well in comparison to the less stratified countries, with Italy being the lowest in mental health disorders of the group.

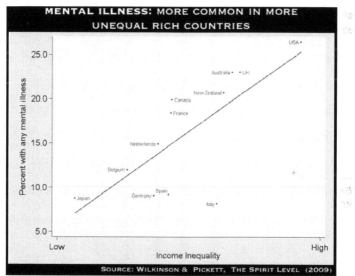

Even *perceived* social status, such as the *caste* relationships found in countries like India, can have a profound effect on confidence and behavior. A study performed in 2004 compared the problem-solving abilities of 321 high caste Indian boys against those of 321 low caste Indian boys. The results demonstrated that when caste was not publicly announced before the problem solving began, both sets of

---

152 *Social dominance in monkeys: dopamine D2 receptors and cocaine self-administration*, Morgan & Grant, Nature Neuroscience, 2002 5(2): p.169-74
153 *Suicide rates rocket in wake of economic downturn recession*, Nina Lakhani, The Independent, Aug 15 2012
154 Chart from *The Spirit Level* by Richard Wilkinson and Kate Pickett, Penguin, March 2009, p.67

boys achieved similar results. The second round, before which the caste of each group was publicly announced, the lower caste group fared much worse, and the higher caste much better, producing very divergent data compared with the first round.[155] People are greatly influenced by their perceived status in their society and often *when we expect to be viewed as inferior, very often we perform as such.*

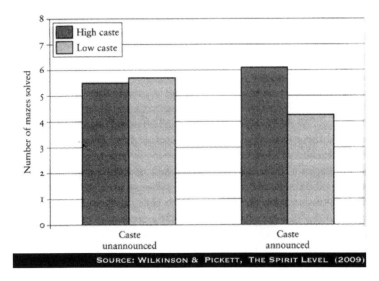

SOURCE: WILKINSON & PICKETT, THE SPIRIT LEVEL (2009)

In conclusion to this subsection regarding the psychosocial, inequality-based phenomenon that shows a clear relationship to psychological wellbeing, it is important to quickly make clear the vast *range of issues* found related. When it comes to education, social capital (trust), obesity, life expectancy, teen birth, imprisonment and punishment, social mobility, opportunity, and even innovation – countries with less income inequality do better than those with more income inequality. Put another way, they are *more healthy* societies.[156]

Case Study: Behavioral Violence

Coupled with the above issues relating to inequality in society, there is one that deserves a deeper look: *behavioral violence.* Criminal psychologist Dr. James Gilligan, former head of the Center for the Study of Violence at Harvard Medical School, wrote a definitive treatment on the subject in his work *Violence: Our Deadly Epidemic and its Causes.* Dr. Gilligan makes it very clear that extreme forms of violence are not random or genetically induced, but rather complex

---

155 *Belief Systems and Durable Inequalities,* Policy Research Working Paper, Waskington DC: World Bank, 2004 | Chart from *The Spirit Level* by Richard Wilkinson and Kate Pickett, Penguin, March 2009, p.113-114
156 Source: *The Spirit Level* by Richard Wilkinson and Kate Pickett, Penguin, March 2009

reactions that originate from stressful experiences, both in the long and short term.

For example, child abuse, both physical and emotional, along with increasingly difficult levels of personal stress, have a direct correlation to both premeditated and impulsive acts of violence and while men have a statistically higher propensity towards violence due to largely endocrinological characteristics that, while *not causing* violent reactions, can *exaggerate* them upon the stress influence,[157] the common theme is the influence of the environment and culture.

This is not to discount the relationship of hormones or even possibly genetic propensities,[158] but to show that at the origin of this behavior is clearly not our biology, but the condition upon which a human exists and the experiences endured. Other common assumptions of causality, such as "instinct" are also far too abstract and vague to hold any operational validity.[159]

Dr. Gilligan states: "I am suggesting that the only way to explain the causes of violence, so that we can learn how to prevent it, is to approach violence as a problem in public health and preventive medicine, and to think of violence as a symptom of life-threatening pathology, which, like all form of illness, has an etiology or cause, a pathogen."[160]

In Dr. Gilligan's diagnosis he makes it very clear that the greatest cause of violent behavior is *social inequality*, highlighting the influence of *shame* and *humiliation* as an emotional characteristic of those who engage in violence.[161] Thomas Scheff, a emeritus professor of sociology in California stated that "shame was *the* social emotion".[162] Shame and humiliation can be equated with the feelings of stupidity, inadequacy, embarrassment, foolishness, feeling exposed, insecurity and the like – all largely social or comparative in their origin.

Needless to say, in a global society with not only growing income disparity but inevitably "self-worth" disparity - since status is

---

157 The hormone testosterone has been commonly "blamed" for male aggression. However it has been found that inter-individual differences in levels of testosterone *do not* result in proportional differences in levels of aggressive behavior when tests on the general population were conducted. It has been found that rather than testosterone causing aggression levels to rise, it is essentially the other way around. See *The Trouble with Testosterone,* Robert M. Sapolsky, Simon & Schuster, 1997, p.147-159

158 Reference: *Violence—A noxious cocktail of genes and the environment, Mariya Moosajee, J R Soc Med. 2003 May; 96(5): 211–214* | Notes a study in New Zealand where an apparent genetic link found to violent behavior would *only* manifest if a great deal of abuse in childhood took place to trigger an expression of that apparent genetic propensity. (http://www.ncbi.nlm.nih.gov/pmc/articles/PMC539471/)

159 Reference: *Violence,* James Gilligan, Grosset/Putnam, New York, 1992, p.210-213

160 Ibid, p.92

161 Ibid, Chapter 5

162 Source: *Shame and conformity: the defense-emotion system,* T.J. Scheff, American Sociological Review, 1988, 53:395-406

touted as directly related to our "success" in our jobs, bank account levels and the like - it is no mystery that feelings of inferiority, shame and humiliation are staples of the culture today. The consequence of those feelings have very serious implications for public health, as noted before, including the epidemic of the behavioral violence we now see today in its various complex forms. Terrorism, local school and church shootings, along with other extreme acts that simply did not exist before in the abstractions they find context today, reveals a unique evolution of violence itself. Dr. Gilligan concludes: "If we wish to prevent violence, then, our agenda is political and economic reform."[163]

The following chart shows rates of homicide across wealthy nations with varying states of social inequality. The United States, which is likely the largest "anti-socialist" advocate with little structural safeguards in place (such as a lack of universal health care), while also pushing the psychological ethic that "independence" and "competition" are the most important ethos - shows a massive level of violence. While debates over gun control and the like still persist in the American political landscape with respect to the epidemic, clearly that has nothing really to do with causality.

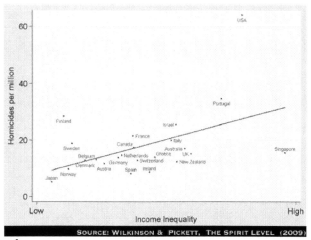

SOURCE: WILKINSON & PICKETT, THE SPIRIT LEVEL (2009)

In Conclusion

This essay has attempted to give a concise overview of core causal relationships to human health on both the psychological level and the physiological level. The theme is how the socioeconomic condition in general improves or worsens public health overall, alluding to ideal conditions which would improve happiness, reduce general disease and alleviate epidemic behavioral problems, such as violence.

While direct economic relationships are very clear in how they reduce human health and wellbeing in the form of *absolute deprivation*, such as an inability to obtain quality food, labor-related

163 Source: *Violence*, James Gilligan, Grosset/Putnam, New York, 1992, p.236

59

time restraints that reduce emotional and developmental support for children, loss of education quality due to regional funding problems, along with case by case turmoil such as the fact that most marriages end due to monetary problems,[164] the *relative deprivation* issue has been more of a focus here due to the fact that it is less understood and more relevant than most understand.

Put into the structural, socioeconomic context, these realities firmly challenges the ethos that competition, class and other "capitalist" notions of incentive and progress are drivers of social progress and health. The more we learn about this phenomenon, the stronger the argument becomes that the nature of our socioeconomic system is somewhat backwards in its focus and intent. Human progress, health and success are clearly not defined by the constant influx of market goods, gadgets and material creations for purchase. Public health and wellbeing are *based on how we relate to each other and the environment as a whole* and market induced stratification is extremely caustic to society.

The result is a *hidden form of violence* against the population and hence the public health issues we see are really *civil & human rights issues,* since they simply do not need to exist. When we see clear genocide in the world we object strongly on purely moral grounds. But what if there existed a constant genocide that is unseen but very real, perpetuated not by a specific person or group but by disorder born out of stress/effects generated by the traditional method of human interaction and economic ordering that has been created and codified?

As will be argued in the following essays, mere adjustments to the current socioeconomic system are not enough in the long-term to substantially resolve these problems. The very foundational principles of our current model are bound by hierarchical economic and competitive orientations and to truly work to remove those attributes and consequences is to completely transform the entire social system.

---

164 Reference: *Money Fights Predict Divorce Rates,* Catherine Rampell (http://economix.blogs.nytimes.com/2009/12/07/money-fights-predict-divorce-rates/)

-HISTORY OF ECONOMY-

It is a telling symptom of our condition that no established school, discipline or general theory of social analysis has grounded itself in life requirements... Instead, some social construct is invariably adopted as the ultimate reference body- set of ideas, the state, the market, a class, technological development, or some other factor than the
life-ground itself.[165]
-John McMurtry

Overview
Economics is likely the most critical, relevant and influential societal characteristic there is. Virtually every aspect of our lives, often without conscious recognition, has a relationship to the historical development and present practice of economic thought on one level or another, molding our most basic social institutions, core beliefs and values. In fact, the very essence of how we as a society think about our *relationship* to each other and the habitat that supports us is, in large part, a direct result of the economic theories and practices we perpetuate.

Thoughtful review of historical religious & moral philosophies, governmental development, political parties, legal statutes and other social contracts and beliefs that comprise a given social system and its culture, reveal the deep impact economic assumptions have and continue to have in shaping of the "zeitgeist" of a time.

Slavery, classism, xenophobia, racism, sexism, subjugation and many other divisive & exploitative notions still common to human cultural history will be found to have kernels of origin or perpetuation in many generally accepted economic philosophies to one degree or another. History is fairly clear with respect to how the social condition is groomed by the prevailing economic assumptions of a given period and this broad sociological consideration is sadly not given much gravity in the world today when thinking about why the world is the way it is and why we think the way we do.

As a preliminary point, a point which will reemerge later in this essay, there has commonly been a duality noted in most modern economic thought where the "capitalist free market", meaning the "free" actions of independent producers, laborer and traders, working in aggregate to buy, sell and employ,[166] is to be contrasted to that of the "state", meaning a unified system of delegated power that has the capacity to set legal policy and economic mandates that can inhibit the actions of the "free market" through interference. Most economic debates today revolved around this duality on one level or another with the "laissez-faire" interests, or those who wish to have a

---

165 Source: *The Cancer Stage of Capitalism*, John McMurtry, Pluto Press, 1999, p.viii
166 A less generalized definition of the "free-market" is as follows: "An economic system in which prices and wages are determined by unrestricted competition between businesses, without government regulation or fear of monopolies." (http://dictionary.reference.com/browse/free+market)

completely non-regulated market economy, constantly at war with the "statists", or those who think some kind of centralized government control and decision making over economic planning and policy is best.

The Zeitgeist Movement takes neither side, even though many who hear TZM's proposals have a knee-jerk reaction to assume the latter association ("statism").[167] As with many traditionalized belief systems, polarized perspectives and defenses are common and the idea that there is no other possible *frame of reference* with respect to how an economic system can be developed and administered, is to close oneself off dogmatically to many relevant and emerging considerations.

The following, brief treatment is about the *historical* development of economics. We will trace the general history of economic thought from roughly the 17th century onward, highlighting the core influences that gave birth to the modern, "free market capitalist" system. However, as will be expanded upon more so in part III, a different perspective will also be alluded to. We will call this the "mechanistic" view. The mechanistic perspective of economic factoring takes a different look at the causal, *scientific* realities of human existence and our habitat and builds a model of economic theory from the standpoint of *strategic reason,* not *historical tradition*.

The bottom line is that modern economic thought is really not modern at all and the vast majority of assumptions still held as 'given', such as "property", "money", "classism", theories of "value", "capital" and other concepts that run through virtually all contextually relevant historical arguments, are really *outdated* in their underlying premises. Rapid development in the industrial, informational and human sciences, which have gone largely ignored by the established economic tradition, are posing critical reconsiderations and new relationships which simply *do not exist* in the traditional models.[168]

With respect to the ever mutating "schools" of thought that have brought the economic debate to where it rests today, the academic, often formulaic traditionalized evolution of established economic theory (and practice) appears to have developed a *self-referring frame of reference.*[169]

---

167 As will be described in later essays, TZM's often false categorization of being "statist" is rooted in its general opposition to market principles, which it finds to be unsustainable and often counterproductive. "Statism", which can take many forms, such as communist, fascist or socialist, advocates a "central authority" to decide how the economic/political process is to unfold, with little to no relevant influence occurring via the general population. TZM supports an open decision making process in general, under the imposition of basic, proven laws of scientific sustainability and efficiency.

168 The notion of an "externality", which will be noted later in this essay, is a case in point. Most environmental and social costs systemic to the market approach, along with arguably the *loss of efficiency* and hence prosperity, are dismissed in the theoretical equation of the market, among many other relevant issues.

169 Economic philosopher John McMurtry stated generally on this issue: "This tendency prevails from the Continental Rationalists on. Leibniz, Spinoza,

In other words, the most common "mainstream" economic considerations discussed/accepted today; those most propagated in the prestigious academic schools and governmental conferences, will be found to derive their importance from the mere fact that they have been *considered* important for so long. As a metaphor, it is similar to viewing the engine of an automobile and assuming the overall structure of that engine is immutable and only variation among existing component parts is possible, as opposed to the radical idea of *redesigning* the entire engine structure from the ground up, perhaps based upon new technology and information that serves the utility more efficiently and successfully.

"Modern" economic thought and practice is an old engine with generations of imminent "experts" working to administer old components parts, refusing to accept the possibility that the entire engine is outdated and perhaps increasingly detrimental. They continue to publish arguments, theories and equations that reinforce the false importance of that old engine (old "frame of reference"), ignoring new advents in science, technology and public health that contradict their traditionalism. It is no different than the long history of other "established" ideas, such as abject human slavery, where the society at large really didn't question the practice, and considered such *established structures,* imposed and codified, as "natural" to the human condition.[170]

Underlying Themes

Taking an historical perspective, Europe of the Middle Ages[171] is generally a decent ideological starting point as the most central ideas characteristic of modern capitalism, which later spread across the world, appear to have taken hold during this period.[172] It is from the 17th century onward that we find most of the influential philosophers

Descartes, Berkeley, Kant and Hegel, for example, more or less entirely presupposed the social regime of their day and its constituent forms as in some way the expression of the divine Mind, which they see it as their rational duty only to accept or to justify." *The Cancer Stage of Capitalism,* Pluto Press, 1999, p.7

170 Aristotle (384 BC– 322 BC), while credited with extensive scientific, logical and philosophical contribution, was also in favor of slavery, justifying the reality with what could be argued as *bias*, not reason. He stated: "But is there any one thus intended by nature to be a slave, and for whom such a condition is expedient and right, or rather is not all slavery a violation of nature? There is no difficulty in answering this question, on grounds both of reason and of fact. For that some should rule and others be ruled is a thing not only necessary, but expedient; from the hour of their birth, some are marked out for subjection, others for rule." *Politics,* Book I, Chapters III through VII

171 The term "Middle Ages" generally refers to the period of European history that lasted from the 5th until the 15th centuries.

172 For a detailed study of the medieval economic system and society, the following work is suggested: *The Agrarian Life of the Middle Ages,* J.H. Chapman and Eileen E. Powers, eds., 2d ed., *The Cambridge Economic History of Europe,* vol. 1 London, Cambridge University Press, 1966

highly regarded today in traditional history books of economics. While historians have found that the basic gestures of "property" and the act of "trading for profit" go back to the second millennium BC,[173] its core developmental foundation and institutionalization appears to rests around the late feudal/early mercantilist periods.

Rather than discuss the various differences between the socioeconomic systems that preceded modern capitalism, it is more worthwhile to note the general similarities. In this broad context, the capitalist system appears to be a manifest evolution of what are mostly deeply ingrained *historical assumptions* of human nature and human social relations.[174]

Firstly, it will be noticed throughout this evolution that a *class divide* has been recognized and employed to one degree or another. People have generally been divided into two groups[175] - those that *produce* for minimal reward and those who *gain* from that production. From ancient Egyptian slavery,[176] to the peasant farmer toiling in subsistence for his lord in medieval feudalism,[177] to the codified oppression of the market merchants by the state monopolies of mercantilism,[178] the theme of *inequality* has been very clear and consistent.

A second feature held in common to these dominant Western socioeconomic philosophies is that of a basic disregard (or perhaps ignorance) of critical relationships between the human species and its governing, supportive habitat. While certain exceptions can be found with indigenous tribes such as with pre-colonial, Native American societies,[179] Western economic thought has been almost devoid of such considerations, absent the more recent and mounting ecological problems which have forced some public/government response and a very general interest in "reform".[180]

---

173 Reference: *Macroeconomics from the beginning: The General Theory, Ancient Markets, and the Rate of Interest*, David Warburton Paris, Recherches et Publications, 2003 p.49

174 The "Emergent" consideration of economic development appears to be a relatively new concept, introduced most popularly by Thorstein Veblen in the early 20th century. Suggested reading on the subject of economic evolution: *The Evolution of Institutional Economics: Agency, Structure and Darwinism in American Institutionalism,* Geoffrey M. Hodgson, London, Routledge, 2004

175 The distinction of "classes" in specific categories is without exact meaning, historically. The point here is the ongoing presence of a clearly dominant class, whether that of ancient nobility, for example, or the modern financial oligarchy.

176 Reference: *The Historical Encyclopedia of World Slavery*, Junius P. Rodriguez, Vol I, Section E

177 Reference: *Mediaeval Feudalism*, Carl Stephenson, Cornell University Press, 1956

178 Reference: *A History of Economic Theory and Method*, Robert B. Ekelund; Robert F. Hébert, New York: McGraw-Hill, 1975

179 Reference: *Defending Mother Earth: Native American Perspectives on Environmental Justice*, Jace Weaver, Orbis Books, 1996

180 To list the ecological problems now facing humanity, from climate

A third and final broad feature to note is the general dismissal of the social recognition of a person's wellbeing on the level of *human need* and hence *public health*. Advancements in the human sciences, which occurred largely after the core doctrines of economic thought were traditionally codified, have found that *human wants* and *human needs*[181] are not the same and the deprivation of the latter can create many negative consequences not only for the individual but for the society itself. Anti-social, "criminal" and violent behavior, for example, have been found sourced to many forms of social deprivation rooted in the socioeconomic tradition.[182] Put more generally, the system ignores such social consequences by design, relegating these outcomes as mere "externalities" in most cases.

This reality was further compounded in the 18th century where the "socially Darwinistic"[183] undertone of the "labor-for-reward" premise increasingly reduced the human being to an object that was to be defined and qualified by his or her contribution to the system of labor. If the average person is unable to obtain labor or engage successfully in the market economy, there exists no real safeguard with respect to one's survival or wellbeing, except for "interference" coming from the "state" in the form of "welfare". In the modern day, this reality is of great controversy where the claim of "socialism" has become a knee-jerk condemnation reaction whenever governmental policy attempts to provide direct support for a citizenry without full use of the market mechanism.

Dawn of Market Capitalism

Medieval Feudalism (roughly from the 9th to 16th centuries) was the dominant socioeconomic system that essentially preceded "free market capitalism" in Western Europe, with what was later to be called "mercantilism" serving as what could be considered a transition stage.

Feudalism was based on a system of mutual obligations and services going up and down a set social hierarchy, with the entire social system resting essentially on an agricultural foundation. Medieval society was mostly an agrarian society and the social hierarchy was based essentially on peoples' ties to land. The basic

---

destabilization, to pollution, to resource depletion, to loss of biodiversity and other invariably *public health* threats, would be too extensive to detail here. In the view of TZM, these issues are largely a result of the Capitalist premise and its accepted approaches and values .

181 Consumption patterns in modern society have shown an arbitrary nature with respect to "Human Wants", such as the powerful shift in values which occurred in the early 20th century with the application of modern Western advertising. "Human Needs", however, are basic necessities, largely shared by all humans, which maintain physical and psychological health.

182 See the essay *Defining Public Health*.

183 "Social Darwinism" is a very general ideology that seeks to apply biological concepts of Darwinism or of "survival of the fittest" type theory to sociology and politics. Historian Richard Hofstadter popularized the term in the United States in 1944. The intuition of this concept, however, appears long before Darwin's time in philosophical thought.

economic institutions were the "guilds" and if someone wanted to produce or sell a good or service, they would generally join a guild. A great deal could be stated in detail about this extensive period of history and as with most history it is subject to various interpretations and debate. However, for the sake of this essay, we will only present a very general overview with respect to the economic transition to market capitalism.[184]

As agricultural and transport technology improved, the expansion of trade occurred and by the 13th century, with the advent of the four-wheeled wagon, for example, the range of market interaction rapidly increased. Likewise, increased labor specialization, urban concentrations and population growth also occurred.[185] These changes, coupled with the resulting, increasing power of the "merchant capitalists", as they could be called, slowly weakened the traditional, customary ties that held the feudal social structure together.

Over time, more complex cities began to emerge which were successful in obtaining independence from the feudal lords and increasingly complex systems of exchange, credit and law began to emerge, many of which are found to mirror many basic aspects of modern capitalism. In the customary feudal system, generally the "handicraft" producer was also the seller to the buyer of use. However, as the evolution of the market continued around these new urban centers, the craftsman began to sell at a discount in mass to non-producing merchants who would resell in distant markets for a "profit"-another feature later to be held common to market capitalism.

By the 16th century, the "handicraft" industry common to feudalism had been transformed into a crude mirror of what we know today, with the outsourcing of labor, singular ownership of production, along with many finding themselves more and more in the position of being "employed" rather than producing themselves. Eventually, the logic surrounding monetary *profit* began to be the core, deciding factor of overall action in a systemic way and the true seeds of capitalism took root.[186]

Mercantilism, which essentially dominated Western European economic policy from the 16th to the late 18th centuries,[187] was characterized by state-driven trade monopolies to ensure a positive "balance of trade",[188] coupled with many other extensive regulations for production, wages and commerce emerging over time, further

---

184 Reference: *Mediaeval Feudalism*, Carl Stephenson, Cornell University Press, 1956

185 Reference: *The Economy of Early Renaissance Europe, 1300–1460*, Harry A. Miskimin, Englewood Cliffs, NJ: Prentice-Hall, 1969, p.20

186 Reference: *Studies in the Development of Capitalism*, Maurice H. Dobb, London, Routledge and Kegan Paul, 1946, Chapter 4

187 Reference: *The Concise Encyclopedia of Economics,* David R. Henderson, Liberty Fund, Inc, 2002, "Mercantilism"

188 A positive balance of trade is also known as a "trade surplus" and it consists of exporting more than is imported in monetary value. This act by the State is often called "Protectionism" today.

increasing the power of the state. Collusion between the state and these emerging industries were common and many wars occurred due to these practices since it was based on trade restrictions between nations that often took the effect of economic warfare.[189]

Adam Smith, who will be discussed later in this essay, wrote an extensive criticism of mercantilism in his classic 1776 text, *An Inquiry into the Nature and Causes of the Wealth of Nations*.[190] It is here where it could be declared that the ideological birth of "free market" capitalism really took root in theory, with the rejection of what is often called "state" capitalism in modern terms, where the state "interferes" with the "freedom" of the market - a defining feature of mercantilism.[191]

Today, "capitalism", as a singular term, is generally defined culturally in the theoretical context of "free market" not "state" capitalism, although many will argue in great detail as to which type of system we really have today, among other variations of the term. In reality, there is no pure "free market" or "state" based system in existence but a complex fusion between the two, generally speaking. Again, as noted at the beginning of this essay, the vast majority of economic debates and blame regarding economic unfolding often revolve around these polarized ideas.[192]

Capitalism Defined

Capitalism[193] as we know it in specifics today, including not only its economic theory but powerful political and social effects, emerged in form, as noted, rather slowly over a period of several centuries. It should be stated upfront that there is no complete agreement amongst economic historians/theorists as to what the essential features of capitalism really are. We will, however, reduce its historical characterization (which some will likely find debatable) to four basic features.

---

189 Reference: *The Growth of Economic Thought*, Henry William Spiegel, Duke University Press, 3rd Ed, 1991, pp.93-118.

190 Reference: A*n Inquiry into the Nature and Causes of the Wealth of Nations*, Adam Smith, 1776, Book IV: Of Systems of Political Economy

191 Murray Rothbard, a featured economist of the modern "Austrian School", summarized the "Statist" perspective and criticism: "Mercantilism, which reached its height in the Europe of the seventeenth and eighteenth centuries, was a system of statism which employed economic fallacy to build up a structure of imperial state power, as well as special subsidy and monopolistic privilege to individuals or groups favored by the state. Thus, mercantilism held exports should be encouraged by the government and imports discouraged." (*Mercantilism: A Lesson for Our Times?*, Murray Rothbard, Freeman, 1963)

192 As argued in the essay *Value System Disorder*, this is a false duality and moot with respect to the underlying problems commonly attributed to the polarized debate.

193 From here on in this essay, we will use the term "capitalism" in its most common cultural form, implying the "free market" theoretical context.

1) Market-based production/distribution: Commodity production is based around rather complex interrelationships and dependencies that do not involve *direct* personal interactions between producers and consumers. Supply and demand is mediated by the "market" system.

2) Private ownership of production means: This means that society grants to private persons the right to dictate how the raw materials, tools, machinery, and buildings necessary for production can be used.

3) Decoupling of ownership and labor: In short, a constant class divide is inherent where on the top level, "capitalists",[194] by historical definition, own the means of production, but yet have no obligation to contribute to production itself. The capitalist owns everything produced by the laborers, who only own their own labor, by legal authority.

4) Self-maximizing incentive assumed: Individualistic, competitive and acquisitive interests are necessary for the successful functioning of capitalism since a constant pressure to consume and expand is needed to avoid recessions, depressions and other negatives. In many ways, this is the "rational" behavioral view held where if all humans acted in a certain assumed way, the system would function without inhibition.[195]

Locke: Evolution of "Property"
A deep philosophical undercurrent to the capitalist system is the notion of "property". English philosopher John Locke (1632-1704) is a pivotal figure. Also sourced in Adam Smith's more influential *Wealth of Nations*, Locke not only defines the idea in general, he presents a subtle yet powerful contradiction.

In Chapter V, entitled "property", of Locke's *Second Treatise of Government* published in 1689, he poses an argument with respect to the nature of property and its appropriation. He states: "The labour of his body and the work of his hands, we may say, are strictly his. So when he takes something from the state that nature has provided and left it in, he *mixes his labour with it*, thus joining to it something that is his own; and in that way he makes it his property."[196] This statement (supporting in gesture what was later to associate with the "labor theory of value"), proposes the logic that since labor is "owned" by the

---

194 While a "capitalist" can be considered a person in favor of this approach to economy, a more accurate definition denotes "a person who has capital, especially extensive capital, invested in business enterprises." [http://dictionary.reference.com/browse/capitalist] In other words, this is a person who owns or invests capital for a return or profit, but yet has no obligation to contribute to actual production or labor in any way.

195 A corollary to this are the various "rational choice" and "utility theories" common to free market microeconomic theory which attempts to quantify human actions around various behavioral models. (more on this later in the essay)

196 Source: *Second Treatise of Government,* John Locke, 1689, Chapter V, Section 27

laborer (since he owns himself), any energy expelled through his labor *transfers* that ownership to the product made.

His philosophical disposition is essentially derived from a Christian perspective, stating: "God gave the world to men in common; but since he gave it to them for their benefit and for the greatest conveniences of life they could get from it, he can't have meant it always to remain common and uncultivated."[197]

Given this declaration of the "common" nature of the earth and its fruits to all of humanity before its "cultivation" via appropriation in the form property, he also derives that owners are required to not allow anything to *spoil* ("Nothing was made by God for man to spoil or destroy.")[198] and they must leave enough for others ("This appropriation of a plot of land by improving it wasn't done at the expense of any other man, because there was still enough [and as good] left for others...").[199]

These values, in simplistic form, seem socially justifiable in general. He makes it clear up until this point that the ownership context is relevant only in so far as the owner's *needs* and ability to *cultivate*, or produce.[200] However, in Section 36, he reveals a unique reality, the implications of which Locke likely did not anticipate and, in many ways, nullifies all prior arguments in his defense of private property. He states: "The 'one thing' that blocks this is the invention of money, and men's tacit agreement to put a value on it; this made it possible, with men's consent, to have larger possessions and to have a right to them."[201]

Now, in effect, his original premise, summarized in part here, that: "Anyone can through his labour come to own as much as he can *use in a beneficial way* before it spoils; anything beyond this is *more than his* share and belongs to others"
[202] becomes very difficult to defend as money now not only allows "[men] to have larger possessions", implicitly voiding in context the idea that "anything beyond this is *more than his* share and belongs to others", it also further implies that money can *buy labor*, which voids the idea that "he [in this case the buyer] *mixes his labour with it*, thus joining to it something that is his own; and in that way he makes it his property."[203]

Finally, the proviso "Nothing was made by God for man to spoil

---

197 Ibid, Chapter V, Section 34, 1689
198 Ibid, Chapter V, Section 31, 1689
199 Ibid, Chapter V, Section 33, 1689
200 Locke States: "Nature did well in setting limits to private property through limits to how much men can work and limits to how much they need. No man's labour could tame or appropriate all the land; no man's enjoyment could consume more than a small part; so that it was impossible for any man in this way to infringe on the right of another, or acquire a property to the disadvantage of his neighbor..." (*Second Treatise of Government*, John Locke, Chapter V, Section 36, 1689)
201 Ibid, Chapter V, Section 36, 1689
202 Ibid, Chapter V, Section 31, 1689
203 Ibid, Chapter V, Section 27, 1689

or destroy"[204] is nullified with a new association that money, being gold or silver at that time, simply *cannot* spoil. "That is how money came into use - as a durable thing that men could keep without its spoiling, and that by mutual consent men would take in exchange for the truly useful but perishable supports of life."[205]

It is here where we find, at least in the medium of literary discourse, the true seed of capitalist *ownership justification* where the use of money, treated as an abstract commodity in and of itself (in effect, an assumed embodiment of "labor"), allowed an evolution of thought and practice to emerge which increasingly shifted the focus from relevant production (Locke's "cultivation") to mere ownership mechanics and the pursuit of profit.[206]

Adam Smith

Adam Smith (1723-1790) is often credited as one of the most influential economic philosophers in modern history. His work, while naturally based on the philosophical writings of many before him, is often considered a starting point for economic thought in the context of modern capitalism. Reaching maturity at the dawn of the Industrial Revolution,[207] Smith lived at a time where it could be argued that the inherent features of the capitalist "mode of production" were becoming ever more striking, given the introduction of concentrated, centralized production factories and markets.

As noted, in 1776 Smith published his now world famous *An Inquiry into the Nature and Causes of the Wealth of Nations*. Among many relevant observations, he appears to be the first to recognize the three principal categories of income at the time - (a) profits, (b) rents and (c) wages - and how they related to the main social classes of the period - (a) capitalists, (b) landlords, and (c) laborers. It is worth noting that the role of *landlords/rent*, which is seldom discussed today in modern economic treatments, was a common point of focus then since the pre-industrial systems where still largely agrarian, highlighting the *landlords* (which later dissolved into the classification of simply *owners* in future market theories).

Smith's most noted contribution to the philosophy of capitalism was his general advocation that even though individuals might act in a narrow, selfish manner on their personal behalf or on the behalf of the class or group to which they are a part, and even though conflict, both

---

204 Ibid, Chapter V, Section 31, 1689
205 Ibid, Chapter V, Section 47, 1689
206 The Stock Market and increasing power of the investment/financial powers around the world in the 21st century reflects this culmination well. It appears that the mere act of ownership and trade via money alone, without any need for production cultivation and human service, has become the most profitable industry in the world today.
207 The Industrial Revolution occurred from about 1760 to some time between 1820 and 1840 starting in Europe, according to various historians, and was essentially the transition/application to new, technology based manufacturing processes.

individual or class based, seemed to be the result of these actions, there was what he called an "invisible hand" that secured a positive social outcome from singular, selfish, non-social intents. This concept was presented both in his works *The Theory of Moral Sentiments*[208] and *The Wealth of Nations.*

He stated in the latter: "As every individual, therefore, endeavors as much as he can both to employ his capital in the support of domestic industry, and so to direct that industry that its produce may be of the greatest value; every individual necessarily labors to render the annual revenue of the society as great as he can. He generally, indeed, neither intends to promote the public interest, nor knows how much he is promoting it...he intends only his own gain, and he is in this, as in many other cases, led by an invisible hand to promote an end which was no part of his intention. Nor is it always the worse for the society that it was no part of it. By pursuing his own interest he frequently promotes that of the society more effectually than when he really intends to promote it."[209]

This nearly religious ideal had a powerful effect on the post-Smith era, giving a very *social* vindication for the inherently self-maximizing, *anti-social* behavior common to capitalist psychology. This basic philosophy was to develop, in part, as the foundation of "neoclassical"[210] economics beginning in the late nineteenth century.

Smith, knowing quite well the class conflicts inherent to capitalism, goes on to discuss the nature of how some men gain "...superiority over the greater part of their brethren",[211] reinforcing what was to increasingly be considered a "law of nature" regarding human power and subjugation by further theorists. His view of property was in harmony with John Locke, elaborating on how society itself is manifest around it. He stated "Civil government, so far as it is

---

208 "The rich only select from the heap what is most precious and agreeable. They consume little more than the poor, and in spite of their natural selfishness and rapacity, though they mean only their own conveniency, though the sole end which they propose from the labours of all the thousands whom they employ, be the gratification of their own vain and insatiable desires, they divide with the poor the produce of all their improvements. They are led by an invisible hand to make nearly the same distribution of the necessaries of life, which would have been made, had the earth been divided into equal portions among all its inhabitants, and thus without intending it, without knowing it, advance the interest of the society, and afford means to the multiplication of the species." [*The Theory of Moral Sentiments* par. IV.I.10, 1790]

209 Source: *An Inquiry into the Nature and Causes of the Wealth of Nations*, Adam Smith, 1776, par. IV.2.9

210 There is no static definition of "neoclassical economics". However, a general, culturally common summary includes the broad interest in "free", unregulated markets, focusing on the determination of prices, outputs, and income distributions in markets through supply and demand, often mediated through a hypothesized maximization of utility by income-constrained individuals and of profits by cost-constrained firms.

211 Source: *An Inquiry into the Nature and Causes of the Wealth of Nations*, Adam Smith, 1776, par. V.1.2

instituted for the security of property, is in reality instituted for the defense of the rich against the poor, or of those who have some property against those who have none at all."[212]

Property, as an institution, also requires a means to justify respective *value*. To this end, various "theories of value" have been and continue to be postulated. Often sourced in origin back to Aristotle's *Politics,* Smith's contribution is still widely referenced as a pivotal influence. In effect, Smith builds upon Locke's "mixing labor" premise of production/ownership and extends from there, creating a "labor theory of value".

He states "Labour was the first price, the original purchase money that was paid for all things. It was not by gold or by silver, but by labour, that all the wealth of the world was originally purchased; and its value, to those who possess it, and who want to exchange it for some new productions, is precisely equal to the quantity of labour which it can enable them to purchase or command."[213] Many chapters of Book I of *Wealth of Nations* work to explain the nature of prices/values respective to his denoted income/class categories of "wages", "rents", and "profits". However, it will be found that his logic is rather circular in specifics as the price assessments are found to originate merely from *other* price assessments in a chain with no real starting point, other than the loose distinction of applied labor, which has, of course, no intrinsic, static monetary qualification. This problem of ambiguity in both the dominant "labor" and "utility" theories of value common to capitalist market theory will be addressed in detail later in this essay.

Overall, Smith's economic theory supported "laissez-faire" capitalism as the highest mode of socioeconomic operation, stating that: it was a "system of natural liberty" and "Every man, as long as he does not violate the laws of justice, is left perfectly free to pursue his own interest his own way, and to bring both his industry and capital into competition with those of any other man, or order of men."[214] This later concept, as will be argued in the essay, *Value System Disorder,* is a rather naive assumption of human behavior and, in effect, a contradiction in terms.

Malthus and Ricardo

Thomas Malthus (1766-1834) and David Ricardo (1772-1823) were two well acknowledged, leading theorists of political economy of the early 19th century. They were "friendly rivals" by some comparison but from the broad view of history they shared virtually the same perspective, closely tied to Adam Smith's.

The late Industrial Revolution in Europe and America was a period of extensive conflict between laborers and capitalist owners. Numerous revolts and strikes in response to abhorrent and abusive working conditions for not only men, but also women and children,

---

212 Ibid.
213 Ibid.
214 Ibid., par. IV.9.51

were common. This gave rapid rise to the now common labor unions and a general battle between "workers and owners" has continued ever since. To emphasize the extent of this class warfare, in England, the *Combination Act of 1799* was imposed which basically outlawed any combination of workers to group together for power in order to, in effect, exert influence or inhibit the interests of their employers.[215]

Historian Paul Mantoux, writing of this period, commented on "the absolute and uncontrolled power of the capitalist. In this, the heroic age of great undertakings, it was acknowledged, admitted and even proclaimed with brutal candor. It was the employer's own business, he did as he chose and did not consider that any other justification of his conduct was necessary. He owed his employees wages and once those were paid the men had no further claim on him."[216] It was in the midst of all this that Malthus and Ricardo invariably contextualized their economic and social views.

Beginning with Malthus, his classic work *An Essay on the Principle of Population* orients around essentially two assumptions. The first is that the class structure of wealthy proprietors and poor laborers would inevitably reemerge no matter what reforms where attempted.[217] He considered it a *law of nature*. The second idea, something of a corollary to first, was simply that poverty and suffering and hence economic divides were inevitable consequences of natural law.[218]

His thesis on population rests upon the very simple assumption that "Population, when unchecked, increases in a geometrical ratio. Subsistence increases only in an arithmetical ratio."[219] Therefore, if the standard of living of everyone in society were increased, the vast majority would respond by increasing the amount of children they have. In turn, population outpacing subsistence would very soon push the population back to poverty. It was only through "moral restraint",[220] a social quality that he implies to belong to the more upstanding upper class, that this problem is checked by behavior.

---

215 This power of capitalist interests to engage and, in many ways, *become* the government to serve their own competitive advantage will also be discussed in the essay: "Value System Disorder"

216 Source: *The Industrial Revolution in the Eighteenth Century*, Paul Mantoux, Harcourt Brace Jovanovich, New York, 1927, p.417

217 He states: "No possible sacrifices of the rich, particularly in money, could for any time prevent the recurrence of distress among the lower members of society, whoever they were" (*An Essay on the Principle of Population*, Thomas Malthus, 1798, Chapter 5)

218 He states: "It has appeared, that from the inevitable laws of our nature some human beings must suffer from want. These are the unhappy persons who, in the great lottery of life, have drawn a blank." (*An Essay on the Principle of Population*, Thomas Malthus, 1798, Chapter 10)

219 Source: *An Essay on the Principle of Population*, Thomas Malthus, 1798, Chapter 1

220 From his 2nd edition of *An Essay on the Principle of Population*, 1836, *Principles of Political Economy*, vol. 1, p.14. New York, Augustus M. Kelley, 1964.

Evidently, the difference between the wealthy and the poor was the high moral character of the former and the base morality of the latter.[221]

Again, as noted prior in this essay, the *intuitive cultural condition* has had a great deal to do with the prevailing premises of thought that have guided economic operations into the modern day. While many today might dismiss Malthus and these clearly outdated ideas, the seeds were deeply planted in the economic doctrines, values and class relationships that occurred during and after his time. In fact, those of a more "conservative" mindset still commonly cite variations of his population theory when dealing with economically less-developed countries.

Malthus, along with Locke and Smith, also held deeply Christian convictions in their frames of reference, whether directly extracted from scripture or based on personal interpretation. Malthus frames his "moral restraint" with the implication that a true Christian would righteously denounce such base vices and also accept the *inevitable* misery necessary to keep population from outstripping resource subsistence. Likewise, just as there is enormous debate today with respect to laws pertaining to the notion and use of "welfare" or "public aid" programs" to help the poor,[222] Malthus, naturally, was a big proponent of the abolition of what were then called the "poor laws", as was David Ricardo.

Moving on to Ricardo, he essentially accepted Malthus' population theory and conclusions regarding the nature and causes of poverty, but disagreed with certain economic theories, such as elements of Malthus' *theory of value, theory of gluts* and certain class assumptions. Since most of these disagreements in detail are superfluous to this broad discussion at hand (and arguably outdated in general), Ricardo's most notable contributions to economic thought will be the point of focus.

In 1821, Ricardo finished the third edition of his influential *Principles of Political Economy and Taxation*. In the preface, he states his interest: "The produce of the earth...all that is derived from its surface by the united application of labour, machinery, and capital, is divided among three classes of the community, namely, the proprietor of the land, the owner of the stock of capital necessary for its cultivation, and the laborers by whose industry it is cultivated. To

---

221 It is worth noting that the Malthusian Population Theory is actually very inaccurate with respect to factors pertaining to population growth, based on statistical understandings today. Apart from the effect technology has played in expanding production capacity and efficiency exponentially, particularly with respect to food production, the generalization that higher standards of living increase population proportionally is not supported by regional comparison. Poor countries statistically reproduce faster today than wealthy countries. The issue appears to be a cultural, religious and educational phenomenon, not a rigid "law of nature" as Malthus concluded.

222 Reference: *Abolishment of Welfare: An Idea Becomes a Cause* (http://www.nytimes.com/1994/04/22/us/abolishment-of-welfare-an-idea-becomes-a-cause.html)

determine the laws which regulate this distribution is the principal problem in political economy."[223]

While critical of certain aspects of Adam Smith's *labor theory of value*, he still supported the basic distinction, stating: "Possessing utility, commodities derive their exchangeable value from two sources: from their scarcity, and from the quantity of labour required to obtain them."[224] In common with Smith, he elaborates: "If the quantity of labour realized in commodities regulates their exchangeable value every increase of the quantity of labour must augment the value of that commodity on which it is exercised, as every diminution must lower it."[225]

Consequently, Ricardo viewed society and the class divisions of his time from the labor perspective and it logically went that the interests of workers and capitalists were opposed. "If wages should rise," he often stated, "then... profits would necessarily fall."[226] Yet, even though this disharmony alludes to an underlying interest of each class to work to gain advantage over the other for their benefit, often resulting in general imbalance in large part due to the power of the capitalist owners to control labor (and set policy), coupled with the advent of mechanization (machine application) which systematically reduced the need for human labor in applied sectors, he alludes to the conviction that the theory of capitalism, if correctly applied, should *always* create full employment in the long run.

On the specific issue of machine application displacing human labor for the advantage of the manufacturer, he states: "The manufacturer...who...can have recourse to a machine which shall... [lower the costs] of production on his commodity, would enjoy peculiar advantages if he could continue to charge the same price for his goods; but he...would be obliged to lower the price of his commodities, or capital would flow to his trade till his profits had sunk to the general level. Thus then is the public benefited by machinery."[227]

However, as with other aspects of his writing, contradiction is common. While maintaining the basic idea that the general public would benefit from the introduction of labor displacing machinery under the assumption that market prices would cleanly decline and those displaced would always smoothly relocate, in the third edition of his *Principles,* Ricardo starts chapter 31 by stating: "Ever since I first turned my attention to questions of political economy, I have been of the opinion that...an application of machinery to any branch of production as should have the effect of saving labour was a general good...[but] that the substitution of machinery for human labor is often very injurious to the interests of the class of laborers."[228]

---

223 Source: *The Principles of Political Economy and Taxation*, David Ricardo, 1821, Dent Edition, 1962, p.272.
224 Ibid., p.5
225 Ibid., p.7
226 Ibid., p.64
227 Ibid., p.53
228 Ibid., pp.263-264

He later re-qualifies the argument by stating "The statements which I have made will not, I hope, lead to the inference that machinery should not be encouraged. To elucidate the principle, I have been supposing, that improved machinery is suddenly discovered, and extensively used; but the truth is, that these discoveries are gradual, and rather operate in determining the employment of the capital which is saved and accumulated, than in diverting capital from its actual employment."[229]

His general dismissal of the issue of humans being displaced by machines, later to be called "technological unemployment" will also be found in common with many other economists that followed him, including John Maynard Keynes (1883-1946), who stated, in line with Ricardo's general assumption of "adjustment": "We are being afflicted with a new disease of which some readers may not yet have heard the name, but of which they will hear a great deal in the years to come - namely, *technological unemployment.* This means unemployment due to our discovery of means of economizing the use of labour outrunning the pace at which we can find new uses for labour. But this is only a temporary phase of maladjustment. All this means in the long run *that mankind is solving its economic problem.'*[230]

The subject is brought up here as an accent of focus because it will be revisited in part III of this text, presenting a context of technological application apparently unrealized or disregarded by the major economic theorists of modern history who, again, are often locked into a *narrow frame of reference.*

As a final point regarding Ricardo, he is also credited for his contribution to international "free-trade", specifically his *Theory of Comparative Advantage,* along with perpetuation of the basic "invisible hand" ethos of Adam Smith. Ricardo States: "Under a system of perfectly free commerce, each country naturally devotes its capital and labour to such employments as are most beneficial to each. This pursuit of individual advantage is admirably connected with the universal good of the whole. By stimulating industry, by rewarding ingenuity, and by using most efficaciously the peculiar powers bestowed by nature, it distributes labour most effectively and most economically: while, by increasing the general mass of productions, it diffuses general benefit, and binds together, by one common tie of interest and intercourse, the universal society of nations throughout the civilized world."[231]

Theories of Value and Behavior

Up until this point, the broad contributions of four major historical figures and inevitably the central characteristics inherent to the capitalist philosophy have been briefly discussed. It will be noticed that

229 Ibid., p.267
230 Source: *Economic Possibilities for Our Grandchildren,* John Maynard Keynes, 1931
231 Source: *The Principles of Political Economy and Taxation,* David Ricardo, 1821, Dent Edition, 1962, p.81

underlying these views rest assumptions of human behavior, social (class) relationships, coupled with a "metaphysical" market logic where everything will work out just fine if certain values and a generally "selfish" perspective is taken by the players of the market game, along with little "restriction" of the market itself.

As a brief aside, nowhere in the writings of these thinkers, nor in the vast majority of works produced by later theorists in favor of free market capitalism, is the actual *structure* and *process* of production and distribution discussed. There is an explicit disconnect between "industry" and "business", with the former related to the technical/scientific process of true economic unfolding; with the latter only pertaining to the codified market dynamics and pursuit of profit. As will be discussed more so in a moment, a central problem inherent to the capitalist mode of production is how advancements in the "industrial approach", which can allow for increased problem resolution and the furthering of prosperity, have been *blocked* by the traditional, seemingly immutable tenets of the "business approach". The latter has governed the actions of the former, to the disadvantage of the former's potential.

This kind of disconnect or *truncated frame of reference* is also to be found in other areas of focus, such as the dominant theories of *labor, value* and *human behavior* which inevitably serve to justify the institution of capitalism. As noted prior, the "labor theory of value", made popular in general by its implications via Locke, Smith and Ricardo, is a generalized proposal stating that the value of a commodity is related to the labor needed to produce or obtain that commodity. As acceptable as this idea is in general from an intuitive perspective, there are many levels of ambiguity when it comes to quantification. Many historical objections have persisted, such as how different types of labor having differing skills and wage rates could not be properly combined, along with how to factor in natural resources and "working" investment capital itself.

The growth of "capital goods"[232] in the 20th century, such as machine automation of labor, also present challenges for the rather simplified labor theories' concept of *labor derived value* since, after a certain point, the labor value inherent to production machines, which today often function to produce *more machines* with diminishing human effort over time, presents an ever diluted *transfer of value* in this context. It has been suggested by some economists today, focusing on the rapidly advancing fields of information and technological sciences, that the use of machine automation, coupled with *artificial intelligence,* could very well move humans out of the traditional labor force almost entirely. Suddenly, *capital* has become

---

232 "Capital goods" are generally defined as: Any tangible assets that an organization uses to produce goods or services such as office buildings, equipment and machinery. Consumer goods are the end result of this production process.
(http://www.investopedia.com/terms/c/capitalgoods.asp#axzz2Gxg1RmR6)

labor, so to speak.[233]

This ambiguity extends also to competing theories of value postulated by economists, including most notably what is called the *utility theory of value.* While the labor theory basically takes the perspective of labor or production, the utility theory takes what we could call the "market perspective", meaning that value is derived not from labor but by the purpose (or utility) derived by its use (use value) by the consumer, as *perceived* by the consumer.

French Economist Jean-Baptiste Say (1737-1832) is notable with respect to utility theory. A self-proclaimed disciple of Adam Smith, he differed with Smith on this issue of value, stating: "After having shown...the improvement which the science of political economy owes to Dr. Smith, it will not, perhaps, be useless to indicate...some of the points on which he erred...To the labour of man alone he ascribes the power of producing values. This is an error."[234]

He goes on to explain how the "exchange value" (price), of any good or service depends entirely on its "use value" (utility). He states: "The value that mankind attaches to objects originates in the use it can make of them...[To the] inherent fitness or capability of certain things to satisfy the various wants of mankind, I shall take leave to affix the name utility...The utility of things is the ground-work of their value, and their value constitutes wealth...Although price is the measure of the value of things, and their value the measure of their utility, it would be absurd to draw the inference, that, by forcibly raising their price, their utility can be augmented. Exchangeable value, or price, is an index of the recognized utility of a thing.[235]

The *utility theory of value* is different from the *labor theory* not only in its derivation of value, but also in its implication regarding a kind of *subjective rationalization* with respect to human decisions in the market. Utilitarianism,[236] which has become deeply characteristic of the microeconomic assumptions put forward by neoclassical economists today, is often modeled in complex mathematical formulas in an effort to explain how humans in the market "maximize their

---

233 Reference: *The End of Work: The Decline of the Global Labor Force and the Dawn of the Post-Market Era,* Jeremy Rifkin, Putnam Publishing Group, 1995
234 Source: *A Treatise on Political Economy,* Jean-Baptiste Say, Philadelphia: Lippincott, 1863, p.xi (Translation is from the fourth French edition, published in 1821)
235 Ibid, p.62
236 Jeremy Bentham, a notable proponent of "Classic Utilitarianism", stated: "Nature has placed mankind under the governance of two sovereign masters, pain and pleasure. It is for them alone to point out what we ought to do... By the principle of utility is meant that principle which approves or disapproves of every action whatsoever according to the tendency it appears to have to augment or diminish the happiness of the party whose interest is in question: or, what is the same thing in other words to promote or to oppose that happiness. I say of every action whatsoever, and therefore not only of every action of a private individual, but of every measure of government." (*An Introduction to the Principles of Morals and Legislation,* Jeremy Bentham, 1789, Dover Philosophical Classics, 2009. p.1)

utility", specifically around the idea of increasing happiness and reducing suffering.

Underlying these ideas of human behavior, as with most of economic theory itself, are, again, traditionalized assumptions. Economist Nassau Senior (1790–1864) supported a common theme reoccurring today that human wants were *infinite*: "What we mean to state is, that no person feels his whole wants to be adequately supplied; that every person has some unsatisfied desires which he believes that additional wealth would gratify."[237] Such declarations of human nature are constant in such treatments, with notions of greed, fear and other hedonistic reflex mechanisms which assume, among other things, that *material acquisition, wealth* and *gain* are inherent to happiness.

Today, the dominant and largely accepted microeconomic perspective is that all human behavior is reducible to rational, strategic attempts to maximize either profits or gain and to avoid pain or loss. Ever expansive utilitarian arguments of this nature continue to be used to morally justify competitive, market capitalism. One example of this is the notion of "voluntarism" and the suggestion that all acts in the market are never coerced and therefore everyone is free to make their own decisions for their own gain or loss. This idea is extremely common today, as though such "free exchanges" existed in a void with no other synergistic pressures; as though the pressures of survival in a system with clear tendencies toward basic class warfare and strategic scarcity would not generate an *inherent coercion* to force laborers to submit to capitalist exploitation.[238]

Overall, the *utilitarian* (hedonistic, and competitive and "forever dissatisfied") model of human nature is likely the most common defense of the capitalist system today. It is, in many ways, both a psychological theory of how people behave and an ethical theory of how they *ought* to behave, arguably supporting a retroactive logic that often puts market theory before human behavioral *reality*, conforming the latter to the former.

In reality, when the utilitarian perspective is fully considered, two serious problems emerge. First, it is virtually impossible to find predictability in such "pleasure and pain" boundaries after a certain degree on the social level. There is no empirical means of comparing the intensity of one individual's sense of pleasure with those of another individual, beyond the very most basic assumption of wanting "gain" over "loss". While the utility theory of value might be logical in a purely abstract, generalized view, without quantification, the mechanics of such emotional dynamics are, in reality, susceptible to severe variation.

The entire life experience of a person, compared to another person, might find some very basic common ground with respect to their personal conditioning to pleasure and pain responses, but seldom

---

237 *An Outline of the Science of Political Economy*, Nassau Senior, 1836, London, Allen and U., 1938, p.27
238 More on this issue will be discussed in the essay *Structural Classicism.*

will a parallel concordance be found in any detail. Since individual pleasures are deemed the ultimate "moral" criteria in utilitarianism, there is really no way one can make such judgments between the pleasures of two individuals. Economist Jeremy Bentham, often considered the father of utilitarianism, actually recognized this in passing, writing: "Prejudice apart, the game of push-pin is of equal value with the arts and sciences of music and poetry. If the game of push-pin furnish more pleasure, it is more valuable than either."[239]

The second problem is the *shortsighted* nature of the assumed emotional reaction. Human beings have historically expressed the rational interest to suffer in the present in order to gain (or hope to gain) in the future. Altruism, which has undergone extensive philosophical debate, might very well be rooted in forms of "pleasure" obtained by the selfless (painful) acts for the benefit of others. As will be discussed later, the pain/pleasure premise put forward by such arguments, reinforced by an impulsive reaction for gain, has become a socially rewarded pattern. This has generated a mentality where *short-term gain* is sought after often at the true expense of *long-term suffering.*

Yet, in abstraction, utilitarianism also offers a bizarre kind of *equalizer*, since it can be identified with the perspective of "mutual exchange" and hence a way to always see capitalism as a system of social harmony, rather than of warfare. Coming back to the labor theory vs. the utility theory of value, the former clearly shows conflict as the labor theory takes into account the cost-efficiency sought by the capitalist, at the expense of wages for the laborers. The utility theory, on the other hand, removes these ideas overall and states that everyone is seeking the same thing and therefore, structure aside, *everyone is equal*. In other words, all exchanges become mutually beneficial to everyone in a narrow, absurdly abstract generalized logic. All human actions are reduced to this system of "exchange" and hence all political or social distinctions disappear in theory.

The "Socialist" Uprising

Socialism, like capitalism, has no universally accepted definition in general public conversation but is often technically defined as "an economic system characterized by social ownership of the means of production and co-operative management of the economy."[240] The root of socialist thought appears to go back to 18th century Europe, with a complex history of "reformers" working to challenge the emerging capitalist system. Gracchus Babeuf (1760-1797) is a notable theorist in this area, with his "*Conspiracy of Equals*" which attempted to topple the French Government. He stated "Society must be made to operate in such a way that it eradicates once and for all the desire of a man to become richer, or wiser, or more powerful than others."[241] French

---

239 *Rationale of Reward,* Jeremy Bentham Book 3, Chapter 1
240 Source: Britannica.com
   (http://www.britannica.com/EBchecked/topic/551569/socialism)
241 Source: *The Defense of Gracchus Babeuf before the High Court of*

Socialist-Anarchist Pierre Joseph Proudhon (1809-1865) is famous for declaring that "Property is Theft" in his pamphlet *An Inquiry into the Principle of Right and of Government.*

By the early 19th century, socialist ideas were expanding rapidly, commonly in response to perceived moral and ethic problems inherent to capitalism, such as class imbalance and exploitation. The list of influential thinkers is vast and complex, so only three individuals, noting their most relevant contributions, will be discussed here: William Thompson, Karl Marx and Thorstein Veblen.

William Thompson (1775-1833) was a powerful influence on socialist thought. He was in support of the idea of "cooperatives", made famous by Robert Owen as something of an alternative to the capitalist business model and philosophically took a utilitarian perspective when it came to human behavior. He was very influenced by Bentham but his use/interpretation of utilitarianism was rather different. For instance, he believe that if all members of society were treated *equally*, rather than engage class warfare and exploitation, they would have equal capacities to experience happiness.[242]

He argued extensively for a kind of *market socialism*, where egalitarianism and equality prevailed in his famous *An Inquiry into the Principles of the Distribution of Wealth Most Conducive to Human Happiness.* He made it clear that Capitalism was a system of exploitation and insecurity, stating: "The tendency of the existing arrangement of things as to wealth is to enrich a few at the expense of the mass of producers, to make the poverty of the poor more hopeless."[243] However, he went on to recognize that even if such a hybrid of capitalism and socialism did emerge, the underlying premise of *competition* was still a serious problem. He wrote at length about the problems inherent to the nature of market competition, outlining five issues that have been common rhetoric of socialist thought ever since.

The first problem was that every "laborer, artisan and trader [viewed] a competitor, a rival in every other...[and each viewed]; a second competition, a second rivalship between...[his or her profession] and the public."[244] He went on to state it would be "in the interest of all medical men that diseases should exist and prevail, or their trade would be decreased ten, or one hundred, fold."[245]

The second problem was the inherent oppression of women and distortion of the family, noting that the division of labor and overarching ethic of competitive selfishness further secured the

---

Vendôme, University of Massachusetts Press, 1967, p.57
242 Reference: *An Inquiry into the Principles of the Distribution of Wealth Most Conducive to Human Happiness*, William Thompson, London, William S. Orr, 1850, p.17
243 Ibid, p.xxix
244 Ibid, p.259
245 Ibid.

drudgery of women in the household and gender inequality.[246]

The third problem associated with competition was the inherent instability generated in the economy itself, stating: "The third evil here imputed to the very principle of individual competition is, that it must occasionally lead to unprofitable or injudicious modes of individual exertion...every man must judge for himself as to the probability of success in the occupation which he adopts. And what are his means of judging? Every one, doing well in his calling, is interested in concealing his success, lest competition should reduce his gains. What individual can judge whether the market, frequently at a great distance, sometimes in another hemisphere of the globe is overstocked, or likely to be so, with the article which inclination may lead him to fabricate?...and should any error of judgment...lead him into an uncalled for, and, therefore, unprofitable line of exertion, what is the consequence? A mere error of judgment...may end in severe distress, if not in ruin. Cases of this sort seem to be unavoidable under the scheme of individual competition in its best form."[247]

The fourth problem noted is how the selfish nature of the competitive market presented insecurity around core life support consequences, such as security in old age, sickness and from accidents.[248]

The fifth problem denoted by Thompson regarding market competition was that it slowed the advancement of knowledge. "Concealment, therefore, of what is new or excellent from competitors, must accompany individual competition...because the strongest personal interest is by it opposed to the principle of benevolence."[249]

Karl Marx (1818-1883), along with many others, was influenced by Thompson's work and is likely one of the most well known economic philosophers today. With his name often used in a derogatory manner to gesture the perils of *Soviet communism* or "totalitarianism", Marx is also likely the most misunderstood of all popularized economists. While most famous in the general public mind for presenting treatises on Socialist-Communist ideas, Marx actually spent most of his time on the subject of Capitalism and its operations.

His contribution to understanding Capitalism is more vast than many realize, with many common economic terms and phrases used today in conversations about capitalism actually finding their root in Marx's literary treatments. His perspective was largely historical, and featured particularly detailed scholarship about the evolution of economic thought. Due to the immense size of his work, only a few influential issues will be addressed here.

One issue to denote was his awareness of how the capitalist characteristic of "exchange" was principled as the ultimate basis for social relationships. He stated in his *Grundrisse*: "Indeed, insofar as

---

246 Ibid, pp.260-261
247 Ibid, pp.261-263
248 Ibid, p.263
249 Ibid, p.267

the commodity or labour is conceived of only as exchange value, and the relation in which the various commodities are brought into connection with one another is conceived of as the exchange of these exchange values...then the individuals...are simply and only conceived of as exchangers. As far as the formal character is concerned, there is absolutely no distinction between them...As subjects of exchange, their relation is therefore that of equality."[250]

"Although individual A feels a need for the commodity of individual B, he does not appropriate it by force, nor vice versa, but rather they recognize one another reciprocally as proprietors...No one seizes hold of another's by force. Each divests himself of his property voluntarily."[251]

Again, as noted prior with respect to the reoccurring theme of human relations and class assumptions (or denials), Marx emphasized what could be argued as three core *delusions:* the delusion of *freedom, equality* and *social harmony,* as reduced to an extremely narrow association around the idea of "mutually beneficial exchange", which was to be the only real economic relationship by which the whole of society is to be assessed.

"It is in the character of the money relation - as far as it is developed in its purity to this point, and without regard to more highly developed relations of production - that all inherent contradictions of bourgeois society appear extinguished in money relations as conceived in a simple form; and bourgeois democracy even more than bourgeois economists takes refuge in this aspect...in order to construct apologetics for the existing economic relations.[252]

His work *Capital: A Critique of Political Economy,* Marx extensively analyzes many factors of the capitalist system, namely the nature of commodities themselves, the dynamics between value, use value, exchange value, labor theory and utility, along with a deep investigation of what "capital" means, how the system evolved and ultimately the nature of roles within the model. An important theme to denote is his view regarding "surplus value", which, in gesture of Ricardo's "labor theory of value", is the assumed value appropriated by the capitalist in the form of *profit,* which is in excess of the value (cost) inherent to labor/production itself.

He stated with respect to dismissing this "Surplus" origin in exchange: "Turn and twist then as we may, the fact remains unaltered. If equivalents are exchanged, no surplus-value results, and if non-equivalents are exchanged, still no surplus-value results. Circulation, or the exchange of commodities, begets no value."[253] He then argues, in short, differentiating between "labor" and "labor power", with the latter consisting of both a "use value" and an "exchange value", that a

---

250 Source: *Grundrisse,* Karl Marx, tr. Martin Nicolaus, Reprint Vintage Books, New York, 1973 p.241
251 Ibid, p.243
252 Ibid, pp.240-241
253 Source: *Capital,* Karl Marx, Foreign Languages reprint , Moscow, 1961, vol. 3, p.163

worker is only compensated for meeting his needs for *subsistence*, which is represented in his wages, while everything past that value is a "surplus", which theoretically translates into the "profit" made by the capitalist, finalized by the price "mark up" in market exchange.[254]

This point, which he further extends in context & dynamics inherent to the circulation/application of different forms of capital (capital defined still as a means of production but in this case mostly in its monetary form), poses the conclusion that an exploitation of the workers was *inherent* to the creation of "surplus value" or "profit". In other words, by implication, this was a form of basic inequality built into the capitalist system and as long as one small group of "owners" controlled the surplus value created by the working class, there will always be rich and poor, wealth and poverty.

Marx further extends this idea to a reassessment of "property", which was essentially now the legal foundation of "capital" itself, explicitly allowing for the coercive expropriation of "surplus labor" (that part of labor which generates the surplus value) stating: "At first the rights of property seemed to us to be based on a man's own labour. At least, some such assumption was necessary since only commodity-owners with equal rights confronted each other, and the sole means by which a man could become possessed of the commodities of others, was by alienating (giving up) his own commodities; and these could be replaced by labour alone. Now, however, property turns out to be the right, on the part of the capitalist, to appropriate the unpaid labour (surplus labour) of others or its product, and to be the impossibility on the part of the labourer, of appropriating his own product. The separation of property from labour has become the necessary consequence of a law that apparently originated in their identity."[255]

Marx develops these kinds of arguments extensively in his writing, including the idea that working class labor cannot be "voluntary" in this system - only coercive - since the ultimate decision to apply labor for a wage was in the hands of the capitalist. He stated, "The worker therefore only feels himself outside his work, and in his work feels outside himself. He is at home when he is not working, and when he is working he is not at home. His labour is therefore not voluntary but coerced; it is forced labour. It is therefore not the satisfaction of a need; it is merely a means to satisfy needs external to it."[256]

In the end, it was this complex, multifaceted degradation, exploitation and dehumanization of the average worker that bothered him so and pushed him toward reform. He even invented a phrase - "The Law of the Increasing Misery" - to describe how the general working population's happiness was inverse to the accumulation of wealth for the capitalist class. In the end, Marx was convinced that

---

254 Ibid, p.176
255 Ibid, vol. 1, pp.583–584
256 Source: *Economic and Philosophic Manuscripts of 1844,* Karl Marx, Moscow, Progress, 1959, p.69

pressures inherent to the system would push the working class to revolt against the capitalist class, allowing for a new "socialist" mode of production where, in part, the working class operated for their own benefit.

Thorstein Veblen (1857-1929) will be the final so-called "socialist" whose influential ideas regarding the development and flaws of capitalism will be explored here. Like Marx, he had the advantage of time with respect to the digestion of economic history. Veblen taught economics at a number of universities during his time, prolifically producing literature on various social issues.

Veblen was very critical of the neoclassical economic assumptions, specifically regarding the applied utilitarian ideas of "human nature", seeing the idea that all human economic behavior was to be reduced to a hedonistic interplay of self-maximization and preservation as absurdly simplistic.[257] He took what we could call an "evolutionary" view of human history, with change defined by the social institutions that took hold or were surpassed. He stated with respect to the current (what he deemed "materialistic") state of the time:

"Like all human culture this material civilization is a scheme of institutions - institutional fabric and institutional growth...The growth of culture is a cumulative sequence of habituation, and the ways and means of it are the habitual response of human nature to exigencies that vary incontinently, cumulatively, but with something of a consistent sequence in the cumulative variations that so go forward - incontinently, because each new move creates a new situation which induces a further new variation in the habitual manner of response; cumulatively, because each new situation is a variation of what has gone before it and embodies as causal factors all that has been effected by what went before; consistently, because the underlying traits of human nature (propensities, aptitudes, and what not) by force of which the response takes place, and on the ground of which the habituation takes effect, remain substantially unchanged."[258]

Veblen challenged the basic foundation of the capitalist mode of production by questioning many of the factors that had been essentially "given" or deemed empirical by the centuries of economic debate. The now ingrained institutions of "wages", "rents", "property", "interest", "labor" were disturbed in their supposed simplicity by a view that none of them could be held as intellectually viable, outside of the purely categorical association with extreme limits of application. He joked about how "a gang of Aleutian Islanders slushing about in the wrack and surf with rakes and magical incantations for the capture of shell-fish are held, in point of taxonomic reality, to be engaged in a

---

257 Reference: "Why Economics Is Not an Evolutionary Science," *Place of Science in Modern Civilization and Other Essays*, Thorstein Veblen, pp.73-74
258 Source: "The Limitations of Marginal Utility," *The Place of Science in Modern Civilization and Other Essays*, Thorstein Veblen, New York, Russell and Russell, 1961, p.241-242

feat of hedonistic equilibration in rent, wages, and interest. And that is all there is to it."[259]

He saw production and industry itself as a *social process* where lines were deeply blurred, as it invariably involved the *sharing of knowledge* (usufruct) and skills. In many ways, he viewed such categorical characteristics of capitalism to be *inherent* to capitalism alone and not representative of physical reality, hence a vast contrivance. He found that the dominant neoclassical theory existed, in part, to obscure the fundamental class-warfare and hostility inherent, to further secure the interests of what he called the "vested interests" or "absentee owners" (aka capitalists).[260]

He rejected the idea that private property was a "natural right", as assumed by Locke, Smith and the others, often joking about the absurdity of thought that leads the "absentee owners" to claim "ownership" of commodities produced, in reality, by the labor of the "common worker", highlighting the absurdity of the long held principle that from labor, comes property.[261] He went further to express the inherent *social nature* of production and how the true nature of skill and knowledge accumulation completely voided the assumption of property rights in and of itself, stating:

"This natural-rights theory of property makes the creative effort of an isolated, self-sufficing individual the basis of ownership vested in him. In so doing it overlooks the fact that there is no isolated, self-sufficing individual...Production takes place only in society - only through the co-operation of an industrial community. This industrial community may be large or small...but it always comprises a group large enough to contain and transmit the traditions, tools, technical knowledge, and usages without which there can be no industrial organization and no economic relation of individuals to one another or to their environment...There can be no production without technical knowledge; hence no accumulation and no wealth to be owned, in severalty or otherwise. And there is no technical knowledge apart from an industrial community. Since there is no individual production and no individual productivity, the natural-rights preconception...reduces itself to absurdity, even under the logic of its own assumptions.[262]

As with Marx, he saw no other way to distinguish the two major classes of society than between those who *work* and those who *exploit* that work[263] with the profit making portion of capitalism (the "business") completely separate from production itself ("industry"). He

259 Source: "Professor Clark's Economics", *Place of Science in Modern Civilization*, Thorstein Veblen, p.193
260 Reference: *Absentee Ownership and Business Enterprise in Recent Times*, Thorstein Veblen, Augustus M. Kelley, New York, 1964, p.407
261 Reference: "The Beginnings of Ownership", *Essays in Our Changing Order*, Thorstein Veblen, p.32
262 Ibid, pp.33-34
263 Reference: "The Instinct of Workmanship and the Irksomeness of Labor", *Essays in Our Changing Order*, Thorstein Veblen, pp.188-190

makes a clear distinction between business and industry and refers to the former as functioning as a vehicle of "sabotage" for industry. He saw a complete contradiction between the ethical intent of the general community to produce efficiently and with high service, and the laws of private property that had the power to direct industry for the sake of profit alone, reducing that efficiency and intent. The term "sabotage" in this context was defined by Veblen as the "conscientious withdrawal of efficiency."[264]

He states: "The industrial plant is increasingly running idle or half idle, running increasingly short of its productive capacity. Workmen are being laid off...And all the while these people are in great need of all sorts of goods and services which these idle plants and idle workmen are fit to produce. But for reasons of business expediency it is impossible to let these idle plants and idle workmen go to work—that is to say for reasons of insufficient profit to the business men interested, or in other words, for the reasons of insufficient income to the vested interests."[265]

Furthermore, Veblen, as opposed to the vast majority of people in the modern day who condemn acts of "corruption" on ethical grounds, did not see any of the problems of abuse and exploitation as an issue of "morality" or "ethics". He saw the problems as inherent, built into the nature of capitalism itself. He states: "It is not that these captains of Big Business whose duty it is to administer this salutary modicum of sabotage on production are naughty. It is not that they aim to shorten human life or augment human discomfort by contriving an increase of privation among their fellow men...The question is not whether this traffic in privation is humane, but whether it is *sound business management*."[266]

With respect to the nature of Government, Veblen's view was very clear: Government by its very political construct existed to protect the existing social order and class structure, reinforcing private property laws and by direct extension reinforcing the disproportionate ownership (ruling) class. "Legislation, police surveillance, the administration of justice, the military and diplomatic service, all are chiefly concerned with business relations, pecuniary interests, and they have little more than an incidental bearing on other human interests",[267] he stated.

The idea of democracy was also deeply violated by capitalist power in his view, stating "constitutional government is a business government."[268] Veblen, while aware of the phenomenon of "lobbying" and the "buying" of politicians commonly seen today as a form of

---

264 Source: *The Engineers and the Price System*, Thorstein Veblen, New York, Augustus M. Kelley, 1965, p.1
265 Ibid, p.12
266 Source: *Absentee Ownership and Business Enterprise in Recent Times,* Thorstein Veblen, New York, Augustus M. Kelley, 1964, pp.220-221
267 Source: *The Theory of Business Enterprise*, Thorstein Veblen, New York, Augustus M. Kelley, 1965, p.269
268 Ibid, p.285

"corruption", did not see this as the real nature of the problem. Rather, government control by business was not an anomaly. It was simply what government had manifested to be by design.[269] By its very nature, as an institutionalized means for social control, government would always protect the "rich" against the "poor". Since the "poor" always greatly outnumbered the "rich", a rigid legal structure favoring the wealthy ("propertied interests") had to exist to keep the class separation and benefit to the capitalist interests intact.[270]

Likewise, he also recognized how the capitalist-state government very much needed to keep *social values* in line with their interests - what Veblen called a "pecuniary culture". Therefore, the predatory, selfish and competitive habits typical of "success" in the underlying social warfare inherent to the capitalist system *naturally reinforced* those values by default. To be giving and vulnerable was of little use to "success" in this context, as the ruthless and strategically competitive were icons of social reward.[271]

In a broad assessment, Veblen worked to critically analyze the core structure and values of the capitalist model, posing what could be argued as some profoundly sociologically advanced conclusions with respect to its inherent contradictions, technical inefficiency and value disorders. His work is very much encouraged for review by all interested in the history of economic thought, specifically for those skeptical of the premise of the free market.

In Conclusion: Capitalism as "Social Pathology"

The history of economic thought is, in many ways, the history of *human social relationships*, with the pattern of certain mere assumptions gaining prominence to the effect of being considered sacrosanct and immutable over time. This element of *traditionalism*, culminating from values and belief systems of earlier periods, has been a core theme in this short review of economic history. The central point being that the attributes taken as "given" to the dominant theories of economy today are actually not based on direct *physical support*, such as would be needed to find validation via the *method of science*, but rather based on the mere perpetuation of an established *ideological* framework which has evolved to intricately *self-refer* to its internal logic, justifying its own existence by its own standards.

Today, it is not what embodies the capitalist ideology in specifics that is most problematic, but rather what it *omits* by extension. Just as early religions saw the world as flat and had to adjust their rhetoric once it was proven round by science, the tradition of market economics is faced with similar trials. Considering the simplicity of the agrarian and eventually primitive approaches to industrial production, there was little awareness or needed concern about its possible negative consequences over time on not only the

---

269 Ibid, pp.286-287
270 Ibid, pp.404-405
271 Reference: *The Theory of the Leisure Class*, Thorstein Veblen, New York, Augustus M. Kelley, 1965, pp.229-230

habitat (ecological) level, but also on the human level (public health).

Likewise, the market system, with its very old assumptions regarding possibility, also ignores (or even fights) the powerful breakthroughs in science and technology that express capacities to solve problems and create elevated prosperity. In fact, as will be explored in the essay *Market Efficiency vs. Technical Efficiency*, such progressive actions and harmonious recognitions regarding the *habitat* and *human well-being* reveals that market capitalism literally *cannot facilitate these solutions,* since its very mechanics disallow or work against such possibilities by default.

Generally speaking, the resolution of problems and hence *increasing of efficiency* is, in many ways, anathema to the market's operation. Solving problems in general means no more ability to gain income from the "servicing" of those problems. New efficiencies almost always mean a reduction of labor and energy needs and while that may seem positive with respect to *true earthly efficiency*, it also often means a loss of jobs and reduction of monetary circulation upon its application.[272]

It is here where the capitalist model begins to take the role of a *social pathogen,* not only with respect to what it ignores, disallows or fights against by design, but also with respect to what it *reinforces and perpetuates.* If we go back to Locke's statement about how the nature of money, given its tacit consent by the community, was to essentially serve as a *community* in and of itself, it is easy to see how this once mere "medium of exchange" has evolved into its present sociological form, where the entire basis of the market serves, in fact, not with the intent to create and assist with human survival, health and prosperity, but to now merely facilitate the act of *profit and profit alone.*

Adam Smith never would have fathomed that in the present day, the most lucrative, rewarded fields would be not the production of life supporting/improving goods, but rather the act of moving money around – hence the "work" of financial institutions such as banks, "Wall St." and investment firms – firms that *literally create nothing,* but hold immense wealth and influence.

Today, the only real *value theory* in place is what could be called the "money sequence of value".[273] Money has taken on a life of its own with respect to the reinforced psychology moving it. It has no direct purpose in intent but to work to manifest more money out of less money (investment).

This "money seeking money" phenomenon has not only

---

272 A simple example of this is the amount of funding and employment that has been generated from the serving of cancer. If cures for cancer where to actually emerge, the downsizing of these massive medical institutions would naturally result. This means that the solving of problems can result in the loss of livelihood for many who worked to service those problems. This creates a perverse reinforcement to keep things the same – avoiding change in general.

273 This phrase was put forward by John McMurtry in his work *The Cancer Stage of Capitalism*, Pluto Press, 1999

created a *value system disorder* where this interest in monetary gain trumps everything, leaving truly relevant environmental and public health issues secondary and "external" to the focus of economy, its constant propensity to "multiply" and "expand" truly has a *cancerous* quality where this idea of needed "growth", rather than steady-state balance, continues its pathological effect on many levels.

Much could be said about the debt system[274] and how virtually all the countries on the planet earth are now indebted to *themselves* to the extent where we, the human species, actually do not have the money in circulation to pay ourselves back from what we have borrowed out of thin air. The need for more and more "credit" to fuel the "market" is constant today due to this imbalance, which means, like cancer, we are dealing with an intent of *infinite expansion and consumption.* This simply cannot work on a finite planet.

Furthermore, the scarcity-driven, competitive ethos inherent to the model continues to perpetuate divisive class warfare that keeps not only the *world* at war with itself via empire imperialism and protectionism, but also within the general population. Today, most walk around *afraid of each other* since exploitation and abuse is the dominant, rewarded ethos. All humans have adapted in this culture, unnecessarily, to see each other as threats to one's own survival in increasingly abstract "economic" contexts. For example, when two people walk into a job interview, seeking life support, they are not interested in the wellbeing of the other, since only one will gain the job. In fact, *empathic* sensitivities are negative pressures in this system of advantage and go completely unrewarded by the financial mechanism.

Likewise, the assumption that "fairness" could ever exist in such a competitive environment, particularly when the nature of "winning" and "losing" means a loss of life support or survival, is a deeply naïve ideal. The legal statutes in existence that work to stop monopoly laws and financial "corruption" exist because there is literally no built in safeguard for such so-called "corruption" in this model. As implied by Smith and Veblen in this essay, the "state" is really a manifestation of the economic premise and not the other way around. The use of state power for legislation to ensure the security and prosperity of one class over another, is not a distortion of the capitalist system, it is a *core feature* of the free market competitive ethic.

Many in the libertarian, laissez-faire, Austrian school, Chicago school and other neoclassical offshoots constantly tend to talk about how "state interference" is the problem today, such as with having protectionist import/export polices or the favoring of certain industries by the state. It is assumed that somehow the market can be "free" to operate without the manifestation of monopoly or the "corruptions" inherent to what has been deemed today "crony capitalism", even though the entire basis of strategy is competitive or, in more direct

---

274 The creation of money out of debt, coupled with its multiplication via the Fractional Reserve lending system, a near universal practice of the central banks of the world, continues to seek infinite growth by its very mechanics.

terms, "warring". Again, to assume the State would not be used as a tool for differential advantage – a tool for business – is absurd.[275]

In the end, these overtly and unnecessarily *selfish* values have been at the root of human conflict since their inception and, as noted, the historical notion of human warfare on the class level is seen by most as "given", "natural" or "immutable". In the existing social model, extracted from an inherently scarcity-driven, xenophobic and racist frame of reference, there is no such thing as peace or balance. It simply isn't possible in the capitalist model. Likewise, the *illusion of equality* between people in the so-called "democratic" societies also persists, assuming that somehow political equality can manifest out of the explicit, *economic inequality* inherent to this mode of production and human relations.

Early in this essay the distinction between the "historical" and "mechanistic" view of economic logic was mentioned in passing. The importance of the "mechanistic" (scientific) perspective, which will be explored in later essays, is critical with respect to understanding how deeply out of date and flawed the market economy really is. When we take the known laws of nature, both on the human and habitat levels, and start to calculate what our options and possibilities are, technically, without the baggage of such historical assumptions, a very different *train of thought* emerges. In the view of TZM, this is the new worldview by which humanity needs to align in order to solve its current, mounting sociological and ecological problems, along with opening the door to enormous possibilities for future prosperity.

---

275 It is worth pointing out that "market discipline", or the corrective nature of the market by which all business are supposed to be susceptible, only really applies to the lower classes today. As noted historically by the "too big to fail" rhetoric and recent (~2008) bank bailouts amounting to well over 20 trillion dollars, the wealthy sectors are protected by the gesture of so-called given "Socialism", not Capitalism.

-MARKET EFFICIENCY VS TECHNICAL EFFICIENCY-

The synergetic aspect of industry's doing ever more work with ever less investment of time and energy per each unit of performance...has never been formally accounted as a capital gain of land-situated society. The synergistic effectiveness of a world-around integrated industrial process is inherently vastly greater than the confined synergistic effect of sovereignly operating separate systems. Ergo, only complete world desovereignization can permit the realization of an all humanity high standard support.[276]
R. Buckminster Fuller

Overview

Scientific development, while evolving in parallel with traditional economic development over the past 400 years or so, has still been largely ignored and seen as an "externality" to economic theory. The result has been a "decoupling" of the socioeconomic structure from the *life support* structure to which we are all tied, and upon which we all depend. In most cases today, apart from certain technical assumptions with respect to how a system not based on market dynamics and the "price mechanism"[277] could function, the most common argument in support of market capitalism is that it is a system of "freedom" or "liberty".

The extent to which this is true very much depends on one's interpretation, even though such generalized terms are often ubiquitous in the rhetoric of proponents of the model.[278] It appears such notions are really reactions to prior attempts at alternative social systems in the past that generated power problems like "totalitarianism".[279] Hence, ever since, based on this fear, any model conceived outside of the capitalist framework is often impulsively relegated to the supposed historical tendency towards "tyranny" - and then dismissed.

Be that as it may, this underlying gesture of "freedom", whatever its implication in subjective use, has generated a *neurosis* or confusion with respect to what it means for a species such as ours to survive and prosper in the habitat – a habitat clearly governed by *natural laws*. What we find is that on the level of our habitat relationship we are simply *not free* and to have an overarching value

---

276 Source: *Operating Manual for Spaceship Earth*, R. Buckminster Fuller, 1968, Chapter 6

277 Ludwig von Mises in his famous work *Economic Calculation In The Socialist Commonwealth* argues that the "price mechanism" is the only possible means to understand how to "efficiently" create and move goods around an economy. This criticism of any kind of "planned" system has been touted as sacrosanct by many today and a vindication of the Capitalist system. This issue will be addressed in part III.

278 Reference: *An Inquiry into the Nature and Causes of the Wealth of Nations*, Adam Smith, 1776, par. IV.9.51

279 A classic text that employed this basic fear was F.A. Hayek's *The Road to Serfdom*. "Human nature" had a very clear implication, justified fundamentally by historical trends of totalitarianism suggested as linked to collaborative/planned economies.

orientation of supposed freedom, which is then applied toward how we should operate our global economy, has become increasingly dangerous to human sustainability on the planet earth.[280]

The difficultly of social relationships aside, humans, regardless of their traditional social customs, are strictly bound by the natural, governing laws of the earth and to stray from alignment with these is to invariably *inhibit* our sustainability, prosperity and public health. It should be remembered that the core assumptions of our current socioeconomic system developed during periods with substantially *less* scientific awareness of both our habitat and ourselves.[281] Many of the negative consequences now common to modern societies simply didn't exist in the past and it is now this *clash of systems* that is further destabilizing our world in many ways.

It will be argued here that the integrity of any economic model is actually best measured by how well *aligned* it is with the known, governing *laws of nature*. This *natural law* concept is not presented here as anything esoteric or metaphysical, but as fundamentally observable. While it is true that the laws of nature are constantly refined and altered in our understandings over time, certain causal realities have stood, and continue to stand, as definitively true.

There is no debate that the human organism has specific *needs* for survival, such as the need for nutrition, water and air. There is no debate with respect to the fundamental ecological processes that secure the environmental stability of our habitat that *must* go undisturbed in their symbiotic-synergistic relationships.[282] There is also no debate, as complex as it is, that the human psyche has, on average, basic predictable reactions when it comes to environmental *stressors* and hence how reactions of violence, depression, abuse and other detrimental behavioral issues can manifest as a result.[283]

This scientific, causal or technical perspective of economic relationships reduces all relevant factors to a *frame of reference* and *train of thought* relating to our current understanding of the physical world and its natural, tangible dynamics. This logic takes the science of

---

280 Reference: "A Safe Operating Space for Humanity", *Nature,* 461, 472-475, 24 September 2009, doi:10.1038/461472a;

281 While some historians often place the dawn of the scientific method in ancient Greece, *The Renaissance,* starting around the 16th century, appears to be a major period of significant discovery and acceleration. Galileo (1564 - 1642) is considered today by some as the "father" of modern science. However, these emerging understandings shared very little interest in the economic realm.

282 The disruption of ecosystem processes by human action has shown clear negative consequences. Pollution, deforestation, loss of biodiversity and many other common characteristics of the current state of the world today reveals a deep misalignment with the immutable symbiotic/synergistic realities of our habitat to which we are bound.
Reference:
http://www.globalchange.umich.edu/globalchange1/current/lectures/kling/e cosystem/ecosystem.html

283 See the essay *Defining Public Health.*

human study, hence, again, the shared nature of *human needs* and *public health*, and combines it with the proven *rules of our habitat,* to which we are synergistically and symbiotically connected. Put together, a "ground up", rational model of economic operation can be generalized with very little need, in fact, for the centuries of traditionalized economic theory.[284]

This isn't to say those historical arguments do not possess value with respect to understanding cultural evolution, but rather to say that if a truly scientific worldview is taken with respect to what "works" or "doesn't work" in the strategy of efficiency demanded by the chess-game of human survival, there is very little need for such historical reference in abstraction. This view sits at the core of TZM's reformist logic and will be reviewed again in part III of this text.

The bottom line is that these points of near-immutable scientific awareness are almost completely without recognition in the economic model dominant today. In fact, it will be argued that the two systems are not only decoupled, they are *diametrically opposed* in many ways, alluding to the reality that the competitive market economy is actually not "fixable" as a whole, and hence a new system based *directly* on these "natural law" realties needs to be constructed from the ground up.

This essay will examine and contrast a series of "economic" considerations from both the perspective of the market system (market logic) and this noted *mechanistic* or "technical" logic. It will express how "efficiency" takes on two very different meanings in each perspective, arguing that "market efficiency"[285] works only to be efficient with respect to *itself*, using man-made rule-sets related mostly to classical economic dynamics that facilitate profit and growth, while "Technical Efficiency", referencing the known laws of nature, seeks the most optimized manner of industrial unfolding possible to preserve the habitat, reduce waste and ultimately *ensure public health,* based on emerging scientific understandings.[286]

Cyclical Consumption & Economic Growth

Market capitalism in basic operation can be generalized as an interaction between *owners*, *laborers* and *consumers*. Consumer demand generates the need to produce via the owners (capitalists), who then employ laborers to perform the act of production. This cycle essentially originates with "demand" and hence the real engine of the market is the *interest, ability* and *act* of everyone buying in the market place. All recessions/depressions[287] are a result, on one level or

---

284 See the essay *History of Economy*
285 The use of the term "market efficiency" here is not to be confused with other historical meanings. The concept is novel to this essay. Traditional meaning:
   http://www.investopedia.com/articles/02/101502.asp#axzz2H9IWIQwR
286 The term 'economy' in Greek [Oikonomia] means "management of a household - thrift"; Hence to e·con·o·mize, or "increase efficiency".
287 Recessions are typically defined as "a significant decline in economic

another, of a loss of sales. Therefore the most critical necessity for keeping people employed and hence keeping the economy in a state of "stability" or "growth" is constant, *cyclical consumption.*

Economic growth, which is generally defined as "an increase in the capacity of an economy to produce goods and services, compared from one period of time to another"[288] is a constant interest of any national economy today and, consequently, the global economy in general. Many macroeconomic tactics are often used during times of recession to facilitate more loans, production and consumption in order to keep an economy functioning at or ideally beyond its current level.[289] The *business cycle*, a period of oscillating expansion and contraction, has long been recognized as a characteristic of the market economy due to the nature of "market discipline", or correction, which, according to theorists, is partly a natural ebb and flow of business successes and failures.[290]

In short, the rate (increase or decrease) of consumption is what generates the business cycle's periods of growth or contraction, with macroeconomic monetary regulation generally increasing and decreasing ease of *liquidity* (often via interest rates) in order to "manage" the expansions and contractions. While modern, monetary macroeconomic policy is not the subject of this essay, it is worth pointing out here, as an aside, that mutual respect toward both the expansion and contraction periods of the business cycle has *not* existed historically. Periods of monetary expansion (often via cheaper credit) that usually correlate to periods of economic expansion (as more money is being put to use) are hailed by the citizenry as national successes for society, while all contractions are seen as policy failures.

Therefore, there has always been an interest by the political establishments (who want to look good) and major, influential market institutions (protecting corporate profits) to *preserve* periods of expansion for as long as possible and fight all forms of contraction. This perspective is natural to the value system inherent to capitalism for "pain" is to be thwarted at all times, often in a shortsighted manner. No company willingly wants to downsize nor does any political party willingly want to "look bad", even though traditional economic theory tells us that these periods of contraction are "natural" and

---

activity spread across the economy."
(http://www.investopedia.com/ask/answers/08/cause-of-recession.asp#axzz2HzEmQsvq)

288 'Economic growth' defined:
http://www.investopedia.com/terms/e/economicgrowth.asp#axzz2H9IWIQwR

289 A common reaction of central banks during times of recession is to increase "liquidity" in the economy. Liquidity is simply the amount of capital that is available for investment and spending. The Federal Reserve, the central bank of the United States, typically manages liquidity, by adjusting interest rates.

290 The 'business cycle' is often thought about in five stages: growth (expansion), peak, recession (contraction), trough and recovery. (http://www.investopedia.com/terms/b/businesscycle.asp#axzz2IGANj1hr)

should be allowed.

The result has been, in short, a constant *increase* in the money supply (i.e. purchasing power and capital) during times of recession, with the end result being massive *global debt*, both public and private.[291] The reality is that all money comes into existence through loans and each of those loans is made with *interest attached*, where the loan must be paid back with the interest fee accrued (bank's profit); meaning that the very nature of money creation automatically entails a *negative balance* by default. There is always more debt in existence than there is money in circulation.[292]

So, returning to the main point with respect to the need for demand/consumption to keep the economy working, this process of exchange and general focus on growth is at the heart of the market's context of "efficiency". It doesn't matter *what* is being produced or the effect on the state of human or earthly affairs. Those are all, again, "externalities". As a concentrated example of this logic, the stock market, which is itself nothing more than the trading of money and its now numerous "derivatives", generates enormous GDP and "growth" through resultant sales/profit.[293]

Yet, these acts arguably produce *nothing* of tangible, life supporting value. The stock market system and the now massively powerful financial institutions are completely *auxiliary* to the real, producing economy. While many argue that these investment institutions *facilitate* businesses and jobs with their application of capital, this act is, once again, only systemically relevant in the current system (market efficiency) and utterly irrelevant in terms of real production (technical efficiency).

In short, when it comes to *market logic*, the more turnover or sales, the better - and that is that - regardless if the item sold is credit, rocks, "hope" or flapjacks. Any pollution, instances of waste or

---

291 According to a 2010 report by the World Economics Forum, global credit (or in effect, debt) doubled from $57 trillion to $109 trillion from 2000 to 2010. It also forecasts $210 trillion in global credit (debt) by 2020. (http://www.weforum.org/reports/sustainable-credit-report-2011)
292 According to the Federal Reserve, as of 2009 total US (Public and Private) debt was about $51 trillion. (https://www.federalreserve.gov/datadownload/Download.aspx?rel=Z1&series=654245a7abac051cc4a9060c911e1fa4&filetype=csv&label=include&layout=seriescolumn&from=01/01/1945&to=12/31/2010) If we compare this to the existing money supply, as measured by M3, which is the broadest measure, we find that as of Dec. 2012 it was about $15 trillion.* (http://www.shadowstats.com/charts/monetary-base-money-supply) *Note: M3 has been discontinued in reporting by the US. However, its numbers can be extrapolated based on component measures.
293 For example, in the US, the "venture capital" industry, which essential invests money in new businesses, was 21% of GDP in 2010. (http://www.nvca.org/index.php?option=com_content&view=article&id=255&Itemid=103) According to a 2012 article in *The New Republic*: "the largest six banks in our (us) economy now have total assets in excess of 63% of GDP" (http://www.tnr.com/article/politics/shooting-banks#)

other such detriments are, again, "external". There is no consideration for the technical role of actual production processes, strategies for efficient distribution, design applications or the like. Such factors are assumed to culminate *metaphysically* in the best interest of the people and the habitat simply because that is what the "invisible hand"[294] of the market implies.

Yet, the growing "more with less"[295] revolution in the industrial sciences has created a new reality where the advancement of industrial technology has reversed the pattern of "cumulative material effort" with respect to efficiency. The logic that "more labor, more energy and more resources" will produce proportionally more effective results has been challenged. In increasingly more circumstances, the *reduction* of energy, labor and materials to accomplish certain tasks has been the outcome, given our modern scientific, technical applications.[296]

For instance, satellite-based communication today, while intellectually sophisticated, embodying a great deal of evolved knowledge, is, in physical reality, rather simple and resource efficient in comparison to the prior alternatives for communication, which in global application, involved enormous amounts of cumbersome materials, such as heavy copper wires, along with the difficult, often risky task of laying out such materials by human labor power. What is accomplished today with a set of generally small, global satellites in orbit is truly amazing by comparison. This *design revolution,* which gets to the heart of what true economic (technical) efficiency means, stands in direct opposition to the cyclical consumption, growth-based economic model.

Again, the intention of the market system is to *maintain or elevate rates of turnover*, as this is what keeps people employed and increases employment and so-called growth. Hence, at its core, the market's entire premise of efficiency is based around tactics to accomplish this and hence any force that works to *reduce* the need for labor or turnover is considered "inefficient" from the view of the market, even though it might be very efficient in terms of the *true definition* of economy itself, which means to conserve, reduce waste and do *more with less*.

If we hypothetically reduced our global society to a single, small island with a respectively small population, with very limited

---

294 See the essay *History of Economy* where Adam Smith's notion of the "invisible hand" is discussed.

295 As an historical note, engineer R. Buckminster Fuller used this phrase ("more with less") in his discussion of the phenomenon in his work *"Operating Manual for Spaceship Earth"*, 1968

296 The famous ENIAC computer of the 1940s contained 17,468 vacuum tubes, along with 70,000 resistors, 10,000 capacitors, 1,500 relays, 6,000 manual switches and 5 million soldered joints. It covered 1800 square feet of floor space, weighed 30 tons, and consumed 160 kilowatts of electrical power. It cost about $6 Million in modern value. Today, a cheap, pocket size cell phone computes substantially faster than ENIAC.
(http://inventors.about.com/od/estartinventions/a/Eniac.htm)

technology as compared to today, finding that only x number of food/survival items were possible in the natural regeneration of the land, would it be a good idea to employ an economic system that sought to increase the use and turnover of the island's resources as fast as possible for the sake of "growth"? Naturally, the ethic of *strategic use* and *preservation* would develop as an ethos in such a condition. The idea would be to reduce waste, not accelerate it, which, again, is what the true definition of "economy" means – to *economize*.

Unnecessary Obsolescence: Competitive and Planned

When we think of obsolescence, we often might consider the rapid technological changes occurring in the world today. Every few years it seems our communication and processing devices, namely computer technology, undergo rapid development. "Moore's Law", for example, which essentially denotes how processing power doubles every 18-24 months, has been extended to apply to other, similar technological applications, illuminating the powerful trend of scientific advancement in general.[297]

However, when it comes to goods production, two forms of (eventual) obsolescence occur today which are *not* based on the natural evolution of technological capacity, but rather result from (a) the contrived, *competitive rule structure* of the market system, along with (b) the driving urge for market "efficiency" in seeking turnover and reoccurring profit.

The first (a) could be called "competitive (or intrinsic) obsolescence". This is obsolescence resulting from the consequential nature of a competitive economy, as each producing entity works to maintain differential advantage over another by reducing expenses in production in order to keep the price "competitively" low for consumer purchase. This mechanism is traditionally termed "cost efficiency" and the result is products that are *relatively inferior* the moment they are made. This competitive need permeates every step of production, with, in effect, a reduction of technical efficiency along the way via using cheaper materials, means and designs.

Imagine, hypothetically, if we took into account all of the material requirements for, say, the creation of a car, seeking to maximize its efficiency, durability and quality in the most *strategically* optimized way, based on the materials themselves - *not* the cost of those materials.[298] The life cycle of the car would then be determined *only* by its natural wear and tear with a very deliberate design focus on upgrading attributes of the car when they have become obsolete or

---

297 Reference: *The Law of Accelerating Returns*, Ray Kurzweil
(http://www.kurzweilai.net/the-law-of-accelerating-returns)

298 The notion of "strategically optimized" will be addressed in part III but it is worth noting here that the equation which decides what is to be used in the construction of anything, technically, not only involves the properties of the "ideal" materials, but the *relative utility* of related materials (with similar properties) which may alter the necessary material component for use due to other "efficiency" related factors, such as resource supply.

damaged by *natural-use* circumstances.

The result would be a production *designed to last*, hence reducing waste and invariably increasing efficacy of utility. It is safe to assume that many in the world today believe this is what actually happens in the design and production of goods but that simply isn't the reality. It is mathematically impossible for any competing company to produce the *strategically best* good, technically, in a market economy, as the "cost efficiency" mechanism *guarantees* a less-than-optimal production.

The second form (b) of obsolescence is known as "planned" and this production technique to ensure cyclical consumption gained interest in the early 20th century when industrial development was advancing efficiency at an accelerating rate, producing better goods, faster. In fact, there was not only a need to encourage *more purchases* by the general public,[299] the problem of resulting increased lifespan and general efficiency of goods was also slowing consumption. Again, the "more with less" phenomenon was surfacing in a rapid way.

Rather than allow for a good's lifespan to be determined by its natural capacity, with the logical *natural law* intention for it to exist as long as possible, given limited resources on a finite planet and a natural interest to save energy, both material and human, corporations decided it was instead best to create their *own* "lifespan" for goods, deliberately inhibiting efficiency for the sake of repeat purchases.[300]

In the 1930s, some even wanted to make it mandatory for all industries, legally, where life cycles were decided not by the natural state of technological ability but by the mere ongoing need for labor and increased consumption. In fact, the most notable historical example of this period was the Phoebus light bulb cartel of the 1930s where, in a time where light bulbs were able to last up to about 25,000 hours, the cartel forced each company to restrict light bulb life to less than 1000 hours to assure repeat purchases.[301] Today, every major manufacturer strategizes to limit good life cycles based on marketing models for cyclical consumption and the result is not only the reprehensible waste of finite resources, but a constant waste of human labor and energy as well.

Outside the dynamics of the market economy, it is extremely difficult to argue against the need for optimum design of goods. Sadly,

---

299 Charles Kettering, Director of General Motors in 1929, wrote of the need to 'keep the consumer dissatisfied' (1929) (http://www.wwnorton.com/college/history/archive/resources/documents/ch27_02.htm). Wall Street banker Paul Mazur wrote: "We must shift America from a needs to a desires culture. People must be trained to desire…to want new things even before the old have been entirely consumed. We must shape a new mentality in America." (Harvard Business Review, 1927)

300 In 1932, industrialist Bernard London propagated a well-known pamphlet entitled *Ending the Depression through Planned Obsolescence,* which outlined the need for the model.

301 Reference: *Planned Obsolescence: The Light Bulb Conspiracy*, ESSA, 2012 (http://economicstudents.com/2012/09/planned-obsolescence-the-light-bulb-conspiracy/)

the nature of *market efficiency* disallows such *technical efficiency* by default.

Property vs. Access
The tradition of *personal property* has become a staple of modern culture with little financial incentive in the long run to utilize a system of sharing or *access*. While a few examples of community sharing of commodities do exist in the modern day,[302] the general ethic of "ownership" and the inherent value/investment characteristics of property itself make such approaches more costly in the long run by the user than to engage in direct purchase.

From the standpoint of *market efficiency*, this is a good thing, as the more direct purchases of goods, the better. Generally speaking, if 100 people wish to drive a car, having 100 people purchase those cars is more "efficient" for the market than if 100 people shared 20 cars in a system of strategically designed access, enabling utilization based on actual *use time*.

If we analyze patterns of actual use of any given good on average, many types of products are found to be used intermittently. Transport vehicles, recreational equipment, project equipment and various other genres of goods are commonly accessed at relatively distant intervals, making the task of ownership not only somewhat of an inconvenience given the need to store these items, but also clearly *inefficient* in the context of true economic integrity, which seeks a reduction of waste at all times.

Every year, countless books are borrowed virtually for free from libraries around the world and returned, not only saving an enormous amount of material resources over time, but also facilitating knowledge *access* to those who might otherwise have no means to obtain it. Yet, this practice is a rare exception in the *market efficiency* driven world today as clearly it is to the disadvantage of the market to have anything available without direct purchase on a per-person basis.[303]

However, let's hypothetically extend this idea of the *sharing of knowledge* to the sharing (enabled access) of material goods. From the standpoint of *market efficiency,* it would be extremely inhibiting. While profit would still be generated in the capitalist model by the loaning of items to people on the basis of their need, it would be enormously disproportionate when compared to the profit/consumption rates of a society based on separate, personal ownership of each good.

Yet, on the other hand, the *technical efficiency* would be profound. Not only would fewer resources need to be utilized (along with less labor power) since less of each good would need to be

---

302 As a simple example, the sharing of bikes in Europe has become common. (http://www.treehugger.com/cars/bike-sharing-now-in-100-european-cities.html)

303 As an aside, the only reason this library exception has persisted is because of a tradition put in place long ago that saw the need for this *sharing of knowledge* as critical to human development. The tradition of shared libraries goes back 1000s of years.

created to meet the *use time* of citizens, the availability of such goods could very well extend to many who otherwise would not have the ability to afford the purchase to begin with, only the "rental" fee (still assuming a market system). In this regard, the *technical efficiency* has two levels – *environmental* and *social*. From the environmental standpoint, a dramatic reduction of resource use; from the social standpoint (all things being equal), an increase in the access availability of such goods could also occur.

So, from the standpoint of *technical efficiency*, at the deep expense of *market efficiency*, a *shared access* rather than *universal property* oriented society would be exceptionally more sustainable and beneficial. Of course, such a practice would naturally challenge some deep value identifications common to the "propertied" culture today.[304]

Competition vs. Collaboration

The question of society pursuing a competitive or collaborative culture has been a running debate for centuries, with assumptions of *human nature* common to the defense of competition.[305] Today, economists mostly discuss competition as an incentive necessary to continue *innovation*,[306] along with the generally implied assumption that there simply isn't enough to go around on this planet and hence everyone has no choice but to fight on some level, with inevitable losers.[307] Such assumptions noted, the themed context here of *market vs. technical efficiency* shall be explored with respect to the competitive benefits and/or consequences.

There are two core angles to consider: the first is (a) how competition affects industrial production itself; the second is (b) how it actually effects innovation or creative development.

(a) If we examine the layout of industrial production today, we see a complex global system of interaction, moving resources, components and goods constantly from one location to another for various

---

304 In his work, *The Age of Access*, Jeremy Rifkin poses similar questions, stating, "In a society where virtually everything is accessed, however, what happens to the personal pride, obligation, and commitment that go with ownership? And what of self-sufficiency? Being propertied goes hand in hand with being independent. Property is the means by which we gain a sense of personal autonomy in the world. When we access the means of our existence, we become far more reliant on others. While we become more connected and interdependent, do we risk at the same time becoming less self-sufficient and more vulnerable?" (P. Tarcher/Putnam, 2000, p.130)

305 Reference: *The Influence of Social Hierarchy on Primate Health*, Robert M. Sapolsky, Science 29 April 2005: Vol. 308 no. 5722 pp. 648-652 DOI: 10.1126/science.1106477 (http://www.sciencemag.org/content/308/5722/648.abstract)

306 Reference: on traditional defenses of competition as a source of innovation: *Competition and Innovation: An Inverted U Relationship* (http://www.nber.org/papers/w9269)

307 See the prior essay, *History of Economy*, and its treatment in Thomas Malthus, who viewed the world as unable to support the population and was influential in his view.

production or distribution purposes. Business, in its pursuit of *profit* and *cost efficiency*, invariably seeks out inexpensive labor, equipment and facilities at all times to remain competitive in the market. This can take the form of local immigrant labor at minimum wage, a "sweatshop" production facility overseas, a relatively cheap processing factory across the country, etc.

The bottom line is that from the standpoint of *market efficiency*, the cost-to-profit ratio is all that matters, even if the actual act of this global processing is using disproportionately wasteful amounts of fuel, transport resources, labor power and the like.[308] The notion of "proximal efficiency", meaning in this case the efficiency derived from the distance between industrial production/distribution points, is not considered and the practice of globalization today engages in a vast amount of wasteful resource movement around the world based almost entirely on the interest of saving money, not optimal, *technical efficiency*.

This ignoring of the importance of "proximal efficiency" in industrial action, whether domestic or international, is the source of some very wasteful realities. Today, industrial production is almost entirely international, especially in the technological age. The degree to which this is needed, from a technical perspective, is slight, at best.

While agricultural production has historically been regional given the propensity of certain regions to produce certain types of goods, or perhaps facilitate a more conducive environment for other such cultivations, these issues are very few in proportion to the vast majority of industrial goods production, discounting as well various technological possibilities today to overcome such regional requirements.[309]

"Localization", meaning the deliberate reduction of distance between and around all facets of production and distribution, is the most technically efficient manner for a community to operate, taking into account the obvious exceptions, such as how, for example, mineral extraction clearly must begin at its point of origin in the earth, etc. It is simple to see, especially with respect to modern technical applications which currently go unused, how the vast majority of life-sustaining goods can be generated in close proximity overall to where they are to be utilized.

As will be described in further detail in part III of this text, there

---

308 Canadian economist Jeff Rubin made this observation well with respect to oil cost trends: "What we're going to find is it's not going to make sense to produce things on the other side of the world, no matter how cheap labor costs are there, when it's so expensive to transport things." (http://www.npr.org/templates/story/story.php?storyId=104466911)

309 This is mentioned in passing to point out the extensive modern breakthroughs in agricultural methods that are not based on traditional arable landmasses. "Vertical farming", for example, has been shown to have immense possibilities on a global scale, removing the common regional restrictions to agricultural production. Suggested Reading: *The Vertical Farm: Feeding the World in the 21st Century*, Dickson Despommier, Thomas Dunne Books, 2010

is a technically efficient train of thought with respect to the utilization of *proximity* when it comes to extraction, production, distribution and recycling/waste disposal. The end result would be enormous levels of resource and human energy preservation – preservation of a *capacity* that, in fact, could be reallocated if need be to further advancing projects, rather than squandered as mere waste via the market model today.[310]

As a final note on this subject of how competition limits the technical efficiency of industrial production, increasing waste - the reality of good "multiplicity" is another issue. While all production by competing companies is typically oriented around historical statistics regarding what their "market share" is and how many goods they can sell on average, per region, the very fact of multiple corporations, working in the same genre of good production, producing nearly *identical* products with only mild variation, only adds to the sources of unnecessary waste.

As will also be described in the next sub-section, the idea of, for example, multiple cell phone companies competing for market share by mere design variation, generating consequentially relative inefficiencies in design due to different strategies to gain cost efficiency, coupled with the general lack of *compatibility* of components given the financial benefit of pushing *proprietary standards* and system compatibilities, creates another complex web of inefficiency.[311]

Clearly, from the standpoint of *technical efficiency*, one collective cell phone company, working to produce the strategically best, most adaptable, universally compatible design, would not only be more respectful of the environment, it would also create a tremendous ease and *use efficiency* as well since the problem of seeking proprietary repair parts and overcoming compatibility problems, would be dramatically reduced.

It is often argued, however, that the pursuit of competition and the product variations that arise in the quest for market share by competing businesses is a way to introduce new ideas to the public. However, such a method could also be achieved by systems of direct, mass feedback from the public with respect to what is needed, coupled with an emergent awareness campaign about what is now possible given the empirical evolution of technological advancement.

---

310 It is critical to note, as will be discussed in part III, that this notion of turning the inefficiency or wasted resources and energy inherent to the market economy into actual productivity sits at the core of human society's ability not only to transcend the scarcity-ridden environment we have today, but far exceed it with an abundance.

311 The closest thing today that attempts to overcome the problems and waste generated by proprietary components, meaning components that can only come from the manufacturer, is the ISO Standard System. However, this system, in reality, does very little to overcome the true problem and is mostly about compliance with basic quality standards, not universal adaptability of components across global industry. (Ref: http://www.iso.org/iso/home.html)

(b) The second issue here, as noted, has to do with how competition affects innovation or creative development itself. While the assumption still persists today that differential reward for one's contribution motivates other people to seek that reward, which is also a common justification of the existence of "classes", modern sociological study finds a number of conflicting views.[312] The idea that humans are motivated inherently by a need to "beat" others by, for example, gaining material-financial rewards in excess of others, is without credible vindication, outside of the intuitive view drawn from the existing, highly competitive, scarcity driven market condition in which humanity finds itself today, by design.

However, once again, the sociological debate can be set aside as the context here is how competition relates to *market & technical efficiency* directly. In short, the competitive system seeks *secrecy* when it comes to business ideas, often universally against the open flow of knowledge. The use of *patents* and *proprietary rights* or "trade secrets" perpetuates not an advance of innovation as many proponents of the competitive market assume – but retardation.

It is very interesting to think about what knowledge means, how it is generated and how odd it is for anyone to rationally claim "ownership" of an idea or invention. At no time in human history has any singular individual culminated an idea that was not *serially* generated by many before them. The historical culmination of knowledge is a social process and therefore, any claim of ownership of an idea by a person or corporation is intrinsically faulty. The common semi-economic term used today is "usufruct", which means "the legal right of using and enjoying the fruits or profits of something belonging to another."[313] In reality, however, all attributes of every idea in existence today, in the past and forever in the future, has without exception a distinctly *social*, not personal point of origin.

It becomes obvious that the notion of *intellectual property*, meaning ownership of mere thoughts and ideas, has manifest out of the vast period of human history where one's creativity has become tied to one's personal survival. In an economic system where people's ideas have the capacity to generate income for them personally, the idea of such ownership becomes relevant. After all, if you "invent" something in the modern system which could generate sales and hence help your personal economic survival, it would be extremely *inefficient*, in the market sense of the word, to allow that idea to be "open-source", since others, seeking survival themselves, would likely quickly seize that invention for their own financial exploitation.

It is also easy to see how the phenomenon of "ego" has manifest around the idea of intellectual ownership as well, since the basis of reward in such a system invariably has a psychological tie to one's personal sense of self-worth. If a person "invents" something, files for

---

312 Reference: *No Contest: The Case Against Competition*, Alfie Kohn, Boston, Boston: Houghton Mifflin, 1986
313 Source: Merriam-Webster.com (http://www.merriam-webster.com/dictionary/usufruct)

intellectual ownership, exploits it for profit and then manifests a large house and extensive property, his or her "status" as a human being is traditionally elevated as far as the standards set by culture – he/she is considered a "success".

Yet, if we were to think about it in general, the sharing of knowledge has no negative recourse outside of the economic premise of ownership for profit exploitation. There is nothing to lose and, indeed, an enormous amount to be gained *socially* by the sharing of information. Coming back to the prior example in this essay of competing cell phone companies, we will notice that within the confines of boardroom meetings where often marketers, designers and engineers consider how to improve their product in general, the *sharing of their ideas* is paramount.

However, imagine if that meeting was extended to all competing cell phone companies at once, where not only could they remove their contrived, utility-less "marketing" angles devised to gain the market share of other competitors (such as aesthetic gimmickry), they could work to produce the cumulative "best" in concert. Extending even more so, what if all designs were "public domain" in the sense that anyone in the world who had an interest to help improve an idea was able to?

The schematics of a cell phone design could be posted publicly with a system of technical interaction where people from all around the world could help, if they had the ability, with the technical efficiency and utility of the design. While this is an abstract hypothetical example, it is clear that the result of such an open approach to the sharing of information could facilitate an *explosion* of creativity and productivity never before witnessed. As will be discussed in Part III, the removal of the monetary-market system is critical to the facilitation of this capacity.

Labor for Income

At the core of the market system is the selling of an individual's labor as a commodity. In many ways, the ability of the market to employ the population has become a measure of its integrity. However, the advent of "mechanization", or the automation of human labor, has become an ever-increasing point of *interference* over time.[314] Historically, the

---

314 A glance at US historical labor statistics by sector shows the pattern of machine automation replacing human labor definitively. In the agricultural sector, almost all traditional workflow is now done by machine. In 1949, machines did 6% of the cotton picking in the South. By 1972, 100% of the cotton picking was done by machines. [Source: *The Cotton Harvester in Retrospect: Labor Displacement or Replacement?*, Willis Peterson, St Paul, 1991, pp 1-2] In 1860, 60% of America worked in agriculture, while today it is less than 3%. (Source: *Why job growth is Stalled*, Fortune, 3/8/93 p.52) In 1950, 33% of US workers worked in Manufacturing, while by 2002 there was only 10%. (Source:http://www.usatoday.com/money/economy/2002-12-12-manufacture_x.htm) The US steel industry, from 1982 to 2002 increased production from 75m tons to 120m tons, while steel workers went from 289,000 to 74,000.(Source: *Will 'Made in the USA' fade away?*, Nelson

application of machine technology to labor has been seen as an issue of not only social progress but also "economic" progress, in the market sense, mainly due to the increase in productivity.

The basic assumption is that mechanization (or more broadly *technological innovation*) facilitates industrial expansion and hence an inevitable reallocation of labor displaced by machine into new, emerging sectors. This is a common defense.[315] Historically speaking, there appears to be some truth to this, where the reduction of the human work force in one sector, such as was the case with the automation of agriculture in the West, has been overcome to a degree by the advancement of other employment sectors, such as the modern service sector. However, this assumption that technological innovation will generate new forms of employment *in tandem* with those displaced by it, creating an *equilibrium*, is actually very difficult to defend when the *rate of change* of innovation, coupled with the *cost saving interests* of business is taken into account.[316]

As for the latter, the "role" of mechanization from the standpoint of *market efficiency* exists almost solely to assist "cost-efficiency". Robotics in the modern day have far exceeded the physical capacity of the average human being, along with rapidly advancing calculation processes which continue to vastly exceed human thought. The result is the ability of industry to employ machines, which invariably have more productive capacity than human labor, coupled with the extremely notable financial incentive of reduced liability for the

---

D. Schwartz, Fortune Nov 24th 2003, p. 102) In 2003, Alliance Capital did a study of the world's largest 20 economies at that time, ranging from the period of 1995 to 2002, finding that 31 million manufacturing jobs were lost, while production actually rose by 30%. (Source: *US Weekly Economic Update: Manufacturing Payrolls Declining Globally: The Untold Story*, Alliance Bernstein Oct 2003) This pattern of *increasing* productivity and profit, coupled with decreasing employment, is a new and powerful phenomenon.

315 See the subsection on economist David Ricardo in the essay: *History of Economy*

316 Economist Stephen Roach warned in 1994, "The service sector has lost its role as America's unbridled engine of job creation." (Source: Interview, 3/15/94, noted in book *The End of Work* by Jeremy Rifkin, Penguin p.143) Examples of this include: From 1983-1993, banks cut 37% of their human tellers, and by the year 2000, 90% of all bank customers used teller machines (ATMs) (Source: "Retooling Lives", Vision, 2000 p. 43) Business phone operators have almost all been replaced by computerized voice answering systems, post office tellers are being replaced by self-service machines, while cashiers are being replaced by computerized kiosks. McDonalds, for example, has been talking about full automation of its restaurants for many years now, introducing kiosks to replace the front of house staff, while using automated cooking tools, such as burger flippers, for the back of house staff. (Source: http://www.techdirt.com/articles/20030801/1345236_F.shtmls) The fact that they haven't done so is likely a public relations issue, for they know how many jobs would be cut in the event that such automation should be adopted in the most uninhibited way..

business owners in many ways. While machines might require maintenance, they do not need health insurance, unemployment insurance, vacations, union protection and many other attributes common to human employment today. Therefore, in the narrow logic inherent to the pursuit of profit, it is only natural for businesses to seek out mechanization at all times, given its long term cost benefits and hence *market efficiency*.

As far as the suggestion that equilibrium will always be found eventually between new labor roles and displaced labor due to technological innovation, the problem is that the *rate of change* of technological development far exceeds the rate of new job creation.[317] This problem is unique as it also assumes that human society would always *want* new employment roles. It is here where subjective *cultural values* should be considered. Given that our current sociological condition demands human employment as the backbone of *market sustainability*, hence market efficiency, the ethic of "work" and its identity associations, culturally, have perpetuated a force where the actual function of the labor role - its true *utility* - becomes less important than the mere act of labor itself.[318]

Just as *market efficiency* has no consideration for what is actually being bought and sold in general, so long as it keeps cyclical consumption at an acceptable rate, the labor roles taken on today in production are equally as arbitrary in the view of the market. In theory, we could envision a world where people are being paid to do what could be considered "pointless" occupations, when it comes to utility, generating high levels of GDP with virtually no true social contribution. In fact, even today we could step back and ask ourselves what the social role of many institutions really is and perhaps come to the conclusion that they serve only to *keep moving money* around, not to create or actually contribute anything tangible for the benefit of society.

These are complex philosophical questions as they challenge dominant traditional ethics and the very nature of what "progress" really means in many ways. For instance, the following thought exercise is worth considering. Imagine if we were to revert our social system back to the 16th century, where many modern (21st century) technological realities were simply unheard of. The population of that era would naturally have expectations of what would be technically

---

317 Reference: *The Law of Accelerating Returns*, Ray Kurzweil (http://www.kurzweilai.net/the-law-of-accelerating-returns) While the context of this article regarding exponentially advancing technological capacity does not reference mechanization, it is clearly axiomatic to assume its relevance in this way, particularly with respect to what could be called "cybernation", which is the combination of machines and computers distinctly, creating "intelligence" in machines.

318 The link between having a "job" and one's self-worth has become increasingly powerful. Reference: *Joblessness And Hopelessness: The Link Between Unemployment And Suicide* (http://www.huffingtonpost.com/2011/04/15/unemployment-and-suicide_n_849428.html)

possible that would be far below what is generally accepted as possible today.

If this society was able to superimpose, overnight, the massive technological capacity of the modern era, there is little doubt that virtually *everything* related to the core survival of the population could be automated. The question then becomes, what do they now do with their newfound freedom? What becomes the cultural focus of their lives if the basic drudgery of fundamental survival was removed? Do they invent new jobs simply because they can? Do they elevate themselves, preserving and embodying this new freedom by altering their social system itself, removing this previously demanded "labor for income" requirement? These questions get to the root of what *progress* and *personal/social goals* and *success* really are.

Nevertheless, a dominant cultural value today is that of "earning a living", and the application of mechanization, in the sense of *market efficiency* is actually a double-edged sword. While cost-efficiency is inherent to mechanization and hence the general improvement of profit by reducing costs for the business owners, the displacement of human workers, known today as "technological unemployment", actually works *against market efficiency* to the extent that those unemployed workers are now *unable to contribute* to the needed cyclical consumption that powers the economy, since they have lost their *purchasing power* as "consumers".

This contradiction within the capitalist model is unique. From the stand point of *market efficiency*, mechanization hence poses both a positive and negative outcome in this sense and when we realize that the rate of technological change will, in all probability, displace people *increasingly faster* than new sectors of employment can be created, mechanization as an inhibiting factor to capitalism becomes ever more apparent. It is, in total, decreasing *market efficiency* in this circumstance.

However, on the other hand, from the standpoint of *technical efficiency*, once again, we see vast improvement and immense possibilities on many levels. The production capacity enabled by this application clearly shows a powerful increase in efficiency regarding not only the effect of industrial production, but also a general increased efficiency of the goods themselves by extension of the accuracy and integrity inherent in production. Also, an implication of this new level of production efficiency is that *meeting the needs of the global population was never more possible*. It is easy to see that without the interference of market logic on this new technical capacity, which invariably inhibits its full potential, what could be relatively deemed an "abundance" of most life sustaining goods could be facilitated for the global population.[319]

---

319 This is not a utopian concept as very basic statistical extrapolations prove this vast improvement of efficiency and production capacity on many levels. A simple example, while not exhaustive in its variables, is the obsolescence of "work hours" in industrial factory production. The 8-hour day common to human labor could manifest to nearly 24-hour labor via machine

Scarcity vs. Abundance

"Supply and demand" is a common market relationship which expresses, in part, how the value of a resource or good is proportional to how much of it is in existence or accessible. For example, diamonds are considered quantitatively more rare and hence of higher value than water, which can be found in a general abundance on the planet. Likewise, certain human creations, if created in short supply, are also subject to this dynamic, even if the perception of rarity is culturally subjective, such as with a single canvas painting by a renowned artist which might fetch many, many times its actual resource value in a sale.[320]

From the standpoint of *market efficiency*, general scarcity is a good thing overall. While extreme scarcity is, indeed, destabilizing both for an industry or an economy as a whole ("shortages"), the most optimized state within which the market system can exist is in a sort of *balanced* scarcity pressure, hence the assurance of sales-producing demand. Again, the life requirements of humans are not recognized in this equation.

Meeting human needs in the form of food, housing, low-stress circumstances for mental health, etc., is utterly "external" here and has no direct relationship to *market efficiency*. Meeting human needs in a direct sense would, again, be inefficient to the market's logic as it would remove the scarcity pressure that fuels cyclical consumption. Put another way, there is a need for *imbalance* in order to fuel this demand pressure and this imbalance can come in many forms.

Debt, for example, is a form of imposed scarcity which puts a person in a position to which they must often submit to labor which may be of a more "exploitative" nature – meaning the reward (usually the wage) is grossly disproportionate to what is needed to keep a healthy standard of living in one's circumstance. In this respect, the debt system facilitates a distinct form of *market efficiency* as it benefits the employer since the ease of lowering wage rates (cost efficiency) naturally increases as private debt levels increase.

The more in debt people are, the more likely they will submit to low wage labor and hence generate more profit for the business owners. In fact, the same logic can be applied to the use of legally unregulated "sweatshop" labor in the third world, which is frequently "exploited" by Western companies. Excessive work hours coupled with notoriously low wages are common - yet these people have literally *no choice* but to submit as there are no other options for survival in their region, often due to debt resulting from austerity measures.[321]

---

automation. This crude example shows how "abundance" can be created of core life supporting goods.

320 Edvard Munch's painting "The Scream" sold for $119 million in 2012. If we were to compare the actual material value of the work in physical form, it was sold for about 10-15,000 times its material value in paint and canvas. (http://www.huffingtonpost.co.uk/2012/05/03/edvard-munchs-the-scream-_n_1473129.html?ref=uk-culture)

321 Reference: *Economic Chaos, Loans, Greece and Corporatocracy*, John

In fact, the regulation of the money supply in total is based on a general scarcity since, as noted before, all money today is *made out of debt* and this debt-money is sold into the market as a commodity through "loans", with the mark-up of interest attached to generate a profit for the banks. Yet, this "interest" profit, which is money itself, is *not created* in the money supply itself. For instance, if an individual takes out a loan for 100 dollars and pays 5% interest on the loan, that individual is required to pay back 105 dollars. But, in an economy where all money comes into existence through loans, which is the reality, only the "principal" ($100) exists in the money supply with the "interest income" ($5) uncreated.

Therefore, there is always more debt in existence than there is money to pay for it. Furthermore, since the poor are responsible for taking more loans in general for their home/cars/etc. than the wealthy, who maintain a financial surplus, this overall debt pressure tends to fall on the lower classes, compounding the inherently insurmountable problem of being in debt and hence with limited options. In this model, bankruptcy, for example, is not a result of some poor business judgments - it is an inevitable consequence - like a game of "musical chairs".[322]

So, coming back to the central point, the reality of scarcity in the current economic system is a source of great *efficiency* in the market sense for if people had their basic needs met, or if they were able to meet those needs without the external pressure of irresolvable debt which keeps the imbalances - cyclical consumption, profit and growth would suffer. As insidious as it may seem to our intuition and humanity, that keeping people deprived is actually a positive precondition for the workings of the market, this is the reality.

Needless to say, from the standpoint of *technical efficiency*, seeing the human being as a bio-chemical machine in universal need of basic nutrition, stability and other psychosocial requirements which, if unattained, can result in sickness both physical and psychological, we can recognize the decoupled state of human/social well-being with this "market logic".[323]

As a final point on this issue, the market seeks the *servicing* of problems at all times. In fact, it could be stated generally that *technical inefficiency is the driver of market efficiency*. Problem resolution is not sought by the market as it then creates an income void and hence a loss of monetary gain and movement. The result of this, in part, is a perverse reinforcement of incentive to seek or even advance problems in general. A century ago the idea of selling bottled water would have been strange given its general, unpolluted abundance. In the modern day, it is a multimillion-dollar industry annually, derived mostly from the water pollution that has occurred

---

Perkins, 2011 (http://www.huffingtonpost.com/john-perkins/economic-chaos-loans-gree_b_901949.html)

322 Reference: *Web of Debt*, Ellen Hodgson Brown, Third Millennium Press, 2008

323 Please see the prior essay *Defining Public Health*

due to irresponsible industrial practices.[324] The profit and jobs now associated with this technically inefficient reality of resource pollution and destruction, has improved, once again, the economic *market efficiency* needed to keep cyclical consumption going.

Conclusion

Market efficiency, generally speaking, takes on a "macro" and "micro" reality. On the macro scale, anything that can increase sales, growth or consumption, regardless of the originating pressure for demand or what is actually being bought and sold, is deemed efficient in this context. On the micro scale, this efficiency takes the form of enabling conditions that can increase profit and reduce input costs ("cost efficiency") on the part of business.

This "efficiency" inherent to capitalism operates without any respect for the social or environmental costs of its process to keep cyclical consumption and profit going and the world you see around you - full of ecological disorder, human deprivation and general social and environmental instability - has been the result. On the other hand, *technical efficiency*, which one could characterize as, in fact, a hindrance to *market efficiency*, seeks to maintain the environment, maintain human health and essentially keep balance in the natural world. The reduction of waste, resolution of problems and the *maintaining of alignment* with natural law is the *common sense* logic embodied.

It is unfortunate to realize that today we have two *opposed* systems of economy working at once – working against each other, in fact. The market system, embodying its archaic, traditionalized logic, is utterly out of sync with the natural (technical) economy as it exists. The result is vast discord and imbalance with ever-mutating problems and consequences for the human species. It is clear which system will "win" in this battle. Nature will persist with its natural rules regardless of how much we theorize this or that validation of the way we have traditionally organized ourselves on this planet.

Nature doesn't care about our vast monetary economic ideas, its theories of "value", sophisticated financial models or detailed equations regarding how we *think* human behavior manifests and why. The *technical reality* is simple: learn, adapt and align to the governing laws of nature, or suffer the consequences. It is absurd to think that the human species, given its evolution within the same natural laws to which our economic practice (and values) must align, would be *incompatible* with such laws. It is merely an issue of maturity and awareness today.

As a final point, as well as a general aside, there has emerged a trend in the 21st century, in the wake of all the growing and persisting ecological problems that claims to seek what is called a "green economy". Some have even divided this economic view into sectors,

---

324 Reference: *Water and Air Pollution,* History.com
    (http://www.history.com/topics/water-and-air-pollution)

including applications for renewable energy, eco-buildings, clean transportation and other categories of focus.[325] It will be noticed that all of those awarenesses and sought applications are generally in line with the *technical* or scientific awareness perspective discussed in this essay.

Sadly, as positive as the intent of these new organizations and business planners may be, the inefficiency *inherent* to the capitalist model of economics - with all its need for certain forms of contrived "efficiency" to maintain itself - immediately pollutes and deeply limits all such attempts, which explains why such *technical efficiency* approaches have still yet to really be applied. The sad reality is that while some improvement can be made, such progress will be inherently limited to an ever-increasing degree since, as described, the very structural basis of the way market capitalism works is actively opposed to the efficiencies inherent in the natural law view. The only logical solution is to rethink the entire structure if any real efficiency, elevated prosperity and problem resolution is to be achieved in the long run.

---

325 Reference: (regarding the "green economy") How do you define the 'green' economy?, MNN, 2009 (http://www.mnn.com/green-tech/research-innovations/blogs/how-do-you-define-the-green-economy)

-VALUE SYSTEM DISORDER-

I believe that greed and competition are not a result of immutable human temperament; I have come to the conclusion that greed and fear of scarcity are in fact being continuously created and amplified as a direct result of the kind of money we are using...The direct consequence is that we have to fight with each other in order to survive.[326]
-Bernard Lietaer

Thought Genes
Given the relatively slow rate of change of the human being with respect to biological evolution, the vast societal changes that have occurred over the past 4000 years of recorded history have occurred due to the evolution of knowledge – hence "cultural evolution". If we were to search for a mechanism for cultural evolution, the notion of the "meme"[327] is useful to consider. Defined as "an idea, behavior, style, or usage that spreads from person to person within a culture", memes are considered to be sociological or cultural analogues to genes,[328] which are "functional (biological) units controlling the transmission and expression of one or more traits".

While genes basically transmit biological data from person to person through heredity, memes transmit cultural data - ideas - from person to person via human communication in all forms.[329] When we recognize, for example, the power of technological advancement over time and how it has dramatically changed our lifestyles and values and will continue to do so, we can view this overall, emergent phenomenon as an *evolution of ideas,* with information *replicating* and *mutating,* altering the culture as time moves forward.

Given this, we could gesturally view the human mental state and its propensities for action as a form of *program.* Just as genes encode a set of instructions which, in concert with other genes and the environment produce sequential results, the processing of memes by the intellectual capacity of human beings, in concert, create patterns of behavior in a similar way. While "free will" is certainly a complex debate to be had with respect to what actually triggers and manifests human decisions, it is fundamentally clear that people's ideas are limited by their input (education). If a person is given little knowledge about the world, their decision process will be equally as limited.[330]

---

326 Bernard Lietaer is an economist, author and professor most notable for his work to help design the EU currency system. Quote from *YES! Magazine,* Interview with Bernard Lietaer, *Beyond Greed and Scarcity*, Sarah van Gelder (http://www.transaction.net/press/interviews/lietaer0497.html)

327 Source: ('meme' defined) Merriam-Webster.com (http://www.merriam-webster.com/dictionary/meme)

328 Source: ('gene' defined) Merriam-Webster.com (http://www.merriam-webster.com/dictionary/gene)

329 Richard Dawkins' book *The Selfish Gene* introduced the term "meme". Dawkins cites as inspiration the work of geneticist L. L. Cavalli-Sforza, anthropologist F. T. Cloak and ethologist J. M. Cullen.

330 The inverse relationship of literacy/knowledge accumulation to superstitious

Likewise, just as genes can *mutate* in ways that are detrimental to their host, such as the phenomenon of cancer,[331] so can memes with respect to ideological/sociological transmissions, generating mental frameworks that serve as detriments to the host (or society). It is here where the term "disorder" is introduced. A disorder is defined as "a derangement or abnormality of function"[332]. Therefore, when it comes to social operation, a disorder would imply institutionalized ideological frameworks that are *out of alignment* with the larger governing system. In other words, they are *inaccurate* with respect to the context in which they attempt to exist, often creating imbalance and detrimental destabilization.

Of course, history is full of initially destabilizing, transitioning ideas and this ongoing intellectual evolution is clearly natural and necessary to the human condition as there is no such thing as an "absolute" understanding. However, the differentiation to be made here is the fact that when ideas persist for a long enough period, they often create *emotional connections* on the personal ("identity") level and *institutional establishments* on the cultural level, which tend to perpetuate a kind of *circular reinforcement,* generally resisting change and adaptation.

Recognizing our intellectual evolution, as a process with no end and being open to new information to help better align ourselves for sustainable practices, is clearly a core ethic needed both on the personal and social level if we expect to keep *adapting* for the better in the context of cultural evolution. Sadly, there are powerful cultural forces that work against this interest in the world today. Structures, both ideological and *encoded* in the current social infrastructure[333] actively work against this critical necessity of cultural adaption. An analogy would be the starvation of our biological cells by removing oxygen from the environment – only in this case we are restricting our vulnerability to *learn and adapt,* with *knowledge* being the "oxygen" by which we as a species are able to solve problems and continue progress.

This disorder is, as will be described, inherent to the market

---

belief is clear. According to the United Nations' Arab Human Development Reports, less than 2% of Arabs have access to the Internet. Arabs represent 5% of the world's population and yet produce only 1% of the world's books, most of them religious. According to researcher Sam Harris: "Spain translates more books into Spanish each year than the entire Arab world has translated into Arabic since the ninth century." It is axiomatic to assume that the growth of the Islamic Religion in Arab Nations is secured by a relative lack of outside information in those societies.

331 Cancer is a term used for diseases in which abnormal cells divide without control and are able to invade other tissues. (http://www.cancer.gov/cancertopics/cancerlibrary/what-is-cancer)

332 Source: ('disorder defined') TheFreeDictionary.com (http://medical-dictionary.thefreedictionary.com/disorder)

333 To clarify the notion of "encoded", this refers to structural attributes such as needing, for example, "to compete" in order to succeed in the market economy. It is built into the system's framework, or *encoded.*

capitalist tradition. It is not only the actual decisions being made against the interests of adaptation, knowingly or not, that perpetuate detrimental effects on many levels – it is also the *value system* – the employment of "identity" and a normalized sense of custom, which bears a powerfully problematic force. This is compounded even more so when the purpose served (or appears to be served) by such intents directly ties to our *survival* and *existence*. There is nothing more personal to us than how we *identify* ourselves and the economic system we encompass is invariably a defining feature of our mentalities and worldview. If there is something wrong with this system, then it implies there is something wrong with ourselves, given that we are the ones who perpetuate it.

Value System Disorder
Just like cancer is, in part, an immune system disorder, sociological traditions which persist with ever-increasing problem generation for society could be called a *value system disorder.*[334] This disorder has to do with a kind of *structured psychology* where certain assumptions have been given credence over time based merely on their cultural persistence, coupled with an inherent *reinforcement of itself* in operation. The larger the social context of the disorder, often the more difficult its resolution, not to mention the difficulty of its mere recognition itself.

On the scale of a social system, it becomes very difficult as the society as a whole is constantly being conditioned into the dynamics of its own framework, often creating powerful *self-preservation* reactions whenever its integrity is challenged. These, what could be called "closed intellectual feedback mechanisms", are what comprise the vast majority of arguments in defense of our current socioeconomic system, just as they have in generations prior. In fact, it appears to be a general sociological trend since, again, people's very *identity* is invariably associated with the dominant belief systems and institutions they are born into.

In the words of John McMurtry, Professor Emeritus of Philosophy at the University of Guelph, Canada: "In the last dark age, one can search the inquiries of this era's preserved thinkers from Augustine to...Ockham, and fail to discover a single page of criticism of the established social framework, however rationally insupportable feudal bondage, absolute paternalism, divine right of kings and the rest may be. In the current final order, is it so different? Can we see in any media or even university press a paragraph of clear unmasking of a global regime that condemns a third of all children to malnutrition with more food than enough available...? In such a social order, thought becomes indistinguishable from propaganda. Only one doctrine is

---

334 To clarify the phrase, the term "value" refers to an ethical preference in a personal or cultural sense, generally considered subjective. It becomes a basis for action. For example, a person who believes in a certain religious philosophy might establish *values* in favor of certain behaviors. A *value system* is a set of consistent values and measures.

speakable, and a priest caste of its experts prescribes the necessities and obligations to all...Social consciousness is incarcerated within the role of a kind of ceremonial logic, operating entirely within the received framework of an exhaustively prescribed regulatory apparatus protecting the privileges of the privileged. Methodical censorship triumphs in the guise of scholarly rigor, and the only room left for searching thought becomes the game of competing rationalizations."[335]

Such reactions are also common with respect to established practices in specific fields. For instance, Ignaz P. Semmelweis (1818 -1865), a Hungarian physician who discovered that puerperal fever could be drastically cut by the use of simple hand washing standards in obstetrical clinics, essentially foreshadowing the now fully accepted germ theory of disease, was shunned, rejected and ridiculed by his finding. It wasn't until long after his death his now very basic realization was respected. Today, some use the phrase, "The Semmelweis Reflex" as a metaphor for the reflex-like tendency to reject new evidence or new knowledge because it contradicts established norms, beliefs or paradigms.[336]

Overall, once a given set of ideas is entrusted by a large enough number of people, it becomes an "institution"- and once that institution is made dominant in some way, such as existing for a certain period of time, that institution could then be considered an "establishment". "Institutional establishments" are simply social traditions given the illusion of permanence and the longer they persist, often the stronger the defense of their right to exist by the majority of culture.

If we examine the institutional establishments we take for granted today – from macro system attributes such as the financial system, the legal system, the political system and major religious systems – to micro system attributes such as materialism, marriage, celebrity, etc. – we must remind ourselves that none of these ideas are actually *real* in the physical sense. These are temporal *meme structures* we have created to serve our purposes given conditions at certain points in time and no matter how much we emotionally *attach* to such issues; no matter how large an institution may become; no matter how many people may believe in such institutions - they are still *impositions of thought* and *transient* by nature.

So, coming back to the context here of the *value system disorder,* market capitalism, while arguably being deeply decoupled from physical reality and a root source of the vast majority of the social woes in the world today, keeps itself in place through a set of *culturally reinforced values* and *power establishments* upon which the society is ultimately conditioned and generally inclined to defend. This is made increasingly powerful in its persuasion since the dominant value system disorder at hand today is born out of assumptions relating to critical *human survival* itself.

---

335 *The Cancer Stage of Capitalism*, John McMurtry, Pluto Press, 1999, p.6
336 General biography of Ignaz P. Semmelweis:
    http://semmelweis.org/about/dr-semmelweis-biography/

Characteristics of Pathology

In order to critically evaluate an existing framework of thought, a basic, mutually accepted benchmark needs to be generated. "Cultural relativism"[337] is an anthropological notion that refers to the fact that different cultural groups generate different perceptions of "truth" or "reality". "Moral relativism",[338] which is a similar notion, has to do with the variance of what is considered "correct" or "ethical". Over the course of human history, these distinctions have become increasingly narrow since the *scientific revolution* of causal thought, from the Renaissance onward, has increasingly reduced the "relative integrity" of various beliefs.

The fact is, beliefs are *not equal* in their validity. Some are truer than others and hence some are more dysfunctional than others in the context of real life. The scientific method of arriving at conclusions is the ultimate benchmark upon which the integrity of human values can be measured and this modern reality demystifies the common "relativism" defense of subjective human belief.

It is not about "right" and "wrong" but what *works* or *doesn't work*. The integrity of our values and beliefs is only as good as how aligned they are with the natural world. This is the *common ground* that we all share.

This concept ties in directly with sustainability in the broad context of human survival itself, as a sustainable social system naturally must have *sustainable values* to facilitate and perpetuate the structure. Unfortunately, the evolutionary baggage of our cultural history has maintained value structures that are so powerful, yet so clearly decoupled from reality, which our personal and societal assumptions of happiness, success and progress itself continue to be deeply perverted and exist in discordance with the governing laws of our habitat and human nature. The human being indeed has a *common nature* and while nothing appears 100% universal across the species, certain pressures and stressors can generate, on average, serious public health problems.[339] Likewise, if our values support behaviors that are not in accordance with our *physical sustainability* on the planet Earth, then naturally we can expect ever-increasing problems on that environmental level as well.[340]

---

337 "Cultural relativism" is a principle that was established as axiomatic in anthropological research by Franz Boas in the first few decades of the 20th century.

338 Similar to "cultural relativism", "moral relativism" is generally defined as: "any of several philosophical positions concerned with the differences in moral judgments across different people and cultures." (https://www.boundless.com/management/definition/moral-relativism/)

339 Please see the prior essay *Defining Public Health*

340 A general example would be the *consumer values* prevalent in the world today. The act of increasing ownership is common as more property is equated to increased success and more consumption is related to economic growth. Yet, such an un-conservative ethic can be considered un-sustainable given we live on a *finite planet* with *finite resources*. In fact, it has been argued by many that the "standard of living" of the United States would be,

The dominant value system, which the capitalist socioeconomic model perpetuates, is arguably deeply *pathological* to the human condition as the mechanisms related to survival and general reward compound emotional attachments and forms of self-preservation which are essentially rooted in a kind of *primitive desperation and fear*. The fundamental ethos is that of an anti-social, scarcity driven pressure, which forces all players of the game to be generally exploitative and antagonistic both of others and the habitat. It also has built-in pressures to avoid socially easing interests due to a resulting loss of profit,[341] furthering this stress-induced emotional disparity. The result is a vicious cycle of general abuse, narrow-minded selfishness, and social and environmental disregard.

Of course, historically, these caustic characteristics are usually defended as simply "the way it is" - as though our evolutionary psychology must be stuck in this state. In fact, if the touted psychological doctrines of traditional market theory hold true ("neoclassical utilitarianism") regarding our apparent limits with respect to a "workable" social structure, then imbalance, environmental destruction, oppression, violence, tyranny, personality disorders, warfare, exploitation, selfish greed, vain materialism, competition and other such divisive, inhumane and destabilizing realities are simply *inalterable* and therefore the whole of society should do nothing but *work around* such inevitabilities with whatever "controls" we can put in place to "manage" these realities of the human condition. It is as though the human being is deemed to have a severe, incurable mental disorder – a firm retardation - that simply cannot be overcome, so everything in society must be altered around it in an attempt to deal with it.

Yet, the more we live as human beings; the more history we are able to see of ourselves over generational time; the more we are able to compare the behaviors of different cultures across the world and across history – the more clear it becomes that our human capacity is being *inhibited* directly by an archaic reward and survival structure which continues to reinforce primitive, desperate values and while such values might have served a positive evolutionary role in the past, the present and foreshadowed future arguably lays these behavioral patterns bare as detrimental and unsustainable, as this overall text has expressed at length.

---

in the current scheme of things, technically impossible to extend to the rest of the world. According to some surveys: "Humanity is now using resources and producing carbon dioxide at a rate 50 percent faster than the Earth can sustain..." Sources: *Living Planet Report: Humanity Now Needs 1.5 Earths,* 2010 (http://www.business-biodiversity.eu/default.asp?Menue=49&News=233); *The Earth Is Full,* 2011 (http://www.nytimes.com/2011/06/08/opinion/08friedman.html)

341 It should be understood that the more problems in the world, the more there is to service and capitalize upon. The more true problem resolution, the less capacity there is to capitalize and hence less to maintain or increase economic growth.

Self-Preservation Paralysis

While each of us generally wishes to survive and do so in a healthy state, naturally prepared to defend that survival when need be, *self-preservation* in the current socioeconomic condition unnecessarily extends this tendency in ways that severely inhibit social progress and problem resolution. In fact, it could be said that this short-term preservation occurs often at the cost of *long-term integrity.*

The most obvious example of this has to do with the fundamental nature of seeking and maintaining *income,* the lifeblood of the market system and, by extension, human survival. Once a business succeeds in gaining market share, typically supporting employees along with the owners, the business naturally gravitates to an interest to *preserve* that income generating market share at all costs. Deep value associations are generated since the business is not just an arbitrary entity that produces a good or service - it is now a means of *life support* for everyone involved.

The result is a constant, socially debilitating battle, not only with the competitors who also seek the same consumer market, but with *innovation* and *change* itself. While technological progress is a constant, fluid progression on the scientific level, the market economy sees this emergence as a threat in the context of existing, currently profitable ideas. Vast levels of historical "corruption", cartel and monopoly generation and other defensive moves of existing businesses can be found throughout history, each act working to secure income production regardless of the social costs.[342]

Another example has to do with the psychological neurosis built out of the credit-based reward incentive inherent to the market system. While it is intellectually clear that no single person invents anything given the reality that all knowledge is *serially* generated and invariably *cumulative* over time, the market economy's characteristic of "ownership" creates a tendency not only to reduce information flow via patents and "trade secrets", it also reinforces the idea of "intellectual property", despite the true fallacy of the notion itself.

On the value system level, this has mutated into the notion of "credit" entitlement and hence often "ego" associations to presented ideas or "inventions". In the world today, this phenomenon has taken a life of its own with a tendency for many who contribute often seeking status elevating "credit" for the idea, even though they are, again, clearly part of a continuum larger than themselves. While appreciation for the time and labor of a given person working towards the progress of an idea is a productive social incentive and fundamental to our sense of purpose in action, the perversion of intellectual ownership and all its contrived attributes extend this operant satisfaction into distortion.

---

342 A well-established example of inhibited progress for the maintaining of existing profit establishments was the successful effort made by the oil industry and, by extension, the US government to slow progress toward fully electric vehicles in the 1990s. Reference: *Who Killed the Electric Car?* (http://www.imdb.com/title/tt0489037/synopsis)

In fact, on the largest scale of knowledge culmination, such acts of "appreciation" inevitably become irrelevant in the memory of history. Today, for instance, when we use a modern computer to assist our lives, we seldom think about the thousands of years of intellectual study that discovered the core scientific dynamics related, nor the enormous amount of cumulative time spent by virtually countless people to facilitate the "invention" of such a tool, in its current form.

It is only in the context of *manifest ego* and *monetary reward security* that this becomes a "natural" value issue with respect to the market system. If people do not claim "credit", they will not be rewarded and hence they will not gain survival from that contribution in the market. So, the condition has compounded this neurosis that is invariably stifling towards progress via the sharing of knowledge.

Furthermore, disorders associated with market "self-preservation" can take many other forms, including the use of government as a tool,[343] the pollution of academia and information itself[344] (since educational institutions are supported by income as well), and even common interpersonal relationships.[345] The fear inherent to the loss of livelihood naturally overrides almost everything and even the most "ethical" or "moral" person, when faced with the risk of non-survival, can usually justify actions that would be traditionally called "corrupt". This pressure is constant and is the source, in part, of the vast co-called "criminality" and social paralysis we see today.

Competition, Exploitation and Class Warfare

Building on the prior point, exploitation, which is inherent to the competitive frame of mind, has permeated the very core of what it means to "succeed" in general. We see this "taking advantage" rhetoric in many facets of our lives. The act of manipulation and exploitation for competitive gain has become an underlying force in modern culture, extending far beyond the context of the market system.

The attitude of seeing others and the world as merely a means for oneself or a particular group to "conquer" and keep ahead of is now

---

343 Corporate lobbying, by its very nature, is a means to use money to influence political decisions. Reference: *Corporate Lobbyists Threaten Democracy*, Julio Godoy, IPS: (http://www.ipsnews.net/2012/08/corporate-lobbyists-threaten-democracy/)

344 A unique example of this was the 2007 case in which Microsoft Corporation, dissatisfied with the information on the public encyclopedia "Wikipedia" worked to hire an editor to change the public information in its favor. Reference: *Microsoft Offers Cash for Wikipedia Edit* (http://www.washingtonpost.com/wp-dyn/content/article/2007/01/23/AR2007012301025.html)

345 A study by a Connecticut wealth management firm showed that many would get married simply for money, with the average 'price' that people would marry for being around $1.5 million. Reference: *Survey: Most People Would Marry For Money,* Tom Miller (http://www.yourtango.com/20072778/survey-most-people-would-marry-for-money)

a driving psychological distortion to be found in romantic relationships, friendships, family structures, nationalism and even how we relate to the habitat we exist within - where we seek to exploit and disregard the physical environment's resources for short term personal gain and advantage. All elements of our lives are necessarily viewed from the perspective of "what can I get out of it personally?"

A study performed at the Department of Psychology at the University of California, Berkeley, in 2011 found that: "...upper-class individuals behave more unethically than lower-class individuals...upper-class individuals were more likely to break the law while driving, relative to lower-class individuals. In follow-up laboratory studies, upper-class individuals were more likely to exhibit unethical decision-making tendencies, take valued goods from others, lie in a negotiation, cheat to increase their chances of winning a prize, and endorse unethical behavior at work than were lower-class individuals. Mediator and moderator data demonstrated that upper-class individuals' unethical tendencies are accounted for, in part, by their more favorable attitudes toward greed."[346]

Studies of this nature are very interesting as they reveal that the common human nature argument in its extreme context, that of people inevitably "being competitive and exploitative", when defending the current social system, is bypassed. Class relationships are not genetic relationships, even though the nuances of individual propensities could be argued. This study expresses a cultural phenomenon overall since it is axiomatic to assume that the general attitude of disregard for external negative consequences, or so-called "unethical behavior" expressed by the upper class, is a result of the type of *values* needed to achieve the position of actually making it to the "upper class".[347]

In common poetic rhetoric, this intuition has held true for centuries, with the observation that those who achieve "success" in the business sense, are often "desensitized" and "ruthless". There appears to be a general *loss of empathy* by those who achieve such "success" and it is intuitively obvious why this is the case, given the value system disorder of *competitive disregard* inherent to the market system psychology. Overall, the more caring and empathic you are, the less likely you are to succeed financially - no different from a general sport where you are not going to help an opposing player achieve their goals for it means you are more likely to lose.

Overall, the lower classes are found to be more socially humane in many ways. For example, it has also been found that the poor give a higher percentage of their income (4.3%) to charity than rich people

346 Reference: *Higher social class predicts increased unethical behavior,* Piffa, Stancatoa, Côtéb, Mendoza-Dentona, Dacher Keltnera, University of Michigan, 2012 (http://www.pnas.org/content/early/2012/02/21/1118373109)
347 Reference: "How Wealth Reduces Compassion", Daisy Grewal, *Scientific American,* 2012 (http://www.scientificamerican.com/article.cfm?id=how-wealth-reduces-compassion)

(2.1%). A 2010 study found that: "...lower class individuals proved to be more generous...charitable...trusting...and helpful...compared with their upper class counterparts. Mediator and moderator data showed that lower class individuals acted in a more prosocial fashion because of a greater commitment to egalitarian values and feelings of compassion. Implications for social class, prosocial behavior, and economic inequality are discussed."[348] [349]

A study conducted by the *Chronicle of Philanthropy* using tax-deduction data from the Internal Revenue Service, showed that households earning between $50,000 and $75,000 a year give an average of 7.6% of their discretionary income to charity. That compares to 4.2% for people who make $100,000 or more. In some of the wealthiest neighborhoods, with a large share of people making $200,000 or more a year, the average giving rate was 2.8%.[350] [351]

Success & Status

Underlying the capitalist model is an implied assumption that those who contribute the most must gain the most. In other words, it is assumed that to become say, a billionaire, you must have done something important and helpful for society. Of course, this is clearly untrue. The vast majority of extremely wealthy people originate their wealth out of mechanisms that are not socially contributive on any direct, creative level when broken down and analyzed.[352]

The act of engineering, problem solving and creative innovation almost always occurs on the level of the laborer in the lower echelons of the corporate complex, only to be capitalized upon by those at the top (owners) who are skilled at the contrived game of generating a "market". This is not to discount the intelligence or hard work of those who hold vast wealth, but to show that the rewards of the system are displaced, allocated to those who *exploit* the mechanisms of the market, not those who *actually* engineer and create. In fact, one of the most rewarded sectors of the global economy today is that of investment and finance.[353] This is a classic example as to be a "hedge fund" manager, moving money around for the mere sake of gaining

---

348 Source: "Having Less, Giving More: The Influence of Social Class on Prosocial Behavior", *Journal of Personality and Social Psychology,* 2010, Vol. 99, No. 5, 771–784, 2012
(http://www.rotman.utoronto.ca/phd/file/Piffetal.pdf)
349 Source: *Study: Poor Are More Charitable Than The Wealthy,* NPR, 2012
(http://www.npr.org/templates/story/story.php?storyId=129068241)
350 Reference: *The Rich Are Less Charitable Than the Middle Class: Study,* CNBC, 2012 (http://www.cnbc.com/id/48725147)
351 Reference: "America's poor are its most generous givers", Frank Greve/McClatchy analysis, 2009
(http://www.mcclatchydc.com/2009/05/19/68456/americas-poor-are-its-most-generous.html)
352 Reference: *The Engineers and the Price System,* Thorstein Veblen, 1921
353 Reference: "The 40 Highest-Earning Hedge Fund Managers", Nathan Vardi, *Forbes* (http://www.forbes.com/sites/nathanvardi/2012/03/01/the-40-highest-earning-hedge-fund-managers-3/)

more money, with zero contribution to creative development,[354] is one of the highest paid occupations in the world today.

Likewise, the very notion of "success" in the culture today is measured by material wealth, in and of itself. Fame, power and other gestures of attention go hand in hand with material wealth. To be poor is to be abhorred, while to be rich is to be admired. Across almost the entire social spectrum, those of high levels of wealth are treated with immense respect. Part of this has to do with a system-oriented survival mechanism, such as the personal interest in gaining insight into how to *also* become such a "success" - but overall it has morphed into a strange fetish where the idea of being rich, powerful and famous, by whatever means necessary, is a guiding force.

The value system disorder of rewarding, in effect, generally the most ruthless and selfish in our society, both by financial means and then by public adoration and respect, is one of the most pervasive and insidious consequences of the incentive system inherent to the Capitalist model. It not only works to bypass true interests in types of innovation and problem-solving which inherently do not have monetary return, it also reinforces the market system's *own existence*, justifying itself by way of high status attainment for those who "win" in the system, regardless of true contribution or the social and environmental costs.

Sociologist Thorstein Veblen wrote extensively on this issue, referring to this value "virtue" as *predatory*: "As the predatory culture reaches a fuller development, there comes a distinction between employments...The "honorable" man must not only show capacity for predatory exploit, but he must also avoid entanglement with occupations that do not involve exploit. The tame employments, those that involve no obvious destruction of life and no spectacular coercion of refractory antagonists, fall into disrepute and are relegated to those members of the community who are defective in the predatory capacity; that is to say, those who are lacking massiveness, agility, or ferocity...Therefore the able-bodied barbarian of the predatory culture, who is mindful of his good name...puts in his time in the manly arts of war and devotes his talents to devising ways and means of disturbing the peace. That way lies honor."[355]

William Thompson, in his *An Inquiry into the Principles of the Distribution of Wealth Most Conducive to Human Happiness* restates the reality of this associative influence:

---

354 There is a common argument that the financial sector is relevant to industrial production because it facilitates the capital by which production is originated by investment. However, that facilitation is a contrivance since the act of production in physical reality, absent the Capitalist model, has nothing to do with money or investment at all – it has to do with education, resources and engineering. Investment and finance is not *real* as it does not produce - it is not needed with respect to the real components of production.

355 "The Instinct of Workmanship and the Irksomeness of Labor," in *Essays in Our Changing Order*, Thorstein Veblen, pp.93-94

"Our next position is, that excessive wealth *excites the admiration and the imitation, and in this way diffuses the practice of the vices of the rich, amongst the rest of the community; or produces in them other vices arising out of their relative situation to the excessively rich.* On this point, nothing is more obvious than the universal operation of the most common principle of our nature – that of association. The wealth, as a means of happiness...is admired or envied by all; the manner and character connected with the abundance of these good things, always strike the mind in conjunction with them..."[356]

Classes and class warfare are a natural outgrowth of this as the value associations to wealth and power, manifest by the current system, become an issue of *emotional identity* over time. The status-interest begins to take on a life of its own and it generates actions of self-preservation on the part of the upper class that seek to maintain (or elevate) their status in ways that might not even relate to money or material wealth anymore. Self-preservation, in this case, extends to a kind of *drug addiction*. Just as a chronic gambler needs the endorphin rush of winning to feel good, those in the upper class often develop similar compulsions in relationship to the state of their perceived status and wealth.

The term "greed" is often used to differentiate between those who exploit modestly and those who exploit excessively. Greed is hence a relative notion, just as being "rich" is a relative notion. The term "relative deprivation"[357] refers to the discontent people feel when they compare their positions to others and realize that they have less of what they *believe* themselves to be entitled to. This psychological phenomenon knows no end and within the context of the material success incentive system of capitalism, its presence as a severe value system disorder is apparent on the level of mental health.

While maintaining a needs meeting, quality standard of living is important for physical and mental health, anything beyond that balance in the context of social comparison has the capacity to create severe neurosis and social distortion. Not only is there no "winning" in the end when it comes to the subjective perception of status and wealth, it often serves to *decouple* those figures from the majority of the human experience, generating alienation and dehumanization in many ways. This empathic loss has no positive outcome on the social level. The predatory reward values inherent to the market system virtually guarantee endless conflict and abuse.[358]

Of course, the myth is that this neurosis of seeking "more and more" status and wealth is the core driver of social progress and

---

356 Source: *An Inquiry into the Principles of the Distribution of Wealth Most Conducive to Human Happiness*, William Thompson, London, William S. Orr, 1850, p.147
357 Source: *Relative Deprivation: Specification, Development, and Integration*, Iain Walker, Heather J. Smith, Cambridge University Press, 2001, ISBN 0-521-80132-X, Google Print
358 More in the essay: *Structural Classism, the State and War*

innovation. While there might be some basic truth to this intuitive assumption, the intent, again, is *not* social contribution but *advantage* and *financial gain*. It is like saying being chased by a pack of hungry wolves ready to eat you is good for your health since it is keeping you running. While certain accomplishments are clearly occurring, the guiding force (intent) again has little to do with those accomplishments and the detrimental byproducts and larger-order paralysis inherent nullifies in comparison the idea that the values of competition, material greed and vain status is a legitimate source of societal progress.

In fact, epidemiologist Richard Wilkinson has extrapolated a comparison of wealthy nations oriented by the income disparity present in each population. It was found that those nations with the least income disparity actually were *more* innovative[359] and when we consider that the competitive value drive has a large role with respect to how severe the gap between the rich and poor is, it is axiomatic to consider that the values of egalitarianism and collaboration have more creative power than the traditional economic incentive rhetoric would claim.

As a final point in this subsection, the subject of materialism and status can be extended to the similar issue of *vanity* as well. While a mild deviation from our point, the vanity-based culture we have today finds a direct relationship to these drives for status and measures of "success" rooted in the psychological value incentives inherent to the capitalist system. Given that the value system of "acquisition" is, in fact, *necessary* for the consumption model to work, it is only natural that marketing and advertising generate *dissatisfaction* continually, including in the way we feel about our physical appearance.

In fact, a study was conducted some years ago on the island of Fiji, in which Western television was introduced to a culture that had never experienced the medium before. By the end of the observation period, the effect of materialistic values and vanity took a powerful toll. A relevant percentage of young women, for example, who prior had embraced the style of healthy weight and full features, became obsessed with being thin. Eating disorders, which were virtually unheard of in this culture, began to spread and women specifically were transformed.[360]

Ideological Polarization & Blame
When the subject of what has "gone wrong" with the world today is broached - given the poverty, ecological imbalance, inhumanity, general economic destabilization and the like - a polarized debate often ensues. Dualities such as "the right or the left" or "liberal or

---

359 Reference: "The Importance of Economic Equality", Eben Harrell, *Time, 2009;* Also See: *The Spirit Level* by Richard Wilkinson and Kate Pickett, Penguin, March 2009

360 "Study Finds TV Alters Fiji Girls' View of Body", Erica Goode, *The New York Times*, 1999 (http://www.nytimes.com/1999/05/20/world/study-finds-tv-alters-fiji-girls-view-of-body.html)

conservative" are common, implying that in the range of human comprehension and preference, there is a rigid guiding line that embodies all known possibilities.

Paired with this is also the older, yet still common duality of "collectivism vs. free market". In short, this duality assumes that all options of economic preference must adhere to the idea that society should either be based on the supposed democratic will of all the people in the form of "free-trade" – or that a small group of people should be in control and tell everyone else what to do. Due to the dark history of totalitarianism that plagued the 20th century, a fear based value orientation, which rejects anything that even remotely hints at the appearance of "collectivism", is extremely common today, with the related word "socialism" often used in a derogatory way.[361]

As noted prior in this essay, people's sense of possibility is directly related to their knowledge - what they have learned. If traditional educational and social institutions present all socioeconomic variation within the confines of such boxed *frames of reference*, people will likely mirror this assumption (meme) and perpetuate it in thought and practice. If you are not "abc", then you *must* be "xyz" - this is the common *thought meme.* Even the political establishment of the United States exists in this paradigm, for if you are not a "republican", you *must* be a "democrat", etc.

In other words, there is a direct inhibition of possibility and, in this context, it often manifests a value structure that builds emotional attachments to false dualities. These values are extreme barriers to progress today on many levels. In fact, as an aside, if the intention of a ruling class were to limit any interference from the lower classes, they would protectively work to limit people's sense of possibility.[362]

For example, the supposed problem of "state intervention" of the free-market, a constant theme of capitalist apologists, essentially says that since various policies and practices of the government limit free trade in some way,[363] this is the source of the problem generating market inefficiency. This blame game actually goes back and forth between those who claim it is the market that is the problem and those who claim it is the state's interference with the market.[364]

---

361 Reference: "Pat Robertson: Obama A 'Socialist,' Wants To 'Destroy' The United States", Paige Lavender, *The Huffington Post*, 2012, (http://www.huffingtonpost.com/2012/12/14/pat-robertson-obama_n_2301228.html)

362 Much controversy has existed with respect to continual decline of Western education, specifically in America. Charlotte Thomson Iserbyt, former Senior Policy Advisor in the U.S. Department of Education, has written about what she calls *The Deliberate Dumbing Down of America,* Conscience Press, 1999

363 Reference: *Ronald Reagan: Protectionist*, Sheldon L. Richman, 1988 (https://mises.org/freemarket_detail.aspx?control=489)

364 A notable statement by the famous economist Milton Friedman on this issue: "Government has three primary functions. It should provide for military defense of the nation. It should enforce contracts between individuals. It should protect citizens from crimes against themselves or their property. When government - in pursuit of good intentions tries to

What isn't talked about is the duality-shattering reality that the state, in its historical form, *is an extension of* the capitalist system itself. The government did not create this system. The system created the government or more accurately - they evolved as one apparatus. All socioeconomic systems root themselves in the basis of industrial unfolding and basic survival. Just as feudalism, being based on an agrarian society, oriented its class structure in relationships to the livelihood-producing land, so do the so-called "democracies" in the world today. Therefore, the very idea the state government is detached or without the influence of capitalism is a purely abstract theory with no truth in reality. Capitalism essentially *molded* the governmental apparatus's nature and unfolding – not the other way around.

So, when people argue that government regulation of the market is the root of the problem and that the market should be "free" without structural or legal inhibition, they are confused in their associative understanding. The entire legal system, which is the central tool of government, will *always* be "infiltrated" and used to assist in competitive tactics by business to maintain and increase advantage since that is the very nature of the game. To expect anything else is to assume that there are actually "moral" limits to the act of competition. Yet, this is completely subjective. Such moral and ethical assumptions have no empirical basis, especially when the very nature of the socioeconomic system is oriented around power, exploitation and competition - all considered to be, in fact, *ideal virtues* of the "good businessman", as noted before.

If a profit seeking institution can gain power in the government (which is the exact intent of "corporate lobbying") and manipulate the governmental apparatus to favor their business or industry to gain advantage, then that is simply *good business.* It is only when the competitive attacks reach peak levels of unfairness that action is taken to preserve the illusion of "balance". We see this with anti-trust laws and the like.[365] These laws are, in reality, not to protect "free-trade" or the like – but to settle extreme acts of competitive intent inherent in the market place, with all sides jockeying for advantage by whatever means possible.[366]

---

rearrange the economy, legislate morality, or help special interests, the costs come in inefficiency, lack of motivation, and loss of freedom. Government should be a referee, not an active player."

365 Even Adam Smith in his writings implies that businessmen use every means at their disposal to avoid competition and to secure monopolies: "People of the same trade seldom meet together, even for merriment and diversion, but the conversation ends in a conspiracy against the public, or in some contrivance to raise prices." Reference: *An Inquiry into the Nature and Causes of the Wealth of Nations*, Adam Smith, New York, Modern Library, 1937 p. 128

366 Economist Thomas Hodgskin wrote in the early 19th century: "It is not enough, in the eyes of legislators, that wealth has of itself a thousand charms, but they have[...]given it a multitude of privileges. In fact, it has now usurped all the power of legislation, and most penal laws are now made

Even the very constituents of all governments in the world today are invariably of the corporate-business class. Hence, deep business values are clearly inherent in the mindsets of those in power. Thorstein Veblen wrote of this reality in the early 20th century:

"The responsible officials and their chief administrative officers - so much as may at all reasonably be called the "government" or the "administration" - are invariably and characteristically drawn from these beneficiary classes; nobles, gentleman or business men, which all come to the same thing for the purpose in hand; the point of it all being that the common man does not come within these precincts and does not share in these counsels that are assumed to guide the destiny of the nations." [367]

So, to argue that the "free market" is not "free" due to intervention is to misunderstand what the nature of "free" really means with respect to the system. The "freedom" is not the freedom of everyone to be able to "fairly" participate in the open-market and all the utopian rhetoric we hear about today by apologists of the capitalist system – the *real freedom* is actually the freedom to dominate, suppress and beat other businesses by whatever competitive means possible. In this, no "level playing field" is possible. In fact, if the government did not "interfere" by way of monopoly/anti-trust laws or the "bailing out" of banks and the like - the entire market complex would have self-destructed a long time ago. In part, this inherent instability of the market is what economists like John Maynard Keynes basically understood, but arguably to a limited extent.[368]

Individuality & Freedom
All too often people speak of "freedom" in a way that is more of an indescribable gesture than a tangible circumstance. We hear this rhetoric in the political and economic establishments constantly today where associations of "democracy" are made to this "freedom", both on the level of the traditional practice of voting and the movement of money itself via independent free trade. These sociopolitical memes are also reinforced in a polarized way, relatively, which often uses

---

for the mere protection of wealth." Source: *Travels in the North of Germany, Describing the Present State of Social and Political Institutions, the Agriculture, Manufactures, Commerce, Education, Arts and Manners in That Country, Particularly in the Kingdom of Hanover*, Thomas Hodgskin, T. Edinburgh, Archibald Constable, 1820, vol. 2, p. 228

367 Source: *An Inquiry into the Nature of Peace and the terms of its Perpetuation*, Thorstein Veblen, Harvard Law, pp.326-327

368 Keynesian economics, unlike the more libertarian, free-market liberation schools of economic thought, such as the Austrian School, sees, in part, government intervention as periodically needed to avoid certain problems. In the words of the online Business Dictionary: "This theory further asserts that free markets have no self-balancing mechanisms that lead to full employment. Keynesian economists urge and justify a government's intervention in the economy through public policies that aim to achieve full employment and price stability." Source: BusinessDictionary.com (http://www.businessdictionary.com/definition/Keynesian-economics.html)

examples of oppression and the loss of freedom and liberty in prior social systems to defend the current state of affairs.

The creative works of philosophers, artists and writers who have been influential in furthering various ideological notions of this "freedom", often at the expense of societal vulnerability, increasing this dogmatic polarization, has further compounded these values.[369] In short, a great deal of fear and emotional power exists around the notion of social change and how it might affect our lives in the way of liberty and individuality.

Yet, if we step back and think about what freedom means away from these cultural memes, we find that notions of freedom can be argued as *relative* given human history, along with *standards of living* and even *personal expression* itself. Therefore, in order to decide what freedom is and how to qualify it, we need to measure it from an (a) historical perspective on one side and with respect to (b) future possibility on the other.

(a) Historically, the fundamental concern is based on the fear of power and the abuse of power. Human history, in part, is certainly one of perpetual power struggles. Fueled by deeply divisive religious and philosophical beliefs and values which manifested abject slavery, the subjugation of women, periodic genocide, prosecution for heresy (free speech, or what was and still is known as "free thought"), the divine right of kings and the like, it could be argued that human history in this context is a history of dangerous, unfounded superstitions made sacrosanct by primitive values/understanding in those periods of time, at the expense of human well-being and social balance. The fear and scarcity of these earlier periods appears to have amplified the worst of what we might consider "human nature", often seeking power as a way to avoid the abuse of power in a vicious cycle.

Yet, it is critically important to notice that we have been in a process of *transition* away from these archaic values and beliefs overall, with the global culture and its institutions slowly embracing scientific causality and its merit with respect what is real and what isn't. With this, certain positive trends have become clear.

We have moved from the "divine", ultimate power of genetically determined kings and pharaohs into a system of very limited, yet general public participation via a so-called "democratic process" in most of the world. Human exploitation, subjugation and abject slavery has lost its common defenses of religious, racial or gender superiority and improved to the extent that the slavery today overall takes the less severe form of "wage labor" - in the larger context of "class" associations - as determined by one's place in the *economic* hierarchy.

---

369 Ayn Rand's famous novel *Anthem* is a notable, influential example of this artistic culmination of values. It takes place in a dystopian future where mankind has entered another dark age characterized by irrationality, collectivism, and socialistic thinking and economics. The concept of individuality has been eliminated. For example, the use of the word "I" is punishable by death.

The market economy, in all its historical forms, has also been able to overcome the race-like "caste" predeterminations as well since it does allow a level of (limited) social mobility in the community where income gained facilitates more general "freedom".[370]

Such progressive realities need to be taken into account as capitalism, with all its flaws, has served to help improve certain things in the social condition. Yet, what hasn't changed is the underlying premise that is still elitist and bigoted in how it favors one group over another, both structurally and sociologically. Only in this case the "group" favored has nothing much to do with gender, race or religion anymore – but to do with a kind of forceful expedience and competitive mentality that pushes itself to the top of the class hierarchy, at the inevitable expense of others.

Capitalism, it could well be argued, is really is a *post-modern slavery system*, with a new value orientation of "competitive freedom" holding it in place. This reinvented notion of "freedom" basically says that we are all "free" to compete with each other and take what we can. Yet, as noted before, such a state of "open freedom", existing without abuse, oppression and structural advantage - is clearly impossible. So, while proponents of capitalism may adduce the social improvements which have occurred since its advent as evidence of its social efficacy, we must acknowledge that its root form is *not* in the interest of human freedom, but an echo of social bigotry which has been polluting culture for thousands of years, rooted in a general psychology of *elitism and scarcity*.

Today, true freedom is directly related to the *amount of money* a person has. Those below the poverty line have severe limitations on personal freedom as compared to the wealthy. Likewise, while proponents of the free market often talk about "coercion" in the context of state power, the reality of *economic coercion* is ignored. Traditional economic theorists constantly use rhetoric that suggests that everything is an issue of *choice* in the market and if a person wishes to take a job or not, it is their choice.

Yet, those in poverty, which is the majority,[371] face a severe reduction of choice. The pressures of their limited economic capacity creates a powerful state of coercion by which they not only must take labor roles they might not appreciate to survive, they are often subject

---

370 'Social mobility' is structurally inhibited in the capitalist system, with a very small percentage actually attaining upward mobility, statistically. Mobility in the United States, home of the "American Dream", has also been increasingly declining. Reference: "Exceptional Upward Mobility in the US Is a Myth, International Studies Show", *Science Daily* (http://www.sciencedaily.com/releases/2012/09/120905141920.htm) Also See: "Harder for Americans to Rise From Lower Rungs", *New York Times*, 2012 (http://www.nytimes.com/2012/01/05/us/harder-for-americans-to-rise-from-lower-rungs.html?pagewanted=all)

371 While the poverty line standard is relative based on the region of application, over 50% of the world as of a 2005 World Bank Study live on less than 2.50 a day, or about $912.00 a year. Source: GlobalIssues.org (http://www.globalissues.org/article/26/poverty-facts-and-stats)

to vast exploitation in the form of low wage rates due to that same desperation. In fact, general poverty, in this context, is a very *positive* condition for the capitalist class for it ensures cost-efficiency in the form of cheaper labor.

So again, while we may have seen some societal improvement over time, this improvement is really just a variation of a common theme of general elitism, exploitation and bigotry. The long history of assumed resource scarcity and limits on production have also compounded this idea, in the Malthusian sense,[372] where the idea of everyone finding some level of economic equality was deemed simply impossible.

(b) Yet, modern science and the exponential development of technical application, along with a deeper awareness of our human condition,[373] has opened the door to future possibilities for social improvement and, in fact, a further elevation of freedom in ways never before seen. This awareness presents a problem since the possibility of achieving this new level is deeply inhibited by the values and establishments set forth by the traditional capitalist social order. In other words, the market system simply cannot facilitate these improvements because the nature of their culmination is against the very mechanisms of the system.

For example, the efficiency made possible on the technical, scientific level today, if correctly applied, could provide a high standard of living for every human on earth, coupled with the removing of dangerous and monotonous labor through the application of *cybernated* mechanization.[374] In the world today, the vast majority of people spend most of their life working an occupation and sleeping. Many of these occupations are not enjoyed[375] and are arguably *irrelevant* with respect to true personal or social contribution and development.

So, if we wish to think about what freedom means on a basic level, it means being able to direct your life in the way you wish, within reason.[376] Being able to live your life without worrying about

---

372 See the section on Malthus and Ricardo in the essay *History of Economy.*
373 Clarification: Socially causal or *psychosocial* effects of the human-society relationship have proven some powerful realities about the origins of aberrant or destructive behavior. See the essay "Defining Public Health" for more explanation.
374 A detailed extrapolation will be presented in part III of this text.
375 Reference: "New Survey: Majority of Employees Dissatisfied", *Forbes,* Susan Adams 2012
(http://www.forbes.com/sites/susanadams/2012/05/18/new-survey-majority-of-employees-dissatisfied/)
376 Naturally, there can be no "pure" freedom in the natural world that is governed by the laws of nature, nor can unlimited freedom exist in a social condition that deals with life standard requirements for social stability. For example, one is not "free" to murder another in a direct sense. Such social contracts and values exist around not abusing others because they ease imbalance and destabilization.

your basic survival and health, or that of your family, is the first step. Likewise, the labor for income system is one of the most "unfree" institutions that could exist today not only with respect to the inherent economic coercion, but also with respect to the corporate structure itself, which is quite literally a top-down, hierarchical dictatorship.

Sadly, even with these possibilities present and real, the *value system disorder* built from the capitalist model and its rather paranoid fear of anything outside of it, has and will continue to fight these possibilities for more elevated states of freedom. In fact, the very idea of providing basic social support in the form of "welfare" or the like is attacked, in part, on the basis of its avoidance of facilitating the open market – the very market that, in reality, likely created the impoverished state of those who need such assistance.

As a final note on the subject of "freedom", capitalist theory, both historical and modern, is devoid of any relationship to the Earth's resources and its governing ecological laws. Apart from the most primitive awareness of scarcity, which is a marker of the common "supply and demand" value theory, the scientific nature of the world is absent in this model - it is "external". This omission, paired with the exploitation and cost reducing reality inherent to the incentive system of the market, is what has generated the vast environmental problems, from soil depletion, to pollution, to deforestation, to virtually everything else we can think of on the ecological level.

In analyzing the early development of this philosophy, we can logically speculate about how this came to be. Given the largely agrarian base of production and the minimalism of early "handicraft" type good production, our capacity at that time to negatively affect the environment was inherently limited. We simply did not pose as much of a threat since the vast edifice of industry as we know it today had not evolved.

This development reveals that under the surface of capitalism is an old perspective, which is growing increasingly out of date, with ever-occurring repercussions resulting as our technological capacity increases our ability to affect the world. A parallel would be the institution of war. Competitive values and warfare were a tolerable reality when the damage done was limited to primitive muskets centuries ago. Today, we have nuclear weapons that can destroy everything.[377] So, taking an evolutionary view, capitalism has been a practice and value orientation that did help progress in certain ways, but all trend evidence now shows that the inherent immaturity of the system will lead to ever increasing problems if it persists.

The "Marketization" of Life.

As a final point of this essay, the trend of the ever-increasing *marketization of life* has created a deep distortion of values in the

---

377 Albert Einstein was quoted as saying, "I know not with what weapons World War III will be fought, but World War IV will be fought with sticks and stones." (*The New Quotable Einstein,* Alice Calaprice, Princeton University Press. 2005 p.173)

world. Since "freedom" has been culturally associated with "democracy" and democracy in the economic sense has been associated with the ability to buy and sell, the *commodification* of just about everything one can think of has been occurring.

Traditional values and rhetoric of prior generations have often viewed the use of money in some ways as something of a "cold" necessity, with some elements of our lives considered "sacred" and not for sale. The act of prostitution, for example, in which people sell intimacy for money is a situation where cultural values usually find alienation. In most countries the act is illegal, even though there is little legal justification since sexual engagement itself is legal. It is only when the element of purchase comes into play, is it deemed reprehensible.

However, such sanctities that have been culturally perpetuated are becoming increasingly overturned by the market mindset. Today, whether legal or not, nearly anything can be bought or sold.[378] You can buy the right to bypass carbon emissions regulations,[379] you can upgrade your prison cell for a fee,[380] buy the right to hunt endangered animals,[381] and even buy your way into a prestigious university without meeting testing requirements.[382]

It becomes a strange state when some of the most normal, natural acts of human life become incentivized by money as well, such as how it is being used to encourage children to read,[383] or encourage weight loss.[384] Psychologically, what does it mean for a child when they are reinforced with money for their most basic actions? How will this affect their future sense of reward? These are important questions in a *world for sale,* with the guiding value principle that it is only when one *makes money* from an action, is that action worth doing.

Such *market values* appear as a clear social distortion as the very essence of human initiative and existence is being transformed. While we might not take much extreme concern over seemingly trivial issues such as the fact one can purchase access to the carpool lane while driving solo,[385] the larger manifestation of a culture built on the

---

378 Reference: *What Money Can't Buy: The Moral Limits of Markets*, Michael J. Sandel, Farrar, Straus and Giroux, 2012

379 Reference: Data can be viewed online with respect to the EU at www.pointcarbon.com

380 Source: "For $82 a Day, Booking a Cell in a 5-Star Jail", *New York Times,* April 29, 2007

381 Source: "Saving the Rhino Through Sacrifice", Brendan Borrell, *Bloomberg Businessweek*, December 9, 2010

382 Source: "At Many Colleges, the Rich Kids Get Affirmative Action: Seeking Donors", Daniel Golden, *Wall Street. Journal*, February 20, 2003

383 Source: "Is Cash the Answer", Amanda Ripley, *Time,* April 19, 2010, pp.44-45

384 Source: "Paying people to lose weight and stop smoking", Kevin G. Volpp, *Issue Brief*, L.D. Institute of Health Economics, University of Pennsylvania, vol. 14, 2009

385 Source: "Paying for VIP Treatment in a Traffic Jam", *Wall Street Journal,* June 21 2007

edifice of everything being for sale, is the *dehumanization* of society as everyone and everything is reduce to a mere commodity for exploit.

Today, as shocking as it is, there are actually *more slaves* in the world than *anytime in human history*. Human trafficking has and continues to be a massive industry for profit, selling men, women and children into various roles.

The US Department of State has published "It is estimated that as many as 27 million men, women, and children around the world are victims of what is now often described with the umbrella term "human trafficking." The work that remains in combating this crime is the work of fulfilling the promise of freedom—freedom from slavery for those exploited and the freedom for survivors to carry on with their lives."[386]

In the end, while most people who believe in the free market capitalist system would ethically stand in outrage at these vast human abuses occurring in the world, usually making distinctions between "moral and "amoral" forms of trade, the fact of the matter is that the commodification concept itself can draw no objective lines and such "extreme" realities are, in truth, simply a *matter of degree* with respect to application. From a purely philosophical standpoint, there is no technical difference between any form of market exploitation. The psychology inherent – the *value system disorder* – has and will continue to perpetuate a predatory disregard within the culture and it is only when that *structural mechanism* is removed from our very approach to societal organization, will the aforementioned issues find resolution.

---

386 Source: *Trafficking in Persons Report 2012*, US Department of State
(http://www.state.gov/j/tip/rls/tiprpt/2012/192351.htm)

-STRUCTURAL CLASSISM, THE STATE AND WAR-

Man is the only Patriot. He sets himself apart in his own country, under his own flag, and sneers at the other nations, and keeps multitudinous uniformed assassins on hand at heavy expense to grab slices of other people's countries, and keep them from grabbing slices of his. And in the intervals between campaigns he washes the blood of his hands and works for "the universal brotherhood of man"- with his mouth.[387]
- Mark Twain

Overview

Human conflict has been a consistent characteristic of society since the beginning of recorded history. While justifications of this have ranged from assumptions of immutable human propensities towards aggression and territoriality, to the religious notion of polarized metaphysical powers at work, such as forces of "good" and "evil", history has revealed that cases of conflict generally have a rational correlation to *environmental circumstances* and/or *cultural conditions*. From the immediate, fearful stress reaction of our "fight or flight" propensity,[388] to the calm, calculated planning of strategic national warfare, there is always a *reason* for such conflict and the general public's interest to reduce conflict naturally requires we fully assess causality as deeply as we can to consider tangible solutions.

This essay will examine two general categories of "warfare": "imperial warfare" and "class warfare". While perhaps seemingly different, it will be argued that the root psychological mechanisms of these two categorizations are basically the same, along with how some of the actual mechanisms of "battle" are actually much more elusive or covert than many recognize. Overall, the central thesis is that the source of these seemingly immutable realities resides within the *socioeconomic premise* itself - in the context of a certain reinforced psychology and hence sociological schemata - not rigid determinations in our genes or lack of some moral aptitude.

Put another way, these present realities are not fueled by ideologically isolated groups such as, for example, a rogue country's government or some exceptionally "greedy" business mentality – but rather by the most fundamental, underlying values inherent to virtually everyone's lives in the current socioeconomic condition we perpetuate as culturally "normal". The only difference is the *degree* to which these values are harnessed and for what purpose.

---

387 Source: "Man's place in the animal world", *What is Man? And other Irreverent Essays*, Mark Twain, 1896, p.157
388 "The fight-or-flight response" (or the acute stress response) was first described by American physiologist Walter Bradford Cannon. His theory states that animals react to threats with a general discharge of the sympathetic nervous system, priming the animal for fighting or fleeing.

Imperial War: Rise of the State

The Neolithic Revolution some 12,000 years ago[389] marked a pivotal turning point for human society as it transitioned us from almost exclusively "living off the land" - limited to the habitat's natural regeneration – to an accelerating trend of environmental control and resource manipulation. The development of agriculture and the creation of labor-easing tools was the beginning of what can be observed today, where the spectrum of the human capacity to utilize *science* for the alteration of the world for our advantage appears virtually unlimited.[390]

However, this initially slow technological adaptation has set in motion certain patterns and changes which have arguably generated many of the problems we recognize as all too common today. An example would be how imbalance through relative poverty and economic stratification has taken hold as an apparent consequence of this new capacity. In the words of neuroscientist and anthropologist Dr. Robert Sapolsky: "Hunter-gatherers [had] thousands of wild sources of food to subsist on. Agriculture changed all that, generating an overwhelming reliance on a few dozen food sources...Agriculture allowed for the stockpiling of surplus resources and thus, inevitably, the unequal stockpiling of them, stratification of society and the invention of classes. Thus it has allowed for the invention of poverty."[391]

Likewise, the rather nomadic lifestyle of the hunter-gatherer slowly became replaced with settled, protectionist tribes and then eventually localized city-type societies. In the words of Richard A. Gabriel in the work *A Short History of War*: "The invention and spread of agriculture coupled with the domestication of animals in the fifth millennium B.C. are acknowledged as the developments that set the stage for the emergence of the first large-scale, complex urban societies. These societies, which appeared almost simultaneously around 4000 B.C. in both Egypt and Mesopotamia, used stone tools, but within 500 years stone tools and weapons gave way to bronze. With bronze manufacture came a revolution in warfare."[392]

This is also the period that the concept of the "state" as we know it and the permanence of the "armed force" emerged. Gabriel

---

389 Sometimes also called the Agricultural Revolution, it was the world's first historically verifiable revolution in agriculture. It was the wide-scale transition of many human cultures from a lifestyle of hunting and gathering to one of agriculture and settlement that supported an increasingly large population and the basis for modern social patterns today.

390 Reference: *Exponentially Accelerating Information Technologies Could Put an End to Corporations* (http://scienceprogress.org/2011/06/exponentially-growing-information-technology-will-put-an-end-to-corporations/)

391 Source: *Why Zebras Don't Get Ulcers*, Robert Sapolsky, W. H. Freeman, 1998, p.383

392 Source: *A Short History of War: The Evolution of Warfare and Weapons*, Richard A Gabriel, Strategic Studies Institute, U.S. Army War College, Chapter 1, 1992

continues: "These early societies produced the first examples of state-governing institutions, initially as centralized chiefdoms and later as monarchies...At the same time, centralization demanded the creation of an administrative structure capable of directing social activity and resources toward communal goals...The development of central state institutions and a supporting administrative apparatus inevitably gave form and stability to military structures. The result was the expansion and stabilization of the formerly loose and unstable warrior castes...By 2700 B.C. in Sumer there was a fully articulated military structure and standing army organized along modern lines. The standing army emerged as a permanent part of the social structure and was endowed with strong claims to social legitimacy. And it has been with us ever since."[393]

Imperial War: Illusions

"Imperialism" is defined as: "the policy, practice, or advocacy of extending the power and dominion of a nation especially by direct territorial acquisitions or by gaining indirect control over the political or economic life of other areas."[394]

While traditional culture might generally think of imperial war as a variation of war in general, assuming other forms of armed, national conflict, it is argued here that the root basis of *all* national wars are actually imperial in nature. The literally thousands of wars in recorded human history have had to do mostly with the acquisition of resources or territory, where one group is either working to expand its power and material wealth, or working to protect itself from others trying to conquer and absorb their power and wealth.

Even many historical conflicts, which on the surface appear to be for the purposes of pure ideology, are often actually hidden imperial economic moves. The Christian Crusades of the 11th century, for example, are often defined as strictly religious conflicts or expressions of ideological fervor. Yet, a deeper investigation reveals a powerful undertone of trade expansion and resource acquisition, under the guise of the "religious" war.[395] This is not to say that religions have not been a source of tremendous conflict historically, but to show that there is often an oversimplification found in many historical texts, with the economic relevance often missed or ignored. Regardless, the notion of the "moral" crusade as a form of *cover* for national, economic imperialism continues to this day.[396]

---

393 Ibid.
394 Source: Merriam-Webster.com (http://www.merriam-webster.com/dictionary/imperialism)
395 Reference: *Economic Development of the North Atlantic Community,* Dudley Dillard, Prentice-Hall, New Jersey, 1967, pp.3-178.
396 The use of religion to generate political support for imperial acts of war is quite common historically. Even in the United States today, politicians, with respect to recent military actions, have consistently made a general undertone of religious war or of acting on the behalf of "God". Islamic and Jewish states appear to do the same thing, along with states. The Israeli-

In fact, there is a deeply *coercive* tendency witnessed throughout history when it comes to gaining public support for the act of national warfare. For instance, a cursory review of history will find that all "offensive" acts of war, meaning war *initiated* by a given power for whatever reason (not a response to direct invasion), originate from the constituents and associates of the *governmental body* - not the citizenry. Wars tend to begin with some kind of announced suggestion emanating from state power; then fueled by the *corporate-state* supported media;[397] with the citizenry slowly groomed to appreciate the suggestion. It also helps the state a great deal if there is some form of emotionally striking provocation as well, which can be manipulated to further justify the intended war.[398]

Such tactics for the manipulation of a citizenry can take many

---

Palestinian conflict, for example, which is generally acknowledged as a deeply religious conflict for "holy" territory, reveals, upon closer inspection, that religion, while perhaps a real factor in the public mind overall, is actually *not* the root of the conflict. The real root appears to be elite imperialism and resource acquisition in general, with religion used as means to foster and maintain public support. Reference: http://www.thejakartaglobe.com/globebeyond/israel-palestine-not-a-religious-conflict/558353

397 *State supported media* is commonly defined as media produced by direct funding from a country's government. While this is still common in the world and often subject to state propaganda, in the United States, a similar yet more obscure form has emerged - something we could call *corporate-state supported media*. Corporate statism is a form of "corporatism" whose adherents hold that the corporate group is the basis of society and the state. The poetic tradition of the "free press" in the US, being without "regulation" or "interference", is a long-standing value and assumption. Yet, when we factor in the reality of the increasing concentration of major media outlets, such as the fact that as of 2012 six corporations control 90% of them* - coupled with the basic understanding that there is little to no separation between the government and its corporations by default in the Capitalist rooted socioeconomic model between the government and its corporations - it is difficult to defend the idea that the most dominant news outlets exist without ideological influence towards preserving the status quo since they are so bound up with it. With respect to the initiation of war, a statistical review of historical media for the past 100 years will show a deep support by all major news outlets towards the government's interests. *Source: (http://www.businessinsider.com/these-6-corporations-control-90-of-the-media-in-america-2012-6)

398 Former US National Security Advisor Zbigniew Brzezinski understood this well, and stated in his famous work *The Grand Chessboard: American Primacy And Its Geostrategic Imperatives*: "The attitude of the American public toward the external projection of American power has been much more ambivalent. The public supported America's engagement in World War II largely because of the shock effect of the Japanese attack on Pearl Harbor. (Basic Books Publishing, 1998, pp.24-25) "...as America becomes an increasingly multi-cultural society, it may find it more difficult to fashion a consensus on foreign policy issues, except in the circumstance of a truly massive and widely perceived direct external threat."(Basic Books Publishing, 1998, p.211)

forms. The use of fear, honor (revenge), patriotic paternalism,[399] morality, and the "common defense" are likely the most common ploys. In fact, invariably all acts of war are justified as "defensive" in the public sphere, even if there is no rational, tangible public threat to be found. Yet, there is, indeed, a core truth to this notion of "defensive" war,[400] since acts of imperial mobilization are based on a very real, yet obscure form of economic and/or political fear – the fear of *losing control* or *power*. In other words, while there may not be a direct, immediate threat to a given, *aggressor* nation – the long term competitive need to continually *re-secure* its existing power from possible *future* loss is a very real and founded fear. So, in effect, this "defense" is that of elitist, upper-class self-preservation and hence usually *morally unjustifiable* to the public in its true terms; hence these ploys are used instead to gain public approval.[401]

Economist and sociologist Thorstein Veblen, in his famous 1917 work *An Inquiry Into The Nature Of Peace And The Terms Of Its Perpetuation* wrote the following on the subject of public persuasion: "Any warlike enterprise that is hopeful to be entered on must have the moral sanction of the community or of an effective majority in the community. It consequently becomes the first concern of the warlike statesman to put this moral force in train for the adventure on which he is bent. And there are two main lines of motivation...the preservation or furtherance of the community's material interest, real or fancied - and vindication of the national honor. To these should perhaps be added a third, the advancement and perpetuation of the nations *culture*."[402]

---

399 The term paternalism is defined as: "a system under which an authority undertakes to supply needs or regulate conduct of those under its control." (http://www.merriam-webster.com/dictionary/paternalism) The term "patriotic paternalism" denotes the assumption that a sovereign nation knows better than another and hence it works to influence and take control of the nation for the supposed benefit of its people.
400 In the modern day, the term "preemptive war" is commonly used to justify an act of aggression by the claim it is a defensive move to thwart a looming attack of some kind by the target.
401 Former US National Security Advisor Zbigniew Brzezinski expresses this "paternalistic defense" clearly in his work *The Grand Chessboard: American Primacy And Its Geostrategic Imperatives.* He states with respect to the need for America to essentially remain in control of the world: "America is now the only global superpower, and Eurasia is the globe's central arena. Hence, what happens to the distribution of power on the Eurasian continent will be of decisive importance to America's global primacy and to America's historical legacy." (Basic Books Publishing, 1998, p.194) "To put it in a terminology that harkens back to the more brutal age of ancient empires, the three grand imperatives of imperial geostrategy are to prevent collusion and maintain security dependence among the vassals, to keep tributaries pliant and protected, and to keep the barbarians from coming together." (Ibid., p.40) "Henceforth, the United States may have to determine how to cope with regional coalitions that seek to push America out of Eurasia, thereby threatening America's status as a global power." (Ibid, p.55)
402 Source: *An Inquiry Into the Nature of Peace and the Terms of Its*

This last point on the perpetuation of the nation's *culture* is best exemplified with the common, modern Western imperial claims of seeking to spread "Freedom and Democracy". This claim takes a *paternal* position, positing the idea that the current political climate of a targeted nation is simply too inhumane and intervention to "help" its citizens becomes a "moral obligation" of the invading power.

Veblen Continues: "Any Patriotism will serve as ways and means to warlike enterprise under competent management, even if [the people are] not habitually prone to a bellicose temper. Rightly managed, ordinary patriotic sentiment may readily be mobilized for warlike adventure by any reasonably adroit and single-minded body of statesmen - of which there is abundant illustration."[403] "...it is [also] quite a safe generalization that when hostilities have once been got fairly underway by the interested statesman, the patriotic sentiment of the nation may confidently be counted on to back the enterprise, irrespective of the merits of the quarrel".[404]

In America, the phrase "I'm against the war but support the troops"[405] is common among those who oppose a given conflict but wish to be viewed as still respectful of their country in general. This phrase is unique as it is actually irrational. To logically "support the troops" would mean to support the *role of being* a "troop", hence the acts that are required by that role. The implicit gesture, of course, is that one supports the need for war and hence supports the men and women of the armed forces who assist that need. Yet, the statement itself is fully contradictory and exists as a form of "doublethink",[406] as to disagree with the existence of a certain war is to wholly disagree with actions of those who engage it. It is similar to saying, "I'm against cancer killing people but I support cancer's right to life".

The armed forces have historically been held in high public esteem by a citizenry and the government continually glorifies this to the extent that the assumption of "honor" takes on an irrational life of its own. In fact, it is compounded psychologically by a built-in *ceremonialism*. Honor is formalized through awards, medals, parades, postures of respect and other adornments which impress the public as to the supposed value of the actions of the soldiers and hence the institution of war. This further reinforces the cultural *taboo* where to insult any element of the war apparatus is seen as showing disrespect for the sacrifice of the armed forces.

From the standpoint of true protection and problem resolution, as would be the "honorable" case of a firefighter who saves a child from a burning building, this admiration is warranted. The selfless,

---

Perpetuation, Thorstein Veblen, Echo Library, 1917 p.16
403 Ibid., p.7
404 Ibid., p.16
405 Reference: *Can You Support the Troops but Not the War? Troops Respond* (http://www.huffingtonpost.com/paul-rieckhoff/can-you-support-the-troop_b_26192.html)
406 "Doublethink" a term coined by George Orwell which describes the act of simultaneously accepting two mutually contradictory beliefs as correct.

altruistic position of putting one's life at risk for the benefit of another is naturally a noble act. However, in the context of historical warfare, the personal altruism of a soldier does not justify broad acts of national, imperial aggression, no matter how well intentioned the soldiers may be.

Furthermore, this fear-oriented *power preservation* by the established governmental apparatus also naturally generates a "sub-war" against the domestic citizenry itself, almost always amplified in times of war. Those who challenge or oppose a given national conflict have historically been met with direct oppression and, by cultural extension, public resentment. The common yet ambiguous legal violations of "treason"[407] and "sedition"[408] are historical examples of this, along with the pattern of suspending the rights of citizens during times of war, sometimes even including free speech.[409]

Socially, the use of "patriotism", as noted before, is also very common to the effect that those who do not support a war are often dismissed as not supporting the national citizenry by extension, creating alienation. More recently, those in opposition and perhaps engaging in protest actions have been considered "terrorists" by the state,[410] a powerful incrimination with severe legal consequences if deemed true by the authorities.

However, this "sub-war" can be deconstructed into an even deeper mechanism - what could be called a kind of *social control* in support of imperial intent. In many countries today, either by obligation from birth[411] or by persuasion to legally binding contracts[412] the pressure or motivation to join the military itself is *manipulative* on many levels. Advertising tactics such as "money for college" or "personal accomplishment" are common, arguably targeting the lower

---

407 "Treason" is defined as: "the offense of attempting by overt acts to overthrow the government of the state to which the offender owes allegiance" Source: http://www.merriam-webster.com/dictionary/treason
408 "Sedition" is defined as: "incitement of resistance to or insurrection against lawful authority" Source: http://www.merriam-webster.com/dictionary/sedition
409 From World War II's Japanese-American Internment camps that imprisoned over 127,000 US citizens, (Source: http://www.ushistory.org/us/51e.asp) to the suspension of civil liberties as such as "habeas corpus", (Source: http://www.salon.com/2009/04/11/bagram_3/) to the prosecution for mere speech, (Source: http://www.history.com/this-day-in-history/us-congress-passes-sedition-act) rights violations during wartime is an historical constant.
410 A recent example of this was the "Occupy Movement" uprising that was later revealed to be considered a possible "terrorist threat" by the FBI. (Source: http://www.justiceonline.org/commentary/fbi-files-ows.html)
411 Israel, for example, enforces near full conscription of its citizens. (Source: http://www.aljazeera.com/news/middleeast/2012/07/20127853118591495.html)
412 Reference: "Why Is Getting Out of the U.S. Army So Tough?", Time, 2012 (http://nation.time.com/2012/05/04/why-is-getting-out-of-the-u-s-army-so-tough/)

rungs of the economic hierarchy.[413] The United States is on record for having at times spent billions a year ($4.7 billion in 2009) on global public relations in assist public image and recruitment.[414]

Imperial War: Source

When the traditional, propagandized illusions in defense of the act of organized human murder and resource theft have been overridden, dismissing such shallow justifications as paternal patriotism, honor and protectionism, we find that war today is actually an inherent characteristic of the propertied, scarcity-driven *business* system. It would be false to say that war is a product of capitalism in and of itself since the practice of war predates capitalism extensively. However, when we deconstruct the premise itself we see that war is, indeed, a central, immutable feature of capitalism as it is simply a more sophisticated manifestation of these same, divisive, competitive, archaic values and practices.

Just as a corporation competes with other corporations of the same genre for income survival, invariably seeking monopoly and cartel when it can, all governments on the planet are fundamentally premised on the same form of survival by extension. Using America as a case study, in 2011 the country gained about $2.3 trillion in federal income tax revenues alone.[415] These revenues are important to the operation of what is, in effect, the *business institution* known as "America", in the same way the annual earnings of Microsoft affect its ability to function. America is, in truth, a *corporation* in function and form; with all the registered businesses existing in its domestic legal web to be considered *subsidiaries* of this *parent* institution we traditionally call the "US government".

Therefore, all actions of the US government, along with all competing governments in the world, must naturally keep an acute *business acumen* in operation. However, what separates this "parent corporation" (America) from its subsidiary sectors (corporations) is the scale of its capacity to preserve itself and keep a competitive edge. Its necessity to preserve the core drivers of its economy is crucial and a cursory glance at history regarding how the US was able to gain and maintain its status of a global "empire", shows this business acumen clearly. The manifestation is really little different in principle than how a specific corporation seeks to gain a commercial monopoly. Only in this case the ideal of *global monopoly* (empire) is not restricted by legal mandate as is commonly claimed by the domestic legal restraint - it is forcefully executed in the theater of imperial war.

---

413 Reference: "Military recruiters target isolated, depressed areas", *Seattle Times*, 2005
(http://seattletimes.com/html/nationworld/2002612542_recruits09.html)
414 Source: "Pentagon Spending Billions on PR to Sway World Opinion", *Fox News,* 2010 (http://www.foxnews.com/politics/2009/02/05/pentagon-spending-billions-pr-sway-world-opinion/)
415 Source: "Federal Revenues by Source", *Heritage.com,* 2012
(http://www.heritage.org/federalbudget/federal-revenue-sources]

In fact, interestingly enough but not unexpectedly, the very act of this self-preservation through military might have *itself* become a powerfully lucrative business venture which often improves the economic state of the nation and hence profits to its corporate constituents. Today, we can extend these economic benefits to the massive military expenditures[416] [417] along with the reconstruction of war-torn areas by the conquering states' commercial subsidiaries,[418] the slow prodding of a country's integrity through trade tariffs, sanctions and debt impositions for the sake of population subjugation for the benefit of transcontinental industries[419] [420] and many other modern "economic war" conventions.

This point was likely best expressed by one of America's most decorated army officers of the 20th century: Major General Smedley D. Butler.[421] Butler was the author of a famous book released after World War I titled *War is a Racket*, and stated the following with respect to the business of war: "War is a racket. It always has been. It is possibly the oldest, easily the most profitable, surely the most vicious. It is the only one international in scope. It is the only one in which the profits are reckoned in dollars and the losses in lives."[422]

He also wrote in 1935: "I spent 33 years and four months in active military service and during that period I spent most of my time as a high class muscle man for Big Business, for Wall Street and the bankers. In short, I was a racketeer, a gangster for capitalism. I helped make Mexico and especially Tampico safe for American oil interests in 1914. I helped make Haiti and Cuba a decent place for the National City Bank boys to collect revenues in. I helped in the raping of half a dozen Central American republics for the benefit of Wall Street. I helped purify Nicaragua for the International Banking House of Brown Brothers in 1902-1912. I brought light to the Dominican Republic for

---

416 Reference: *The 25 Most Vicious Iraq War Profiteers,* BusinessPundit.com, 2008 (http://www.businesspundit.com/the-25-most-vicious-iraq-war-profiteers)

417 Reference: *Ten Companies Profiting Most from War,* 247WallSt.com, 2012 (http://247wallst.com/2012/02/28/ten-companies-profiting-most-from-war/)

418 Reference: *Advocates of War Now Profit From Iraq's Reconstruction,* LATimes.com, 2004 (http://articles.latimes.com/2004/jul/14/nation/na-advocates14)

419 Reference: *Deadly Sanctions Regime: Economic Warfare against Iran,* GlobalResearch.ca, 2012 (http://www.globalresearch.ca/deadly-sanctions-regime-economic-warfare-against-iran/5305921)

420 Reference: *Confessions of an Economic Hit Man: How the U.S. Uses Globalization to Cheat Poor Countries Out of Trillions,* DemocracyNow.org, 2004 (http://www.democracynow.org/2004/11/9/confessions_of_an_economic_hit_man)

421 Reference: *Banana Wars: Major General Smedley Butler,* About.com (http://militaryhistory.about.com/od/1900s/p/Banana-Wars-Major-General-Smedley-Butler.htm)

422 Source: *War is a Racket*, Smedley D. Butler, William H Huff Publishing, 1935, Chapter 1, p.1

the American sugar interests in 1916. I helped make Honduras right for the American fruit companies in 1903. In China in 1927 I helped see to it that Standard Oil went on its way unmolested. Looking back on it, I might have given Al Capone a few hints. The best he could do was to operate his racket in three districts. I operated on three continents."[423]

John A. Hobson's (1858-1940) monumental work *Imperialism: A Study* described the tendency as a "social parasitic process by which a moneyed interest within the state, usurping the reins of government, makes for imperial expansion in order to fasten economic suckers into foreign bodies so as to drain them of their wealth in order to support domestic luxury."[424]

Now, many would think about these acts of abuse as a form of "corruption" but this reasoning is difficult to justify in the broad view. The ethical and moral argument of "fair" and "unfair" has no cogent integrity *within* the system framework inherent to capitalism. This is one of the unfortunate failures of realization by those who are active in the message of "world peace" or "anti-war" activism but yet still defend the competitive market model. In other words, "world peace" appears simply not a possibility within the currently accepted model of economic practice.

Every step of the application of global capitalism, starting from its European inception, has been associated with vast violence, exploitation and subjugation. European colonialism,[425] the capture of African "slaves" for use and sale, the forced subjugation of countless colonial peoples, and the creation of privileged sanctuaries of profiteering and power for the many government-created or government-protected businesses, only touches the surface of its inherent character as a "war system" of thought.

Thorstein Veblen, again writing from 1917, makes the direct connection to what he called the "pecuniary" or monetary foundation of war: "It has appeared in the course of the argument that the preservation of the present pecuniary law and order, with all its incident of ownership and investment, is incompatible with an unwarlike state of peace and security. This current scheme of investment, business, and [Industrial] sabotage, should have an appreciably better chance of survival in the long run if the present conditions of warlike preparation and national "insecurity" were maintained, or if the projected peace were left in a somewhat problematic state, sufficiently precarious to keep national animosities alert..."[426] "So, if the projectors of this peace at large are in any degree

---

423 Originally in *Common Sense*, 1935. Reproduced in Hans Schmidt's *Maverick Marine: General Smedley D. Butler and the Contradictions of American Military History*. University Press of Kentucky, 1998 p.231
424 Source: *Imperialism: A Study*, J.A. Hobson, University of Michigan Press, Ann Arbor, 1965, p.367
425 Reference: Western Colonialism defined:
   http://www.britannica.com/EBchecked/topic/126237/colonialism-Western]
426 Source: *An Inquiry Into the Nature of Peace and the Terms of Its*

inclined to seek concessive terms on what the peace might hopefully be made enduring, it should evidently be part of their endeavors from the outset to put events in train for the present abatement and eventual abrogation of the rights of ownership and of the price-system in which these rights take effect."[427]

Further evidence of this context can be found in the more modern forms of *indirect violence.* These include "economic warfare" approaches, as mentioned before, which can serve as complete acts of aggression in and of themselves, or as a part of a procedural prelude to traditional military action. Examples come in the form of trade tariffs, sanctions, debt by coercion, and many other lesser-known, covert methods to weaken a country.[428]

Global financial institutions such as the World Bank and IMF have heavy vested state and hence business interests behind them and they have the power to allocate debt to "bailout" suffering countries at the expense of the quality of life of its citizenry, often taking charge of natural resources or industries through select privatization or other manners which can weaken a country's ability to the effect that it becomes reliant on others, to the advantage of commercial outsiders.[429]

This is simply a more covert manner of subjugation than was seen, say, with the British Empire's imperial expansion through its "East India Company" - the commercial force that took advantage of the newly conquered regional resources and labor in Asia in the 17th century.[430] However, unlike British Empire expansion, American empire expansion did not gain its status through military action alone, even though such a presence is still enormous globally.[431] Rather, the use of complex economic strategies that repositioned other countries into subjugation to US economic and geo-economic interests was made

Perpetuation, Thorstein Veblen, B.W. Hubsch, 1917 pp.366-367

427 Ibid. p.367

428 Reference: *Our Economic Warfare, ForeignAffairs.com* (http://www.foreignaffairs.com/articles/70162/percy-w-bidwell/our-economic-warfare)

429 As noted by research by the STWR regarding the World Bank: "In most of its client countries, it is virtually the only doorway to access international trade, development finance and private investment capital. It derives its power and policy agendas from its wealthiest shareholders – governments that comprise the G-7...who routinely use the Bank to secure lucrative trade and investment deals in developing countries for their respective transnational corporations (TNCs)." Source: *IMF, World Bank & Trade,* STWR (http://www.stwr.org/imf-world-bank-trade/corporate-power-and-influence-in-the-world-bank.html)

430 Reference: *East India Company,* Britannica.com (http://www.britannica.com/EBchecked/topic/176643/East-India-Company)

431 As of 2011, it has been reported that the US military exists in over 130 countries, with an estimated 900 bases. Source: *Ron Paul says U.S. has military personnel in 130 nations and 900 overseas bases,* politifact.com, 2011 (http://www.politifact.com/truth-o-meter/statements/2011/sep/14/ron-paul/ron-paul-says-us-has-military-personnel-130-nation/)

common.[432]

Class War: Inherent Psychology

Moving on to the "class war" this notion has been noted in historical literature for centuries based partly on assumptions of human nature, partly on assumptions of a lack of capacity of the Earth and production means to meet everyone's needs and partly on the more relevant awareness that the system of market capitalism inevitably *guarantees* class division and imbalance due to its inherent mechanisms, both structurally and psychologically.

Founding free market economist David Ricardo's statement that "If wages should rise...then... profits would necessarily fall"[433] is a simple acknowledgment of the structural assurance of class conflict as the *wage* relates to the lower "working class" and the *profits* the upper "capitalist class" and as one gains, the other loses. Likewise, even Adam Smith in his canonical *The Wealth of Nations* clearly expresses the nature of power preservation on the behavioral (psychological) level, stating: "Civil government, so far as it is instituted for the security of property, is in reality instituted for the defense of the rich against the poor, or of those who have some property against those who have none at all."[434]

However, the true *use* of government for the purposes of the upper or business class seems to be stubbornly ignored by Smith, Ricardo and even many of today's economists, who seem unable or unwilling to take into account present-day events. Even the most committed, laissez-faire market economist still expresses the need for government and its legal apparatus to exist as something of a "referee" to keep the game "fair". Terms such a "crony-capitalism" are often used under the assumption that "collusion" between a governmental constituency and the *seemingly* detached corporate institutions is of an unethical or "criminal" nature.

Yet again, as noted before, it is illogical to assume that the nature of government is anything else at its core than a vehicle to support the businesses that comprise the wealth of that country. The business apparatus really *is* the country in technical form, regardless of the surface claim that a "democratic" country is organized around the interests of the citizenry itself. In fact, it can be well argued that no government in recorded history has ever offered its citizens a legitimate place in governance or legislation and within the context of modern capitalism, which is still a manifestation of centuries old values and assumptions with a clear elitism in intent, it is interesting how this myth of "democracy" perpetuates itself today in the way that it does.

To further this point, one of the architects of the US

---

432 Reference: *Why the Developing World Hates the World Bank,* TheTechOnline, 2002 (http://tech.mit.edu/V122/N11/col11parek.11c.html)
433 Source: *The Principles of Political Economy and Taxation,* David Ricardo, 1821, Dent Edition, 1962,p.64
434 Source: *An Inquiry into the Nature and Causes of the Wealth of Nations,* Adam Smith, 1776, par. V.1.2

Constitution of the United States, James Madison, expressed his concern very clearly regarding the need to oppress the political power of those in the lower classes. He stated: "In England, at this day, if elections were open to all classes of people, the property of landed proprietors would be insecure. An agrarian law would soon take place. If these observations be just, our government ought to secure the permanent interests of the country against innovation. Landholders ought to have a share in the government, to support these invaluable interests, and to balance and check the other. They ought to be so constituted as to *protect the minority of the opulent against the majority*. The senate, therefore, ought to be this body; and to answer these purposes, they ought to have permanency and stability."[435]

So, starting with this awareness that the very premise of global "democracy" is deeply inhibited by the capitalist incentive system to competitively maintain power on the level of the state to assist the upper class in preserving political and, by extension, financial power, a clearer picture of how deep this class war runs is obtained. Likely the most striking aspect of this is how such mechanisms of class division exist in our every day lives but yet go unseen since they are structurally *built in* to the financial, political and legal apparatus itself.

Class War: Structural Mechanisms

In the modern day, with 40 percent of the planet's wealth being owned by 1 percent of the world's population,[436] we find that both in terms of *system structure* and *incentive psychology*, powerful mechanisms exist to maintain and even accelerate this grossly disproportionate global wealth imbalance. Needless to say, given the financial basis of everything in the world today, with great wealth comes great *power.* Hence, as described prior, this power enables a more robust strategy for competitive gain and self-preservation and consequently it has hence extended into the very *structure* of the social system itself, assuring that the upper class has great ease in maintaining their vast wealth security, while the lower classes face enormous structural barriers to attaining any basic level of financial security.

Some mechanisms of this class war *oppression* are fairly obvious. For instance, the debate over taxation, and how there has been an historical favoring of the corporate rich over the working poor, is one example.[437] The argument of the establishment usually revolves around the idea that since the rich are also the "ownership class" and

---

435 Source: *Notes of the Secret Debates of the Federal Convention of 1787,* Robert Yates, Alston Mygatt, p.183

436 Reference: *One percent holds 39 percent of global wealth,* RawStory.com, 2011 (http://www.rawstory.com/rs/2011/05/31/one-percent-holds-39-percent-of-global-wealth/)

437 Reference: *Poor Americans Pay Double The State, Local Tax Rates Of Top One Percent,* HuffingtonPost.com, 2012 (http://www.huffingtonpost.com/2012/09/21/poor-americans-state-local-taxes_n_1903993.html)

are partly responsible for the generation of general employment, they should be given more financial freedom.[438] As an aside, it is easy to see that there is very little true merit in this one-sided argument since the financial oppression through public taxation is actually *limiting* the purchasing power of the general public, creating an arguably more powerful impediment to economic growth than the mere limiting of the coffers of the corporate "employers".[439] The only exception to this, which transcends the argument of the rich as "job creators", is the advent of *plutonomy*, which will be addressed towards the end of this essay.

Class favoring taxation aside, four other more critical structural factors will be discussed: (a) debt, (b) interest, (c) inflation and (d) income disparity.

(a) Debt is a misunderstood social practice in that most assume debt is an *option* in society today. In reality, the entire financial system is built out of debt, quite literally. All money is brought into existence through loans in the modern economy, coming from central and commercial banks who essentially create the money out of demand itself.[440] This basic mechanism of monetary creation is a powerful force of economic oppression. Household debt today tends to consist of credit card loans, housing loans, car loans and student (educational) loans. Those in the lower classes naturally hold higher levels of this *consumer* debt than the upper class since the very nature of being unable to pay outright for basic social staples, such a car or home, forces the need for banks loans.

The result is that the pressure of debt is constant in the lives of the vast majority.[441] [442] [443] The general wage and income rates being what they are on average, naturally as low as possible to assist with the dominant capitalist ethos of cost-efficiency upon which the entire society is engineered, the wage income made by the average employee tends to only barely meet the basic loan servicing requirements while in concert with meeting basic, everyday survival

438 Reference: *Don't Tax the Job Creators,* Cnbc.com, 2012
  (http://www.cnbc.com/id/48290347/Don039t_Tax_the_Job_Creators_Romn
  ey)
439 Reference: *Private Debt Kills the Economy,* GlobalResearch.ca, 2012
  (http://www.globalresearch.ca/private-debt-kills-the-economy/5303842)
440 For a full treatment on the creation of money, see: *Modern Money
  Mechanics,* Federal Reserve Bank of Chicago, 1961
441 Reference: *U.S. Credit Card Debt Grows, Fewer Americans Make Payments
  On Time,* HuffingtonPost.com, 2012
  (http://www.huffingtonpost.com/2012/11/19/us-credit-card-debt-
  grows_n_2158010.html)
442 Reference: *Drowning In Medical Debt? Filing For Bankruptcy Could Be Your
  Life Raft,* BusinessInsider.com, 2012
  (http://articles.businessinsider.com/2012-01-
  27/news/30669714_1_bankruptcy-filers-medical-debt-credit-score)
443 Reference: *The Debt That Won't Go Away,* cnbc.com, 2010
  (http://www.cnbc.com/id/40680905)

needs. Hence a form of "running in place" is constant and the possibility of social mobility up the class hierarchy is deeply impeded, let alone the difficulty of simply getting out of debt itself.[444]

(b) Interest: Coupled with debt is the profit attribute associated the sale of money itself. Since the Capitalist market economy supports the general commodification of virtually everything, it is no surprise that money itself is sold into existence for profit and this comes in the form of *interest*. Whether it is a central bank creating money in exchange for government securities or a commercial bank making a mortgage loan to an average person, interest fees are almost always attached.

As mentioned in previous essays, this creates the condition where more debt is generated than actual money in circulation to cover it. When a loan is made, only what is termed the "principal" is produced. The money supply of any country consists of this principal in form, which is the aggregate value of all loans made (money creation). The interest fee, on the other hand, is not in existence. This means that, on the social level, all those taking interest bearing loans must find money from the *preexisting* money supply in order to cover it when paying the loan back. In this process, since all interest paid is being pulled from the principal, it is a mathematical eventuality that certain loans simply cannot be repaid. There simply isn't enough money in the system at any one time.[445]

The result is an even more powerful downward class pressure on those holding such basic, common loans since there is always this basic *scarcity* in the money supply itself and everyone working to service their loans have to contend with the inevitable reality that someone is going to fail to meet their loan repayment in the long run. Bankruptcy is a common result in those segments of society that get this "short end of the stick". Even more troubling is how the banking mechanism reacts to those who are unable to fulfill their loan obligation. The loan contract and legal system support the power of banks, in most cases, to "repossess" the physical property of those who cannot pay.[446]

---

444 Reference: *The American Household Is Digging Out of Debt in the Worst Possible Way,* TheAtlantic.com, 2013
(http://www.theatlantic.com/business/archive/2013/01/the-american-household-is-digging-out-of-debt-in-the-worst-possible-way/272657/)

445 A common objection to this analysis is the assumption that interest *income* is also output into the money supply through savings accounts, C.D.s and other such investments. However, this assumes that that money is being *created* during the time of payment. This is not true. Interest income payments are generated by the existing profits of the financial institution so the assumption does not change the equation. The interest fee required for payment simply doesn't exist in the money supply.

446 It is interesting to point out as an aside that banking institutions by which loans are obtained for a purchase - such as a home – are able to take the *full* property regardless of the value paid in prior. Even if 99% of the loan is paid off, they can still take 100% of the property if the final payments are not made.

If we think deeply about this ability to "repossess", it is arguably an indirect form of *theft*. If it is inevitable that some will succumb to not meeting their loan repayment due to the inherent scarcity in the money supply, with the possible result of the physical property obtained from that loaned money being repossessed by the bank via contractual agreements, then the bank's acquisition of such true, physical property is inevitable over time. This means the banks, which are always owned by members of the upper class to be sure, are taking houses, cars and property of the lower classes, simply because the money they created out of thin air in the form of a loan is not being returned to them. This is, in essence, a covert form of physical wealth transfer from the lower to the upper class.

However, returning to the subject of interest itself, such realities are of little direct concern to the upper class. Given the wealth surplus inherent to their financial status, coupled with the lack of necessity to even take loans most of the time due to this surplus, the scarcity pressure inherent to the money supply due to interest fees always falls on the shoulders of the lower classes. Also, the wealthy are actually further class-protected as the phenomenon of *investment income* via interest earned from large savings accounts, certificates of deposit and other means, turns this vehicle of social oppression for the poor into a vehicle of financial advantage for the rich.[447]

(c) Inflation is generally defined as "The rate at which the general level of prices for goods and services is rising, and, subsequently, purchasing power is falling."[448] Unfortunately this common definition gives no insight into its true causality. While there has been debate as to the true causes of inflation in different economic schools,[449] the "Quantity Theory of Money"[450] has been proven as the most relevant. In short, this theory simply recognizes that the more money in circulation, the more inflation or rising prices. In other words, all things being equal, if we double the money supply, price levels will also double, etc. The new money dilutes the value of the existing money in a variation of the supply-demand theory of value.

The consequence of this is what we could call a "hidden tax" on people's savings and fixed income rates. For example, let us assume the inflation rate is 3.5% a year. If you have $30,000, in ten years it will only buy about $21,000 worth of goods.[451] While this

---

447 For example, a person who deposits $1 million into a C.D. at 3% interest annually will generate $30,000 a year merely for that deposit alone. In terms of percentage, 3% may not seem as that dramatic. In terms of absolute value, compared to the income of the vast majority, it is quite dramatic.
448 Source: Investopedia.com
(http://www.investopedia.com/terms/i/inflation.asp#axzz2JypjmRJs)
449 Reference: *Macroeconomics: Theory and Policy*, Robert J. Gordon, "Modern theories of inflation" McGraw-Hill, 1988
450 "Quantity Theory of Money" defined source:
http://www.investopedia.com/articles/05/010705.asp#axzz2JypjmRJs
451 3.5% annual depreciation after 10 years. Original value $30,000 - Year 1:

might appear to have an equal effect for the whole of society, the reality is that it deeply affects the poor much more than the rich when it comes to survival. A person with 3 million dollars in savings is not much hindered by the 3.5% loss of purchasing power. However, a person with only $30,000 in savings, working to perhaps put a down payment on a home in the future, is deeply affected by this hidden tax.

In the context of *structural classism,* where fixed attributes of the system itself assist in the oppression of the poor and helping of the rich, the mechanism of this hidden tax in also immutably built in. The inherent scarcity in the money supply forces new loans constantly in the economy. Coupled with that is the now globally utilized monetary expansion process known as the *fractional reserve lending* system.[452]

Contrary to popular belief, most loans are not given from a bank's existing deposits. They are invented in real time, limited only by a set percentage of their existing deposits.[453] In short, due to this process over time, it is currently possible that for every $10,000 deposited, about $90,000 can be created from it through the process of ongoing loans and deposits across the entire banking system.[454] This *pyramiding* of money, coupled with the interest pressure that creates scarcity in the money supply, reveals that the system is *inherently* inflationary.

(d) Income differences across society also have both a psychological and structural causality. Psychologically, they are driven, in part, by the basic profit and cost preservation incentive necessary to remain competitive and functional in the market. In many ways this incentive could be considered *cognitively structural*, as there is a behavioral threshold that all players in the market economy must adhere when it comes to survival. In turn, this interest of self-preservation though cost-efficiency and maximizing profits, while basic to the capitalist

---

$28,950; Year 2: $27,937; Year 3: $26,960; Year 4: $26,017; Year 5: $25,107; Year 6: $24,229; Year 7: $23,381; Year 8: 22,563; Year 9: $21,774; Year 10 $21,012

452 For a full treatment on the Fractional Reserve Lending, see: *Modern Money Mechanics*, Federal Reserve Bank of Chicago, 1961

453 To quote *Modern Money Mechanics,* a text produced by the Federal Reserve Bank of Chicago: "Of course, they [the banks] do not really pay out loans from the money they receive as deposits. If they did this, no additional money would be created. What they do when they make loans is to accept promissory notes in exchange for credits to the borrowers' transaction accounts...Reserves are unchanged by the loan transactions. But the deposit credits constitute new additions to the total deposits of the banking system" (*Modern Money Mechanics*, Federal Reserve Bank of Chicago, 1961)

454 To quote *Modern Money Mechanics*: "The total amount of expansion that can take place...Carried through to theoretical limits, the initial $10,000 of reserves distributed within the banking system gives rise to an expansion of $90,000 in bank credit (loans and investments) and supports a total of $100,000 in new deposits under a 10 percent reserve requirement." (*Modern Money Mechanics*, Federal Reserve Bank of Chicago, 1961)

game at its core, shows a clear tendency to extend as an overall survival philosophy or human value system in general.

In other words, social values become altered by this economic need for constant self-preservation and very often it manifests itself into behavior which, in abstraction, might be condemned as "excessive", "selfish" or "greedy" - when, in fact, such deemed characteristics are mere extensions or *matters of degree* with respect to this basic conditioning to "stay ahead".

Therefore, the overall trend of increasing income inequality in general should not be a surprise.[455] While the United States, with its deeply competitive nature, is a highlight of extreme class inequality today,[456] the trend is still very much a global phenomenon.[457] While the debate about historical trends vs. current trends can be made regarding why this period of time, the early 21st century, is showing such extensive increases in the wealth gap – we might conclude that certain *structural factors* have made their way into the system and these factors are assisting the disparity. We may also conclude that these mechanisms are not *anomalies* of the system - but rather represent a natural *evolution* of capitalism through time.

For example, the vast income now coming from "capital gains" is a case in point. While seemingly a minor nuance of general income, some economic analysts have deemed capital gains to be the "key ingredient of income disparity in the US".[458] Capital gains are defined as "[t]he amount by which an asset's selling price exceeds its initial purchase price. A realized capital gain is an investment that has been sold at a profit."[459] Its most common context is with respect to the selling of stocks, bonds, derivatives, futures and other abstract "trading" vehicles.

It has been found that in the United States alone, the top 0.1 percent of the population earns about half of all capital gains,[460] and

455 Reference: *U.S. Income Inequality: It's Worse Today Than It Was in 1774,* TheAtlantic.com, 2012 (http://www.theatlantic.com/business/archive/2012/09/us-income-inequality-its-worse-today-than-it-was-in-1774/262537/)
456 Reference: *The Unequal State of America: a Reuters series,* Reuters.com, 2012 (http://www.reuters.com/subjects/income-inequality/washington)
457 Reference: *Income Inequality Around the World Is a Failure of Capitalism,* TheAtlantic.com, 2011 (http://www.theatlantic.com/business/archive/2011/05/income-inequality-around-the-world-is-a-failure-of-capitalism/238837/)
458 Reference: *The Top 0.1% Of The Nation Earn Half Of All Capital Gains,* Forbes.com, 2011 (http://www.forbes.com/sites/robertlenzner/2011/11/20/the-top-0-1-of-the-nation-earn-half-of-all-capital-gains/)
459 Source: Investorwords.com (http://www.investorwords.com/706/capital_gain.html)
460 Reference: *Capital gains tax rates benefiting wealthy feed growing gap between rich and poor,* WashingtonPost.com, 2011 (http://www.washingtonpost.com/business/economy/capital-gains-tax-rates-benefiting-wealthy-are-protected-by-both-parties/2011/09/06/gIQAdJmSLK_story.html)

such gains account for about 60 percent of the income of the top 400 richest citizens.[461] The class mechanism of capital gains is interesting because it is a privileged form of income. While the stock market might be used for conservative mutual fund and retirement investment by the general public, it is really an upper class person's game when it comes to substantial returns due to the high level of capital initially needed to facilitate such high value returns. Like the elitism of high level interest income, capital gains are a class securing mechanism fueled by preexisting substantial wealth.

Then we have the differences in income with respect to one's position in the corporate hierarchy. In a study performed by the Canadian Centre for Policy Alternatives, it was found that Canada's top CEOs make an average worker's yearly salary *in 3 hours*.[462] In the United States, according to research by the *Economic Policy Institute* "the average annual earnings of the top 1 percent of wage earners grew 156 percent from 1979 to 2007; for the top 0.1 percent they grew 362 percent. In contrast, earners in the 90th to 95th percentiles had wage growth of 34 percent, less than a tenth as much as those in the top 0.1 percent tier. Workers in the bottom 90 percent had the weakest wage growth, at 17 percent from 1979 to 2007."[463]

They continue: "The large increase in wage inequality is one of the main drivers of the large upward distribution of household income to the top 1 percent, the others being the rising inequality of capital income and the growing share of income going to capital rather than wages and compensation. The result of these three trends was a more than doubling of the share of total income in the United States received by the top 1 percent between 1979 and 2007 and a large increase in the income gap between those at the top and the vast majority. In 2007, average annual incomes of the top 1 percent of households were 42 times greater than incomes of the bottom 90 percent (up from 14 times greater in 1979), and incomes of the top 0.1 percent were 220 times greater (up from 47 times greater in 1979)."[464]

Similar patterns can be found in other industrialized nations. In fact, in 2013 even China has been discussing their growing income gap problem with proposals to ease the disparity.[465] The *Organization for Economic Co-operation and Development* in a 2011 report found that

461 Reference: *Questioning the Dogma of Tax Rates,* NYTimes.com, 2011 (http://www.nytimes.com/2011/08/20/business/questioning-the-dogma-of-lower-taxes-on-capital-gains.html?pagewanted=all&_r=0)
462 Reference: *Top Canadian CEOs make average worker's salary in three hours of first working day of year,* FinancialPost.com, 2012 (http://business.financialpost.com/2012/01/03/top-canadian-ceos-make-average-workers-salary-in-three-hours/)
463 Reference: *CEO pay and the top 1%,* Epi.org, 2012 (http://www.epi.org/publication/ib331-ceo-pay-top-1-percent/)
464 Ibid.
465 Reference: *China Issues Proposal to Narrow Income Gap,* NYTimes.com, 2013 (http://www.nytimes.com/2013/02/06/world/asia/china-issues-plan-to-narrow-income-gap.html)

countries with historically low levels of income inequality have experienced significant increases over the past decade.[466] [467]

Causality in the form of clearly defined structural mechanisms are more difficult to pin down with respect to this general trend of employment related income imbalance. The combination of the psychological incentive of self-preservation and self-maximization inherent to the value system of capitalism, coupled with the ever-changing legal, tax and financial policy related variables in play, along with the basic strategic edge maintained by the upper classes due to their existing wealth security, creates a complex, synergistic mechanism of class preservation and external oppression.

A subtle yet revealing statistical point to also note is how during recent recessions in the United States, the wealth gap has actually *widened.*[468] It is axiomatic to conclude that if the system of economy was without structural interference in favor of the wealthy, a national recession on the scale of the what occurred from 2007 onward should have affected most everyone negatively, regardless of social class. Yet, it was reported in 2010 that "the wealthiest 5 percent of Americans, who earn more than $180,000, added slightly to their annual incomes last year...Families at the $50,000 median level slipped lower."[469]

As a final point on the issue of income inequality, it is important to note how national economic growth often relates to those of the upper class itself, reducing the general economic relevance of the lower classes. The term "plutonomy" is appropriate in this case. A "plutonomy" is defined as "Economic growth that is powered and consumed by the wealthiest upper class of society. Plutonomy refers to a society where the majority of the wealth is controlled by an ever-shrinking minority; as such, the economic growth of that society

---

466 Reference: *Society at a Glance 2011 - OECD Social Indicators,* Oecd.org, 2011 (http://www.oecd.org/social/socialpoliciesanddata/societyataglance2011-oecdsocialindicators.htm)

467 Reference: *10 Countries With The Worst Income Inequality: OECD,* HuffingtonPost.com, 2011 (http://www.huffingtonpost.com/2011/05/23/10-countries-with-worst-income-inequality_n_865869.html#s278244&title=1_Chile)

468 U.S. Census data revealed:"The top-earning 20 percent of Americans – those making more than $100,000 each year – received 49.4 percent of all income generated in the U.S., compared with the 3.4 percent made by the bottom 20 percent of earners, those who fell below the poverty line, according to the new figures. That ratio of 14.5-to-1 was an increase from 13.6 in 2008 and nearly double a low of 7.69 in 1968. At the top, the wealthiest 5 percent of Americans, who earn more than $180,000, added slightly to their annual incomes last year, the data show. Families at the $50,000 median level slipped lower." Source: http://www.huffingtonpost.com/2010/09/28/income-gap-widens-census-_n_741386.html

469 Reference: *Income Gap Widens: Census Finds Record Gap Between Rich And Poor* (http://www.huffingtonpost.com/2010/09/28/income-gap-widens-census-_n_741386.html)

becomes dependent on the fortunes of that same wealthy minority."[470]

Perhaps the best way to describe the nature of plutonomy and its relevance to the modern day, is to consider the words of those who embrace it. In 2005, Citigroup, a powerful global banking institution, produced a series of internal memos on the subject and it was quite candid in its analysis and conclusions.

They stated: "The world is dividing into two blocs - the Plutonomy and the rest. The U.S., UK, and Canada are the key plutonomies - economies powered by the wealthy."[471] "In a plutonomy there is no such animal as "the U.S. consumer" or "the UK consumer", or indeed the "Russian consumer". There are rich consumers, few in number, but disproportionate in the gigantic slice of income and consumption they take. There are the rest, the "non-rich", the multitudinous many, but only accounting for surprisingly small bites of the national pie."[472] "We should worry less about what the average consumer - say the 50th percentile - is going to do, when that consumer is (we think) less relevant to the aggregate data than how the wealthy feel and what they are doing. This is simply a case of mathematics, not morality."[473]

With 20% of the American population controlling 85% of the country's wealth,[474] it is clear that those utilizing that 85% are more important to the GDP or growth of the economy. What this means is that the financial system has little incentive to *care* about the actions or financial wellbeing of most of the public.

It continues: "the heart of our plutonomy thesis [is] that the rich are the dominant source of income, wealth and demand in plutonomy countries such as the UK, US, Canada and Australia... Secondly, we believe that the rich are going to keep getting richer in coming years, as capitalists (the rich) get an even bigger share of GDP as a result, principally, of globalization. We expect the global pool of labor in developing economies to keep wage inflation in check, and profit margins rising – good for the wealth of capitalists, relatively bad for developed market unskilled/outsource-able labor. This bodes well for companies selling to or servicing the rich."[475]

With respect to the relevance of the rest of the population, the memo states: "We see the biggest threat to plutonomy as coming from a rise in political demands to reduce income inequality, spread the wealth more evenly, and challenge forces such as globalization which

---

470 Source: Investopedia.com
  (http://www.investopedia.com/terms/p/plutonomy.asp#axzz2K4wDOCp1)
471 Source: *Plutonomy: Buying Luxury, Explaining Global Imbalance*, Citigroup Internal Memo, October 16th 2005, p.1
472 Ibid, p.2
473 Source: *The Plutonomy Symposium — Rising Tides Lifting Yachts*, Citigroup Internal Memo, September 29, 2006, p.11
474 Reference: Wealth, Income, and Power, UCSC.edu, 2013
  (http://sociology.ucsc.edu/whorulesamerica/power/wealth.html)
475 Source: *Revisiting Plutonomy: The Rich Getting Richer*, Citigroup Internal Memo, March 5th, 2006, p.11

have benefited profit and wealth growth."[476] "Our conclusion? The three levers governments and societies could pull on to end plutonomy are benign. Property rights are generally still intact, taxation policies neutral to favorable, and globalization is keeping the supply of labor in surplus, acting as a brake on wage inflation."[477] [478]

While plutonomy itself might not exactly be a source of class conflict it is certainly a result. Chrystia Freeland, author of *Plutocrats: The Rise of the New Global Super-Rich and the Fall of Everyone Else* makes a point about the nature of this framed psychology inherent to those of the opulent minority:

"You don't do this in a kind of chortling, smoking your cigar, conspiratorial thinking way. You do it by persuading yourself that what is in your own personal self-interest is in the interests of everybody else. So you persuade yourself that, actually, government services, things like spending on education, which is what created that social mobility in the first place, need to be cut so that the deficit will shrink, so that your tax bill doesn't go up. And what I really worry about is, there is so much money and so much power at the very top, and the gap between those people at the very top and everybody else is so great, that we are going to see social mobility choked off and society transformed."[479]

In Conclusion
A great deal more could be said with respect to the multi-level battling occurring on the planet Earth, mostly centric to financial and market power and its institutional preservation. From physical violence to subtle legal manipulation, the theme is consistent and dominant. It could even be argued that *progress itself* has war waged against it since established corporate institutions who maintain powerful market share in a given industry, will often work to ruthlessly shut down anything that can compete with them, even if the product is progressively better or more sustainable in utility.[480] Change and progress itself, in real terms, are not readily welcomed in the capitalist system as it often disturbs the success of established institutions. The

---

476 Source: *The Plutonomy Symposium - Rising Tides Lifting Yachts*, Citigroup Internal Memo, September 29, 2006, p.11

477 Source: *Plutonomy: Buying Luxury, Explaining Global Imbalance*, Citigroup Internal Memo, October 16th 2005, p.24

478 For a more detailed analysis of these documents by Citigroup, see: http://www.insideriowa.com/en/opinion/index.cfm?action=display&newsID=17761

479 Source: *National Public Radio* (October 15, 2012) "A Startling Gap Between Us And Them In 'Plutocrats'" (http://www.npr.org/2012/10/15/162799512/a-startling-gap-between-us-and-them-in-plutocrats)

480 A well established example of inhibited progress for the maintaining of existing profit establishments was the successful effort made by the oil industry and, by extension, the U.S. government to slow progress toward fully electric vehicles in the 1990s. (Suggested viewing: "Who Killed the Electric Car?": http://www.imdb.com/title/tt0489037/synopsis)

incredibly slow rate of application of new, sustainability improving technological methods is a case in point.[481]

In fact, on the corporate level, there is not only a perpetual war to reduce such competition but there is also the ongoing exploitation of the public in general. Adam Smith actually made this point in his *The Wealth of Nations*, stating: "The interest of the dealers, however, in any particular branch of trade or manufactures, is always in some respects different from, and even opposite to, that of the public...To narrow the competition is always the interest of dealers...But to narrow the competition...can serve only to enable the dealers, by raising their profits above what they naturally would be, to levy, for their own benefit, an absurd tax upon the rest of their fellow-citizens."[482]

On the national level, "peace" today seems to be merely a pause between conflicts on the stage of global civilization. There is a war going on somewhere virtually all the time and when there isn't, the major powers are busy building more advanced weapons and/or selling off the old ones to other countries who are posturing in the same way, all under the name of not only protection but in the name of "good business" as well.[483] Even nations themselves have taken on a form of class hierarchy with dominant 1st world nations subjugating poor 3rd world nations. Common gradient terms such as superpowers, powers, sub-powers and vassal states can be found in historical literature with respect to the national class hierarchy and the structural mechanisms which keep this gradient in form are not very different in intent than what keeps the social classes in order.

For example, while the debt and interest systems, as described, do very well to keep downward pressure on the lower classes, structurally limiting prosperity and social mobility, the same effect occurs to repress a nation via the World Bank and International Monetary Fund.[484] Even John Adams, the second president of the United States pointed this out with his statement: "There are two ways to conquer and enslave a country. One is by the sword. The other is by debt."[485]

On the broadest scale, the real war being waged is on problem resolution and human harmony. The real war is on a balance of power and social justice. The real war, in effect, is on the institution of

481 Reference: *Oil Giants Loath to Follow Obama's Green Lead* (http://www.nytimes.com/2009/04/08/business/energy-environment/08greenoil.html?pagewanted=all&_r=0)
482 Source: *An Inquiry into the Nature and Causes of the Wealth of Nations,* Adam Smith, Modern Library Reprint, 1937, New York, p.250
483 Reference: *The U.S.: Arms Merchant to the Developing World,* Time.com 2012 (http://nation.time.com/2012/08/28/theres-no-business-like-the-arms-business-2/)
484 Reference: *Structural Adjustment - a Major Cause of Poverty,* GlobalIssues.org, 2013 (http://www.globalissues.org/article/3/structural-adjustment-a-major-cause-of-poverty)
485 Source: Heritage.com (http://www.john-adams-heritage.com/quotes/)

economic equality.[486] [487] In the words of former Supreme Court justice, Louis D. Brandeis: "We can have democracy in this country, or we can have great wealth concentrated in the hands of a few, but we can't have both."[488]

All across the world today people talk about the need for equality. Most literate people in the world have no respect for gender or racial bias. The idea of being sexist or racist has become a deeply abhorred view, even though it was not that long ago in the Western world such cultural views were considered "normal". There appears to be a course of evolution that wishes to equalize society that is, by definition, what the underlying gesture of "democracy" is supposed to denote.

Yet, in the midst of all this, the most oppressive form of segregated human suffering continues largely unnoticed in its true context. Today, it is not race, gender or creed that keeps one most oppressed – it is the institution of class. It is now an issue of "rich" and "poor" and, like racism, these ideological and ultimately structural forms of oppression discriminate and divide the human species in deeply powerful and destructive ways.

In the broad view, this theatre of multidimensional warfare – truly a *world* at war with itself – is wholly unsustainable. It is becoming more and more clear, given the accelerating social problems at hand, that the ethos of all-out competition and narrow self-preservation at the expense of others - whether on the personal, corporate, class, ideological or national level - will not be the source of any resolution or long-term human prosperity. It is going to take a new type of thinking to overcome these sociological trends and at the heart of such dramatic cultural change rests the change of the socioeconomic premise itself.

---

486 Reference: *'Extreme' Poverty in US Has More Than Doubled, Study Says*, MoneyNews.com, 2012 (http://www.moneynews.com/Economy/Extreme-Poverty-US/2012/03/06/id/431627)

487 Reference: *Of the 1%, by the 1%, for the 1%*, VanityFair.com, 2011 (http://www.vanityfair.com/society/features/2011/05/top-one-percent-201105)

488 Source: Quoted by Raymond Lonergan in *Mr. Justice Brandeis, Great American*, 1941, p.42

PART III: A NEW TRAIN OF THOUGHT

-INTRODUCTION TO SUSTAINABLE THOUGHT-

Action is the product of the qualities inherent in Nature.
It is only the ignorant man who, misled by personal egotism, says:
'I am the doer.'[489]
-The Bhagavad Gita

Socioeconomic Spectrum

As alluded to in prior essays, sustainable practices can only come about by a value re-orientation towards *sustainable thought*. While the notion of sustainability is often reduced to an ecological context, the real issue under the surface is *cultural*. This hence becomes a process of education. It is the perspective of The Zeitgeist Movement that the economic system utilized in a society is the greatest influence on the values and beliefs of its people. For instance, deeply rooted in even the seemingly separate politico-religious doctrines of our time, resides an undercurrent of values set forth by economic assumptions.[490]

The term "socioeconomic", which is the social science that links the effects of economic activity to other social processes,[491] could have its meaning more specifically extended to also include religious views, political biases, military initiatives, tribal loyalties, cultural customs, legal statutes and other common societal phenomena. It appears that the very fabric of our lives and hence our value system is born, most dominantly, from the cultural perception of our survival, social relationships and ideas of personal/social success.

Moreover, it is critical to restate that political systems, which most in the world still seem to award priority of importance when it comes to the state of affairs in society, are, at best, *secondary* in relevance (if not, in fact, entirely obsolete) when the true ramifications of the economic structure are factored in. In fact, as will be argued in future essays, "political" governance as we know it is really nothing more than an outgrowth of *economic inefficiency*. Very few would care much about "who was in power" or other such traditional notions if they clearly understood the process of economic unfolding and were able to contribute and gain without conflict. Therefore, there is no greater issue of importance than the system of economic unfolding when it comes to the conduct and stability of human beings on both the personal and social level.

---

489 Source: *The Bhagavad Gita,* Chapter 3, Verse 27, Translation: Shri Purohit Swami

490 An example would be this Old Testament scripture which seems to imply that the "poor" will always exist no matter what society does: "There will always be poor people in the land. Therefore I command you to be openhanded toward your brothers and toward the poor and needy in your land." -Deuteronomy 15:11

491 "Socioeconomic" is defined as: "of, relating to, or involving a combination of social and economic factors" (Source: http://www.merriam-webster.com/dictionary/socioeconomic)

Ephemeralization

Generally speaking, an economic system exists to meet the "needs and wants"[492] of the population. The degree by which it is able to do so depends on the state of *usable resources* and the *technical strategy* utilized to harness those resources for a given purpose. In this context, notable engineer and thinker R. Buckminster Fuller argued that true economic "wealth" is not money or even the material outcome of a given production.[493] Rather, true wealth is the level of energy/production *efficiency enabled*, coupled with knowledge development that furthers the *intelligent management* of the Earth's resources. In this view, he defined and expressed a trend termed "ephemeralization"[494] which tracks humanity's technical ability to increasingly do "more with less".

Historically speaking, ephemeralization is, in gesture, a contradiction of the still deeply held "Malthusian"[495] consideration which, in part, claims that humanity is forever out of balance with nature and there will always be a section of the population that *must* suffer, as the available resources simply do not add up to meet everyone's needs.

As noted in prior essays, this worldview is ever apparent in the economic system we still embrace today globally, forging deep

---

492 Consumption patterns in modern society have shown an increasingly arbitrary nature with respect to human "wants", such as the powerful shift in values that occurred in the early 20th century with the application of modern Western advertising. Human "needs", however, are basic necessities, largely shared by all humans, which maintain physical and psychological health. While many still argue subjective interpretations of such terms, "needs" are essentially static and "wants" are essentially variable. Generally speaking, "wants" are a consequence of one's value system and are culturally derived. Therefore, "needs" are hence of greater priority in meeting than "wants".

493 Fuller States: "Wealth...is inherently regenerative. Experimentally demonstrated wealth is: energy compounded with intellect's knowhow." From *Utopia or Oblivion*, R. Buckminster Fuller, Bantam Press, NY, 1969, p.288

494 Ephemeralization, a term coined by R. Buckminster Fuller, is the ability of technological advancement to do "more and more with less and less..." over time. This trend can be noticed in many areas of industrial development, from computer processing (Moore's law) to the rapid acceleration of human knowledge (information technology). A common example would be the computation power and size relationships of computers over time. The ENIAC computer of the 1940s covered 1800 square feet of floor space, weighed 30 tons, consumed 160 kilowatts of electrical power and cost about $6 Million in modern value. Today, an inexpensive, pocket size cell phone computes substantially faster than ENIAC. Hence - less material and yet more power. [http://inventors.about.com/od/estartinventions/a/Eniac.htm]

495 Malthusianism is a perspective often linked to economist and cleric Thomas R. Malthus that, in short, has to do with the need to control/limit population growth due to an empirical assumption of relative resource scarcity. Ideas such as "not helping the poor" as "it only gives false hope" and the like are common to this view. [Suggested Reading: *An Essay on the Principle of Population,* Thomas Malthus, 1798]

structural biases[496] that have inevitably favored one "class" of people over another in survival advantage. In other words, a "war game" has culminated, built out of the assumption of universal, perpetually reinforced scarcity, which moves forward today on its own momentum, largely absent of its original causal reasoning.

The vast majority of what we define as "corruption" today, more often than not, finds its psychological root in this competitive awareness both on the personal level, the corporate (business) level & on the level of government in the form of war, tyranny and self-preserving collusion. In fact, it can be well argued that the very notion of "ethical" in a world decidedly working to gain at the expense of others becomes a highly relative and almost arbitrary distinction.

Yet, this trend of ephemeralization, having increased rapidly from the 20th century's almost sudden industrial/scientific advancements, deeply challenges this protectionist, elitist, scarcity-driven worldview, suggesting new, paradigm-shifting possibilities for human organization.

These possibilities, in part, statistically reveal that we are now able to take care of the entire world's population at a standard of living unknown to the vast majority of humanity today.[497] However, in order for this new reality of *efficiency* to be harnessed, the archaic barriers ingrained in our everyday way of life, specifically our perception of economics, need to be reevaluated and likely overcome entirely.

As noted in prior essays, the term "utopia" commonly arises as a pejorative term amongst those who tend to dismiss large scale social improvement due to either a cynicism of so-called "human nature" or an outright disbelief in humanity's technical capacity to now adjust greatly with new technical means.

For example, an objection common to the current culture, specifically the "wealthy" First World nations, rests in the value of what could be termed the "violence of mass acquisition". At its root, this view takes the Malthusian concept of need-oriented resource insufficiency and transposes it to assume a pressure of *acquisitive irrationality*.

In other words, it assumes human beings empirically have *infinite* material "wants" and even if, say, every human being could

---

496 See prior essay: *Structural Classism, The State and War*
497 While this reality will be discussed in the following essay "Post-Scarcity Trends, Capacity and Efficiency", highlighting the accelerating efficiency of transportation, energy, industrial design, food cultivation technology and the like, the following conclusion by R. Buckminster Fuller in 1969 is worth stating for historical reference: "[Man] developed such intense mechanization in World War I that the percentage of total world population that were industrial "haves" rose by 1919 to the figure of 6%. That was a very abrupt change in history...By the time of World War II 20% of all humanity had become industrial "haves"...At the present moment the proportion of "haves" is at 40% of humanity...if we up the performances...of resources from the present level to a highly feasible overall efficiency of 12% [more]...[all humanity can be provided for]". From *Utopia or Oblivion*, R. Buckminster Fuller, Bantam Press, NY, 1969, pp.153-155

exist with what the West today would deem an upper class lifestyle, with no one falling short, an element of our psychology would never be satisfied in the material sense and the interest in "more and more" material gain would thus always create a destabilizing imbalance in society. Therefore, the existence of "haves" and "have-nots" is perceived to be a consequence of our inherent, status-driven psychology and greed, not availability of resources and means.

To the extent that this is actually true is dubious at best given the extreme cultural condition we find ourselves in today, compared with the historical fact that outside of Western (aka Capitalistic) influence, the concept of "vain material success" is far from universal for the human being.[498] In truth, the relationship of "success" and "property" has been culturally manufactured based upon system necessity and is now a staple value of our consumer-based society.[499]

In a world now driven by "economic growth" to keep employment at a reasonable level; in a world which overtly praises those with great financial wealth as a measure of success; in a world that actually rewards behaviors of human indifference and ruthless competition for market share (rather than honest social contribution for overall human betterment); it is no mystery as to why the idea of a single human owning, say, a 400 room mansion on 500,000 acres of private land with 50 cars and five planes parked in the front yard has become part of an ideal, coveted vision of personal (and social) success.

Yet, from the perspective of true human sustainability, this view is *pure violence* and exists in nearly the same category of one who hoards food and resources he or she doesn't need and refuses to allow others access for the sake of abstract principle.[500] If we imagine a small island of ten people were two people decide to extract and hoard 1,000% more than they need to be healthy, leaving eight people to live in abject poverty and/or dying - would you find this

---

498 Given that the "infinite want" assumption of human craving is still a core component of the monetary-market based economic view of scarcity and resource inequity, it is interesting how the very basis of its assumption implies an empirical irrationality of human behavior. It would have to be irrational given the basic knowledge of humanity dependence on the Earth's finite resources. Contradiction of this assumption is replete in human history, specifically with cultures that developed in less industrialized societies, in more direct association with the land, outside of the influence of our now common consumer culture. Early Native American cultures, for example, held the value of balance as a virtue rather than acquisition. Suggested Reading: *The High Price of Materialism*, Tim Kasser, A Bradford Book, 2003

499 Reference: *Propaganda,* Edward Bernays, Ig Publishing, 1928

500 The socially destabilizing ramifications of a society with great wealth imbalance were best recently exemplified by the rise of what was globally recognized as the "Occupy Wall Street" protests. (http://occupywallst.org/) Wealth imbalance has become recognized increasingly as less of an issue of subjective "moral fairness" but rather an issue of dire public health and social stability.

arrangement an act of "personal freedom" by those two - or an act of social violence against the eight?

This is brought up here to dismiss the "utopian abundance fallacy" reaction common to many regarding, in part, the implications of ephemeralization. Just as we as a global society are realizing the inherent physical limitations of our industrial behaviors, slowly adjusting away from ecologically destabilizing consequences, the understanding that an "infinite wants"-based value orientation is *equally* as detrimental to social balance is critical to realize.

System Limitation
When it comes to cultural philosophies, the human population must gain, in part, a clear understanding of its limitations and derive its expectations and values from this physical reality. The limitations imposed by our environment exist irrespective of human values, interests, wants or even needs in abstraction. If we were to remove humanity from planet Earth and observe the Earth's natural ecological operations with the causal, scientific understandings we have today, we would witness a synergistic/symbiotic system governed by the universal dynamics of nature.

Hence, no matter what we think about ourselves, our intentions or our "freedoms",[501] once we are placed into this *system of physical law* we are bound to it regardless of our beliefs or the cultural norms we have taken for granted, or which have been imposed as "inevitable" or "immutable" by our various cultures. If we choose to learn and align with the logic inherent, we find sustainability and hence stability. If we choose to ignore or fight these pre-existing rules, we will inevitably decrease stability and problems will arise, as is the near-constant state of affairs today in the early 21st century.

This awareness of natural limitations, as we have come to understand them today via the scientific method, expresses perhaps the most profound shift in human "loyalties" in history. In short, we now understand that we either align with the natural world, or we suffer. Sadly, this firm referential association still stands at odds with many common philosophies today, such as established religious and political perspectives. Remarkably also, it is a common rejoinder to label this very firmly based realization as "totalitarian" or "black-and-white", a seemingly rigid and arbitrary imposition upon human life,

---

501 The word "freedoms" is in parenthesis due to the prolific cultural use. Patriotic slogans about "freedom" and "liberty", born out of, in part, the historical problem of tyranny and government abuse, exist today often creating an almost neurotic and misleading view of human behavior. In reality, there is no such thing as universal freedom in the world as rigid physical laws bind us. The cultural notion of "freedom", as most propagated by the Capitalist ideology, can be argued as intrinsically dangerous to species sustainability in many ways - specifically with respect to its absolute ignoring of larger order synergistic system factors, assuming the fallacy that a detached, self-interest based pursuit secures social and ecological balance.

rather than simply the undeniable, scientifically demonstrable state of affairs.

Intriguingly, the nearly paradoxical punch line of the whole consideration of natural law is that within this rational "box" of system limitation we define as the "governing laws of nature" *our range of possibility within these boundaries via the scientific method also reveals an ever-increasing technical efficiency and incredible potential to create an abundance to meet human needs, globally.*

Furthermore, since humanity is the only species on Earth with the mental capacity to alter/affect its ecosystem in truly profound ways, this necessity for alignment becomes critical for species sustainability, public health and true problem solving advancement. Nothing could be more dangerous than a world culture that, given the exponential increase in our capacity to affect ecological and social balance with technology, misunderstands its power and effects. In many ways, humanity is faced with an *educational race against time* with respect to its current *immaturity* in handling the incredible, newfound powers it has realized via science and technology.[502]

As an aside, it is important to remember that when it comes to the history of economic thought itself, the frame of reference has had more to do with *assumptions of human behavior* than intelligent resource management and general physical science/natural law understandings.[503] While our most innate behavioral reflexes and genetic propensities are certainly relevant to the consequences of a socioeconomic system and are very much a part of the equation, assumptions of human behavior cannot rationally be held as a structural starting point of an economic system. Humans are a *consequence* of the same ecological system conditions and not the other way around.

So, in conclusion to this introduction, if the purpose of a social system is to create an ever increasing standard of living, while also maintaining environmental and social balance to assure we do not reduce this quality in the future due to possible resulting consequences of irresponsible choices - such as resource depletion, pollution, disease, negative stress, "wealth" imbalance and other issues – it then becomes critical to base our methodology on the most relevant set of technical parameters we can, oriented around the current state of *scientific awareness* on both an ecological and human level.

---

502 Later in his life, astronomer Carl Sagan made a video commentary which can be found in later releases of his PBS series "Cosmos", stating (paraphrased here):"It is almost as though there is a God and he has given humanity the choice to use the power of science to improve life... or destroy it. It is up to us."

503 See prior essay *History of Economy.*

-POST SCARCITY TRENDS, CAPACITY AND EFFICIENCY-

The world's present industrial civilization is handicapped by the coexistence of
two universal, overlapping, and incompatible intellectual systems: the
accumulated knowledge of the last four centuries of the properties and
interrelationships of matter and energy; and the associated monetary culture
which has evolved from folkways of prehistoric origin.[504]
-M. King Hubbert

Evaluating Design

Examining the surface of Earth today, a network layer of communities,
industrial centers, transport routes, recreational areas, agricultural
systems and the like dominate much of the landscape. Whether
intended as a total system construct or not, this result, at any given
point in time, constitutes the appearance of a topographical *design.*

Yet, on the other hand, given that this resulting "design" today
is, actually, a *consequential amalgamation* of mostly business
dynamics - moving money around for personal or group self-interest,
based around decision-making mechanisms such as profit, cost-
efficiency and the prevailing logic surrounding property relationships –
it could also be argued that what has manifest is actually *not* a
"design" at all. Rather, it is rooted in a mechanism that has created the
appearance of design *ex post facto*[505] since the structural outcome
recognized was not fully anticipated as a whole prior to its
construction.

In other words, the technical order we see in the world today
is mostly the result of financial processes that have little to no
perception of larger scale structural outcomes. It is more of a *proxy
system*[506] and while there are some relative exceptions, such as the
placement of highways, pipelines and the like by funded city planners
who simply *must* take a broad physical view to be functional, even
those circumstances are often working *around* pre-existing property
claims and other forms of interference which tend to reduce *design
efficiency* on the whole.

This is an interesting observation, as once it is recognized that
our society operates *without a large scale preconception of its own
physical design*, one might begin to realize the enormous level of
unnecessary waste and technical inefficiency inherent to such a short-

---

504 Source: *Two Intellectual Systems: Matter-energy and the Monetary
    Culture*, M. King Hubbert, 1981
505 "Ex Post Facto" is a Latin term that means "done, made, or formulated after
    the fact".
506 "Proxy", defined as "the agency, function, or office of a deputy who acts as
    a substitute for another" (http://www.merriam-
    webster.com/dictionary/proxy), is used in this context to describe the
    market economy as a system that serves to assist industrial and, in many
    ways, societal operations *indirectly.* In other words, the system of trade,
    profit, competition and all other such monetary-market attributes are
    merely mechanisms that orient behavior in a certain, arguably short-sighted
    way, absent any kind of larger system perspective.

sighted process.

To consider this more so, two points are worth considering:

a) Existing yet Unapplied Solutions

b) Broad Conception vs. Spontaneous Conception

a) Existing yet Unapplied Solutions:

This first point concerns the tendency of many new innovations for problem resolution to go unapplied within the current economic tradition.[507] If further life improving methods or technologies have not found their way into a system within a *respectable amount of time* (or at all) after general validation, we can rightly assume there are inefficiencies, if not deficiencies, with the very process of economic incorporation and development.

In other words, this delay between proven solutions, and their application in the real world, gauges the ability of the socioeconomic system to *adapt* properly to improved methods and applications. If, for some reason, the social order in question is not able to incorporate such new means to further ecological balance, improve public health, solve problems and increase prosperity, then there is likely a *structural* problem inherent.[508]

b) Broad Conception vs. Spontaneous Conception:

Secondly, from a strictly formulaic viewpoint, direct, total system considerations will always be more efficient and effective than "spontaneous" generation by processes blind to the final outcome or

---

507 A classic example is the electric car that has been around since the 19th century, showing large-scale efficacy in the 21st century via technological improvements. However, the global shift from the polluting gas engine to the clean electric engine has clearly been stifled by established, profit preserving industries related to the automobile manufacturers and energy providers. It is also worth noting that the very foundation of market efficiency is the *mechanism of profit*. With this "proxy" mechanism, actions are only taken if they are "profitable". In real life, we can see a vast array of needed actions to assist social and environmental integrity that have no relevance to the pursuit of profit. In other words, if money cannot be made on a given act, that act isn't deemed of value in the view of the proxy.

508 A classic, large-scale example is the existence of *poverty*. In order to justify poverty, physically, there must be a clear deficiency in the natural world's capacity to meet the needs of those who have resulted to exist in poverty. If it is found that there is a capacity to eliminate poverty as we know it, hence meaning enough food, shelter, water and other resources and services that can, indeed, be made available without removing those basic, life supporting means from others, then the justification of poverty must find another source. In the current system, this justification is essentially theoretical and determined only by the mechanism of the market itself, implying that if a person is incapable of competing sufficiently to obtain his or her own viable standard of living, then they are hence not deserving of that standard of living. Therefore, the reason poverty exists, as per this example, is the result of the market system and its structure, not real life, physical realities.

purpose.[509]

In other words, as gestured before, a basic good, such as a car, has a design that is conceived of in advance, before physical production. Once this design is decided upon, it is then followed by applying real life materials and processes to create the actual physical product. This may seem obvious to most as a logical process but the relevance of such preconception is often lost when it comes to larger order contexts.

We have to wonder what the outcome would be if we applied the pseudo-democratic market process of bidding, buying and selling for short-term profit, if even possible on such a scale, to the creation of high integrity *goods systems*, such as an airplane, computer, car, home or the like. While today the resources, labor and sub-component systems of these items are certainly in play in the open market, the *design itself* is not.

The design is relegated, necessarily, to the discipline of *science* overall. It could be said that a line is intuitively drawn in this way between what is susceptible to monetary opinion and what is tangibly needed to keep some basic level of technical, system integrity. (Please note that this notion of design is not to be confused with subjective "style" interests. Design, as used here, is not an aesthetic consideration but a technical one.)

Imagine, hypothetically, if people "bid and offered" for the physical design construction of a house in each tiny physical detail, ignoring scientific principles. In other words, instead of referencing the basic laws of physics and the natural science that defines the core structural integrity of any building, we let the *market* decide, with everyone "buying" and "selling" such premises for their personal gain, regardless of their technical understanding. Of course, such an idea is truly absurd in such abstraction and most reading this probably can't even imagine such an irrational interplay.

However, this is exactly what is occurring as a result of our economic system in many other less obvious ways. For example, on the "macroeconomic" scale, the global commercial network created by what is termed *globalization*[510] - with its basis in cost efficiency which, among other things, utilizes cheaper labor in often distant regions,[511] while wasting large amounts of energy sending resources all over the world and back - reveals this loss of efficiency well.[512]

---

509 The main exception to this would be a situation where the assumed system design is simply not understood properly at that time. In other words, if the goal or function of a given system is not fully realized, then naturally that system can only be designed to that level of understanding.

510 Globalization is defined as: "the development of an increasingly integrated global economy marked especially by free trade, free flow of capital, and the tapping of cheaper foreign labor markets". (http://www.merriam-webster.com/dictionary/globalization)

511 Reference: *Globalization: Between Fairness and Exploitation* (http://www.pbs.org/wnet/wideangle/episodes/land-of-wandering-souls/globalization-between-fairness-and-exploitation/3073/)

512 Reference: *Why globalization is energy intensive and wreaks havoc on oil*

From the perspective of *preconceived design,* given the more logical possibility of localization of labor, production and distribution in most all cases, globalization, in its current form, is highly inefficient compared to other possibilities. This is not to deny that globalization and this integration of international economies has generally been a productive occurrence within the evolution of economics. In that context, it has served global industrial development fairly well. However, if we step out of the box of market logic and examine how we could *directly* design a more technically efficient and localized set of systems, within the global setting, we find that the current method is not only inferior, it is rather offensive.

On the "microeconomic" scale, this can be exemplified with respect to the inefficiency inherent to the *quality* of basic good components, also due to the practice of cost efficiency and the inherent interest to produce the so-called "best" at the "lowest cost" which, quite simply, does not produce the best at all.

For example, a proposed schematic design of, say, a laptop computer might be reasonably efficient, technically. However, if the actual materials used to generate that final good are relatively poor in quality, no matter how intelligent the overall, basic design, it will incur relative weakness and will likely break down more rapidly than if the same design was also optimized to use the most "appropriate" materials from a technical point of view, rather than those materials decided upon as per the proxy of "market efficiency".[513]

Another example is the market phenomenon of *proprietary technology*. While we see, ostensibly, an enormous amount of variety in the world today with respect to good production, a closer look shows a vast and wasteful multiplicity,[514] along with problematic structural incompatibility between producers' components of the same good

---

prices (http://www.csmonitor.com/Environment/Energy-Voices/2013/0228/Why-globalization-is-energy-intensive-and-wreaks-havoc-on-oil-prices)

513 This is a rather subjective example as, ideally, a planned design should be thorough enough to take into account the actual, physical materials and their characteristics, decided upon down to the smallest relevant part. In truth, this only happens to a certain degree, with many components of a given good included as a means to keep a product "cheap" and competitive in the open market. An example would be tires on a car. While general specification of tire grade may be suggested, the use of "cheap" tires could prevail due to an interest to limits costs by the consumer or even the producer.

514 An example of multiplicity is how good production today grades quality based on a targeted demographic. There are deliberately poor goods continuously designed for those with limited purchasing power and there are more optimized goods, which are longer lasting and effective, designed for those who can afford such quality. While native to the logic of the market system's inherent and resulting class stratification, this type of waste is actually unneeded if society had the intention to share design ideas in totality, seeking optimization as strategically as possible. In a NLRBE, this would be the case, removing the market and hence the enormous waste produced by this kind of demographic based multiplicity.

genre.

In other words, competing corporations today tend to create *custom systems* (such as a computer system and its required components) that are incompatible with the developments of other producers in that same *good genre*. "Universal compatibility",[515] or lack thereof, is yet another example that the byproduct of this market "proxy" game and the larger order system inefficiency and waste is enormous. This pattern is also common to generational development of existing commercial product systems (aka "models"), such as when improvements are made to a given machine, unnecessarily making obsolete older components of that machine, in the interest of assuring further purchases from the consumer.[516]

It is critical to note that there is no such thing as a *single product* in the closed system of Earth with respect to planetary resources and their use, nor are any product designs or production *methods* existing in a vacuum. Each good and its process of production is merely an extension of the whole of industry. Hence, the materials utilized, along with designs, find their true context only with respect to the *whole of industry and resource management* on all levels. This understanding forces the constant need to view industry (and hence economics itself) as a single system process to ensure maximum technical efficiency.

So with this in mind, coupled again with the first point regarding the question of why certain realities are not put into practice even though they are clearly doable at a given point in time, this essay will examine socially relevant technological trends and design capacities which, if applied *properly*, could radically transform the world into a "post-scarcity", highly abundant condition that would alleviate the vast majority of the world's problems we see as commonplace today.

Moreover, it is a conclusion of TZM that the current model not only disallows (or too slowly incorporates) new advents in efficiency due to the very nature of business and its tendency to preserve inefficiency for the sake of an establishment's profit,[517] the very detached and segregated nature of market activity inherently ignores larger order considerations to source and solve problems or accelerate

---

515 See essay *True Economic Factors* for more on this subject.
516 Here is an example: *Fury at Apple's 'rip-off' plan to make ALL iPhone accessories obsolete by changing design of socket* (http://www.dailymail.co.uk/sciencetech/article-2162867/Apple-slammed-iPhone-5-charger-Rip-plan-make-ALL-accessories-obsolete.html)
517 A classic historical example of this propensity was what was later termed the "War of Currents". In short, knowing that his direct current (DC) distribution of electricity was inferior to the emerging alternating current (AC) system put forward by Nikola Tesla, inventor Thomas Edison engaged in an extensive disinformation campaign to suppress AC's popularity, to preserve his financial stake in the existing AC infrastructure. Edison even went so far as going to the United States Congress seeking to *outlaw* alternating current, along with publicly killing animals by AC electrocution.

improvement.[518]

Design Efficiency

If we break down the everyday complexity of our lives today, dissecting what interplay is most critical to human survival, sustainability and prosperity, we might find three basic things: science, natural law & resources. 'Science' is the *mechanism* for discovery and validation; 'natural law' is the pre-existing *rule set* which we are continually learning about via science and necessarily adapting; while 'resources' exist in the context of both raw *Earthly materials* and the power of the *human mind* to comprehend. With respect to the development of *design*, these three attributes are naturally indispensable to each other.

Furthermore, the term *industrial design*,[519] for the purposes of this essay, will be used to denote the process of economic oriented industry in all its facets, from singular good creation to the total order of the global economy in form. The history of industrial design is, in many respects, the *true history* of economic development. As our ever-emerging scientific understandings generate logical inference with respect to how best utilize our resources and time, the global landscape, both physical and cultural, has undergone perpetual change.

In this context, the core interest of industrial design is essentially *efficiency* and it could be argued that there are three central efficiency contexts related: (a) labor efficiency (b) material efficiency and (c) system efficiency.

(a) *Labor efficiency* has a unique history. Since the early 20th century there has been a relatively rapid transition from the dominant use of human and animal muscle as the source of labor power, to the use of powered machines. This phenomenon, which is termed *mechanization*, was able to elevate the workforce from much strenuous toil, to operate in more of a position of tool utilization.

However, by the end of the 20th century, this pattern continued to advance, where such machines were not only capable of moving heavy loads and performing complex physical acts, they were also merging with *computerization* and degrees of *artificial intelligence* (AI) and hence were able to make *decisions* as well. In short, the accelerating trend today has proven that these modern machines are

---

518 While the existence of government has served as both a regulator of business matters as well as an active colluder of such matters given its existence as a business in and of itself, there have been very few global actions that have united the industrial system. One example was the *Montreal Protocol,* which, perhaps for the first time in history, united the world in a basic interest in environmental protection (Ozone Layer Depletion).

519 Industrial design is traditionally defined, as "is the use of both applied art and applied science to improve the aesthetics, ergonomics, functionality, and/or usability of a product."

now greatly surpassing, in productivity, the vast majority of the actions historically held by human beings and there appears to be no slowing down of this trend.[520] Overall, TZM views this trend as suggesting a powerful means by which the human species can further maximize its productive ability to meet the needs of all human beings, while generating a level of human freedom never before seen, if adapted properly.[521]

(b) *Material efficiency* is how well we utilize the raw materials of the Earth. *Materials science*[522] *also* has a unique history unto itself, with each period of time discovering new patterns and possibilities. Metallurgy, a domain of materials engineering that studies the physical and chemical behavior of metallic elements and their mixtures,[523] was a very important development historically, enabling a vast spectrum of possibility through the creation of compounds and alloys. For example, the term "Bronze Age",[524] which was the period in Europe of around 3200-600 BC, is characterized by the common use of copper and its alloy bronze for many purposes.

However, perhaps the most important discovery in materials science understanding (and perhaps one of the most important discoveries in human history) was the set of chemical elements that comprise all matter, as we know it. Recognized by most as organized via the "periodic table", 118 elements have been identified as of 2013, with about 92 known to occur naturally on Earth.[525] In short, these chemical elements are the building blocks of everything we experience as tangible in the world around us and each respective atom has certain properties and hence idiosyncratic applications.

---

520 This issue will be addressed at the end of this essay. Suggested reading: *Report Suggests Nearly Half of U.S. Jobs Are Vulnerable to Computerization* (http://www.technologyreview.com/view/519241/report-suggests-nearly-half-of-us-jobs-are-vulnerable-to-computerization/)

521 Viewing the world with a "success" and "status" association to material possessions, as is common today, often pollutes considerations of the positive stress reducing, free time enabling, conflict relieving possibilities of labor automation. Does one want to have a life of freedom from monotony, stress and toil or does want to have vast, excess material possessions? This question presents a value system conflict and the term "adaptation" here is to suggest that people may be willing to reduce the complexity of industry a bit by having less material "wants", in favor of a more "simplified" lifestyle. This isn't to suggest everything we have today could not be available in a NLRBE. It is to say that a worldview which is less materialistic could prevail to make such a transition to a kind automated economy more simple, not to mention be more ecologically sustainable, given the inherent waste.

522 Materials science is an interdisciplinary field involving the properties of matter and its application to various areas of science and engineering. (http://www.sciencedaily.com/articles/m/materials_science.htm)

523 Metallurgy defined: http://www.sciencedaily.com/articles/m/metallurgy.htm

524 Reference: Bronze Age: http://www.thefreedictionary.com/Bronze+Age

525 Source: "New Element 115 Takes a Seat at the Periodic Table", *Time,* 2013 (http://science.time.com/2013/08/28/new-element-115-takes-a-seat-at-the-periodic-table/)

This knowledge, which is extremely new relative to the totality of human understanding,[526] has not only allowed for a deeper understanding of how chemistry can work to create an incredibly vast range of materials for increasingly efficient industrial use, it has also facilitated a powerful understanding of the very nature of matter itself and prospects for manipulation at the atomic scale.

Nanotechnology,[527] which is very much in its infancy, appears quite concrete in its theoretical basis of assembling and disassembling different materials, and even systems of materials (i.e. goods themselves), from the atomic level up and down.[528]

Of course, as profound as that is, the current, relatively crude state of nanotechnology applies mostly in the context of what are called "smart materials"[529] or "meta-materials".[530] As will be touched upon later in this essay, the current state and trends of materials science hold profound possibilities for the present and future.

(c) *System efficiency* is likely the most crucial and important of all concepts for, as abstract as it may seem, everything we know of is a system *itself* or an interaction of two or more systems. Perhaps the best way to express system efficiency is to consider any commonplace act and think about how that act could either reduce waste or increase productivity on any and all levels, not just within the context of the perceived singular act itself. System perspectives are rather obscure to most since we tend to view most functions and processes within the

---

526 In 1789, Antoine Lavoisier published a list of 33 chemical elements, grouping them into gases, metals, nonmetals, and earths. In 1870, Russian chemistry professor Dmitri Mendeleev produced the first "periodic table" with about twice as many, with a new element being discovered about ever year on average thereafter.

527 Nanotechnology defined: the science of manipulating materials on an atomic or molecular scale.

528 Reference: *Michio Kaku: Can Nanotechnology Create Utopia?* (http://betanews.com/2012/11/08/star-trek-replicator-is-closer-to-reality-than-you-think/)

529 "Smart Materials", as a term, is rather new and ambiguous. A common definition would be: "Materials that can significantly change their mechanical properties (such as shape, stiffness, and viscosity), or their thermal, optical, or electromagnetic properties, in a predictable or controllable manner in response to their environment. Materials that perform sensing and actuating functions, including piezoelectrics, electrostrictors, magnetostrictors, and shape-memory alloys." However, a "smart" material isn't necessarily a product of nanotechnology, even though nanotechnology can be common as a means of production.

530 "Metamaterials" are defined generally as "exotic composite materials that display properties beyond those available in naturally occurring materials. Instead of constructing materials at the chemical level, as is ordinarily done, these are constructed with two or more materials at the macroscopic level." One of their defining characteristics is that the electromagnetic response results from combining two or more distinct materials in a specified way that extends the range of electromagnetic patterns because of the fact that they are not found in nature.

bounds of their intended purpose only, in a categorical manner.

For example, when we consider a modern fitness center (aka "gym"), with people exercising on various machines in one location, we tend to think only of the purpose of that institution and hence how to better facilitate the health interests of those people using those machines, etc. We rarely think more broadly and propose: "What if all those people pedaling and pushing and pulling had that exerted energy run into a conversion system where the building itself could be powered, in whole or in part, by that energy in the form of electricity?"[531]

This manner of thought stands at the heart of a *systems theory* type worldview. Perhaps a useful way to think of this *network* perspective is through the synergy of nature itself. In the Earth's biosphere, minus current human interference, there is virtually no such thing as waste. Virtually everything we find in nature is deeply integrated and in balance due to the refining nature of evolution itself.

This is a powerful observation and the term biomimicry[532] is worth mentioning in this context as, in many ways, our development as a species has been to learn from the natural processes in existence already, even though we appear to have decoupled greatly in many ways. Hence, working to facilitate the most *optimized integration* we can, ideally *reusing everything* on all levels, just as nature does, should be a societal goal to ensure sustainability and efficiency.

Established and Potential Trends

There are two broad, basic trends/realities to consider in the world today. For the purposes of this essay, we will refer to them as "established" and "potential". *Established trends* are the socioeconomic trends in play at the time of this writing and these, in the context of public health and ecological balance, are shown to be almost entirely negative.[533] The *potential trends,* on the other hand, reveal life-improving and balance-creating possibilities that *could* occur, if larger

---

531 Actually, this idea was indeed realized but has been applied very rarely as of now. "In the Gym: Clean Energy from Muscle Power", *Time*, 2010 (http://content.time.com/time/business/article/0,8599,2032281,00.html)

532 Biomimicry (from *bios*, meaning life, and *mimesis*, meaning to imitate) is a design discipline that seeks sustainable solutions by emulating nature's time-tested patterns and strategies, e.g., a solar cell inspired by a leaf. (http://www.asknature.org/article/view/what_is_biomimicry)

533 Two broad trends worth noting would be ecological & social. Regarding the ecological, it has been noted that most, if not all major life supporting systems are currently in decline. Ref: *Data Shows All of Earth's Systems in Rapid Decline* (http://www.ipsnews.net/2011/07/data-shows-all-of-earths-systems-in-rapid-decline/) Regarding social trends - a worthy statistical observation is the apparent general increase in social destabilization or "uprisings" that have been occurring in the past 30 years. A program tracking new reports called (GDELT), shows a startling increase in such events. Ref: *Data Map Shows Protests Around the World Increase, With Caveat* (http://theglobalobservatory.org/analysis/576-mapping-some-of-the-worlds-unrest-.html)

order social changes were made. As noted before, these two trends arguably appear to operate in system contradiction of each other.

In the essay titled *Social Destabilization & Transition,* an in-depth look at the current state of societal affairs will be addressed in detail. However, let it be stated that the efficiencies defined, defended and suggested here are not done so simply to show how much better the world "could be", as though what we are doing today is still okay. On the contrary, these basic observations actually demand alignment if we intend to *maintain stability* in our world given its current, degrading patterns.

With a population expected to reach over 9 billion by 2050,[534] with reported trends of looming food,[535] water[536] and energy shortages,[537] these suggestions not only seek to improve but to actually *change course*. Overall, it is the view of TZM that if these current, so-called *established* trends persist with the shortsighted market-based practice and all the characteristics that go along with it, human culture will not only not achieve the positive application of the *potential* trends expressed, increased destabilization will continue to occur.

Post-Scarcity Worldview
In this section, basic statistics and trends will be presented to show how we can, as a global society, achieve a "post-scarcity"[638] social

---

534 Source: *U.N. Raises "Low" Population Projection for 2050*
(http://www.worldwatch.org/node/6038)
535 Reference: *Yield Trends Are Insufficient to Double Global Crop Production by 2050*
(http://www.washingtonpost.com/blogs/wonkblog/wp/2013/07/01/this-unsettling-chart-shows-were-not-growing-enough-food-to-feed-the-world/)
536 Reference: *The Coming Global Water Crisis*
(http://www.theatlantic.com/international/archive/2012/05/the-coming-global-water-crisis/256896/)
537 The hydrocarbon economy and its degree of scarcity has been a controversial subject for many decades. The debate over the current state of supply, globally, has vast disagreement. "Peak Oil", which has been the categorical context of this debate, spans many decades, with the main conclusion being that this form of energy is finite. Regional depletion, such as the United States peak in the 1970s with respect to conventional oil fields, provides axiomatic evidence that other regions and hence the world itself will eventually peak, with many analysts seeing this occur in the very near future. This, coupled with population growth and increased demand, compounds the problem, if accurate. Ref:
(http://www.independent.co.uk/news/science/world-oil-supplies-are-set-to-run-out-faster-than-expected-warn-scientists-6262621.html)
538 The term "post-scarcity" denotes a state that eliminates access scarcity of a given resource or process, usually by means of optimized efficiency regarding production design and strategic use. Needless to say, the idea of achieving total post-scarcity - meaning an infinite, abundant amount of everything for everyone - is rightfully considered an impossibility, even in the most optimistic views. Therefore, this term, as used here, really highlights a point of focus.

system. While scarcity in absolute terms will always be with humanity to one degree or another in this closed system of Earthly resources, scarcity on the level of *human needs* and *basic material success* is no longer a viable defense of the market system's allocation methods.[539]

As a brief aside, a common defense of the price system and the market is that if *any* scarcity exists, it makes void any other approach. The argument goes that since not everyone can have xyz, xyz is scare and hence people need money (or have a lack thereof) to filter out who gains xyz and who doesn't.

The problem with this assumption is that it ignores how certain resources and hence goods have more *relevance* than others when it comes to *public health*. Comparing the scarcity of a very expensive, luxury car which draws status satisfaction from its owner more than its basic purpose as a mode of transport - with the scarcity of food, which is a core life requirement for health, is not legitimate in real life terms. The former interest, while perhaps important to the ego satisfaction of the owner who likely already has his or her basic needs met to afford such a product, is not equivalent to the latter interest of those who have little or nothing to eat and hence cannot survive. One cannot arbitrarily conflate such "needs" and "wants", as though they are simply the same, in theory. Sadly, this is how the market system behaves.

Likewise, with great wealth and material imbalance,[540] comes inevitable social destabilization. Virtually every large-scale public dissent and revolution we have seen in the past couple hundred years have had some economic basis, usually revolving around societal imbalance, exploitation and class separation.[541] The same goes for the roots of crime, terrorism, addictions and other social problems. Virtually all of these propensities are born out of deprivation, whether

---

539 Monetary economics is rooted in viewing the world from the standpoint of shortages or inefficiencies. It is based around managing scarcity through a system of price and value relationships. The more an item is scare, the more it is valued.

540 The following quotation by historian Jerry Z. Muller embraces this reality well: "Inequality is indeed increasing almost everywhere in the postindustrial capitalist world. But despite what many on the left think, this is not the result of politics, nor is politics likely to reverse it, for the problem is more deeply rooted and intractable than generally recognized. Inequality is an inevitable product of capitalist activity, and expanding equality of opportunity only increases it -- because some individuals and communities are simply better able than others to exploit the opportunities for development and advancement that capitalism affords." (http://www.foreignaffairs.com/articles/138844/jerry-z-muller/capitalism-and-inequality)

541 Both relative and absolute deprivation, meaning abject poverty and relative socioeconomic status, show a powerful historical correlation to social destabilization and protest. "Occupy Wall St" which sparked a global protest movement in 2011, was based, most specifically, around income inequality. Its most notable slogan, "We are the 99%", denoted the vast wealth differences between 99% of the population and the 1%, coupled with the power abuse inherent because of this imbalance.

absolute or relative and this deprivation is inherent to the nature of a society based on competition and scarcity.

So, to simply reduce our economic reality down to mere trade, coupled with the claim that any degree of scarcity justifies the use of the market, price and money for allocation, is to ignore the true nature of what ensures social harmony, stability, and public health. Would it seem reasonable to forgo the technical ability to, say, elevate 80% of humanity to the material capacity currently held by only 10% today, simply because "not everyone can own a 500 room mansion"? Again, the absurdity of this objection is quite clear when a *system perspective* is taken with respect to what underscores true public health and social stability.

That aside, below is a list of current life support realities available to the global population that have gone unharnessed due to inhibiting factors inherent to the market economy. Each point will be addressed in its own sub-section.

1) Food Production: Current production methods already produce more than enough food to feed all human beings on earth. Furthermore, current trends toward more optimized technology and agricultural methods also show a capacity to further increase production efficiency and nutrition quality to a state of *active abundance*, with minimal human labor and increasingly less energy, water and land requirements.

2) Clean Water: Desalination and decontamination processes currently exist to such a vast degree of application that no human being, even in the present state of pollution levels, would ever need to be without clean water, regardless of where they are on earth.

3) Energy: Between geothermal, wind, solar, and hydro, coupled with system-based processes that can recapture expelled energy and reuse it directly, there is an absolute energy abundance which can provide for many times the current world's population.

4) Material Production/Access: The spectrum of material production, from buildings to transport to common goods, has experienced a powerful *merging* of capital goods, consumer goods and human labor. With proper *system incorporation* of each genre of production, coupled with *optimized regeneration* processes and a total transformation from the use of property rights to a system of *access rights*, it is clear that all known good functions (in the form of product) can be utilized by 100% of humanity, on a per need basis, in access abundance.

Carrying Capacity
However, before these four issues are addressed in detail, an analysis of the Earth's "carrying capacity" is in order. Carrying capacity is defined as "the maximum, equilibrium number of organisms of a particular species that can be supported indefinitely in a given

environment."[542]

Speculation on the Earth's carrying capacity with respect to human beings, meaning how many people the Earth and its biosphere can support, has been a controversial subject for many centuries. For example, a 2001 United Nations report said that two-thirds of the estimates they noted at that time fell in the range of 4 billion to 16 billion with a median of about 10 billion.[543]

However, technological change, and its capacity to increase efficiency with respect to how our resources are used,[544] presents an ongoing interference in such attempts to arrive at a tangible, empirical figure. The reality is that the number of people the Earth can support is highly variable and based, in part, on the current state of technology at a given time and the more we progress our scientific and technical understanding, the more people we tend to be able to support, with less energy and resources applied per person.

Of course, this isn't to imply that within the closed system of the Earth we have some infinite capacity to reproduce. Rather, it highlights the relevance of what it means to be strategic, intelligent and efficient with our resource use and, by extension, the industrial/economic process itself.

Today, there is no evidence that we are at or are closely approaching the Earth's carrying capacity, if we take into account the trends that reveal our vast potential to "do more with less", coupled with a *value system* that clearly recognizes that we, as a species, occupy a closed Earth system with natural limitations overall and that it is our personal responsibility to ourselves, each other and future generations to keep an interest in balance, efficiency and sustainability.

This *educational* imperative suggests that a conscious, informed global culture can stabilize its reproduction rate if need be, *without* external force, if this basic relationship is properly understood. Of course, much could be said about the influence of old, traditional beliefs, such as religious doctrines that appear to suggest that ongoing and constant procreation is a virtue. These views, which originated in the absence of the knowledge we have today regarding our shared existence on a finite planet, will likely be overcome naturally, with education.[545]

Likewise, if current regions of accelerating population growth

---

542 Carrying capacity defined:
http://dictionary.reference.com/browse/carrying+capacity
543 Source: *World population monitoring 2001*, United Nations
(http://www.un.org/esa/population/publications/wpm/wpm2001.pdf)
544 See essay *Introduction to Sustainable Thought*, section "Ephemeralization"
545 Presently a great fear persists that curtailing or attempting to control the population into more stable reproductive patterns is per se a necessarily violent imposition. Future generations will understand, as a result of access to more information about the planet's carrying capacity, that unchecked "freedom" of reproduction is, in many ways, itself a violent act against the unborn children, and the human race itself, when resource provision and environmental integrity are not factored into the process.

are analyzed, it is found that those existing in deprivation and poverty are reproducing faster than those who are not in poverty. While there is some controversy as to why this pattern prevails, the correlation appears to still be accurate. This evidence suggests that increasing people's standard of living can curtail their rates of reproduction and this furthers the social imperative to create a more equitable system of resource allocation.

(1) Food Production
According to The United Nations Food and Agriculture Organization, one out of every eight people on Earth, (nearly 1 billion people) suffer from chronic undernourishment. Almost all of these people live in developing countries, representing 15 percent of the population of these counties.[546] Poverty is, needless to say, clearly linked to this phenomenon.

Yet, politics and business aside, world agriculture today actually produces 17 percent more calories per person than it did 30 years ago, despite a 70 percent population increase. There is enough food to provide everyone in the world with at least 2,720 kilocalories (kcal) per day, which is more than enough to maintain good health for most.[547] [548] Therefore, the existence of such a large number of chronically hungry people in the developing world today reveals, at a minimum, that there is something fundamentally wrong with the global industrial and economic process itself and not the Earth's carrying capacity, or humanity's ability to process enough resources.

According to the Institution of Mechanical Engineers, "[W]e produce [globally] about four billion metric tonnes of food per annum. Yet due to poor practices in harvesting, storage and transportation, as well as market and consumer wastage, it is estimated that 30–50% (or 1.2–2 billion tonnes) of all food produced *never reaches a human stomach*. Furthermore, this figure does not reflect the fact that large amounts of land, energy, fertilizers and water have also been lost in the production of foodstuffs which simply end up as waste."[549]

In the words of food waste researcher Valentin Thurn, "the number of calories that end up in the garbage in North America and Europe would be sufficient to feed the hungry of this world three times over."[550]

Economically, First World waste patterns can create price

---

546 Source: *Globally almost 870 million chronically undernourished - new hunger report*, FAO
(http://www.fao.org/news/story/en/item/161819/)
547 Source: *Reducing poverty and hunger...*, FAO
(http://www.fao.org/docrep/003/y6265e/y6265e03.htm)
548 Source: *How Many Calories Should I Eat?*, MNT
(http://www.medicalnewstoday.com/articles/245588.php)
549 Source: *Feeding the 9 Billion: The tragedy of waste*, IME,
(http://www.imeche.org/knowledge/themes/environment/global-food)
550 Source: *Author: European food waste adds to world hunger*, dw.de
(http://www.dw.de/author-european-food-waste-adds-to-world-hunger/a-15837215)

increases for the global food supply due to increased demand resulting from those very waste patterns. In other words, the First World *adds* to the world hunger epidemic by its waste patterns on the consumer end because the resulting demand from increased waste increases price values past what is affordable for many.

While there is certainly an educational imperative for the consuming world to consider the relevance of their waste patterns in the current climate, both in terms of real food waste and its effect on global prices due to increased demand because of this waste, it appears that the most effective and practical means to overcome this global deficiency is to "update" the system of food production itself with modern methods. This, coupled with deliberate *localization* of the process itself in order to reduce the vast spectrum of waste caused by inefficiencies in the current *global food supply chain,*[551] would not only reduce such problems in general, it would dramatically increase productivity, product quality and output overall.

While the active use of arable land and land-based agriculture should remain (ideally, of course, with more sustainable practices than we are using today),[552] a great deal of pressure can be alleviated at this time with advanced *soilless* methods, which require less water, less fertilizer, fewer (or no) pesticides, less land, and less labor. These facilities can now be built in urban city environments or even off coastlines, at sea.[553]

Perhaps the most promising of all such arrangements is what is known today as *vertical farming.*[554] Vertical farming has been put to test in a number of regions, with extremely promising results regarding efficiency. Extrapolating these statistics, coupled with parallel trend advancement (increases in efficiency) of the associated mechanisms of this process, reveals that the future of abundant food production will not only (compared to the current land-based tradition) use fewer resources per unit output, cause less waste, have a reduced ecological footprint, increase food quality and the like; it will also use less of the surface of the planet and enable types of food that where once restricted to certain climates or regions to be grown virtually

---

551 Reference: *Food waste within food supply chains: quantification and potential for change to 2050*
(http://www.ncbi.nlm.nih.gov/pmc/articles/PMC2935112/)

552 Topsoil is the top layer of soil that possesses the greatest concentration of organic matter and microorganisms and it is from which plants obtain the overwhelming majority of their nutrients. Today, it is disappearing at an alarming rate primarily due to conventional agricultural practices such as monoculture (the practice of planting one single crop over and over again). Likewise, soil erosion is increasing rapidly with a large number of problematic effects due to inefficient farming practices. Reference: (http://www.ewg.org/losingground/)

553 Ref: http://newearthdaily.com/floating-vertical-farms-could-feed-the-world-with-cheap-plentiful-produce/

554 Dickson Despommier, a professor of environmental health sciences and microbiology at Columbia University, made notable the idea of vertical farming around 1999.

anywhere in enclosed, vertical systems.

While approaches vary, common methods include rotating crop systems in transparent enclosures to use natural light, coupled with hydroponic,[555] aeroponic[556] and/or aquaponic[557] water and nutrient servicing systems. Artificial light systems are also being used, along with other means to distribute natural light, such as the use of parabolic mirror systems that can move light without electricity.[558] Many "waste to energy"[559] systems approaches to these structures are increasingly common, as with advanced power systems based on regenerative processes or localized sources. Between various approaches, the capacity is dramatically increased since food can be grown almost 24 hours a day, seven days a week.

Common objections to this type of farming have mostly been concerns over its energy footprint, criticizing the use of artificial light in some arrangements as too power intensive. However, the use of renewable energy systems, such as photovoltaics, coupled with regional placement most conducive to renewable methods, such as near wave, tidal or geothermal sources, presents plausible solutions for sustainable, non-hydrocarbon based powering.

However, it is best to think about this in a comparative context. In the U.S., up to 20 percent of the country's fossil fuel consumption goes into the food chain, according to the UN's Food and Agricultural Organization (FAO), which points out that fossil fuel use by the food systems in the developed world "often rivals that of automobiles".[560]

In Singapore, a vertical farm system, custom built in a transparent enclosure, uses a closed loop, automated hydraulic system to rotate the crop in circles between sunlight and an organic nutrient treatment, costing only about $3 *a month* in electricity for each enclosure.[561] This system is also reported as *ten times* more productive per square foot than conventional farming, with much less water, labor and fertilizer used, as noted above. There is also no real transport cost

---

555 Defined: "Cultivation of plants in nutrient solution rather than in soil."
(http://www.thefreedictionary.com/hydroponics)
556 Defined: A technique for growing plants without soil or hydroponic media. The plants are held above a system that constantly mists the roots with nutrient-laden water. Also called *aeroculture*.
(http://www.thefreedictionary.com/aeroponic)
557 Defined: Aquaculture is the symbiotic cultivation of plants and aquatic animals in a re-circulating system.
(http://www.growingpower.org/aquaponics.htm)
558 Source: *What is Vertical Farming?*, Jake Cox, 2009,
(http://www.onearth.org/blog/what-is-vertical-farming)
559 Reference: *Waste to Energy*, alternative-energy-news.info
(http://www.alternative-energy-news.info/technology/garbage-energy/)
560 Source: All About: Food and fossil fuels, cnn.com
(http://edition.cnn.com/2008/WORLD/asiapcf/03/16/eco.food.miles/)
561 Source: *Feeding 9 Billion: Vertical Farming – Singapore*
(http://www.offgridworld.com/feeding-9-billion-vertical-farming-singapore-video/)

given all produce is distributed locally, saving more resources and energy.

Overall, there is a spectrum of applications as of now and, in many cases, these preexisting structures, not intended for such work, are being utilized.[562] In Chicago, IL, USA, the worlds largest certified organic vertical farm is in operation. While producing mostly greens for the local Chicago market, this 90,000 square foot facility uses an *aquaponic* system,[563] with waste from tilapia fish providing nutrients for the plants. The farm reportedly saves 90% of its water, compared to conventional farming techniques, and produces no agricultural runoff. Additionally, all of its waste, such as plant roots, stems and even biodegradable packaging, is recycled in collaboration, making it a zero-waste facility.[564]

Current statistics vary with respect to the efficiency, often due to monetary-based limitations and inherent profitability concerns. As with much in the market system, promising technology finds development only if it proves competitive. Given how new these ideas are, we cannot expect to see many examples nor can we expect to see an optimization of such methods to a high degree for measurement without "market acceptance".

However, we can extrapolate the realized potential of existing systems, scaling the application out as if it were incorporated in every major city, in its most relatively efficient form. The following list confirms the superiority of this approach to the current, traditional land based model, not only showing a more sustainable practice, but a more productive practice which can, in concert with existing methods, provide the entire world's population with vegetable based nutrition many times over.[565]

Versatile:
Unlike traditional farming, vertical farms can be constructed anywhere, even on water, using upward layers to multiply output capacity. (i.e. a ten-storey farm will produce 1/10 of a 100-storey farm.) This space

---

562 Source: *'Mega' Indoor Vertical Farm: Chicago Suburb New Home To Nation's Largest Such Facility*
(http://www.huffingtonpost.com/2013/03/28/mega-indoor-vertical-farm_n_2971328.html)

563 Aquaponics is a food production system that combines conventional aquaculture (raising aquatic animals such as snails, fish, crayfish or prawns in tanks), with hydroponics (cultivating plants in water) in a symbiotic environment.

564 Source: *World's largest vertical farm is certified organic*
(http://www.forumforthefuture.org/greenfutures/articles/world%E2%80%99s-largest-vertical-farm-certified-organic)

565 It is worth noting that all major nutritional requirements are technically available in the genre of plant production. Contrary to popular belief, animal products are not required to maintain a high quality human diet. The six major classes of nutrients (carbohydrates, fats, dietary fiber, minerals, proteins, vitamins), omitting water, can all be found in the plant community. (This is not an argument for "vegetarianism", it is just a fact.)

utilization is limited mostly to architectural possibility. Likewise, the plants grown can be "on demand" in many ways, since region based restrictions have been lifted since these farms can grow virtually anything.

Reduced resource use:
Vertical Farming uses substantially less water and pesticide, and is more conducive to non-hydrocarbon based nutrient/fertilizer methods. Its energy use can vary based on application, but in its most efficient setting it uses dramatically less energy both to power the farm itself, and with respect to the now removed need for excess hydrocarbon fertilizer and oil-fueled transport, which is a heavy burden in the current, farm-based process.

More sustainable/less ecological damage:
The current tradition of farming has been recognized as one of the most ecologically destructive processes of modern society. In the words of environmental writer Renee Cho:

"As of 2008, 37.7 percent of global land and 45 percent of U.S. land was used for agriculture. The encroachment of humans into wild land has resulted in the spread of infectious disease, the loss of biodiversity and the disruption of ecosystems. Over-cultivation and poor soil management has led to the degradation of global agricultural lands. The millions of tons of toxic pesticides used each year contaminate surface waters and groundwater, and endanger wildlife.

Agriculture is responsible for 15 percent of global greenhouse gas emissions, and accounts for one-fifth of U.S. fossil fuel use, mainly to run farm equipment, transport food and produce fertilizer. As excess fertilizer washes into rivers, streams and oceans, it can cause eutrophication: algae blooms proliferate; when they die, they are consumed by microbes, which use up all the oxygen in the water; the result is a dead zone that kills all aquatic life. As of 2008, there were 405 dead zones around the world...more than two-thirds of the world's fresh water is used for agriculture."[566]

Post-scarcity capacity:
Students at Columbia University working on vertical farm systems determined that in order to feed 50,000 people, a 30-storey building the size of a "New York City" block would be needed.[567] A New York City block, loosely speaking, is about 6.4 acres.[568] If we extrapolate

---

566 Source: *Vertical Farms: From Vision to Reality*
(http://blogs.ei.columbia.edu/2011/10/13/vertical-farms-from-vision-to-reality/)

567 Source: *Country, the City Version: Farms in the Sky Gain New Interest*
(http://www.nytimes.com/2008/07/15/science/15farm.html?_r=0

568 Generally, in NYC the average length of a north-south block is 1/20th of a mile, or 264 feet. An east-west block is about 1/5th of a mile, or 1,056 feet. So, a square block would be 264 x 1056 = 278,784 square feet, which is equal to 6.4 acres.

this into the context of the city of Los Angeles, CA, USA, with a population of about 3.9 million,[569] with a total acreage of about 318,912,[570] it would take roughly 78 thirty-storey, 6.4 covering land acre structures to feed the local residents. This amounts to about 0.1% of the total land area of Los Angeles to feed the population.[571]

The Earth, being about 29% land, has roughly 36,794,240,000 acres and a human population of 7.2 billion as of late 2013.[572] If we extrapolate the same basis of a 30-storey vertical farm covering 6.4 acres to feed 50,000 people, we end up needing 144,000 vertical farms, in theory, to feed the world.[573] This amounts to 921,600 acres of land to place these farms.[574] Given roughly 38% of all the Earth's land is currently being used for traditional agriculture (13,981,811,200 acres),[575] we find that we need only 0.006% of the Earth's *existing farmland* to meet production requirements.[576]

Now, these extrapolations are clearly theoretical and obviously many other factors need to be taken into account with respect to placement of such farm systems and critical specifics. Also, within the 38% land use statistic, much of that land is for livestock cultivation, not just crop production. However, the raw statistics are quite incredible with respect to possible efficiency and capacity. In fact, if we were to theoretically take only the *crop production land alone* currently being used, which is about 4,408,320,000 acres,[577] replacing the land based cultivation process by placing these 30-storey vertical farm systems only (side by side), the food output would be enough to feed 34,440,000,000,000 people.[578] (34.4 Trillion)

Given that we will *only* need to feed 9 billion by 2050, we only

---

569 Source: *United States Census Bureau*, 2013 (http://www.census.gov/)
570 The city of Los Angeles is 498.3 sq miles that converts to 318,912 acres.
571 78 Buildings occupying 6.4 acres each equals 499.2 acres used total. 499.2 acres is 0.15% of the total acreage of Los Angeles (318,912)
572 Source: worldometers.info (http://www.worldometers.info/world-population/)
573 7.2 billion (total population) divided by 50,000 (production capacity of one 30 story vertical farm) equals 144,000 needed structures.
574 6.4 (acres used per farm) times 144,000 (vertical farms) = 921,600 acres
575 Source: *Farming Claims Almost Half Earth's Land, New Maps Show* (http://news.nationalgeographic.com/news/2005/12/1209_051209_crops_map.html)
576 921,600 (acres of land needed to place vertical farms) is 0.006581% of 13,981,811,200. (Total acres of land on earth used for traditional agriculture, both crop and livestock)
577 Source: *Farming Claims Almost Half Earth's Land, New Maps Show* (http://news.nationalgeographic.com/news/2005/12/1209_051209_crops_map.html)
578 6.4 acres (which is what has been determined as enough space to feed 50,000 people) goes into 4,408,320,000 (total land used currently for only crop cultivation on earth) 688,800,000 times. 688,800,000, which represent the number of possible facilities where each can produce enough food to feed 50,000 people, translate into an output capacity of 34,440,000,000,000 people that can be fed. (688,800,000 x 50,000 = 34,440,000,000,000)

need to harness about 0.02% of this theoretical capacity, which, it could be argued, likely makes rather moot any seemingly practical objections common to the aforementioned extrapolation. As a final note, proteins, which are readily available in the vegetative realm, are still brought into question in the modern day with respect to interest in meat production. From a sustainability standpoint, ignoring the common moral issues and arguably inhumane practices still common to industrialized livestock cultivation, the production of meat is an environmentally unfriendly act today.

According to the ILRI, livestock systems occupy about 45% of the Earth's surface.[579] According to the FAO, livestock sector produces more greenhouse gas emissions than modern gas consuming transport.[580] Given that 90% of all the large fish once thriving in the ocean are gone due to overfishing as well,[581] new solutions are needed.

One such solution is aquaculture, which is the direct farming of fish, crustaceans and the like. This direct approach, if sustainably driven, can provide farm raised, protein rich fish for human consumption, replacing the demand for land-based meat. Another approach is the production of "in vitro meat". In vitro meat may be produced as strips of muscle fibre, which grow through the fusion of precursor cells, either embryonic stem cells or specialized satellite cells found in muscle tissue. This type of meat is usually cultured in a bioreactor.

While still experimental, in 2013 the world's first lab-grown burger was cooked and eaten in London.[582] Other benefits include the reduction of livestock sourced disease which is very common, along with being able to avoid certain negative health characteristics of traditional meat, such as the removal of fatty acids in production.

(2) Clean Water

Given that the human body can only survive a few days without fresh water,[583] making this most basic resource abundantly available to all is critical. Likewise, it is the backbone of many industrial production methods, including agriculture itself. Fresh water is naturally occurring water on the Earth's surface in ice sheets, ice caps, glaciers, icebergs, bogs, ponds, lakes, rivers and streams, and underground as groundwater in aquifers and underground streams. Of all the water on Earth, 97% of it is saline and not directly consumable.

---

579 Source: *Livestock and climate change*
(http://cgspace.cgiar.org/bitstream/handle/10568/10601/IssueBrief3.pdf)
580 Source: *Livestock a major threat to environment*
(http://www.fao.org/newsroom/en/News/2006/1000448/index.html)
581 Source: *Big-Fish Stocks Fall 90 Percent Since 1950, Study Says*
(http://news.nationalgeographic.com/news/2003/05/0515_030515_fishdecli ne.html)
582 Source: *World's first lab-grown burger is eaten in London*
(http://www.bbc.co.uk/news/science-environment-23576143)
583 Freshwater is defined as water that does not contain salt and can be used for human consumption and other processes, such as agriculture.
(http://www.merriam-webster.com/dictionary/freshwater)

According to the World Health Organization: "About 2.6 billion people – half the developing world – lack even a simple 'improved' latrine and 1.1 billion people have no access to any type of improved drinking source of water. As a direct consequence:

• 1.6 million people die every year from diarrhoeal diseases (including cholera) attributable to lack of access to safe drinking water and basic sanitation and 90% of these are children under 5, mostly in developing countries;

• 160 million people are infected with schistosomiasis causing tens of thousands of deaths yearly; 500 million people are at risk of trachoma from which 146 million are threatened by blindness and 6 million are visually impaired;

• Intestinal helminths (ascariasis, trichuriasis and hookworm infection) are plaguing the developing world due to inadequate drinking water, sanitation and hygiene with 133 million suffering from high intensity intestinal helminths infections; there are around 1.5 million cases of clinical hepatitis A every year."[584]

According to the United Nations, by 2025, an estimated 1.8 billion people will live in areas plagued by water scarcity, with two-thirds of the world's population living in water-stressed regions.[585] As with most all of the world's current resource problems, it is an issue of both *poor management* and a lack of *industrial application*. From the standpoint of management, the amount of water wasted in the world due to pollution, overuse and inefficient infrastructure is enormous. About 95% of all water that enters most people's homes goes back down the drain in one shot.[586]

A systems-based solution to optimize this use is to design kitchens and bathrooms so they recapture water for different purposes. For example, the water running through a sink or shower can be made available for a toilet. Various companies have slowly put such ideas to practice recently but overall most infrastructures do nothing of the sort as far as reuse schemes. The same is true of large commercial buildings, which can create reuse networks throughout the whole structure, coupled with capture of rainwater for other purposes, etc.

Water pollution is another problem, which affects both developed and developing nations on many levels. The American Environmental Protection Agency (EPA) estimates that 850 billion gallons of untreated discharges (waste) flow into water bodies

584 Source: *Health through safe drinking water and basic sanitation*
(http://www.who.int/water_sanitation_health/mdg1/en/)
585 Source: *Freshwater Crisis*
(http://environment.nationalgeographic.com/environment/freshwater/fresh water-crisis/)
586 Source: *Water: Use Less-Save More,* Jon Clift & Amanda Cuthbert, 2007

annually, contributing to over 7 million illnesses each year.[587] The Third World Centre for Water Management estimates that only about 10 to 12 percent of wastewater in Latin America is treated properly. Mexico City, for example, "exports" its untreated wastewater to local farmers.

While the farmers value this because the water increases crop yields, the wastewater is heavily contaminated with pathogens and toxic chemicals, representing a serious health risk for both farmers and consumers of the agricultural products grown in this area. In India, major cities discharge untreated wastewater into the bodies of water that serve as their drinking water. Delhi, for example, discharges wastewater directly into the Yamuna River—the source of drinking water for some 57 million people.[588]

Solutions to this problem, in part, must address the issue of the vast inefficiency, likely driven by the monetary limitations of most governments, to institute proper waste systems, coupled with an industrial design imperative to include reuse system techniques to better preserve and utilize our existing resources.

That aside, the most notable, broad solution to compensate for these emerging problems, to facilitate not only an alleviation of the current water problems affecting over 2 billion people but also to transcend into a condition of relative abundance of fresh water for all humans, is to utilize modern (a) *purification* and (b) *desalination* systems both on the macro-industrial and micro-industrial scale.

(a) Purification:

Advancements in water purification have been accelerating rapidly with many technological variations of approach. Perhaps one of the most efficient today is what is called "ultraviolet (UV) disinfection". This process is highly scalable, low energy and works quickly.

According to engineer Ashok Gadgil, inventor of portable UV systems, "In terms of energy use, 60 watts of electrical power – which is comparable to the power used in one ordinary table lamp – is enough to disinfect water at the rate of one ton per hour, or fifteen liters per minute...This much water is enough to meet the drinking water needs of a community of 2,000 people."[589] This device Gadgil developed for rural, poor areas can run off of solar panels and weighs only 15 pounds and has no toxic discharge.

Of course, there is no silver bullet. While UV disinfection works very well for bacteria and viruses, it is less effective with other types of pollution such as suspended solids, turbidity, color, or soluble

587 Source: *Compliance and Enforcement National Priority: Clean Water Act, Wet Weather, Combined Sewer Overflows* (http://www.epa.gov/compliance/resources/publications/data/planning/prior ities/fy2008prioritycwacso.pdf)

588 Source: *Water Quality: An Ignored Global Crisis* (http://www.businessweek.com/articles/2013-03-21/water-quality-an-ignored-global-crisis)

589 Source: *Ashok Gadgil on safe drinking water* (http://www.renegademedia.info/books/ashok-gadgil.html)

organic matter.[590] In large-scale applications, UV is often combined with more standard treatments, such as chlorine, as is the case with the world's largest UV drinking water disinfection plant in New York, which can treat 2.2 billion US gallons (8,300,000 cubic meters) per day.[591] That is 3,029,500,000 cubic meters a year.

The average person in the United States uses 2842 cubic meters a year.[592] This includes fresh water used for industrial purposes, not just for direct (drinking) consumption. The global average is 1385 cubic meters per year.[593] China, India and the United States are currently the largest freshwater users in the world and the majority of that water is used in production, mainly agriculture.[594] In fact, about 70% of all freshwater is used for agriculture globally.[595]

For the sake of pure statistical argument, ignoring the highly needed revisions towards strategic water use, reuse systems and conservation possibilities through more advanced and efficient industrial applications, let us assess the simple question of what it would require to disinfect (assuming it was needed) *all the fresh water* currently being used in the world on average by the population, in all contexts. Given the global average of 1385 cubic meters and a population of 7.2 billion, we arrive at a total annual use of 9.972 trillion cubic meters.

Using the New York UV plant's output capacity of roughly 3 billion cubic meters a year as a base per installation of such a plant, we find that 3,327 plants would be needed globally.[596] The New York plant is about 3.7 acres (160k sq. ft.).[597] This means about 12,309 acres of land is needed, in theory, to facilitate a purification process of all the fresh water currently used globally by the population. Of course, needless to say, there many other "footprint" factors that come into play, such as power needs, coupled with the critical importance of location.

However, let's put this into a larger, more thoughtful comparison. The United States military alone, with its roughly 845,441 military buildings and bases, occupies about *30 million acres* of land globally.[598] Only 0.04% of that land would be needed to disinfect the

---

590 Source: *Ultraviolet Disinfection*
(http://www.nesc.wvu.edu/pdf/dw/publications/ontap/2009_tb/ultraviolet_d wfsom53.pdf)
591 Source: *Multi-barrier Disinfection Strategy - New York City (Case Study)*
(http://www.trojanuv.com/uvresources?resource=403)
592 Source: waterfootprint.org (http://www.waterfootprint.org/?
page=cal/waterfootprintcalculator_national)
593 Source: Ibid.
594 Source: *Which Nations Consume the Most Water?*
(http://www.scientificamerican.com/article.cfm?id=water-in-water-out)
595 Source: worldometers.info (http://www.worldometers.info/water/)
596 9 trillion 972 billion divided by 3 billion
597 Source: *Catskill-Delaware Water Ultraviolet Disinfection Facility*
(http://en.wikipedia.org/wiki/Catskill-
Delaware_Water_Ultraviolet_Disinfection_Facility#cite_note-nyc_pr-1)
598 Source: *The Worldwide Network of US Military Bases*

total fresh water use of the entire world, if it were even needed at scale, which it is not.

(b) Desalination

The realistic possibility of mass, global purification of polluted fresh water aside, likely the most powerful means to assure usable, potable water is to convert directly from a saline source, namely the ocean. With a planet comprised of mostly salt water, this technique, if done properly, assures global abundance alone.

The most common method of desalination used today is *reverse osmosis*, a process that removes water molecules from salt water, leaving salt ions in a leftover brine waste by-product. According to the International Desalination Association: "Currently, reverse osmosis (RO)...accounts for nearly 60 percent of installed capacity, followed by the thermal processes multi-stage flash (MSF) at 26 percent and multi-effect distillation (MED) at 8.2 percent."[599] As of 2011, there were roughly 16,000 desalination plants worldwide, and the total global capacity of all plants online (e.g., in operation) was 66.5 million cubic meters per day, or approximately 17.6 billion US gallons per day.[600]

As with everything technological, many advancing methods currently considered "experimental" suggest a powerful increase in efficiency as the trends unfold. One such method called *capacitive desalination* (CD), also known as capacitive deionization (CDI), has been shown to operate with greater energy efficiency, lower pressures, no membrane components and it does not produce a waste discharge like conventional practices. It can also be easily scaled-up simply by increasing the number of flow electrodes in the system.[601]

Overall, if we examine the existing methods in general, coupled with emerging methods, we see a general trend of increasing efficiency in both power conservation and performance.[602] That briefly noted, the focus of this extrapolation towards a "post-scarcity" utilization of desalination will consider only current, proven, in-use methods, namely the reverse osmosis system.

The Wonthaggi Desalination Plant is an advanced reversed osmosis seawater desalination plant on the Bass Coast near Wonthaggi, in southern Victoria, Australia. It was completed in December 2012. It can produce, conservatively, about 410,000 cubic

(http://www.globalresearch.ca/the-worldwide-network-of-us-military-bases/5564)

599 Source: *Desalination Overview* (http://www.idadesal.org/desalination-101/desalination-overview/)

600 Source: Ibid.

601 Source: *Flow electrodes may enable large-scale sea water desalination* (http://www.rsc.org/chemistryworld/2013/03/sea-water-desalination-capacitive-deionisation)

602 Source: *Advancements in Desalination* (http://www.weat.org/sanantonio/files/06%20-%20Summer%20Seminar%202013%20-%20Jim%20Lozier%20-%20Adv%20in%20Desal.pdf)

meters of desalinated water a day (150 million cubic meters a year),[603] while occupying about 20 hectares (about 50 acres of land).[604] Since, as noted before, the total, annual water use of the world today is about 9 trillion, 972 billion cubic meters, this means that it would take 60,000 plants[605] to process all potable water usage. Once again, this extreme extrapolation is to make a relative point, since we do not need to desalinate that much water in reality.

However, assuming that we did need to desalinate seawater constantly to match current global use, 3 million acres of land would be needed total. Earth has about 217,490[606] miles of coastline which means, loosely using the Wonthaggi model of roughly 20 hectares (roughly 50 acres) with 100 meters per hectare (or 328 feet), assuming the construction was four hectares deep and five hectares long, parallel to the coastline, the plant would take up 1640 feet along the coast. This means, assuming 60,000 plants of the same dimension, it would take up 98,400,000 feet or 18,636 miles of coastline (8.5% of the world's coastline).

Of course, that is a great deal of coastline and naturally many other factors come into play when choosing an appropriate location for such a plant. Again, it is not the purpose of this extrapolation to suggest these statistics are of any other use than to gauge a broad sense of what such capacity means, in light of the water scarcity/stress issues occurring today. Yet, the fact is, it is clearly *within the range* of such application to meet the needs of people suffering from water scarcity via desalination alone, coupled with an infrastructure and distribution system to move water inland.

As a final example, let's reduce this abstract extrapolation more so and apply it to a real life circumstance. On the continent of Africa, for example, which has about 1 billion people as of 2013,[607] roughly 345 million people lack sufficient access to potable water.[608] If we apply the noted global average consumption rate of 1385 cubic meters a year, seeking to provide each of those 345 million people that amount, we would need 477,825,000,000 cubic meters produced annually.

Using the Wonthaggi annual capacity of 150 million cubic meters produced as the base figure, Africa would need 3185 50-acre plants along its coast line to meet such demand, taking up about (25,158 miles of coastline in Africa) 5,223,400 feet or 989 miles. This

---

603 Source: *Victorian Desalination Plant*
    (http://en.wikipedia.org/wiki/Wonthaggi_desalination_plant)
604 Source: *Wonthaggi Desalination Plant*
    (http://www.onlymelbourne.com.au/melbourne_details.php?
    id=31996#.UljSCWRDp94)
605 9 trillion, 972 million divided by 150 million
606 Source: *The Coastline Paradox*
    (http://grokearth.blogspot.com/2012/04/coastline-paradox.html)
607 Source: *World population* (http://en.wikipedia.org/wiki/World_population)
608 Source: water.org (http://water.org/water-crisis/water-facts/water/)

takes up only 3.9% of Africa's coastline.[609]

However, if we divided this number in half, and used UV purification systems for one section and desalinization for the other, the desalinization process would need about 1.9%, or 494 miles of coastline for desalination facilities and only about 296 acres of land for purification facilities, which is a minuscule faction of Africa total landmass (of about 7 billion acres). This is highly doable and obviously, in this case and in all cases, we would strategically maximize purification processes since it is more efficient, while using desalination for the remaining demand.

Such crude statistics reveal that between UV and traditional decontamination, coupled with traditional desalination processes, as they currently exist, even ignoring the rapid advancements occurring in both fields[610] which will likely have an exponentially advanced level of efficiency in the coming decades, the idea of enduring water scarcity on planet Earth is absurd. Both of these isolated extrapolations have assumed only one or the other was applied, in only large scale form, assuming there are no other existing sources of potable water.

In reality, given the existing level of freshwater still available, coupled with a simple, intelligent re-ordering of use-reuse water network schemes to further preserve the existing capacity, coupled with both large and small scale desalination *and* decontamination processes as regions require (many of which can be powered by rapidly advancing renewable energy processes as well), we have the technical capacity to bring potable water availability to absolute global abundance.

(3) Energy

Renewable energy sources are sources that are continually replenished. Such sources include energy from water, wind, solar and geothermal. In contrast, fuels such as coal, oil, and natural gas are non-renewable as they are based on Earth stores which show no near-term regeneration.

As of the early 21st century, the recognition of clean, renewable energy possibilities has been substantial.[611] The spectrum of application, scalability and degree of efficiency, coupled with advancing methods for energy storage and transfer, have arguably made our current, mostly hydrocarbon-based energy methods appear outdated, especially given the ongoing negative consequences of their use. Nuclear energy, while effective and considered a "renewable" form by

609 It is also worth noting that floating, off shore plants are also technically possible. (http://www.bmtdesigntechnology.com.au/design-solutions/floating-desalination-plant/)
610 An advanced technology called the "Slingshot", invented by Dean Kamen, is a small-scale water purification system that can produce clean water from almost any source, including seawater, by means of vapor compression distillation. It requires no filters, and can even operate using cow dung as fuel.
611 Source: Types of Renewable Energy (http://www.renewableenergyworld.com/rea/tech/home)

some, works at very high risk given the unstable materials involved and the large scale accidents on record have brought the safety of this form of production into question as well.[612]

In the world today, the five most commonly used renewable sources are hydropower (via dams), solar, wind, geothermal and biofuels. Renewable energy sources currently represent about 15% of global energy use, with hydro-power accounting for 97% of this figure.[613]

Given that over 1.2 billion people are without access to electricity worldwide,[614] coupled with the ongoing pollution and periodic crises associated with traditional, non-renewable methods, the purpose of this subsection is to show how the dangerous realities associated with fossil fuels and nuclear energy are no longer needed. We can now power the world many times over with clean, renewable, relatively low impact methods, largely localized as per the needs of a single structure, city or industrial application.

However, it is important to point out upfront that there is *no single* solution at this time. Given that different areas of the Earth have different propensities for renewable energy harnessing and use, application must be seen as a *system* or network development of a combination of mediums. That noted, narrowing down the most relevant of these abundance producing possibilities, it is perhaps best to think of renewable energy extraction/harnessing and use in two categories: (a) Large scale/Base-load & (b) Small Scale & Total Mixed-Use systems.

(a) Large Scale/Base-load:

Large-scale generation, such as for "base-load" needs required to power a city or high energy industrial center, includes four main mediums: (a1) geothermal plants, (a2) wind farms, (a3) solar fields, and (a4) water (ocean/hydropower).

(a1) Geothermal:

Geothermal power[615] is energy harnessed essentially from the natural heat of the Earth's molten core, with plants usually placed around areas where the distance to large heat centers is fairly shallow.[616] [617] A

---

612 Source: *Fukushima nuke pollution in sea 'was world's worst'*
    (http://phys.org/news/2011-10-fukushima-nuke-pollution-sea-world.html)
613 Source: *Renewable Energy*
    (http://www.energyzone.net/aboutenergy/renewable_energy.asp)
614 Source: *Energy – The Facts*
    (http://web.worldbank.org/WBSITE/EXTERNAL/TOPICS/EXTENERGY2/0,,con
    tentMDK:22855502~pagePK:210058~piPK:210062~theSitePK:4114200,00.
    html)
615 Geothermal power in this context isn't to be confused with small scale, geothermal heating/cooling processes that utilizes heat from a few feet below the surface. (i.e. geothermal heat pumps)
616 Source: *Geothermal Energy Facts*
    (http://geothermal.marin.org/pwrheat.html#Q1)
617 Source: *Back to Basics Video: What Is Geothermal Energy Anyway?*

2006 MIT report on geothermal energy, promoting an advanced extraction system called EGS, found that 13,000 zettajoules of power are currently available in the Earth, with the possibility of 2000 zettajoules being harvestable with improved technology.[618]

The total energy consumption of all the countries on the planet is about half a zettajoule (0.55) a year[619] and this means thousands of years of planetary power could be harnessed in this medium alone. The MIT report also estimated that there was enough energy in hard rocks 10km below the US alone to supply *all the world's* current needs for 30,000 years.

Even with an expected 56% increase of consumption by 2040, geothermal's capacity is enormous if property tapped.[620] [621] Likewise, the extraction of heat taking place from within the Earth appears quite minor in comparison to its store, making the source *virtually limitless* in proportion to actual human consumption.[622] Also, since the energy is produced constantly, there are no intermittency problems and this type of energy can be produced constantly without the need for storage.

The environmental impact of geothermal is relatively very low. Iceland has been using it almost exclusively for some time and their plants produce extremely low emissions (no carbon) when compared to hydrocarbon-based methods.[623] Apart from some sulphur produced, small earthquakes can occur as a result of drilling techniques. This problem has been acknowledged as human induced[624] and improvement in the engineering process is the solution, coupled with clear understanding of the nature of the location for drilling.

As far as location, it is theoretically possible to place geothermal energy extraction plants anywhere, if the capacity to drill deep enough was there, coupled with other advancements in technology.[625] However, today most plants need to exist near where

---

(http://www.renewableenergyworld.com/rea/video/view/back-to-basics-video-what-is-geothermal-energy-anyway)

618 Source: *Future of Geothermal* Energy
(http://geothermal.inel.gov/publications/future_of_geothermal_energy.pdf)

619 *Source: EIA projects world energy consumption will increase 56% by 2040*
(http://www.eia.gov/todayinenergy/detail.cfm?id=12251)

620 Source: Ibid.

621 Source: *Geothermal Energy Could Provide All the Energy the World Will Ever Need*
(http://www.renewableenergyworld.com/rea/news/article/2010/09/geothermal-energy-is-the-solution-for-the-future)

622 Source: *Geothermal FAQs*
(http://www1.eere.energy.gov/geothermal/faqs.html)

623 Source: *Geothermal energy emissions of little concern*
(http://thinkgeoenergy.com/archives/1733)

624 Source: *How Does Geothermal Drilling Trigger Earthquakes?*
(http://www.scientificamerican.com/article.cfm?id=geothermal-drilling-earthquakes&page=2)

625 Source: *First Google.Org-funded geothermal mapping reportconfirms vast coast-to-coast clean energy source*
(http://www.smu.edu/News/2011/geothermal-24oct2011)

tectonic plates[626] meet on Earth. A geothermal map of the surface of the Earth taken by satellite can show such ideal spots very clearly based on heat emitted.[627] These maps show possibilities near most coastlines around the world[628] and while most studies are ambiguous with respect to exactly how many locations could be made available, the potential recognized, in general, is enormous.

The U.S. Department of Energy has noted that geothermal energy also uses much less land than other energy sources, including fossil fuel and currently dominant renewables. Over 30 years, the period of time commonly used to compare the life cycle impacts from different power sources, a geothermal facility uses 404 meters squared of land per gigawatt hour, while a coal facility uses 3,632 meters squared per gigawatt hour.[629] If we were to do a basic comparison of geothermal to coal given this ratio of meters squared to gigawatt hour, we find that we could fit about nine geothermal plants in the space of one coal plant.[630] [631]

Likewise, it is important to note that new, more efficient methods to tap geothermal appear to be just starting with respect to possible output potential. In 2013 it was announced that a 1000 MW power station was to begin construction in Ethiopia.[632] A megawatt is a unit of *power,* and power capacity is expressed differently from *energy* capacity, which is expressed, in this context of megawatts, as *megawatt hours* (MWh). Put another way, *energy* is the amount of work done, whereas *power* is the rate of doing work. So, for example, a generator with one MW capacity that operates at that capacity consistently for one hour will produce 1 MW-hour (MWh) of electricity.

This means if a 1000 MW geothermal power-station operated at full capacity 24 hours a day, seven days a year (365 days), it would

---

626 Source: *Plate* Tectonics
  (http://science.nationalgeographic.com/science/earth/the-dynamic-earth/plate-tectonics-article/)
627 Source: *First Google.Org-funded geothermal mapping reportconfirms vast coast-to-coast clean energy source*
  (http://www.smu.edu/News/2011/geothermal-24oct2011)
628 Source: geni.org (http://www.geni.org/globalenergy/library/renewable-energy-resources/geothermal.shtml)
629 Source: geo-energy.org (http://geo-energy.org/geo_basics_environment.aspx)
630 3626 m2 / 404 m2 = 8.975 square meters
631 It is worth noting that geothermal, and, in fact, all other renewables addressed in this text, inherently combine the extraction or harnessing location *with* the processing and power distribution location. All hydrocarbon sources, on the other hand, require both extraction (i.e. coal) and processing/power production facilities (i.e. refineries/power plants), almost always in separate locations. As per the current example, the mining land required for coal extraction is omitted from the equation. In short, renewables take up substantially less land and have a exceptionally lower environmental impact in this regard.
632 Source: *The Carbon Capture Report*
  (http://www.dailyethiopia.com/index.php?aid=1498)

produce 8,760,000 MWh/year.[633] The world's current annual usage in MWh is about 153 Billion,[634] which means it would take, in abstraction, 17,465 geothermal plants to match global use.[635]

According to the World Coal Association, there are over 2,300 coal power plants in operation worldwide.[636] Using the aforementioned plant size/capacity comparison of about nine geothermal plants fitting into one coal plant, the space of 1,940[637] (or 84% of the total in existence) coal plants would be needed, in theory, to contain the 17,465 geothermal plants. Also, given coal today accounts for only 41% of the world's current energy production,[638] this theoretical extrapolation also shows how in 84% of the current space usage by coal plants alone (which only produce 41%), geothermal *could* supply 100% power capacity as per global use instead.

All this without the pollution from coal, which has been considered one of the most polluting practices in the world along with being likely the largest contributor to the human-made increase of CO_2 in the atmosphere.

(a2) Wind Farms

U.S. Department of Energy studies have concluded that wind harvesting in the Great Plains states of Texas, Kansas, and North Dakota could provide enough electricity to power the entire USA.[639] More impressively, a 2005 Stanford University study published in the Journal of Geophysical Research found that if only 20% of the wind potential on the planet was harnessed, it would cover the entire world's energy needs.[640]

In corroboration, two more recent studies by unrelated organizations published in 2012 calculated that with existing wind turbine technology the earth could produce hundreds of trillions of watts of power. This, in effect, is many more times what the world currently consumes.[641] Wind power is perhaps one of the most simple and low impact forms of renewable energy and its scalability is limited only to location.

Using the 9,000-acre Alta Wind Energy Center California as a basis, which has an active capacity of 1,320 MW of power, a theoretical

---

633 8760 (hrs in a year) x 1000 (MWh) = 8,760,000 Mwh/year.

634 0.55 zettajoules coverts to about 153 billion MWh

635 153 billion MWh (total global use) / 8,760,000 MWh (geothermal plant capacity) = 17,465 geothermal plants.

636 Source: worldcoal.org (http://www.worldcoal.org/resources/frequently-asked-questions/)

637 17,465 / 9 = 1940.5

638 Source: worldcoal.org (http://www.worldcoal.org/coal/uses-of-coal/coal-electricity/)

639 Source: "U.S. National Renewable Energy Laboratory". February 6th 2007

640 Source: *Evaluation of global wind power* (http://www.stanford.edu/group/efmh/winds/global_winds.html)

641 Source: *The Earth Has Enough Wind Energy Potential To Power All Of Civilization* (http://www.businessinsider.com/the-earth-has-enough-wind-energy-potential-to-power-all-of-civilization-2012-9)

annual output of 11,563,200 MWh is possible.[642] This means 13,231 9000-acre wind farms would be needed to meet the current output figure of 153 billion MWh. This means 119,079,000 acres of (wind sufficient) land would be required.[643] This amounts to 0.3% of the Earth's surface that would be needed to power the world, in abstraction.[644] Once again, this is not to suggest such a thing is ideal given what land is feasible for wind farms, along with other important factors. This is simply to give a general perspective of possibility.

However, one unique reality of wind power generation is the potential of *offshore* harnessing. Compared to land-based wind power, offshore wind power has, on average, a much larger yield, as wind speeds tend to be higher. This reality also alleviates land-based pressures given land scarcity and regional restrictions.

According to the *Assessment of Offshore Wind Energy Resources for the United States*, 4,150 gigawatts (4,150,000 MW) of potential wind turbine capacity from offshore wind resources are available in the United States.[645] Assuming this power capacity was consistent for a year, we end up with an energy conversion of 36,354,000,000 MWh/yr. Given the United States, in 2010, used 25,776 TWh of energy (25.78 billion MWh),[646] we find that offshore wind harvesting *alone* exceeds national use by about 10.6 billion MWhs, or 41%.

Intuitively, extrapolating this national level of capacity to the rest of the world's coastlines, also taking into account the aforementioned land-based only statistic research that found we can power the world many times over onshore as well,[647] the possibilities of wind-based energy abundance is exceptionally impressive.

(a3) Solar Fields
The upper atmosphere of Earth receives about 1.5 × 1021 watt-hours of solar radiation annually. This vast amount of energy is more than 23,000 times that used by the human population of the planet.[648] If humanity could capture one tenth of one percent of the solar energy striking the Earth we would have access to six times as much energy as we consume in all forms today, with almost no greenhouse gas emissions. The ability to harness this power depends on the technology and how high the percentage of radiation absorption is.

---

642 8760 (hrs in a year) x 1320 (MW) = 11,563,200 MWh/year.

643 13,231 x 9000 acres = 119,079,000

644 119,079,000 acres is 0.32% of 36,794,240,000 acres (total land on Earth)

645 Source: *Assessment of Offshore Wind Energy Resources for the United States* (http://www.nrel.gov/docs/fy10osti/45889.pdf)

646 Source: *Energy in the United States* (http://en.wikipedia.org/wiki/Energy_in_the_United_States#cite_note-IEA2012-13)

647 Source: *The Earth Has Enough Wind Energy Potential To Power All Of Civilization* (http://www.businessinsider.com/the-earth-has-enough-wind-energy-potential-to-power-all-of-civilization-2012-9)

648 Source: thefreedictionary.com (http://encyclopedia2.thefreedictionary.com/solar+energy)

Conventional photovoltaics, currently the most common form used mostly for smaller applications, use silicon as the semiconductor and exist in something of a flat cell or sheet. Concentrated photovoltaics (CPV) are generally more efficient than non-concentrated on average; however they tend to require more direct exposure to focus the light properly.

Concentrated solar power (CPS) is a large-scale approach that uses mirrors or lenses to concentrate a large area of sunlight, or solar thermal energy, onto a small area. Electrical power is produced when the concentrated light is converted to heat, which drives a heat engine (such as a steam turbine) connected to an electrical power generator or the like. Unlike photovoltaics, which convert directly to electricity, this technology converts to heat. Recently, large-scale storage methods have also been used to prolong access at night.

A variation of CPS is STE, or Solar Thermal Energy. The Ivanpah Solar Electric Generating System in California, USA is a 3500 acre field[649] with a stated annual generation of 1,079,232 MWh.[650] While Ivanpah does not use any form of storage, it serves about 140,000 homes in the region. If we were to extrapolate using Ivanpah as a basis, it would take 141,767 fields or 496,184,500 acres to theoretically meet current global energy use based on output. This is 1.43% of total land on Earth.[651]

Once again, this is not to suggest such a thing is practical nor is it to ignore the radiation yield differences found on different areas of the Earth. However, deserts, which tend to be highly conducive for solar fields while often less conducive to life support for people, are roughly 1/3 of all the land mass in the world or about 12 billion acres. Compared to the roughly 500 million acres theoretically needed to "power the world" as per our extrapolation, only 4.1% of the world's desert land would be needed.[652]

Likewise, other projects similar to the Ivanpah field have been incorporating storage systems. The Solana 280MW solar power plant in Arizona combines parabolic trough mirror technology with molten salt thermal storage and is able to continue outputting up to six hours after the sky goes dark.[653]

In general, the rate of advancement of photovoltaic, solar

---

649 Source: World's biggest solar thermal power plant fires up for first time (http://reneweconomy.com.au/2013/worlds-biggest-solar-thermal-power-plant-fires-first-time-89135)

650 Source: Ivanpah Solar Electric Generating System (http://www.nrel.gov/csp/solarpaces/project_detail.cfm?projectID=62)

651 153 billion MWh / 1,079,232MWh = 141,767 plants @ 3,500 acres = 496,184,500 acres. 496,184,500 acres is 1.43 % of 36,794,240,000 (total land)

652 Reference: Is Anything Stopping a Truly Massive Build-Out of Desert Solar Power? (http://www.scientificamerican.com/article.cfm?id=challenges-for-desert-solar-power)

653 Source: Solar Plant Generates Power For Six Hours After Sunset (http://www.kcet.org/news/rewire/solar/concentrating-solar/solar-plant-generates-power-for-six-hours-after-sunset.html)

thermal, storage methods and other existing and emerging technologies continue to rapidly advance, revealing that many installations seen as highly efficient today will be grossly inefficient in a decade or two. As will be addressed more so with respect to *smaller scale* renewable energy solutions, the use of solar power localized in the very construction of buildings and domiciles is likely to be where true future efficiency will take place. The issue is making the technology compact and efficient enough for localized, per case use.

However, solar field power stations, just like geothermal and wind, have an enormous global potential in and of themselves and there is little doubt that given proper resources and attention, these fields alone could theoretically establish an infrastructure and efficiency level to power the world alone.

(a4) Water/Hydro Energy

Water-based renewable energy extraction could generally be said to have two broad sources: the *ocean* itself and river-type water flows which use the gravitational force of falling or flowing water, usually in an inland watercourse. The latter is generally referred to in practice as *hydroelectric* and, as noted before, it is currently a fairly large part of the existing renewable energy infrastructure.[654]

On the other hand, the vast potential of the *ocean* has yet to be harnessed within a fraction of its capacity. It is not far-fetched to suggest that the intelligent harvesting of both the various mechanical movements of ocean water coupled with exploiting the differences in heat, known as *ocean thermal energy conversion* (OTEC), that ocean water power couldn't also power the world alone.[655] [656] [657] Given the existing, fairly large-scale use of hydroelectric power (dams) already, this section will instead focus on the ocean potentials.

The most pronounced sea-based potentials at this time appear to be *wave, tidal, ocean current, ocean thermal and osmotic*. Waves are primarily caused by winds; tides are primarily caused by the gravitational pull of the moon; ocean currents are primarily caused by the rotation of the Earth; ocean thermal results from solar heat absorbed by the surface of the ocean; and osmotic power is when fresh water and salt water meet, exploiting the difference in salt concentration.

---

654 Source: *Use and Capacity of Global Hydropower Increases*
   (http://www.worldwatch.org/node/9527)
655 Source: *Ocean currents can power the world, say scientists*
   (http://www.telegraph.co.uk/earth/energy/renewableenergy/3535012/Ocean-currents-can-power-the-world-say-scientists.html)
656 According to Michael Bernitsas, a professor at the University of Michigan Department of Naval Architecture and Marine Engineering: "...if we could harness 0.1 percent of the energy in the ocean, we could support the energy needs of 15 billion people."
   [http://michigantoday.umich.edu/2009/01/story.php?id=7334#.UmB1B2RDp94]
657 Source: *Our Current Technologies*
   (http://voith.com/en/Voith_Ocean_Current_Technologies(1).pdf)

Wave:

It has been found that wave power's *usable* global potential is about 3 TW[658] or about 26,280 TWh/yr assuming constant harnessing. This is almost 20% of current global use. This amount of power has been ascertained essentially by analyzing deep-water regions off continent coastlines. The theoretical power estimate has been estimated at 3.7 TW, with the final net estimate reduced by about 20% to compensate for various inefficiencies related to a given region, such as ice coverage. Energy output is basically determined by wave height, wave speed, wavelength, and water density.

Wave farms, or the construction of wave harnessing plants off a coastline, have seen limited large-scale application at this time, with only about six countries sparsely applying the technology.[659] Locations with the most potential include the western seaboard of Europe, the northern coast of the UK, and the Pacific coastlines of North and South America, Southern Africa, Australia, and New Zealand.

Tidal:

Tidal has two sub-forms: range and stream. Tidal range is essentially the "rise and fall" of areas of the ocean. Tidal streams are currents created by periodic horizontal movement of the tides, often magnified by the shape of the seabed.

Different locations of Earth have large differences in range.[660] In the United Kingdom, an area with high levels of tidal activity, dozens of sites are currently noted as available, forecasting that 34% of all the UK's energy could come from tidal power alone.[661] Globally, older studies have put tidal capacity at 1800TWh/yr.[662] More recent studies have put the theoretical capacity (both range and stream) at 3TW, assuming only a portion would be extractable.[663]

Tidal, while very predictable, is also subject to daily periods of intermittency based around tidal shifts. Assuming only 1.5 TW could be harnessed in a year based on advanced technology, this means about 7% of the world's power could come from tidal.

Ocean Current:

Similar to tidal streams, ocean currents have shown great potential. These currents flow consistently in the open ocean and various emerging technologies have been developing to harness this largely

---

658 Source: *Assessing the Global Wave Energy Potential* (http://www.oceanor.no/related/59149/paper_OMAW_2010_20473_final.pdf)

659 Source: *Wave farm* (http://en.wikipedia.org/wiki/Wave_farm)

660 Source: *Tidal Energy* (http://ei.lehigh.edu/learners/energy/tidal2.html)

661 Source: lunarenergy.co.uk (http://www.lunarenergy.co.uk/factsFigures.htm)

662 Source: Ocean Energy: Prospects & Potential, Isaacs & Schmitt, with 15% utilization factor & 50% capacity factor. [http://www.crpm.org/pub/agenda/1384_nathalie_rousseau.pdf]

663 *Renewable Energy Sources and Climate Change Mitigation*, Ottmar Edenhofer, 2012, pp505-506

untapped medium.

As with all renewables, the capacity to harness such potential is directly related to the efficiency of the technology employed. The EOEA estimates the current potential at 400 THW/yr.[664] However, there is good reason to assume this figure is outdated. Prior applications of turbine/mill technologies to capture such water flows have needed an average current of five or six knots to operate efficiently, while most of the Earth's currents are slower than three knots.[665] However, recent developments have revealed the possibility to harness energy from water flows of less than two knots.[666] Given this potential, it has been suggested that *ocean current alone* could power the entire world.[667]

The Gulf Stream[668] potential has been estimated at 13GW of actual output, assuming a 30% conversion efficiency using more traditional turbine technology.[669] This means 13,000 MW or, assuming constant harnessing of the stream all year, about 113,880,000 Mwh/yr.[670] The United States, in 2011, is estimated to have used 4.1 billion MWh in electricity.[671] This means 30%[672] of the US's electrical consumption could be generated by the Gulf Stream alone. Once again, this is assuming the use of only established technology.

Osmotic:
Osmotic power or salinity gradient power is the energy available from the difference in the salt concentration between seawater and river water. The Norwegian Center for Renewable Energy (SFFE) estimates the global potential to be about 1,370 TWh/yr.[673] with others putting it at around 1,700 TWh/yr[674] or the equivalent of half of Europe's entire

---

664 Source: *Ocean Energy: Position Paper for IPCC*
(http://ec.europa.eu/research/energy/pdf/gp/gp_events/wrec/wrec_2008_o cean-hydro_alla_weinstein_en.pdf)

665 Source: *Ocean currents can power the world, say scientists*
(http://www.telegraph.co.uk/earth/energy/renewableenergy/3535012/Ocea n-currents-can-power-the-world-say-scientists.html)

666 Source: *'Fish Technology' Draws Renewable Energy From Slow Water Currents* (http://michigantoday.umich.edu/2009/01/story.php? id=7334#.UmB1B2RDp94)

667 Source: *Ocean currents can power the world, say scientists*
(http://www.telegraph.co.uk/earth/energy/renewableenergy/3535012/Ocea n-currents-can-power-the-world-say-scientists.html)

668 Source: *Gulf Stream* (http://en.wikipedia.org/wiki/Gulf_Stream)

669 Source: *Theoretical Assessment of Ocean Current Energy Potential for the Gulf Stream System*
(http://www.researchgate.net/publication/256495742_Theoretical_Assessm ent_of_Ocean_Current_Energy_Potential_for_the_Gulf_Stream_System)

670 8760 (hrs a year) x 13000 MW = 113 million 880 thousands MWhs/yr

671 Source: *Energy in the United States*
(http://en.wikipedia.org/wiki/Energy_in_the_United_States#Consumption)

672 4.1 billion / 133.880 million

673 Source: *Osmotic Power* (http://www.sffe.no/?p=2446)

674 Source: *First osmosis power plant goes on stream in Norway*
(http://www.newscientist.com/article/dn18204-first-osmosis-power-plant-goes-on-stream-in-norway.html#.UmCJ-WRDp94)

energy demand.[675]

While still largely in its infancy, osmotic power harnessing through advancing technology is promising. Power plants can, in principle, be built anywhere freshwater meets seawater. They can generate power 24/7, regardless of weather conditions.

Ocean Thermal:
The final ocean-based means for energy harnessing worth noting is ocean thermal energy conversion (OTEC). Exploiting the differences in heat existing around the surface of the ocean and below, warmer surface water is used to heat a fluid, such as liquid ammonia, converting it into vapor, which expands to drive a turbine which, in turn, produces electricity. The fluid is then cooled using cold water from the ocean depths, returning it into a liquid state so the process can start all over again.

Of all the ocean-based energy sources, OTEC appears to have the most potential. It has been estimated that 88,000 TWh/yr could be generated without affecting the ocean's thermal structure.[676] While this figure may not express total, usable capacity, it implies that well over half of all current global energy consumption could be met with OTEC alone. As of 2013, most of the existing OTEC plants are experimental or very small scale. However, a few major industrial capacity projects have been set in motion, including a 10 MW plant off the coast of China[677] and a 100MW near Hawaii.[678] One 100MW offshore plant can theoretically power Hawaii's entire Big Island alone,[679] meaning 186,000 people as of a 2011 census.

Now, in conclusion to this subsection of ocean energy harnessing, keeping consistent with the prior categorical estimations set forward for solar, wind and geothermal, it is worthwhile to consider the total, combined (largely conservative) potential of each noted medium. While this will, of course, be a crude extrapolation since there are many complex variables, including the fact that some applications are still semi-experimental and difficult to properly assess, this general figure still helps to digest the broadest perspective of the potential of

---

675 Source: *Osmotic Power Play: Energy Recovery Teams with GS Engineering & Construction Corp to Develop Highly Available Renewable Energy Source* (http://www.marketwatch.com/story/osmotic-power-play-energy-recovery-teams-with-gs-engineering-construction-corp-to-develop-highly-available-renewable-energy-source-2013-10-15?reflink=MW_news_stmp)
676 *Renewable Energy Sources and Climate Change Mitigation*, Ottmar Edenhofer, 2012, p507
677 Source: *Ocean Thermal Power Will Debut off China's Coast* (http://www.scientificamerican.com/article.cfm?id=ocean-thermal-power-will-debut-off-chinas-coast)
678 Source: *100-mw OTEC project planned for West Oahu* (http://www.bizjournals.com/pacific/print-edition/2012/10/05/100-mw-otec-project-planned-for-west.html?page=all)
679 Source: *Ocean Thermal Energy Conversion Could Power All Of Hawaii's Big Island* (http://www.huffingtonpost.com/2013/09/16/ocean-thermal-energy-conversion-hawaii_n_3937367.html)

ocean renewables. Here is a list of the noted global potentials:

Wave: 27,280 TWh/yr
Tidal: 13,140 Twh/yr (1.5 TW x 8760hr)
Ocean Current: 400 Twh/yr (old estimate with old tech)
Osmotic: ~1,500 TwH/yr (average of noted statistics)
Ocean Thermal: 88,000 Twh/yr

Added together we arrive at 130,320 TWh/yr or 0.46 ZJ a year. This is roughly 83% of current global use (0.55 ZJ). It is important to note that such numbers are derived, in part, from traditional technologies, with no adjustment made for more recent improvements. If we bring traditional Hydroelectric (watercourse based) back into the equation, which, according to the IEA has a potential of 16,400 TWh/yr,[680] this brings the figure up to 146,720 TWh/yr or 96% of current global use.

(b) Small Scale & Total Mixed-Use Systems
The prior section described the vast potential of large-scale, base-load renewable energy harnessing. Wind, solar, water/hydro and geothermal have all shown that they are capable, *individually*, of meeting or vastly exceeding the current 0.55 ZJ annual global energy consumption at this time.

The true question is how are such methods to be intelligently put into practice. Given the regional limitations coupled with other native issues such as intermittency, the real *design initiative* to create a workable combination of such means is needed. Such a *systems* approach is the real solution, harmonizing an optimized fraction of each of those renewables to achieve global, total use abundance.

For example, it is not inconceivable to imagine a series of man-made floating islands off select coastlines which are designed to possibly harness, at once, wind, solar, thermal difference, wave, tidal and ocean currents – all at the same time and in the same general area. Such *energy islands* would then pipe their harvest back to land for human use. Various combinations could also be applied to land-based systems as well, such as constructing wind/solar combinations to compliment the fact that often wind is more present at night, while solar is more present during the day.

Likewise, creative ingenuity with respect to how we can intelligently combine various methods also extends to what we could consider *localized* energy harnessing. Smaller scale renewable methods that are conducive to single structures or small areas find the same systems logic regarding combination. These localized systems could also, if need be, connect back into the larger, base-load systems as well, revealing a total, mixed medium integrated network.

A common example today is the use of single structure solar

---

680 Source: *Renewable Energy Essentials: Hydropower*
(http://www.iea.org/publications/freepublications/publication/Hydropower_E
ssentials.pdf)

panels, such as for home use. While the efficiency of these panels is still improving, coupled with imposed cost limitations as per the investment/profit mechanism of the market, most people utilizing these solar power systems are only able to compliment their home's electricity use rather than gain 100% utilization. (For example, most systems are applied to power the home during the day, while pulling power from the regional base-load grid at night.) This kind of approach that seeks to *maximize localized possibilities first*, before resorting to larger scale energy use, in a system approach, is the key to practical energy abundance, efficiency and sustainability.

To understand the relevance of this more thoroughly, let's expand the example of household solar array application to it possible theoretical potential. In 2011, the average annual electricity consumption for a U.S. residential utility (household) customer was 11,280 kWh.[681] Given 114,800,000 households in 2010,[682] this means 1295 TWh/yr was used. Total electrical energy consumption in 2012 for the USA was 3,886,400,000 MWh/yr.[683] This equates to 3,886 TWh/yr. This means 33% of all electric consumption occurred in people's homes, with the vast majority of that energy coming from fossil fuel power stations.

If all households in the United States were able to power themselves for electricity using solar panels alone, localized energy utilization that is simply wasted at this time, the base-load stress reduction would be dramatic. Contrary to popular belief, as of 2013 this is a real possibility given the state of solar cell efficiency and storage technology.[684] The problem is that the current energy industry is not prepared for such efficiency and consumer solar systems available suffer from high financial expense as a result of limited mass production, competition and a lack social initiative to forward advancement.

It worth stating here that the financial system and its price oriented mechanisms exist as *barriers* to ubiquitous and optimized household solar development in the broad view (along every other

---

681 Source: eia.gov (http://www.eia.gov/tools/faqs/faq.cfm?id=97&t=3)
682 Source: *Total Number of U.S. Households*
(http://www.statisticbrain.com/u-s-household-statistics/)
683 Source: *List of countries by electricity consumption*
(http://en.wikipedia.org/wiki/List_of_countries_by_electricity_consumption)
684 While the current state of CPV solar efficiency, as of 2013 is 44.7%
[http://www.soitec.com/en/news/press-releases/world-record-solar-cell-1373/], with consumer available products averaging only about 18%
[http://sroeco.com/solar/most-efficient-solar-panels], more advance methods are suggesting upwards of 80%.
[http://www.extremetech.com/extreme/168811-new-nano-material-could-boost-solar-panel-efficiency-as-high-as-80] Likewise, battery storage for household use has been advancing via emerging *graphene super capacitors* [http://www.gizmag.com/graphene-based-supercapacitor/28579/] which can charge faster, last many times longer than conventional batteries and are less polluting and take up less space. Another advancing battery technology is termed the LMB, as developed by Donald Sadoway and MIT.

developing technology after a certain point of proven efficacy). While defenders of capitalism argue that the process of investment-to-market of an in-demand good generally reduces the cost of that good over time, making it more available to those who could not afford it before, it is forgotten that the entire process is a *contrivance*.

If price and profit were removed from the system, focusing only on the technology and its statistical merit, both at the current time and its longer term efficiency trends (future improvements), proper resource allocation strategies and research could be employed to bring promising technology to the population much more rapidly. In the case of solar arrays for home power generation, given the incredible capacity it has to alleviate base-load energy stress which would, today, further reduce emissions and fossil fuel pollution, it is a very unfortunate circumstance this technology and its application is subject to the whims of the market.[685]

If we survey the commercial expense of an average solar array as of 2013, an average home using 11,280 kWh a month would require about 30 panels, with a solar cell efficiency of about 9-15% and a night time battery system. This would cost well over $20,000.[686] Such an expense is unaffordable for the vast majority of the world, even though the basic materials used in traditional PV systems are simple and abundant, along with ever-increasing manufacturing ease.

Likewise, it is equally as disappointing to notice how modern home construction has made little to no use of other basic, localized renewable methods that can further facilitate the real world capacity to bring all households (not only in the USA but the in the world) to a place of energy independence.

Noting the power of solar, other nearly universal applications also apply. Small wind harvesting systems[687] and geothermal heating and cooling technology,[688] combined with architectural design making

---

685 It is worth mentioning once again that all business establishments perpetuate themselves mostly by the markets they have created *prior*. A new invention that can interfere with the existing income infrastructure of a given business is often subject to influences that slow or even suppress that income interfering technology. While many see this kind of behavior as a form of "corruption", the truth of the matter is that the very mechanism of bringing a given good to the market is subject to imposed financial limitations which achieve the same goal. For example, if the new good cannot be considered profitable during the course of its development, regardless of its true merit, it will be hindered. The extremely slow pace of renewable energies on the whole, even though the principle of most means has been understood for hundreds of years, is a direct result of monetary investment or lack thereof and the more efficient a technology, the less profit with be realized in the long-term.

686 Source: *Off-Grid System Cost Guide*
   (http://www.wholesalesolar.com/StartHere/OFFGRIDBallparkCost.html)

687 Example: *Saving Energy in West Michigan Honeywell Wind Turbine*
   (http://www.freepowerwindturbines.com/honeywell_wind_turbine.html)

688 Reference: *Geothermal Heat Pumps*

better use of natural light and heat/cool preservation efficiency,[689] there is a spectrum of design adjustments which could make apartments and houses not only self-sufficient, but more ecologically sustainable. Coupling this with use-reuse designs for water preservation, along with other approaches to optimize energy/resource efficiency, it is clear that our current methods are enormously wasteful when compared to the possibilities.

Extending outwards to city infrastructure, we see the same failures almost everywhere with respect to such applied systems. For example, an enormous amount of energy is used in the process of transportation. While the electric vehicle has proven viable for full global use, even though lobbying efforts and other market limitations have continued to keep its application well behind the gasoline powered norm, many system-based methods also go unharnessed.

Apart from a general necessity to reorganize urban environments to be more conducive to convenient mass transit networks, removing the need for numerous autonomous vehicles, simply *re-harnessing* the powered movements of all transport mediums could dramatically alleviate energy pressures.

A technology called *piezoelectric,*[690] which is able to convert pressure and mechanical energy into electricity, is an excellent example of an energy reuse method with great potential. Existing applications have included power generation by people walking on piezo engineered floors[691] and sidewalks,[692] streets which can generate power as automobiles cross over them[693] and train rail systems which can also capture energy from passing train cars through pressure.[694] Aerospace engineer Haim Abramovich has stated that a stretch of road less than a mile long, four lanes wide, and trafficked by about 1,000 vehicles per hour can create about 0.4 megawatts of power, enough to power 600 homes.[695]

(http://energy.gov/energysaver/articles/geothermal-heat-pumps)
689 A design approach called "passive solar" is a good design example.
[http://en.wikipedia.org/wiki/Passive_solar_building_design]
690 Reference: thefreedictionary.com
(http://www.thefreedictionary.com/piezoelectric)
691 Reference: *Energy-Generating Floors to Power Tokyo Subways*
(http://inhabitat.com/tokyo-subway-stations-get-piezoelectric-floors/)
692 Reference: *Six Sidewalks That Work While You Walk*
(http://www.treehugger.com/clean-technology/six-sidewalks-that-work-while-you-walk.html)
693 Reference: *Israel Highway Equipped With Pilot Piezoelectric Generator System* (http://www.greenoptimistic.com/2009/10/06/israel-piezoelectric-highway/#.UmHNTmRDp94)
694 Reference: *New Piezoelectric Railways Harvest Energy From Passing Trains* (http://inhabitat.com/new-piezoelectric-railways-harvest-energy-from-passing-trains/)
695 Reference: *Under Highway Piezoelectric "Generators" Could Provide Power to Propel Electric Cars*
(http://www.greenprophet.com/2010/09/piezoelectric-generators-electric-cars/)

Other theoretical applications extend to pretty much anything that engages pressure or action, including minor vibrations. For example, there are projects working to harness the seemingly small-scale energy production; such as texting on a cellphone in a effort to charge the phone while the phone is simply being touched or moved;[696] [697] applications to harvest energy from airflow from airplanes;[698] and even an electric car that uses piezo tech, in part, to charge itself as it travels.[699]

If we think about the enormous mechanical energy wasted by vehicle transport modes and high traffic walking centers such as downtown streets, the potential of that possible regenerated energy is quite substantial. It is this type of *systems thinking* that is needed in order maintain sustainability, while actively pursuing a global energy abundance.

(4) Material Production/Access

Unlike the prior three sub-sections, which have taken only existing, established methods into consideration with respect to humanity's potential to achieve an abundance[700] of each given focus, this section will necessarily be approached differently.

The problem with creating a basis for an overall *material abundance* extrapolation in a similar manner, taking into account general raw materials, is that the level of industrial revision needed to embrace the high degree of efficiency sought, is radically different from current traditional practices. In other words, we cannot definitively extrapolate in the same way, using an existing, singular process or genre technology in order to draw such a conclusion about the level of productivity possible on the whole.

This is because the true abundance-generating efficiency mechanism is to be found in the large- scale *system orientation*, taking into account the *synergy* present between the sustainability laws inherent to the natural world and the level of efficiency incorporated within the entire

---

696 Reference: *Piezoelectric kinetic energy harvester for mobile phones* (http://www.energyharvestingjournal.com/articles/piezoelectric-kinetic-energy-harvester-for-mobile-phones-00002142.asp?sessionid=1)

697 Reference: *Cisco's Laura Ipsen: Smart grid success requires infotech, energy tech savvy* (http://www.smartplanet.com/blog/science-scope/charge-your-phone-by-typing-on-it/8797)

698 Reference: *Harvesting energy from vehicle air flow using piezoelectrics* (http://www.gizmag.com/harnessing-vehicle-air-flow-energy/13414/)

699 Reference: *P-Eco Electric Concept Vehicle Powered by Piezoelectricity* (http://psipunk.com/p-eco-electric-concept-vehicle-powered-by-piezoelectricity/)

700 As will be explained more so in this section, the abundance state sought has to do with use-time and access, not outright property. An access society is very different from a propertied one in many profound ways, especially when it comes to sustainability, values and human behavior itself. Food, energy and water already assume an access state since such "items" are perishable or part of an continuum that separates it from physical "good" ownership as we traditionally think of it.

societal operation.

For example, today there are over one billion automobiles in the world.[701] From a narrow view, the idea of an "abundance" of automobiles would perhaps imply, based on the current property oriented framework, that every human being on the planet should then own a private automobile. Put bluntly, this is the wrong perspective and an outgrowth of a non-synergetic conditioning which is common to the market system's reinforcement of property as value. From the standpoint of efficiency and sustainability it is extremely wasteful to employ 'one automobile per person' due to the fact that a person actually only drives, on average, only about 5% of the time. Otherwise, the automobile sits in parking lots, driveways and the like.

In the city of Los Angeles, California about 1,977,803 automobiles are reported as in use as of 2009.[702] In abstraction, based on this use-time average of 5%, only 98,890 automobiles would actually be needed to meet the transport time needs of the current use demand, assuming a sharing system. In other words, in principle, only 98,890 automobiles would be needed to meet the transport needs of 1,977,803 people.

Furthermore, for the sake of argument, with all other modes of public transport ignored and with the entire population of Los Angeles (3.9 million people)[703] needing to be mobile for 5% a month, only 195,000 automobiles would be needed, in abstraction, to meet the average use time of 3.9 million people.

Likewise, in the United States in 2008, it was recorded that 236.4 million consumer vehicles were being used. With a U.S. population of 313 million, using the 5% use statistic once again, it would take 15.6 million automobiles to meet use demand. That is an 83% decrease in automobile output to meet the needs of *all* Americans (a 32.4% increase in use or access based on total population), in theory.

Of course, please note that it is well acknowledged here that such an extrapolation is merely for speculation as obviously many other complicating factors come into play in real life that would adjust this equation greatly. The point here is to give the reader a sense of *synergy*. What should be pointed out is the noted *increase in efficiency*, where substantially fewer automobiles are needed to meet the transport needs of substantially more people, due to a system-based, synergetic reorientation (in this case, a car "sharing" system).

Again, this is not to dismiss the need for improved urban or public transport, nor does it address the importance of an automobile's

---

701 Source: *Number Of Cars Worldwide Surpasses 1 Billion; Can The World Handle This Many Wheels?* (http://www.huffingtonpost.ca/2011/08/23/car-population_n_934291.html)

702 Source: The City of Los Angeles Transportation Profile (http://www.gu.se/digitalAssets/1344/1344071_city-of-la-transportation-profile.pdf)

703 Source: United States Census Bureau, 2013 (http://www.census.gov/)

design.[704] At the root of this issue is really the subject of "transportation" itself, the reasons why people need such mobility, and how the environment is designed to cater for (or bypass) such needs. This is an enormous, dynamic subject to consider.

Also, let it be stated upfront that no matter what real or assumed efficiencies may exist in real life, the goal of seeking post-scarcity, as both a means to relieve human suffering and as a method to adapt to truly efficient and hence sustainable practices, *is without debate as a critical point of focus for an expanding society.* It could be well argued that only a perverse society would wilfully choose to persevere with a system that knowingly preserves scarcity for profit and establishment preservation when it is intellectually clear that such a condition is no longer needed and hence any such related human suffering resulting is also no longer needed.

As argued prior, the market economy is not just a response to a scarcity-based worldview, it is also a *preserver* of it. The market structurally requires a high degree of scarcity, as an abundance focused society would eventually mean less labor-for-income, less turnover and less profit on the whole. If society woke up tomorrow to a world where 50% of the human job market was automated and where all food, energy and basic goods could be made available without a price tag due to increased efficiency, needless to say the job market and monetary economy as we know it would collapse.

Value Shift
In order to think properly about the state of our productive capacity to produce life-supporting and standard of living improving goods today, we need to first rationally separate *human needs* from *human wants,* with the priority of meeting *needs* first.

While this distinction may appear like a controversial opinion to many, in a world where now 46% of the total wealth is owned by 1% of the population;[705] in a world where roughly 1 billion do not get basic nutrition;[706] in a world where 1.1 billion people live without clean drinking water and 2.6 billion people lack adequate sanitation;[707] in a

---

704 Many other influences and outcomes can arise to the effect of increasing efficiency in such a context. For example, with about 1.2 million deaths occurring annually from automobile accidents, many design initiatives to assist future safety could dramatically alter that reality. The use of sensor rigged, driverless cars, which are now a reality, could end such deaths immediately. Given about 50 million auto accidents worldwide each year, the result is not only saved lives, but saved medical expenses, insurance claims, lawsuits, data entry, resources, time, the toil of stress and grief that result from injury or death, and a massive array of other alleviations.

705 Source: *46 per cent global wealth owned by richest 1 per cent: Credit Suisse* (http://profit.ndtv.com/news/economy/article-46-per-cent-global-wealth-owned-by-richest-1-per-cent-credit-suisse-369109)

706 Source: *U.N.: One billion worldwide face starvation* (http://www.cnn.com/2009/WORLD/europe/11/15/un.hunger/)

707 Source: *Water Crisis: Towards a way to impove the situation* (http://www.worldwatercouncil.org/library/archives/water-crisis/)

world where 100 million people do not have shelter;[708] in a world where 3 billion live on less than $2.50 a day[709] and in a world where 1.2 billion do not even have electricity[710] - perhaps our priorities as a global civilization need to be addressed with respect to the true maintenance of what we might questionably term "civilization". The truth is, this priority is not a mere poetic gesture; it is a public health requirement.[711]

The process of our physical and psychological evolution has created human needs. Not meeting these virtually empirical needs results in a destabilizing spectrum of physical, mental and social disorders. Human wants, on the other hand, are cultural manifestations that have undergone enormous, subjective change over time, revealing something of an arbitrary nature, in truth. Now, this isn't to say neurotic attachments can't manifest into wants, so much so that they start to take the role of needs, emotionally. However, that is still mostly a cultural condition.

Sadly, again, the market does not separate needs from wants in its basic psychology, which is why scarcity arguments can be extended infinitely in defense of its existence and hence the proposed need to have a competitive, trade-based society, no matter the degree of abundance that can be achieved. This has arguably created a type of neurosis, in fact, where people assume having "infinite wants" and "more and more" is a virtue or even a driver of human progress itself.

Of course, "infinite possibilities" are certainly a reality in many ways, as society cannot predict what technology will materialize many years down the line as influences change and preferences change. However, infinite possibility is about vulnerability and creativity, while still being strategic and intelligent about resource management and use. This is not the same as infinite wants, which sees the human being as insatiable and indiscriminate.

Therefore, part of this *value shift* will be "undoing" the sociological damage done by the psychology inherent to market-based living. A relatively high standard of living can be made available for all human beings assuming, in part, a basic, responsible value shift away from our troubling patterns of wasteful, frivolous acquisition. It is important to restate that the materialism we endure as a society today

---

708 Source: *An estimated 100 million people worldwide are homeless. Source: United Nations Commission on Human Rights, 2005.*
(http://www.homelessworldcup.org/content/homelessness-statistics)
709 Source: *Causes of Poverty* (http://www.globalissues.org/issue/2/causes-of-poverty)
710 Source: *Here's why 1.2 billion people still don't have access to electricity* (http://www.washingtonpost.com/blogs/wonkblog/wp/2013/05/29/heres-why-1-2-billion-people-still-dont-have-access-to-electricity/)
711 Social stability is directly correlated to public health. For example, social inequality can, as it often does, manifest as violent behavior, civil protest and even war, just as poor sanitation and poverty stricken areas can bring disease that could spread to areas which do have good sanitation, yet cause infection (perhaps even an epidemic). Easing economic stress and improving public health is a global imperative for true safety.

is a direct response to the economic need to keep money *circulating* as much as possible. The role of business as we know it is either to service people's existing wants/needs or to invent them in the hope people will conform by showing new demand.

A new "widget" put forward by the market is only as viable as the interest of others to purchase it and the use of advertising and marketing has been very influential in *creating* a culture which sees ownership and acquisition as a sign of social status.[712] This directly assists the need to keep high levels of consumerism in play as GDP and employment are directly related to this pressure. Again, the less interest there is to consume, the less economic growth and hence less demand for jobs. This slows the existing state of a market economy and creates a systemic loss of wellbeing for many.

It can be well-argued that a culture which has decided that acquisition and expansion is the path of progress/success, promoting constant consumption and seemingly infinite "economic growth", is going to eventually hit the limits of sustainability on a finite planet.[713] In clear terms, this trend is one of *disorder*.

Social success and progress can only mean, in part, finding *balance* with the habitat and the other human beings who share the habitat. Sadly, the market system's entire premise contradicts this sustainable value, as the mechanism of economic unfolding does not reward conservation and the reduction of consumption in a direct sense. Put another way, *the market is a scarcity-based structural approach that paradoxically seeks increased levels of consumption to operate "efficiently"*.

So, an analysis of our material capacity to bring common goods into a "post-scarcity" abundance to exceed the needs of all humans on Earth cannot be discussed without also understanding necessary, sustainability oriented revisions which will substantially reduce our resource-use footprint at the same time.

In short, the new industrial design approach is to *deliberately increase the performance, per unit, of how we use our resources*, seeking to always move along the route of doing "more with less". Within this logic, as noted, a series of "pressure" alleviations toward increased sustainability and production simplification/efficiency would occur.

---

712 See the essay *Value System Disorder*.
713 Source: *Ongoing global biodiversity loss and the need to move beyond protected areas: a review of the technical and practical shortcomings of protected areas on land and sea* (http://www.int-res.com/articles/theme/m434p251.pdf)

Efficiency Amplifiers

We will call these "efficiency amplifiers" and the following list presents examples of needed structural economic and social changes which assist this optimized efficiency.

1) The pressure for employment for income or "earning a living" is removed.

In the market model, everyone is structurally coerced to engage some form of trade for survival, whether it is trading labor for a wage or creating a product to distribute for profit.[714] This overall pressure, while often touted as an incentive mechanism for social "progress", actually reduces overall *efficiency* greatly, as it does creativity and innovation as well. This creates a spectrum of resource and time waste since the interest in income generation and the pressure to produce is often absent existing demand.

The intent and need to do "something" to gain income for survival persists regardless of our modern reality that society *may not need* everyone to participate in the economic process. In a NLRBE, the idea of everyone being required to produce or sell something is viewed as counterproductive given the trends of ephemeralization and the necessity of now orienting society toward sustainability.

2) Production targeting social classes is removed.

Social stratification, which is a natural consequence of market capitalism, creates the need to produce a spectrum of qualities for a given good genre.[715] This spectrum is not based on utility or having variation of a good as per the personal needs/interests of individuals. Rather, each quality standard is intended to be purchased by (or made "affordable" to) a given income class.

This creates poor quality goods to meet affordability requirements of lower income consumers and hence generates unnecessary waste. In this new strategically sustainable model, no good is created to be "cheap" by relative standards simply because it fits lower class demographic buying patterns. In a NLRBE, there is no lower class demographic.

---

714 The only two exceptions to this are either to go live outside of the civilization itself which, due to property laws, is essentially impossible, or to obtain enough wealth to begin with via the market or inheritance where there is no need for further trade for survival. The latter, of course, is not open to all in a market economy of any kind.

715 All goods created assume a class relationship. The spectrum could range from the type of extreme poor production found at a "99 Cent" store where one could purchase a plastic watch which has little integrity, vs an extreme luxury item which can only be afforded by the most wealthy in the world. Thorstein Veblen inspired the term "Veblen Good" due to his observation of prestige generated from extremely high priced goods, which transcend utility. http://www.investopedia.com/terms/v/veblen-good.asp

3) Inefficiency inherent to the competitive practice is removed.

Competition between businesses produces four basic forms of unnecessary inefficiency and hence resulting waste:

(a) Proprietary incompatibility of related goods components (lack of standardization)
(b) Wasteful multiplicity of goods by competing businesses of the same genre
(c) Incentivized good weakness to encourage turnover (planned obsolescence)
(d) Inherent good weakness due to seeking cost efficiency (intrinsic obsolescence)

With respect to (a), in a sustainable economy there would exist a universal standardization of all related genre components wherever possible. In 1801, a man named Eli Whitney was perhaps the first to apply standardization in an impacting way. He produced muskets, and during his time there was no way to interchange the parts of different muskets, even though they were the same overall design. If a musket part broke, the whole gun was useless. Whitney developed tools to do this and after 1801, all parts were full interchangeable.
　　While most would assume this common sense idea to be prolific across the global industrial community today, the perpetuation of proprietary components by companies that want the consumer to re-purchase any such needed component from them directly, ignoring the possibility of compatibility with other producers, creates not only great waste but also great inconvenience.

Similarly, with respect to (b), a wasteful multiplicity of genre goods by competing businesses is generated at all times in the current model. While less obvious to many, the general competitive nature of the market keeps new ideas invisible from competitors during development. Then, a good is produced for purchase that likely has some overall improvement of a given feature. Once that feature is on the market, it is then acknowledged and assessed by competing businesses and the race to continue improvement moves forward, back and forth.
　　While many argue this "creative warfare" is a driving force of development/innovation of a given product or purpose, the negative and unnecessary consequence is the rapid, wasteful physical obsolescence inherent to each "cycle" of output. In other words, if a notable cell phone feature improvement is obtained by one company, on the heels of a major release by another company that has already started mass production of their phone version without this upgrade, an immediate state of obsolescence is produced, resulting in less optimized products, which could have been avoided if the producers had been working together, as an industrial whole, rather than hiding progress and competing.

While it may be argued also that it is only through price and the patterns of consumer interest that the knowing of what is in "demand" or not can be obtained, the truth of the matter is that communication could be made more readily between the design mechanism and the consuming public as well.[716] This bypasses the "price-demand" acceptance/rejection technique that is also wasteful as well since it requires production to occur, in many cases, *before* the actual demand is fully understood.

As a final point, a globally interlinked, shared data, non-competitive oriented design/production system would also further facilitate the ability to foreshadow component feature improvement over time. This means industry would be able to understand what changes are coming based on progressive trends and design more efficiently, in anticipation of those looming changes.

Regarding (c), or what has been termed "planned obsolescence", the interest to see products fail or be less optimized to motivate repeat purchases of the same basic good would no longer be incentivized. The practice of deliberately designed obsolescence has been a hidden part of the industrial approach since the mid-20th Century when interest in creating economic growth was high.[717]

In a NLRBE, this interest is removed as there is no market incentive to pursue repeat purchases and therefore more optimized efficiency, durability and sustainability strategies can be applied.

Regarding (d) or "intrinsic obsolescence" as it is termed here, all competition for market share seeks to reduce input costs to whatever degree possible in order to remain affordable in the marketplace and hence persuade the consuming public to purchase one version or "brand" of one good over another. This has been gestured in American marketing culture as "producing the best possible goods at the lowest possible prices."

This inherent inefficiency of seeking to reduce costs creates, as a systemic result, less efficient goods immediately upon production, in the technical sense. Cutting corners in design and production for the sake of preserving money might be considered "economically efficient" in a *market context* but it is clearly economically inefficient in the real world (*physical context)* as it creates unnecessary waste over time. This is not to say that there are no limits to production optimization given the fact that true design can only be taken on the whole, with respect to the state of resources at any given time and associated limitations. This is to say that the use of mere profit-oriented "cost efficiency" to limit product quality is a wholly unscientific means for such decision-making.

---

716 This will be discussed in the essay *The Industrial Government*
717 Reference: *Ending the Depression Through Planned Obsolescence,* Bernard London, 1932

4) Property relationships that create use-isolation are removed in favor of shared access.

As expressed in the prior example regarding automobiles and their use-time, in a NLRBE the property system is replaced by an access system which creates a more fluid means of shared use goods which are not needed at all times by a single person. Common examples would be vacation domicile use, transport, seasonal equipment, tools, production equipment and the like.

As an aside, apart from a general overall reduction of production per use time per person, this can assist larger forms of efficiency as far as convenience as well. We can imagine airport or train travel, for example, being redesigned to assist access to various goods locally, so much so that the idea of "packing" a suitcase was no longer needed. This seemingly minor change alone would positively impact queuing, as well as storage in transit, luggage processing machinery, etc. The *chain of alleviation* is actually quite extensive when given detailed thought.

Clothes, communication tools, recreational items and the like could all be made available at the destination airport or similar facility upon arrival. While this is foreign to many as an idea, especially given the "personalized" oriented nature of our culture, the strife reduced in no longer having to carry large bags and the like could persuade those modern values, given the increased ease. Either way, it comes down to personal choice. In abstraction, a person could literally live without needing to move property around at all, moving around the world at will, without property-oriented inconvenience.

Again, facilitating a means of access, where things can be shared, will allow many more to gain use of goods they otherwise would not in the current model, along with less being produced in proportion. A NLRBE seeks to create access abundance, not a property abundance.

It is also important to note that property is not an empirical concept, only access is. Property is a protectionist contrivance. Access is the reality of the human/social condition. In order for one to truly "own", say, a computer, one would have had to personally come up with technological ideas that made it work, along with the ideas that comprise the tools of its production. This is literally impossible. There is no such thing as empirical property in reality. There is only access and sharing, no matter what social system is employed.

5) Design-based recycling is mandated and incentivized, maximizing resource reuse.

Contrary to our intuition, there is no such thing as waste in the natural world. Humanity has given very little consideration to the role of material regeneration and how all of our design practices must account for this.

As an aside, the highest state of this recycling will eventually come in the form of nanotechnology. Nanotechnology will eventually facilitate the ability to create goods from the atomic level up and disassemble goods back into raw atoms. Of course, while this approach appears to be on pace for the future, it is not suggested that such nanotechnology is even needed at this time for us to be successfully regenerative or abundant.

Today, industrial recycling is more of an afterthought than a focus. Companies continue to do things such as blindly coat materials with certain chemicals that actually distort the properties of that material, making the material less salvageable by current recycling methods. Overall, strategic recycling is a core seed of maintaining abundance. Every landfill on Earth is just a waste of potential.

The law of conservation of mass states that for any system closed to all transfers of matter and energy, the mass of the system must remain constant over time, as system mass cannot change quantity if it is not added or removed. The quantity of mass is "conserved" over time. This natural law implies that mass can neither be created nor destroyed. Human society's use of resources is perhaps best thought of as a process of intelligent rearrangement, rather than of "using" and "discarding".

6) Material use per a given production output is strategically calculated to assure using the most *conducive* & *abundant* materials known.

As will be expressed more so in the essay "The Industrial Government", a new model of evaluation is created which orients materials based on certain efficiency parameters. Two critical ones are material "conduciveness" and a material's overall state of "abundance".

Conduciveness relates to how appropriate the proposed use is, based on the material's properties. Abundance refers to how much of it is available and hence its state of scarcity. Put together, you weigh the value of conduciveness against the value of how accessible and low impact the material is, as compared to other materials that may be more or less conducive and more or less abundant. In other words, it is a synergistic efficiency comparison that makes sure the materials used are optimized for the purpose.

Probably the best example of this is home or domicile construction. The common use of wood, brick, screws, and the vast array of parts typical of a common house, is comparatively inefficient to more modern, simplified, abundant prefabrication or molded-able materials.

A traditional 2000 square foot home is reported to require about 40 to 50 trees. Compare that with houses that can now be created in prefabrication processes, like mold extrusion, with simple, Earth-friendly polymers, concrete and other easily formable and movable methods. Such new approaches have a very small footprint, as compared to our destruction of global forests for wood. Home construction today is one of the most resource intensive and wasteful industrial mediums in the world today and it doesn't need to be that way.

7) Design conduciveness for labor automation.
The more we conform to the current state of rapid, efficient production processes, the more abundance we can create. Most manufacturing approaches typically divide labor into three categories: human assembly, mechanization and automation. Human assembly means hand- made. Mechanization means using machines to assist the human worker. Automation means no human interaction in the process.

Imagine if you needed a chair and there were three designs. The first is elaborate and complex and could only be done by hand at that time. The second is more streamlined where its parts could be made mostly by machines, but would need to be assembled by hand in the end. The third is a chair that is produced by one machine process, fully automated.

This latter chair design type would be the design goal in this new approach. What this would do is reduce the variety of automation machine configurations needed. Imagine, if you will, a robotic-based processing plant that can not only produce cars, it can produce virtually any kind of industrial machine/good comprised of the same basic set of raw materials. This would increase output substantially.

An easy way to understand this trend of simplification is to consider the power of digital software and how one piece of hardware (i.e. computer) can now serve an enormous number of programmable roles. This "dematerialization", as it could be termed, is best exemplified by the modern cell phone. Due to the vast program applications now available for such "smart phones", from medical measurements to full musical synthesizers, the functionality of these small, handheld computers can now take on almost countless roles.

Such roles long ago, before the digital age, would have usually required one hardware configuration for each task. Today, any basic operating system can run a dramatically large number of programmed functions, all contained in a small device. This logic applies to the nature of physical machine production as well as it is simply a matter of time before the act of producing a vast array of goods can be accomplished by small, modular mechanical systems, just like a digital operating system can conduct almost countless programmed functions.

8) Serviceable problems resulting from the prior, inefficient economic process are reduced if not eliminated.

This idea is often difficult to fully comprehend, as the chain of causality resulting from one general inefficiency can be vast and complex. For example, the resolution of water scarcity alone has enormous preventative potential for disease. The amount of labor and resources once used for treating those then resolved diseases can find other roles. Energy abundance has the same reality since energy is the driver of all human activity. A clean, reliable, renewable state of absolute energy abundance would have enormous effects on the production and abundance capacity of this future society.

Likewise, the pursuit of meeting human needs and the removal of "labor-for-income" occupations, which often have no real technical function, would set in motion a new educational possibility, reinforced by an incentive to pursue personal interests and hence the freedom not to feel pressured away from fields of interest since survival and well-being are already taken care of by the social model itself. It is hard to imagine the explosion of creativity possible when this pressure is removed and society is set free to think clearly.

9) Invigorating the "group mind", meaning human connection and the sharing of ideas, will bring ever-accelerating progress.

Similar to the prior point, the Internet has become a powerful tool for research and idea expansion. While "open-source" research and development gets a fair amount of attention today, the ability to harness the communicative power of the internet to create a global dialogue about any given technology or idea will facilitate a type of interactive development never before seen, once focused.

The Game Changers
The discussion of advanced technologies which can dramatically transform the unfolding of the future and assist the pursuit of post-scarcity have not been a focus of this essay as it becomes too easy to simply assume the reality of the speculations. A great number of "futurists" have done just this with mixed results and often times it leaves the audience with looming, premature expectations, waiting around for this or that new technology to finally progress.

However, to dismiss these potentials is equally as hasty. The truth of the matter is that our capacity to accelerate such change comes down to our focus. Just as the Manhattan Project was able to bring countless scientists together for a single output goal (as violent as it may have been to build the atom bomb), the idea of global network projects to rapidly accelerate new technical possibilities is merely a matter of choice. We can only imagine the progress of any given project if enough minds came together to pursue it at once, in an organized way. This "open-source" world approach alone will likely have limitless possibilities.

Likewise, there is no shortage of transformational or "disruptive" technologies on the horizon that could radically alter the industrial landscape. Artificial intelligence, robotics, biotechnology, 3D printing, infinite computing and nanotechnology are just a few. Each of these developing mediums has vast implications for efficiency increases. It is very difficult to know exactly how they will unfold or, more importantly, how they will find synergy, but we do know the trends of development are increasing exponentially in most cases.

For example, a fusion of 3D printing, nanotechnology, AI and robotics will forever alter the state of manufacturing, so much so that a person could perhaps have a garage size manufacturing system in their home to produce virtually anything they may need. Again, while such futuristic and seemingly "science-fiction" speculations are unneeded to justify our modern, tangible capacity to create abundance, these new and emerging mediums should not be overlooked as they are set to have a great impact, if embraced properly.[718]

In the 19th century, aluminum was more valuable than gold, even though it is technically one of the most abundant elements in the world. However, before the discovery of electrolysis, it was extremely difficult to extract. Once this technical process was discovered, almost overnight the scarcity of the material plummeted. Today, we tend to use aluminum with a throwaway mindset. Such dramatic historical changes are important to keep in mind as the same kind of advancement is occurring across many disciplines, often hidden from most people's comprehension and far beyond their expectations. Likewise, the aforementioned technologies are on pace to dramatically change the world.

Raw Resource Assessment
As noted, assessing the state of natural resources to gauge the degree of total/maximum use capacity as per the human population cannot be done by simply extrapolating around current methods. We need to get both a general sense of current inventory levels of all relevant Earthly, resources and then digest them with respect to the aforementioned efficiency amplifiers which, in effect, radically change the way industrial practice and consumption unfolds. It is also worth noting that modern science has brought a great deal of *synthesis* into play and the use of polymers, meta-materials and other rapid advancements in chemistry, physics and engineering are accelerating. The end result is that many resources considered problematic, such as *rare Earth metals,* are finding replacements via highly abundant means.

It is important to point out that most perspectives on current resource use trends are quite negative by those thinking within the context of the current model.[719] There is no shortage of negative reports and rightly so. We have been abusing and misusing our

---

718 With respect to such materials, emerging nanotechnology, such as carbon nanotubes (CNT), which can be arranged to create what has been termed "Buckypaper", is an example of tremendous potential. "Buckypaper" is a macroscopic aggregate of carbon nanotubes that owes its name to R. Buckminster Fuller. Paper-thin and lightweight, it is one- tenth the weight yet potentially 500 times stronger than steel when its sheets are stacked to form a composite. It can also conduct electricity like copper or silicon. This synthetic material, made out of abundant carbon, could be at the foundation of a new, scarcity transcending synthetic materials revolution.
719 Reference: *Two-thirds of world's resources 'used up'* (http://www.theguardian.com/science/2005/mar/30/environment.research)

resources to a vast degree, locked into a life-blind paradigm which has little structural comprehension of its consequences.[720] However, again, this is actually a *mismanagement* problem, not a quantitative or empirical one.

It is also important to note that it is not how much or how little there is of any one thing in absolute terms. Rather, the qualifier has to do with how we are to achieve the *purpose sought*. For instance, the available amount of oil in the Earth, as would be needed for its non-energy uses today (since in this model it isn't needed for energy, as noted), is only as relevant as our incapacity/capacity to find other ways to achieve the same goals oil has achieved, but without it.

Another example is lumber. If home construction completely transcended the use of wood frame houses, globally, using Earth-friendly concrete and polymer processes instead, coming from ubiquitous and abundant raw materials, suddenly a once potentially scarce resource becomes exceptionally abundant, relatively speaking.

Moving on, natural resources are best organized initially by dividing them into (a) biotic and (b) abiotic. Biotic resources are derived from the biosphere and are often called "living resources".[721] Examples of biotic resources are forests, plants, animals, etc. By some definitions, it also includes resources originating from life in the distant past, such as fossil fuels. Abiotic resources are often considered "non-living" resources and include water, soil, minerals and the like.

(a) Overall, the biotic resources of the planet have been suffering greatly due to ever-increasing industrialization. Forest depletion, the loss of biodiversity, loss of fish populations and other issues have brought the sustainability of many such resources into question. In all cases, the problem is not a limited supply of these resources; it is a blatant disregard for any equilibrium with natural regeneration and basic environmental respect. The solution to these declines is to obviously deviate from their rates of use. This can be done by simply substituting other *comparable materials* for those being harvested at unsustainable rates.

In the essays *True Economic Factors* and *The Industrial Government*, this process is described in detail. In short, there is no biotic resource being used today which cannot have its rate of consumption subsided by conscious, strategic adjustment. Wood does not need to be used today for all the current purposes. Not everyone needs to eat fish from the wild ocean as advanced and humane aqua-farming processes now exist. We have already discussed the ability to

---

720 In a 2011 study entitled *"Ongoing global biodiversity loss and the need to move beyond protected areas: a review of the technical and practical shortcomings of protected areas on land and sea"* the following conclusion was made: "In a business-as-usual scenario, our demands on planet Earth could mount to the productivity of 27 planets by 2050." There is no shortage of other negative resource "overshoot" statistics in peer review as well.
721 Source: biology-online.org (http://www.biology-online.org/dictionary/Biotic_resource)

produce a vegetarian abundance with vertical farming and the move to in-vitro meat can be more healthy and sustainable than livestock methods that are damaging the environment.

With such alleviations, we would see a vast improvement in overall resources, biodiversity, the preservation of life-saving medicine derived from the rainforests and so forth. The other, largely untapped renewables mentioned prior, can also rapidly displace fossil fuels for energy use today. So, the issue is really a matter of *intelligent choice.*

(b) Abiotic resources have a different, yet similar management reality. We have already addressed our technical ability to circumvent or solve the problem of water scarcity with purification methods and our rapidly depleting topsoil[722] with soilless farming. Overall, the main resources we are left with are the valuable minerals we utilized to build many of the goods we use. These minerals are mostly compounds of Earthly elements and are extracted from rocks from the Earth's crust. Much progress in use-versatility has also been achieved by industry by extracting elements and forming metal *alloys.* An alloy is a metal *mixture* made by combining two or more metallic elements, such as the formation of *steel.*

There are close to 5,000 known minerals[723] and the number of alloys possible is enormous, with many thousands in use today. As far as analysis, the British Geological Survey (BGS) outputs a statistical assessment of world minerals/elements/chemical compounds each year regarding global extraction/production use.[724] 73 are documented in their 2007-2011 report and hence these can be considered the most utilized for global industrial production.[725] Of those, the BGS in turn updates a "risk list" of such materials based on stressed or anticipated stressed supply.

The following chart expresses the medium risk to very high-risk elements, as per their analysis.

---

722 Source: *The lowdown on topsoil: It's disappearing*
(http://www.seattlepi.com/national/article/The-lowdown-on-topsoil-It-s-disappearing-1262214.php)
723 Source: *Mineral* (http://en.wikipedia.org/wiki/Mineral)
724 Source: *World mineral statistics*
(http://www.bgs.ac.uk/mineralsuk/statistics/worldStatistics.html)
725 Source: *World Mineral Production 2007-2011*
(http://www.bgs.ac.uk/downloads/start.cfm?id=2701)

Element or element group	Symbol	Relative supply risk index	Leading producer	Top reserve holder
rare earth elements	REE	9.5	China	China
tungsten	W	9.5	China	China
antimony	Sb	9.0	China	China
bismuth	Bi	9.0	China	China
molybdenum	Mo	8.5	China	China
strontium	Sr	8.6	China	China
mercury	Hg	8.6	China	Mexico
barium	Ba	8.1	China	China
carbon (graphite)	C	8.1	China	China
beryllium	Be	8.1	USA	Unknown
germanium	Ge	8.1	China	Unknown
niobium	Nb	7.6	Brazil	Brazil
platinum group elements	PGE	7.6	South Africa	South Africa
colbalt	Co	7.6	DRC	DRC
thorium	Th	7.6	India	USA
indium	In	7.6	China	Unknown
gallium	Ga	7.6	China	Unknown
arsenic	As	7.6	China	Unknown
magnesium	Mg	7.1	China	Russia
tantalum	Ta	7.1	Brazil	Brazil
selenium	Se	7.1	Japan	Russia
cadmium	Cd	6.7	China	India
lithium	Li	6.7	Australia	Chile
vanadium	V	6.7	South Africa	China
tin	Sn	6.7	China	China
fluorine	F	6.7	China	South Africa
silver	Ag	6.2	Mexico	Peru
chromium	Cr	6.2	South Africa	Kazakhstan
nickel	Ni	6.2	Russia	Australia
rhenium	Re	6.2	Chile	Chile
lead	Pb	6.2	China	Australia
carbon (diamond)	C	6.2	Russia	DRC

Reproduced from the British Geological Survey's *Risk List* 2011[726]

The BGS states "The...list provides a quick and simple indication of the relative risk in 2012 to the supply of...elements or element groups that we need to maintain our economy and lifestyle. The position of an element on this list is determined by a number of factors that might affect availability. These include the natural abundance of elements in the Earth's crust, the location of current production and reserves, and the political stability of those locations...recycling rates and substitutability of the elements has been

---

726 Source: *Risk list 2012: An updated supply risk index for chemical elements or element groups which are of economic value* (http://www.bgs.ac.uk/mineralsuk/statistics/risklist.html)

considered in the analysis."[727]

The qualifier of *political stability/governance* is actually not relevant, empirically. This is a cultural problem. It should be stated upfront that a NLRBE is achieved by global cooperation and the common war patterns, the "resource curse" and disruptions in the supply chain by such contrived, self-preserving pressures common of world powers would no longer be a problem.

Overall, the BGS rightfully concludes that *substitutability* and *recycling* are the solutions and the scarcest resources essentially suffer from a lack of recycling and a lack of adequate substitutions being made. Rather than address each material noted, the first one listed, rare Earth metals, will be used as the example by which problem resolution can be considered with all the others.

There are seventeen rare earth metals that are considered the most scare of all elements.

Recycling:
The first great failure is that only *one percent* of all rare Earth minerals are recycled today, according to some estimates.[728] Given their common use in electronics, electronic waste recycling has also been dismal. Based on EPA statistics in the US, in 2009 only 25% of consumer electronics were collected for recycling.[729] Likewise, the goods created that hold most of these valuable materials are also *not even intended* to be recycled for the most part.[730]

According to an organization called SecondWave Recycling, "for every one million cell phones recycled, we can recover 75 pounds of gold, 772 pounds of silver, and 33,274 pounds of copper...If the United States recycled the 13 million cell phones that are thrown away annually, we could save enough energy to power more than 24,000 homes for a year."[731]

Substitutions:
Perhaps more importantly, it is now possible to manufacture synthetic versions of these metals in the context of their properties out of very common, abundant materials, in a lab.[732] [733] Nanotechnology is proving

---

727 Ibid.
728 Source: *Rare Earth Recycling* (http://www.molycorp.com/technology/rare-earth-recycling/)
729 Source: *Statistics on the Management of Used and End-of-Life Electronics* (http://www.epa.gov/osw/conserve/materials/ecycling/manage.htm)
730 Source: *Dirty, dangerous and destructive – the elements of a technology boom* (http://www.theguardian.com/commentisfree/2011/sep/26/rare-earth-metals-technology-boom)
731 Source: *Why Recycle Cell Phones? Why not just throw it away?* (http://secondwaverecycling.com/why-recycle-cell-phones-why-not-just-throw-it-away/)
732 Source: *Nanosys: We Can Replace Some Rare Earth Metals* (http://www.fastcompany.com/1705030/nanosys-we-can-replace-some-rare-earth-metals)
733 Source: *Thin Film Solar Cells Using Earth-Abundant Materials*

to be very strong in this approach.[734] Many different industries have been actively working to address the issue in each application, such as now being able to make LED light bulbs without these metals.[735] Overall we see the push to solve this problem ramping up and the fact is, resolution is simply a matter of ingenuity, focus and time.[736]

Industrial reorientation is also important to add to this problem solving equation as a larger tier form of substitutability. While this may not currently apply to rare Earth metals as much at this time, larger scale components in various technologies are changing rapidly. It is a design initiative in engineering to actively focus on component innovation that can bypass such needs. However, given the rate of change for rare Earth metal substitution through synthesis, it appears to be simply a matter of time before this issue is resolved through a combination of strategic use, recycling and synthesis.

Beyond that, it cannot be reiterated enough that the great failure of global industry has been not to make proper *purpose comparisons* when it chooses to use a certain material. In other words, it is not intelligent to use a very rare metal in a generally arbitrary and fleeting product. Since there is no referential database that shows active rates of use, decline and the like, companies make their decisions based merely on cost relationships which have very little value in the sense of *strategic use by comparison*. While it is true that price can reflect scarcity and difficulty of acquiring a certain mineral or element, such a dire reality arises only as the problem acutely materializes. In other words, no real foresight exists in price and by the time price reflects what was actually an observable technical reality at any time, it is often too late and the scarcity becomes a real problem.

In an actively aware resource management system, this would not occur. Not only would such materials be constantly compared to draw assessment as to what is the most appropriate material for a given use, any foreshadowed problem can be seen from a long period away and hence efficiency can be better maximized.[737]

Land

Unlike prior assessments, the issue of land access takes a different consideration. Earth has a finite amount of inhabitable land and hence the *method* by which humans gain access to and share land over time is the real issue. Needless to say, not every human being can have his

---

(http://www.intechopen.com/download/get/type/pdfs/id/39155)

734 Source: *New Nano Material Could Replace Rare Earth Minerals In Solar Cells and OLEDs* (http://inhabitat.com/new-nano-material-could-replace-rare-earth-minerals-in-solar-cells-and-oleds/)

735 Source: *New material could lead to cheaper, more eco-friendly LEDs* (http://www.gizmag.com/silicon-led-rare-earth-element-alternative/27933/)

736 Source: *Rare-earth mineral substitutes could defeat Chinese stranglehold* (http://www.wired.co.uk/news/archive/2013-07/31/race-for-rare-earth-minerals)

737 This is expanded upon in the essay *The Industrial Government*.

or her own private Earth. Likewise, the sickness bred by materialism, wealth and status, which manifests vast and enormous estates by the super rich, fall in the same irrational category – utterly oblivious to sustainability and social balance.

Today, the property system creates a static orientation to land access, with people typically acquiring land and staying on it indefinitely. This tendency to "settle" seems compounded by the labor roles and location requirements of most in the world as well. The tradition of commuting to one's job in a city center is still very common and hence one's home needs to be nearby. In a NLRBE, such pressures are greatly alleviated and the idea of traveling the world constantly is a tangible option.

Analysts have found that if we needed to fit the world's 7 billion people into a single city, modeled after New York City, all Earthly inhabitants would fit in the US state of Texas.[738] While clearly impractical, this simple statistic reveals the vast degree of variance possible regarding how human beings can organize themselves topographically in a global society. The problem isn't the amount of physical space needed for 7 billion or many times more. The problem is intelligent organization, design and education.

That noted, the *method of access* for a NLRBE is to create an interactive sharing system. The foundation of this idea will be expanded upon greatly in the essay "The Industrial Government". In short, people are able to travel from destination to destination, enjoying a given location for a period, before likely moving on. Such systems already exist in the current system, where a network of people and domiciles is available for sharing.[739]

Of course, many used to a "home" oriented frame of mind, which has a traditional romanticism, should not be fearful of losing such emotional security. There is no reason why a "permanent" location for a person or family cannot exist, as we find in the world today. In fact, in a society predicated on access abundance, finding and living in a permanent abode would likely be far easier than in a property ownership society.

Yet, statistics prove that today people very much enjoy moving around, exploring and enjoying new places. If it weren't for their labor-for-income job and monetary limitations, it is clear a great deal more traveling would occur by the vast majority. Once such an access system is set in motion, the network of available places to stay and visit would open up and close down in a natural flow, just as hotels work. When a hotel is booked and full for a given day, naturally others seeking to visit that region look elsewhere. As demand ebbs and flows, feedback is used to produce new structures and the like, no different, again, than how it is done today in the vacation market.

The educational and value imperative is the idea of *sharing the*

738 Source: *If the world's population lived in one city…* (http://persquaremile.com/2011/01/18/if-the-worlds-population-lived-in-one-city/)
739 Reference: airbnb.com (https://www.airbnb.com/)

world. Many today would consider this to be grossly idealized. The idea of freely moving about the planet, staying virtually anywhere, with no obligation to feel the need to return to any central place, seems like a fantasy. Yet, it is very possible. Also, since remote communication is exponentially increasing, engaging in any social/community task or creative interest can occur virtually anywhere as well.

Again, this is a value choice. If a person wishes to keep his family in one place for the rest of their lives, there is more than enough space on the planet (given the Texas statistics noted) to provide for both possibilities, assuming an intelligent revision of city layouts, responsible conservation and an earnest interest to be efficient. Either way, the same access system can be employed to find and settle a certain location, whether it is *temporary* or *permanent*.

Oil

In conclusion to this essay, issues surrounding modern society's addiction to the use of oil are important to address. Oil is likely the most industrial resource utilized on the planet today, used most notably for transport. As described prior, between battery technology, improved design and the vast renewable mediums we have today, there is no legitimate technical reason we need gasoline to power automobiles anymore. The handful of currently available electric cars today is also a clear testament to this fact. Airplanes and other extremely large powered machines might still need such oil force currently but the trends show it is simply a matter of time and focus before planes are able to use solar energy[740] coupled with advanced storage means for large scale, heavy weight commercial needs.

Yet, we should always try to think *outside of the box* when it comes to efficiency and sustainability. In the context of this large-scale, high-energy transport, the question arises: "is there a replacement for plane travel which bypasses such high concentration energy needs?" The answer is yes. Maglev technology is many times faster and uses a fraction of the energy.[741]

So, even if some oil was used for power purposes here and there, such new approaches could reduce its use footprint exponentially, if pursued correctly. In America alone, 70% of the oil used in total goes towards transport in the form of gasoline, diesel and jet fuel.[742] Likewise, if a new condition of peace can be negotiated on planet Earth, with a concentrated pressure to reduce armaments and preparations for war, an extensive oil savings would also occur.

The United States Department of Defense is one of the largest single consumers of energy in the world, responsible for 93% of all US

---

740 Reference: *Solar-Powered Airplane Completes First Leg Of U.S. Flight* (http://www.npr.org/blogs/thetwo-way/2013/05/05/181407952/solar-powered-airplane-completes-first-leg-of-u-s-flight)

741 Reference: *New York to Beijing in two hours without leaving the ground?* (http://www.gizmag.com/et3-vacuum-maglev-train/21833/)

742 Reference: *Petroleum* (http://www.instituteforenergyresearch.org/energy-overview/petroleum-oil/)

government fuel consumption in 2007.[743] The US military uses more energy than most countries. The military is also one of the greatest polluters in the world.[744] So, working to shut down all military establishments would facilitate a vast increase in this resource's abundance.

Yet, as noted, oil is still polluting in multiple ways so using it as we have for combustion is not environmentally intelligent. The real solution is social revision. While the edifice of human society today has a vast dependence on oil and gas in general, generating all sorts of products from plastics and fertilizers, creative engineers have been slowly challenging this core chemical foundation need for many years.

Plastics, which are ubiquitous in the world today, have been almost exclusively in the territory of petroleum for some time. However, recently Dutch scientists have invented means to replace oil-based plastics by using plant matter.[745] [746] Likewise, an organization called Evocative has been able to use mushrooms to generate fully sustainable materials which can also serve to replace many petroleum uses for insulation and the like.[747]

Overall, a great deal of scientific work is going into substitutes for petroleum and most are plant oils and fats because they have essentially the same base chemical structure as petroleum. So, the real issue again is *focus*. Today, commercially available, non-petroleum based plastic bottles ("bioplastic") are becoming much more common[748] so it is clear that the real solution to evolving out of our material petroleum dependence is an issue of intention by the scientific community.

Agriculture is another concern. Fertilizers and pesticides require oil and natural gas and it is well argued that modern civilization, given its rate of food consumption and growth, based on current methods, would not be able to function without these base means. This is likely true. However, that is partly why the prior vertical farming section is so important. Rather than seek to replace these mediums, within the context of *traditional* agricultural, the solution is

---

743 Source: Colonel Gregory J. Lengyel, USAF, The Brookings Institution, Department of Defense Energy Strategy, August 2007.

744 Reference: *The Elephant in the Room: The U.S. Military is One of the World's Largest Sources of C02* (http://www.washingtonsblog.com/2009/12/removing-war-from-global-warming.html)

745 Source: *Who Needs Oil When Scientists Can Make Plastic From Plants?* (http://gizmodo.com/5885953/who-needs-oil-when-scientists-can-make-plastic-from-plants)

746 Source: *Supported Iron Nanoparticles as Catalysts for Sustainable Production of Lower Olefins* (http://www.sciencemag.org/content/335/6070/835.abstract)

747 Source: *Mushroom Materials* (http://www.ecovativedesign.com/mushroom-materials/)

748 Reference: *Coke, Ford join forces to juice supply of plant-based plastic* (http://www.greenbiz.com/blog/2012/06/14/coca-cola-nike-ford-join-forces-juice-supply-plant-based-plastic)

to bypass the problem with the new methods.

Overall, if you think of anything oil and hydrocarbons do today, you can either find an establishment-preserving replacement for it (i.e. the plant oil-based plastics which work in most existing industrial contexts) or a completely new approach based on revised methods which bypass the problem altogether (i.e. vertical farming and its little need for such fertilizer). Not to mention, if we remove oil and gas simply from the main combustion purposes, you then free up so much of it that, apart from environmental concerns, the resource becomes that much more abundant, giving even more time to find further solutions to eliminate any and all environmentally unsustainable realities.

TechnoCapitalist Apologetics

At the root of the increased capacity for abundance, as noted prior, is ephemeralization or doing "more with less". Moore's Law, which is the phenomenon that computer power or chip performance essentially doubles every 18 months, has been found in the modern day to also include any kind of information-based technology.[749] For example, the application of labor automation, which is a combination of robotics and programming, both of which are defined by information in origin, reveals how the means of production itself is becoming an information technology and hence subject to exponential growth as well.

In financial terms, the result of this pattern has been cheaper price values as the efficiency inherent reduces costs to whatever degree allowed. This can be seen in the sharp rise in inexpensive and now ubiquitous technologies, such as cell phones. In absolute abstraction, with all things being equal, assuming society maintained only its current spectrum of use goods, many production trends have the capacity to approach "near zero" value. Given this, the question arises: at what state of such exchange value reduction (price) does value itself become so miniscule as to become moot in and of itself, as an economic factor? Can we expect that potential to occur to such an anticipated high degree in the market system?

The answer is no. The market will never create such large scale, dramatic, post-scarcity implying reductions overall due to its central need for scarcity to keep monetary turnover and hence keep people employed. It is worth noting that many in the modern technology movements still justify the existence of market capitalism, as a means towards "abundance", by observing this general cost reduction phenomenon. As the argument goes, the unfolding of a given production and its increased demand facilitates "better" production methods and hence more savings by the company means more savings by the consumer. This then makes some goods available, over time, to those who would not have been able to afford them prior. If taken at face value, this observation suggests all goods will

---

749 Reference: *Big Idea: Technology Grows Exponentially*
(http://bigthink.com/think-tank/big-idea-technology-grows-exponentially)

approach zero in value overtime, as a given market increases in demand.

The first problem, however, is that this argument simply ignores the vast array of general technical inefficiency which can also, if addressed and solved, create those same reduced costs. In other words, it conflates, erroneously, "market efficiency" and "technical efficiency". Globalization is a common example. While cheap, primitive, Third World labor might be helpful to bring the cost down of a given product for the American consumer market, the wasted energy, wasted resources and possibly inhumane conditions created/exploited to facilitate that "price advantage" really present deep and caustic inefficiencies, in the broad view.

As an aside, while it is indeed true that certain types of technology, usually computer related, are today widely available for many who otherwise would not be able to afford it, this is a result of scientific ingenuity, not the market. Many traditional economists today make the assertion constantly, that "if it weren't for capitalism...", etc. The truth is that the market is nothing more than an incentive and delivery system and while the profit motivation may, at times, incorporate high levels of technical advancement which achieve a higher output potential, invigorating this "more with less" phenomenon, this is but one possible outcome amongst many. Many other highly profitable means can be utilized which have zero to negative value in the pursuit of post-scarcity itself.

Perhaps the best way to think about it is as a self-limiting threshold. The profit goal of cost efficiency is to remain "competitive" against other producers, while naturally seeking maximum income to keep employees paid and the structure of the company intact. That is the incentive equation. Obviously, no company wants to make itself obsolete by pursuing a state of extreme efficiency.

Likewise, profit culture is shortsighted by nature. This means that when faced with a decision for cost efficiency, the easiest and most immediate path to realize this change will likely be pursued. That can, again, mean the difference between updating a technical operation to be more efficient in its process of actual production - or simply outsourcing to a developing country which can be paid so little due to existing poverty - if it looks best on paper as far as cost savings. The market sees no difference between the two. Decisions are based merely on the trade value and the end tends to justify the means.

So, as time progresses, the market process may, indeed, continue to make certain high demand goods more accessible to those who couldn't afford them prior. However, that is not evidence that the fruits of a true, post-scarcity oriented society can be obtained on the whole in the same framework. It will only be through a direct revision of society to accept the post-scarcity intent, removing the interest to preserve scarcity, which is common today, that true progress in abundance will be realized. This conclusion is also avoiding the vast array of other large-scale efficiency problems inherent to market capitalism with respect to cultural and environmental sustainability, which have been discussed at length in other essays.

As a final note, the debate over "technological unemployment" has proven to be a powerful revelation in this clash of perceived intentions as well. Capitalist apologists have been hiding behind the idea that while technology does replace human labor, it is also creating it. While this may have been true in the slower moving past, a highly skewed reality has become ever more apparent.[750]

For one, the exponential increases occurring today have proven to be outpacing human educational adaptation greatly. There is no 1:1 job loss to job creation process unfolding in the modern world. Job losses today and job loss possibilities for the future are enormous when the machine applications are reviewed objectively, given the exponential trends. The interesting thing is that this very process of automation is a huge part of creating abundance, even though companies, in the logic of seeking profit, are using it to save money. The result is a complex dichotomy, with fewer human workers and hence less money available as purchasing power.

Of all the symptoms of failure of the capitalist model, this technological unemployment phenomenon just might be the most profound as it really reveals a clash of system functions. Capitalism presupposes that human labor demand will be near constant and all encompassing. Yet, if it is cheaper to employ machines to do human roles, how do we get "spending money" to humans who have now been removed from the labor force due to those very machines? How can the machines continue to produce without the "fuel" of monetary circulation?

In the end, the reduced value argument within the capitalist context simply doesn't work as it assumes a direct balance adjustment between cost reduced price value (saving of money due to mechanization to lower final good price) to meet the ever decreasing purchasing power of the now poorly employed consumers (those jobs removed due to mechanization).

The only way this could work is if the profit motive itself was removed, which is essentially impossible if we are to still think within the context of a market economy. The only reason companies employ technology to replace human labor to begin with is to save money and increase their competitive place in the overall economy by some degree. This intention undermines any kind of distribution balance between buying power and cost-savings.

---

750 Reference: *Coming to an office near you*
(http://www.economist.com/news/leaders/21594298-effect-todays-technology-tomorrows-jobs-will-be-immenseand-no-country-ready)

-TRUE ECONOMIC FACTORS-

The world has changed far more in the past 100 years than in any other century in history. The reason is not political or economic but technological - technologies that flowed directly from advances in basic science.[751]
-Stephen Hawking

Overview

In Greek, *economy* means the management of a household.[752] The defining qualitative attribute of an economy is its level of "efficiency". As opposed to the practice of "market efficiency" common today, this form of efficiency relates to *physical systems* – not the inter-workings of "money", the "market" and other arguably cultural contrivances.[753]

In this process of physical evaluation, we inevitably end up with a set of interrelated components appropriately called *economic factors*. Again, these components, unlike the vast financial theories in play in the modern world today, have nothing to do with the act of commerce or the like. Rather, they factor in the *actual* technical processes, hence trends, potentials and measurement requirements, needed for optimized system organization of industrial extraction, production, distribution, design, recycling protocols and the like.

However, for the sake of comprehension, even though this manner of economic thought is a vast departure from the traditional monetary-based economic theories we endure today, this essay will still frame these *resource-based* economic components in the context of traditional "microeconomic" and "macroeconomic" categorical distinctions, as would be found in common textbooks with respect to monetary economics.

The *macroeconomic components* have to do with the largest possible physical system degree associations we can comprehend. The *microeconomic components* relate to specific industries or sectors, usually associated with singular good production, regional distribution and regenerative specifics. (This will be expanded upon more so later in this essay.) By *system* extension, *macroeconomic* components naturally govern the logic related to the *microeconomic components* as well. For example, the macroeconomic attribute of *global resource management* has a universal bearing on the proper unfolding of microeconomic operations such as product design efficiency (which invariably use such global resources).

However, before these component factors are addressed, a further discussion of *systems* is in order, along with a declaration of what our societal *goals* actually are.

---

751 Steven Hawking, *A Brief History of Relativity*, Time Magazine, December 31st, 1999
752 The term 'economy' in Greek [Oikonomia] means the "management of a household; thrift" - hence to e·con·o·mize, or "increase efficiency".
753 See the essay *Market Efficiency vs. Technical Efficiency.*

General Systems Theory

General Systems Theory is an idea likely made most famous by biologist Ludwig Von Bertalanffy. He stated: "...there exist models, principles, and laws that apply to generalized systems or their subclasses, irrespective of their particular kind, the nature of their component elements, and the relationships or "forces" between them. It seems legitimate to ask for a theory, not of systems of a more or less special kind, but of universal principles applying to systems in general."[754] While systems theorists throughout the years have put a great deal of intellectual complexity and elaboration forward, the basic recognition is rather simple and intuitively easy to grasp.

The human body, for example, is composed of various system interconnections which not only natively regulate specific processes for a given purpose (such as the heart and its role in blood circulation), these systems always have smaller and larger *degree relationships* as well. In the case of the heart, the *blood* it circulates has its own set of defined chemical properties and system behaviors (smaller degree system relationship) while the heart itself is also a component part of the total human *organ array* (larger degree system relationship) and hence connects with, for example, the *lungs* which assist in oxygen distribution throughout the *blood stream*.

Extending this example to *larger degree* relationships, this human system is connected to an ecological system,[755] which invariably has a direct correlation to human health. For instance, poor industrial methods existing within this ecological system can introduce, for example, pollution into the air, causing conditions that might set the stage for lung problems or other detriments to human health.

Of course, system relationships to human health are not only "physical" in the traditional sense of the term, they are also *psychologically* and *sociologically* causal. Science has come to better understand how human learning and behavioral propensities are generated through both genetic and environmental influences, invariably engaging a larger systems context. For example, as noted in prior essays, addiction problems, such as with drugs or alcohol, can often be found linked to early life stress and emotional loss.[756] In truth, the very basis for *understanding public health is of a systems recognition, without exception.*

Now, binding all systems are what could be termed "generalized governing principles". In scientific terms, a "generalized" principle or theory is a foundational characteristic or assumption that

---

754 Ludwig Von Bertalanffy, *General System theory: Foundations, Development, Applications*, New York: George Braziller, 1976, p.32

755 Ecology is defined as: the branch of biology dealing with the relations and interactions between organisms and their environment, including other organisms. (http://dictionary.reference.com/browse/ecology)

756 Dr. Gabor Maté in his work *In the Realm of Hungry Ghosts* (North Atlantic Books, 2012) presents an enormous amount of research regarding how 'emotional loss' occurring at young ages affects behavior in later life, specifically the propensity for addictions.

governs an entire system. A notable, ongoing quest of modern science has been the search for universally governing principles that apply to all known systems in the universe, as gestured in the prior quotation by Ludwig Von Bertalanffy.

While a great deal of theoretical debate exists with respect to the complex behavior of certain systems, (finding clashes of perspective between, for example, "classical mechanics" and "quantum mechanics") the understandings relevant to efficient economic organization - a system *design* intended to optimize human well-being and long term ecological/social sustainability - need not get lost in such abstraction. Thus, the economic relationships presented in this essay are fairly obvious and easy to validate.

However, let it be stated that when the *systems worldview* is truly understood in its profound ramification of immutable interconnectedness and hence interdependence/co-responsibility of literally everything in the known universe, traditional cultural notions based on human or social division - such as religious loyalty, race loyalty, class, nation states, patriotism and other manifestations born from a world arguably ignorant of this reality in the past – can create nothing but confusion, maladjustment and conflict in the long-term.

Realizing and striving to *think* in the context of interconnected systems is critical for intellectual development, hence creating an educational imperative for people to also learn more as "generalists" as opposed to rigid "specialists", which is the current pattern due to the structure of our traditional labor roles. Sadly, our educational system today has been shaped and structured *not* to create well-rounded understandings of the world, but rather directs focus to isolated and narrow specialties, which reduce systems comprehension consequently.[757]

So, returning to the specific context of the creation of an economic model, this system relevance inherently creates an essentially "self-generating" causality that reduces subjectivity greatly. When we relate current understandings of the *human system* to the *ecological system,* we find a process of objective calculation with respect to what is possible and sustainable, both in the general structure of industrial processes and the *value structure* of society itself.

In the end, once this reality is understood, knowing that we may never have an absolute understanding of the total, universal governing system, our task is hence to derive an economic model that best *superimposes* upon such known properties and relationships of the physical world, adapting and adjusting as efficiently as possible, as new feedback (information) continues to prove valid. Put another way, the creation of an economic model is really a process of structural alignment with the existing ecological system already in play on the

---

757 Reference: "Education and the Market Model", John McMurtry, *Journal of Philosophy of Education* Volume 25, Issue 2, pps 209–217, 1991 Online: http://onlinelibrary.wiley.com/doi/10.1111/j.1467-9752.1991.tb00642.x/abstract

planet earth. The degree to which we are able to achieve this, defines our success.

Social Goals

While diverse global cultures today show many unique features and interests, there is still a basic, virtually universal set of shared *needs* which revolve around survival. In concert, this essentially comprises the basis of "public health", in its broadest definition.

Below is a list of general, seemingly obvious social "goals" which this new economic model would work to meet, with detailed explanations following. Overall, they are component goals of the pursuit to *increase quality of life* for the whole of humanity, while maintaining true sustainability in the long run.

Goals:
(1) Optimized Industrial Efficiency; Active Pursuit of "Post-Scarcity Abundance".
(2) Maintain Optimized Ecological/Cultural Balance & Sustainability.
(3) Deliberate Liberation of Humanity from Monotonous/Dangerous Labor.
(4) Facilitate Active System Adaptation to Emerging Variables.

(1) Optimized Industrial Efficiency; Active Pursuit of "Post-Scarcity Abundance":

Unlike the current, structural economic mandate to *preserve inefficiency* for the sake of monetary circulation, economic growth and power preservation,[758] this goal seeks to optimize, both technically and structurally, all industrial processes to work towards and create what could be gesturally termed a *post-scarcity abundance*.

In short, a *post-scarcity abundance* is an idealized state that eliminates scarcity of a given resource or process, usually by means of optimized efficiency regarding production design and strategic use. Needless to say, the idea of achieving *universal* post-scarcity - meaning an abundant amount of everything for everyone - is rightfully an impossibility, even in the most optimistic views. Therefore, this term, as used here, really highlights a *point of focus*.[759]

Common examples of current post-scarcity realities, which will be addressed at length in a later essay,[760] include the statistically proven ability to generate an abundance of nutrition for the world's population, an abundance of energy for responsible human use, an abundance of domiciles to shelter, at a high level of quality, every family on earth, along with an abundance of goods, both needs-based

---

758 See the essay *Market Efficiency vs. Technical Efficiency*.
759 The matter of degree, in fact, becomes arbitrary. Even if only possible with a few resource sets, it does not change the goal and importance of the pursuit of post-scarcity. Social improvement in general has been based upon such alleviations.
760 See the essay *Post-Scarcity Trends, Capacity and Efficiency*.

(i.e. tools) and *reasonable*[761] want based (luxury/specialty items) to facilitate an ever-easing and improving quality of life unknown by likely 99% of humanity today.

These and many other possibilities have been proven as statistical realties for the Earth's current population and beyond, accomplished through what R. Buckminster Fuller gesturally called the "Design-Science Revolution",[762] or the re-design of our social infrastructure to enable this new and profound efficiency.

Needless to say, this societal redesign suggests a radical departure from current social norms and established traditions, including the very nature of our socioeconomic/governmental structure itself. (The complex subject of transition will be discussed in a later essay.)[763]

(2) Maintain Optimized Ecological Balance & Sustainability:

Maintaining environmental sustainability is of obvious importance given the human species has no independence from its habitat and is strictly supported by it. In fact, evolution itself reveals that we are actually *generated from the habitat*, further expressing the deeply symbiotic/synergistic connection.

Any negative disturbance of these interconnected ecological systems will likely result in proportional negative disturbances of our wellbeing over time. Therefore, making sure the economic system in practice has a structural, built-in respect for these natural orders is critical to public health and sustainability in the long term. This aspect itself is, in fact, a gauge of an economic system's own practical validity as a life-support structure.

It is worth reiterating that the current market model of economics maintains literally *no structural acknowledgment* of these natural order laws. The market simply *assumes* such balance will be maintained through what are rightly deemed *metaphysical* mechanisms related to monetary-market dynamics alone -[764] A false assumption.

(3) Deliberate Liberation of Humanity from Monotonous, Dangerous & Irreverent Labor:

As will be described in technical detail in a later essay[765] with respect to the powerful, ephemeralization oriented trend of what is termed

---

761 The physically unsustainable, excessive property and "hoarding" mentality common to the current culture's ideal of high social status and success today needs alleviation.

762 Suggested Reading: R. Buckminster Fuller, *Critical Path*, St. Martin's Press, 1981

763 See the essay *Transition & The Hybrid Economy*.

764 See the essay *History of Economy*, where Adam Smith's notion of the "Invisible Hand" is discussed.

765 See the essay *Post-Scarcity Trends, Capacity and Efficiency*

mechanization (meaning the application of machines, displacing labor roles commonly held by humans) the need for human toil and suffering in monotonous, irrelevant or dangerous occupations has become increasingly less needed.

This new technical reality has also created trends which were once unimaginable, such as the fact that the application of automation has proven to now be more efficient than human labor, making the persistent tradition of "earning a living" an increasingly irresponsible social convention given that we can now do *more with less people* in virtually every sector today.

Likewise, it is also important to consider the pattern of human employment over generational time, recognizing that the current social detriment of "unemployment" is entirely manifest from the application of technology to labor.[766] The great myth of the 20th century, propagated by market economists is that technology creates jobs in the same proportion as jobs are taken away by it.[767] This is now proven as statistically incorrect as the exponential increase in information technology and its translation into ever-advancing machine efficiency proves the fallacy of this once *seemingly* true observation.[768] Today, the 21st century labor crisis shows no sign of subsiding[769] and

---

766 Economists would likely dispute this statement today, with the claim of "outsourcing" and other issues brought into the equation (along with other narrow, truncated distinctions). In truth, looking at human labor without borders, on the global scale, over generational time, we see that it has been technology and only technology that has shifted both production methods and what is of interest to produce. If this progress were not seen, humanity would never have experienced the Neolithic Revolution and hence would still be hunting and gathering in a primitive way.

767 This assumption is part of what has been historically termed the "The Luddite Fallacy". It is worth noting that even if one were to entertain the Luddite Fallacy's claim that new jobs are created to equally compensate for displaced labor in a now-mechanized sector, increasingly it is becoming realized that such jobs arguably have little to no actual relevance to the viability and function of life-support. Hence, the "new jobs created" invariably serve as a kind of waste of human energy. It is one thing to perform acts of interest in one's life, on one's own accord. It is another to be coerced into such meaningless labor simply because you must "work for a living". Suggested Reading: David Graeber, *On the Phenomenon of Bullshit Jobs*, Strike Magazine, 2013 (http://www.strikemag.org/bullshit-jobs/)

768 The issue here is the rate of technological acceleration. One hundred years ago, this rate of change was much less rapid, while today the rate of change is increasing exponentially forward. While social shifts in industry and labor were able to dynamically compensate for this change in the past due to the relatively slow pace, as time moves forward, it will become ever more difficult to maintain "labor for income" as we know it in the current tradition. This is also because the exponential growth curve reduces the cost of machine automation tools over time, setting up a general inevitability that human labor in a certain sector will not only be outdone in performance by machine but they will be cheaper in the long run. Suggested Reading: http://www.kurzweilai.net/the-law-of-accelerating-returns

769 News and statistical reports on an emerging Global Unemployment Crisis

will only find resolution through a restructuring of industrial labor methods, altering the "work for a living" tradition dramatically.[770]

(4) Facilitate Active System Adaptation to Emerging Variables:

While this goal might seem more abstract than prior goals, acknowledging the emergent reality of intellectual and industrial evolution is critical. We must *structurally* allow for adaptation.

The aggregate intellectual culmination of human knowledge is and, as the trends currently show, will always be, incomplete. Many practices that might be deemed "sustainable" or in accord with public health today, might very well be found to be detrimental in a relative or absolute sense in the future. An example would be the decades past of oil combustion. While little negative retroactions were found during its early use, today there is a strong push to move away from hydrocarbon energy use due to the growing consequences resulting from its employment as the primary energy source for society – especially given the current state of more clean and more abundant alternatives.

Therefore, the industrial/economic system must be dynamically updatable, enabling rapid error correction and improvement as progress unfolds. Again, this type of flexibility is currently missing in the market economy today, since any such changes often have a destabilizing effect on the profitability of related industries. Change in general is extremely slow in the modern period in this regard due to the *paralysis* that originates from the preservation of market share and group power. It can be well argued that progress is often *detrimental* to existing profit schemes.

Macroeconomic Factors:

In traditional, market-based economic theory, *macroeconomics* deals with the broadest influences and policies that affect, in part, the dynamics and probable outcomes of the *microeconomic* condition. This usually relates to growth measures, employment levels, interest rates, national debts, currencies and the like.

In the context of a NLRBE, we can also establish economic components which could be categorically thought about in the same way, only this time it has to do with the largest order *governing* pressures of the physical world directly, along with how these *physical principles* relate to the more "microeconomic" actions of good production, design, distribution and the like. In other words, it is an

---

have been prolific in the early 21st century, specifically with young adults. Reference: *Generation jobless*
(http://www.economist.com/news/international/21576657-around-world-almost-300m-15-24-year-olds-are-not-working-what-has-caused)

770 Reference: *Could Automation Lead to Chronic Unemployment? Andrew McAfee Sounds the Alarm*
(http://www.forbes.com/sites/singularity/2012/07/19/could-automation-lead-to-chronic-unemployment-andrew-mcafee-sounds-the-alarm/)

overarching *rule structure*, supported by essentially physical science, to ensure true economic efficiency is maintained and optimized.

At the core of the macroeconomic (and, by extension, microeconomic) approach rests the method of thought and analysis itself. This is "The Scientific Method". It is often said that nothing in science can be proven, only disproven. This is the beauty of the method as its inherent skepticism of its own conclusions, if uninhibited by human bias, can assure continual progress and adjustment. Science gives a vehicle to *arrive at conclusions*, not "make them", and it is this *system-based logic* where all economic decisions are to be oriented regarding both possibilities and restrictions.[771]

Inherent to The Scientific Method in the context of "macroeconomic policy" for a NLRBE are what we could consider *Earth-wide* recognitions. These components have to do essentially with the following:

(1) Global Resource Management
(2) Global Demand Assessment
(3) Global Production and Distribution Protocols.

These three factors are considered "macroeconomic" since they embody core, near universal infrastructure considerations, regardless of what a given production specifically entails or where it is on the planet. (It should also be immediately recognized that the concept of a "national economy" is no longer viable in this perspective, nor was it ever, in truth, technically speaking.)

(1) Global Resource Management:

Global Resource Management is the process of tracking resource use and hence working to predict and avoid shortages and other problems. In effect, it is no different than the logic underlying most common inventory systems we might find in the commercial arena today. However, this system has to do primarily with tracking the rate of natural generation to maintain *dynamic equilibrium*.[772]

All known natural resources - whether lumber, copper ore, water, oil, etc. - have their own rates of natural regeneration, if any. In certain cases, such as the state of certain metals or minerals, regeneration rates are so large scale that it would be more appropriate to simply assume a finite supply outright.[773] Overall, this process would begin with a total Earth survey to whatever degree technically possible, tracked in real-time to whatever degree technically possible.

The catalogue of tracked resource components would include

---

771 See the essay *The Scientific Worldview*.
772 Dynamic Equilibrium is defined as: "A condition in which all acting influences are cancelled by others, resulting in a stable, balanced, or unchanging system." Source:
http://www.thefreedictionary.com/dynamic+equilibrium
773 For example, metals such as copper are now widely accepted to have originated in stars, with the earth collecting these materials as it formed.

all forms, from biotic resources such as trees, to abiotic resources such as iron ores and the like. Pollution and other ecological disturbances of resource integrity would also be accounted for. While such a total systems approach to this Earth-wide resource accounting and tracking system might seem like a difficult task, it is actually very feasible in the modern day, with such technology already being employed by respective industries in the corporate setting.

(2) Global Demand Assessment:
Global Demand Assessment is the process of realizing the demands of the human population. In short, this process would be broken up into a series of regional surveys, coupled with the release of publications that inform the public as to new designs possible in consumer or industrial production.

Whereas from the current cultural practice, which consists of public advertising by profit seeking corporations, often impose status/vanity oriented values on the population in many respects rather than serving to assist them with existing needs, the process of engagement in a NLRBE deals explicitly with creating awareness of new technical possibilities as they emerge, while also allowing public consensus to decide what is of interest to produce and what isn't.[774]

This could be termed the "market" of a NLRBE. In many ways, it can also be considered the mechanism of societal "governance" itself since this type of social interaction towards decision-making does not have to be restricted to mere good design and production.[775] After all, at the core of any society are *really* the technical mechanisms that enable order, well-being and quality of life.

We often forget what the purpose of a government really is in the modern day. At its core, it is a means to assist economic organization to improve life, ease stress and create safety. The problem is that government today has necessarily turned into a system of essentially organized corruption and "mafia" type protectionism rather than a facilitator of life support.

In this new approach, a purely technical/interactive system is established which works, in gesture, similar to how the notion of "direct democracy"[776] has been proposed to work in the modern day, where decision-making processes involve group participation in a *direct* way, goal by goal. With the exponential increase in computer-based calculation power, this type of aggregate societal "thinking" is now possible.

The details of this interactive system, along with an expansion

---

774 Today, it is only through price and profitability that demand is accessed. Very rarely is the public invited to participate in future designs.

775 This will be addressed further in the essay: *The Industrial Government*

776 Unlike "Representative Democracy" where elected representatives make decisions, Direct Democracy allows individuals to vote on issues. This association is used loosely here as the traditional notion of direct democracy is too primitive. The suggested system has to do with public participation in cumulative design of goods to meet needs, in part.

of an integral concept termed as "automated design" or the calculation of *utility-based systems* (in this context the *system* being a good in question), will be addressed in a following essay.[777] However, let it be stated that all designs have a built-in logic towards what works, what is sustainable and what reduces negative retractions (or problems). It is this new, technical referential benchmark that guides the process of industrial design.

Now, a final note worth mentioning in passing is that in the current market economy, the demand assessment process is orchestrated in a deeply haphazard manner via what is traditionally termed the "price mechanism".[778] Many in traditional economic schools have even argued that the dynamic variability of human interests makes it technically *impossible* to calculate such demand without the price mechanism. While this may have been somewhat true in the early 20th century when these claims were made, the age of advanced computer calculation, coupled with modern sensing and tracking technology, has removed this barrier of complexity.[779]

(3) (a) Global Production & (b) Distribution Protocols:
Global Production and Distribution Protocols address the reasoning by which the overall industrial system is to be laid out in the context of Earth surface infrastructure. This simple notion has to do with where these facilities are located and why. A basic economic factor to consider here is what we will call the "proximity strategy".

In the current system, the property orientation forces facilities for production and distribution to be scattered and rather random in placement. The advent of globalization and the constant search for cost efficiency by corporations via cheap labor and resources creates enormous inefficiency and waste, not to mention a basis for inhumane labor exploitation and other problems.

In a NLRBE, the organization of global industrial processes are based on optimizing efficiency at all times, creating a *network* of facilities, logically based around factors related to the *purpose* of those facilities. This is actually simple to consider since the variables related can be quantified in importance fairly easily. Since the shortest distance between two points is a straight line, coupled with the modern technical capacity to produce many goods without the need for regional conditions (e.g. advanced, enclosed food production systems), a core concern to reduce energy and waste is to localize, as much as possible.

---

777 See the essay *The Industrial Government*.
778 Ludwig von Mises in his famous work *Economic Calculation in the Socialist Commonwealth* argues that the "price mechanism" is the only possible means to understand how to "efficiently" create and move goods around an economy. This criticism of any kind of "planned" system has been touted as sacrosanct by many today and as a vindication of the capitalist system.
779 See the essay *The Industrial Government*.

(3a) Global Production Protocols: The best way to express this is to provide a specific example by which variations can find a common context. We will use the example of the textile industry, specifically the manufacturing of clothing.

Today, 98% of the clothing Americans wear is imported, mostly from China.[780] Most clothes are still made from cotton today. Where does China like to get a great deal of its cotton? - the United States.[781] So, today, the United States produces a core raw commodity for the textile industry, ships to China to make the clothes, only to have it shipped back to the US when done.

We can use our imagination with respect to the millions of barrels of oil alone wasted over time on this movement of materials, when such harvesting and production could be localized very easily. Again, this is a product of the market economy's internal economic mechanisms that have *no regard* for true, Earthly economic relationships - which require physical efficiency and waste reduction - not financial efficiency and a reduction of monetary costs. This is a clear disconnect.

(3b) Global Distribution Protocols: The same basic logic applies to post-production distribution. Once goods are created, they are to be made available regionally in the most efficient way possible, based on *demand* and *proximity*. Once established per regional needs, distribution has three basic components:

3b1) Facility Location
3b2) Method of Access
3b3) Tracking/Feedback.

3b1) Facility Location:
Facility Location is based on logical proximity of a population concentration. This is best exemplified with the current practice today of (usually) placing grocery stores in average convenience about a community, though even this strategy is often compromised by the market's inherent logic.[782] However, other technological factors could come into play to ease the movement of goods and reduce waste, along with more convenient access. While local facilities containing the most commonly needed goods might exist in close proximity around a community, delivery systems, such as automated *pneumatic tube* structures for medium-sized products, could be installed into homes in

---

780 Source: Clothing 'Made in America': Should U.S. Manufacture More Clothes? (http://abcnews.go.com/Business/MadeInAmerica/made-america-clothes-clothing-made-usa/story?id=13108258)

781 Source: China Said to Buy 1 Million Tons of U.S. Cotton for Reserves (http://www.bloomberg.com/news/2012-06-15/china-said-to-buy-1-million-tons-of-u-s-cotton-for-reserves-1-.html)

782 Reference: *Why do competitors open their stores next to one another? - Jac de Haan* (http://ed.ted.com/lessons/why-do-competitors-open-their-stores-next-to-one-another-jac-de-haan)

the same manner as plumbing is built into a home today.

Other variations could include systems of access based on specific, regional needs, such as the case with recreational activities. Access facilities can be placed on location for various interests, such as sports resources, supplying needed equipment at the time and place of use.

3b2) Method of Access:

Method of Access is best described as a shared "library" system. This isn't to imply that all items retrieved must be "returned" to these access facilities, but to show that they *can be* for convenience. It is certainly a welcomed practice since this process of "sharing" is a powerful enabler of both *preservation* efficiency and public *access* efficiency. In other words, fewer goods are needed to meet the interests of more of the population through sharing systems, as compared to the 1:1 universal property system practiced today.

A common example would be specialized tool needs that are used relatively sparsely in the population. Production equipment for a specific project and recreation equipment that might be used only a few times a year, are simple examples. On the other side of the spectrum, everyday needs, such as personal communication technology and the like, are made available in the same way, with an expectation of return likely only when the item fails, so it can be recycled or repaired. This concept of moving from a *property-oriented* to an *access-oriented society* is a powerful notion. Today, certain "rental" industries have already seen the fruits of this concept in the form of convenience, even in a market system.[783]

Again, comparing to the current model, these facilities exist like "stores" do today, with regional demand dynamically calculated to ensure supply abundance and avoid shortages and overruns. The difference is that nothing is "sold" and the ethos is of an strategically efficient, interactive system of sharing, with, again, returns occurring also when product life expires or when the good is no longer needed.

As an aside, there is a common reaction to this idea that problems such as "hoarding" or some kind of abuse would ensue. This assumption is basically superimposing *current* monetary-market consequences on the new model, erroneously. People in the scarcity driven world today hoard and protect impulsively when they have something to fear or wish to exploit goods for their market value. In the NLRBE, there is no resale value in the system since there is no money.[784] Therefore, the idea of hoarding anything would be an

---

783 Bike and Car sharing systems are common examples. The "ZipCar" is a company that provides localized access to car rentals in a regional context, based on need. Likewise, Europe has seen a rise in on-location street bike rentals as well, with various docking/access stations strategically located around a city.

784 A summarized explanation of why a monetary economy is structurally incompatible with the level of efficiency and goals of this new model is detailed in the essay: "Post-Scarcity Trends, Capacity and Efficiency"

inconvenience rather than an advantage.[785]

3b3) Tracking/Feedback:

Tracking and Feedback, as implied above, is an integral part of keeping the system, both regional and global, as fluid as possible, when it comes to not only the meeting of regional demand through adequate supply, but also keeping pace with changes in extraction, production, distribution technology and new demands. Naturally, these factors are highly synergistic. Sensor systems, programs and other resource tracking technology have been rapidly developing for various industrial uses.[786] Modern commercial inventory systems are already quite advanced in the proper context when it comes to demand and distribution. The issue is merely its scalability in certain contexts to account for all necessary attributes.

In conclusion to this section on macroeconomic factors, the overarching consideration is *efficiency on all levels* and this has its own causal logic as noted before, when considered in the larger ecological and physical system interconnectivity inherent to the natural world. This efficiency has to do with waste reduction and meeting human needs, always oriented in its possibilities by the current state of technology via the scientific method.

Microeconomic Factors:

Given these so-called *macroeconomic* concepts, it is important to restate that the underlying principles regarding optimum efficiency, productivity and sustainability are the same throughout the whole model, from top to bottom. This is, again, the *train of thought* coming from the scientific method, calculated within the near-empirical framework of natural law logic itself.

Now, while traditional market-based economic theory considers "microeconomics" as something of a study of the behavior of individuals, households and businesses making decisions around markets, price determinations and other factors based essentially around the movement of money in various ways, the microeconomic context of a NLRBE is quite different.

Microeconomic considerations in this new model revolve around the actual methods of good design and production itself. This is basically organized around two factors:

1) Product Design Efficiency
2) Means of Production Efficiency

(1) Product Design Efficiency relates to the integrity of design itself.

---

785 The subject of seemingly unpredictable, human behavioral aberration (i.e. "crime") is addressed in the essay "Lifestyle, Freedom and The Humanity Factor"
786 Reference: *HP invents a central nervous system for earth.*
http://www.fastcompany.com/1548674/hp-invents-central-nervous-system-earth-and-joins-smarter-planet-sweepstakes

Today, cost efficiency and the resulting technical inefficiencies, coupled with the corporate process of competition and the vast unnecessary duplication of specific goods, has created a climate of unnecessary waste and limited product lifespans. There are also, as will be discussed in greater detail in a moment, few built-in recycling protocols, if any, during these production designs as well. This is important because advanced recycling would assist in more preservation of materials in the long run, adding to long-term efficiency.

Likewise, *proprietary* technologies, serving the interest to preserve market share for a particular business, have created an environment where there is very little compatibility of component parts across multiple manufacturers of the same basic products.

Therefore, five component factors are relevant here:

1a) Optimized Durability
1b) Optimized Adaptability
1c) Universal Standardization
1d) Integrated Recycling Protocols
1e) Conducive for Automation

1a) Optimized Durability:

Optimized Durability simply means that any good produced is done so with the intention to last as long as possible, in this most strategic manner possible. The notion of *strategic* is important here for this is not to imply that all, for example, computer enclosures should be made out of titanium, simply because it is very strong. Once again, this is a *synergistic design calculation* where the notion of the "best" material for a given purpose is always relative to parallel production needs which also might require that type of material. Therefore, the decision to use a specific material is to be assessed not only for its use for the specific good, but also by comparing it to the needs of other productions which require similar efficiency. Nothing exists outside this system-centric comparison. All industrial decisions are made with consideration of the largest system degree of relevance.

This interest to create the "strategically best" is critical to human sustainability, especially when it has been reported that we are using our natural resources today *faster* than the planet is generating them, due to such inefficiencies.[787] The modern "throwaway" culture is not only driven by a hedonistic, short-sighted value system imposed by modern advertising and current measures of "wealth" and "success", it is also needed to maintain the paid labor system, a pivotal part of keeping the market economy going.

---

787 Source: *Report: Consumption of Earth's resources unsustainable*
(http://www.cbsnews.com/8301-205_162-57434525/report-consumption-of-earths-resources-unsustainable/)

242

1b) Optimized Adaptability:

Optimized Adaptability is really a sub-component of "Optimized Efficiency" in the context of design engineering. Today, from automobiles to cell phones, efficiency increasing technological advancements continue rapidly. Yet, even with this rapid rate of change, other larger order attributes remain the same for relatively longer periods of time, as per historical trends. In other words, different production components have different rates of change and this means a system of "adaptability" and active "updating" can be foreshadowed through trend analysis, with the resulting expectations *built into* an existing design to the best degree possible.

An example would be the rate of change of a computer system's chip processor (CPU). The advancement of chip power has been accelerating rapidly due to Moore's law. As a result, many software applications, as they improve to embrace these new speeds enabled, will not work on computer system with older chips. This typically forces the user to buy a new computer system, even though the only true issue is the CPU, not the whole system. While other factors can come into play such as system compatibility with the new chip, seldom do people update these chips alone, even though it is feasible.

This kind of adaptability is critical today on all levels, which alludes to the next economic component, "universal standardization".

1c) Universal Standardization:

Universal Standardization is a set of optimized protocols, generated from mass industrial feedback in a collaborative way that works to create uniform, universal compatibility of all components associated to a given good genre. Today, this lack of standardization is a source of not only great waste, but great instability in the functioning of common goods, since the competitive ethos and proprietary intent restricts efficiency in a powerful way.

This practice has been justified under the guise of "progress" in design with the premise that competing corporations, incentivized by financial gain, will "outdo" each other and hence be more productive with advancement. While there might be some truth to this, the retardation, waste and instability caused does not justify the practice. Furthermore, it has, and will always be, the sharing of information in the long run that has led to advancement, both personal and societal.

Creating a research database of known component parts by industry, actively shared across the world as a point of design reference and feedback in the creation of common parts and goods, is not a difficult task and certainly would not inhibit technological advancement or ingenuity. If anything, it would present more diverse information and perspectives and hence better decisions could be made faster.

1d) Integrated Recycling Protocols:

This simply means that the current state of component and material reuse is optimized directly and strategically considered in the very design of the product itself. Again, this does not happen in the modern day, in any efficient way. A survey of landfills in the world finds many useful component parts that have been discarded in association with larger systems (goods). Since a normal corporation who makes such items rarely encourages them to be returned for direct reprocessing, this is the inevitable outcome.

Furthermore, while traditional plastic, glass, paper and other recycling systems are in place with moderate efficiency, this process is really crude and ineffective in comparison to direct, industry-connected regeneration. In a NLRBE, optimized recycling considerations to reuse materials, preformed or not, would be standard. In the end, "landfills" would not exist in this approach, as there is a way to reuse virtually *everything* we produce, if we had the interest to do so.

1e) Conducive for Automation:

This means that a given good design accounts for the state of labor automation, seeking to remove human involvement whenever possible by more efficient, often less complex design. In other words, part of the efficiency equation is to make the production easy to produce by automated means, taking into account the current state of automation techniques. We seek to simplify the way materials and production means are used so that the maximum number of goods can be produced with the least variation of materials and production equipment. More on this in the next section.

(2) Means of Production Efficiency:

Means of Production Efficiency as an economic component refer to the actual tools and methods used in industrial production itself. While this could also be considered a macroeconomic factor in many ways, it is considered microeconomic based on the fact that it relates to direct, specific production as well, along with human labor roles.

The means of production of anything is directly related to the state of technology. From the Neolithic Revolution, with the advent of stone tools, to the birth of "cybernation" today and "thinking" machines that can assess, execute and problem solve, the core foundation of all "labor" has been an engagement with available, assisting technological tools.

The trend has been an easing of labor overall, with a general reduction of the human workforce in each sector as related to capacity. Two hundred years ago, the agricultural industry employed most of the people in the United States. Today, only a very small fraction is working in agriculture due to machine application and automation. This phenomenon and trend of "mechanization" is important because today it is challenging the very basis of the labor for income system, along with foreshadowing productivity moving towards a point of what could be termed "post-scarcity".

Today, we are more productive with less people in any given sector, relative to time and capacity, due to the application of machine technology. In many ways, this reality marks one of the most significant shifts in our social evolution, challenging the very fabric of our current social system, revealing immense possibilities for the future as far as the creation of a *strategic abundance*.

So, in a NLRBE, this ability is *maximized*, reducing the human work force as we know it by a liberal application and expansion of automation, increasing productivity vastly. Human labor involvement, while still necessary even in more advanced phases, is reduced to broad oversight of these automated systems as they are established. Factories are also no longer bound by traditional restrictions due to an eight hour long, five day a week schedule since there is no reason, given the massive reduction of human contribution possible. These systems could now function 24 hours a day, seven days a week, if needed.

As an aside, the question is often posed: "How many people are needed to oversee fluid operations and handle problem resolution?" This kind of question can be answered by assessing current statistical trends, averaging them and then extrapolating them forward.

However, there is a common confusion between "work" in the sense of common drudgery by which the monetary incentive is a common reward, and the "work" which all humans, due to pure creative interest and contributive intent, perform as well. A deep value shift assumed by TZM is that progress in the classic distinction of "work" will morph into a type of social contribution that is actually of enjoyment and interest to people. Today, all across the world, the human interest to explore, create and improve exists, regardless of the monetary imposition.

However, due the constant pressure for income in the current model, nearly all such acts assume the needed context of a pursuit of money for survival. It could be argued that this has polluted the more natural human incentive system to explore, learn and create, without such a pressure.

That noted, the notion of "work" then in the context of overseeing operations, repairing systems and other maintenance would likely not be reduced to the type of drudgery we so often considered the "work" reality in the modern day. Rather, the act is respected as a form of personal contribution for personal and social gain, since every act engaged in this type of system has a direct personal benefit to the people working to keep it operating smoothly.

Again, this incentive is almost non-existent in the current mode since the capitalist system is designed for all the core profit benefits to go to the *owners* of the businesses, with the fruits of production often never relating to the worker in a direct sense, absent mere wage rewards. Today, employee/owner relations exist as something of a "class war", with animosity between the groups a common occurrence.[788] In this new approach, all acts of contribution benefit the person performing the act, and the community at large. They are connected directly.

That being understood, only a very small fraction of the population would be "required", as it were, to engage in maintaining the core systems, likely about 5% of the population when industrial methods reach modern possibilities. This 5% could then be broken-up across the population. So, if a given population of a city region is 50,000 people, the industrial system would require 2500 people, assuming a traditional work week of eight hours a day for five days per week. This translates into 100,000 hours being worked a week. In terms of the total population this work responsibility amounts to a mutual obligation of each person "working" only two hours a week.

Clearly, this is a hypothetical as in such an advanced system, a system that serves everyone, human values would change greatly and many would likely be honored to take on more hours, reducing the obligation of others. Once again, we are talking about barebones maintenance here, as opposed to an immersive "job" as is currently understood and required. In reality, a free society of this nature could create an eruption of creative advancement and progress never before seen, with people working to contribute in vast, robust ways. Why? - Because, again, such individuals would also be helping themselves directly in the process. Any invention, or breakthrough in efficiency serves the entire community in this model. Self-interest becomes social interest.

So, to conclude this point, this new means of production is about focusing core labor on true technical productivity that has a direct social/personal return, with the most liberal focus on automation and such efficiency increasing technology and automation as much as possible.

Conclusion

As with anything of this brevity, we have an inevitable incompleteness. Other factors, both macro and micro, could be expressed in further detail. However, if one follows this basic train of thought, a train of thought governed by scientific logic to ensure optimized *physical efficiency* and *sustainability,* these other parameters inevitably make themselves known.

In short, the outcome of this NLRBE system requires the same type of respectful engagement as with any other natural system. Just as our understanding of the forest and its regeneration and biodiversity has led a basic philosophy to engage this ecosystem with respect to its vulnerabilities to ensure its long-term integrity, the same logic applies to the NLRBE as a whole.

This social model is an attempt to *mirror* the natural world in the most direct way possible and could be considered a "natural system" just like anything else we find in nature, such as an

---

788 See the essay *Structural Classism, the State and War.*

ecosystem. Would it ever be perfect? No. But the logical foundation is there for constant improvement, far beyond the state of affairs today.

The following summary tree, as a general outline for this essay, has been generated for review:

NLRBE: An Economic Model Overview:

-System (Social) Goals
       (1) Optimized Industrial Efficiency; Active Pursuit of "Post-Scarcity" Abundance.
       (2) Maintain Optimized Ecological/Cultural Balance & Sustainability.
       (3) Deliberate Liberation of Humanity from Monotonous/Dangerous Labor.
       (4) Facilitate Active System Adaptation to Emerging Variables.
-Macroeconomic Components
       (a) Global Resource Management
       (b) Global Demand Assessment
              -Creating awareness of new technical possibilities
              -Public consensus to decide what is of interest to produce
       (c) Global Production and Distribution Protocols
              -Global Production
                    -Strategic Localization
              -Global Distribution
                    -Facility Location
                    -Method of Access
                    -Tracking & Feedback
-Microeconomic Components
       (a) Specific Good Efficiency
              -Optimized durability
              -Optimized adaptability
              -Universal standardization
              -Integrated Recycling Protocols
              -Conducive for Automation
       (b) Means of Production Efficiency
              -Applied Mechanization

-THE INDUSTRIAL GOVERNMENT-

Modern politics is business politics...This is true both of foreign and domestic policy. Legislation, police surveillance, the administration of justice, the military and diplomatic service, all are chiefly concerned with business relations, pecuniary interests, and they have little more than an incidental bearing on other human interests.[789]
-Thorstein Veblen

Political vs. Technical Governance
The nature and unfolding of the politically driven model of representative democracy, legislation creation and the sanctioned enforcement of law, are all borne out of natural tendencies inherent to the act of commerce and trade, operating within a scarcity-driven social order.

The development of this commercial regulation and the rationale behind the very existence of "state governance" is quite easy to trace historically. After the Neolithic revolution, humanity's once nomadic patterns shifted toward a new propensity to farm, settle and create towns. Specialization flourished and trade was hence inevitable. However, given the possibility for imbalance and dispute, as regional populations grew and regional resources often became more scarce, a security and regulatory practice manifested to protect a community's land, property, trade integrity and the like.

The use of an "army", which is sanctioned to protect by public decree, became standardized, along with an adjacent legal or regulatory authority complex, sanctioned to essentially give power to a set group of officials which facilitate such policy creation, enforcement, trials, punishment practices and the like.

This is mentioned here as there are many schools of economic thought in the early 21st century that talk about reducing or even removing the state apparatus entirely, falsely assuming the state itself is a separate entity and the starting point of blame for current societal woes or economic inefficiencies. Yet, on the other side of the debate spectrum is a general cry for increased state regulation of the market to ensure more limits on business manipulation and hence work to avoid what has been often perceived as "crony capitalism"[790]. The truth of the matter is that this polarizing, false duality between the "state" and the "market" is blind to the true root cause of what is actually causing problems, not realizing that the dyad of state and market

---

789 The Theory of Business Enterprise, Thorstein Veblen, p.269
790 "Crony Capitalism" is defined as "A description of capitalist society as being based on the close relationships between businessmen and the state. Instead of success being determined by a free market and the rule of law, the success of a business is dependent on the favoritism that is shown to it by the ruling government in the form of tax breaks, government grants and other incentives."
[http://www.investopedia.com/terms/c/cronycapitalism.asp] It is important to note that TZM does not believe in this distinction as it falsely assumes such collusion is avoidable.

synergy is, in reality, a single power system in play, at once.

Irrespective of the merit of any specific argument as to the favoring of the "free market" vs. the favoring of "state regulation", all business dealings have historically required some level of legal mediation. This is because all transactions are a form of competition and all competition invites the possibility of fraud or abuse, given the natural pressure of external circumstances and the nature of survival itself, within the bounds of the scarcity-based market. The fact is, any form of commerce that exists in this scarcity-reinforced worldview, will manifest so-called "corrupt" or dishonest behavior constantly. It is firmly incentivized. The degree of corruption itself even becomes a matter of opinion, in fact. The line between accepted business acumen and blatant dishonest persuasion is not an easy distinction to make today in the broad view.

Therefore, some type of overriding decision-making power has always been granted to some group body to mediate conflicts and this is the seed of governmental power, as we know it. Yet, the punch line of the whole circumstance is that in a world where everything is powered by money; in a world where, in truth, everything is for sale, the rapid "corruption" of any such regulation or power establishment is also essentially guaranteed over time, to one degree or another.[791]

Put another way, there will always be a need for legal regulation of transactions in the market by some publicly sanctioned institution, and the market ethic will always corrupt such regulation to some extent with the influence of money because money and business are actually what make the world move. This is simply what is to be expected when the entire psychological foundation of existence is based on survival through acts of competitive self-interest, oriented by the universal assumption of empirical scarcity, with no real structural safeguards given to members of society for some reassurance in survival. To think any regulatory agency would not be susceptible to such corruption; to think state policy and hence coercion could not be 'purchased' like any other commodity is to deny the basic philosophical foundation inherent to the market's notion of "freedom" itself.

Therefore, complaining about state regulation or lack thereof is ultimately a moot issue in the broad scheme of long-term societal change. True social change will not come about by the illusive preference of one of these over the other. It will only come about by installing a completely different system which eliminates both the market and the state as we know it, elevating the entire framework

---

791 Corporate Lobbying, which is legal across the world, is a perfect example. This is legal because commercial institutions are the backbone of economic development. Government gains income from taxation and the level of gain coming from that taxation is directly tied to the businesses that hire people and sell goods. Therefore, it is only natural to assume they should have input in political decisions, at least in theory. Yet, the moral hazard is obvious since their input will inevitably work to serve their business interests. Civil government is, in truth, business government.
Ref: http://www.opensecrets.org/lobby/

out of the narrow, competitive focus of managing scarcity in the current "earn a living or suffer" system, to a focus on facilitating a sustainable abundance and the meeting of human needs directly.

So, the following economic and management information presents a vast departure from the current, day-to-day unfolding of life as we know it when it comes to commerce and social management. What this model does is literally remove the edifice of representative government and replace it with a kind of participatory democracy. This participation is mediated through digital communication methods that can bring the interests of the whole community into calculation, whether dealing with interests of the so-called "public" sector or the "private" sector. In actuality, there is no difference in the process of participation and hence there would no longer be a public or private sector.

The importance of this kind of management resides in several areas. For one it assures that human social operation is in accord with basic sustainability principles needed to operate with generational longevity, whilst also maintaining a vigilant focus on producing the most strategically necessary goods at the peak technical capacity known at the time of production. Such management is also about removing the vast incentive and requirement for corruption and corrupt behaviors, abuse and business/government collusion which has plagued civilization since antiquity. The active pursuit of abundance through these sustainable means ensures not only survival and efficiency, but stability, ease and a higher state of public health on a vast scale.

Economic Model Defined

An economic model is a theoretical construct representing component processes by a set of variables or functions, describing the logical relationships between them. If one has studied traditional or market-based economic modeling, a great deal of time is often spent on things such as price trends, behavioral patterns, inflation, the labor market, currency fluctuations, and so forth.

Rarely, if ever, is anything said about public or ecological health. Why? - Because the market is life-blind and decoupled from the actual science of life support and sustainability. It is a proxy system that is based only around the act of exchange and exchange preferences.

Therefore, the best way to think about a NLRBE is not in the traditional terms of any form of market-oriented economic model common today. Rather, this model can best be thought about as an *advanced production, distribution and management system*, which is democratically engaged by the public, through a kind of "participatory economics".

This type of approach facilitates input processes, such as design proposals and demand assessment, while also filtering all actions through what we could call *sustainability* and *efficiency* protocols. These protocols are the basic rules of industrial action set by natural law, not human opinion. As noted, neither of these two interests is structurally inherent in the capitalist model.

Goals, Myths & Overview

All economic systems have structural goals and often times these goals are not exactly apparent in the theories set forward in principle. The market system and a NLRBE have very different structural goals.

-Market capitalism's structural goal is growth and maintaining rates of consumption high enough to keep enough people employed at any given time. Likewise, employment itself requires a culture of real or perceived inefficiency and that often means the preservation of scarcity in one form or another.

-A NLRBE's goal is to optimize technical efficiency and create the highest level of abundance possible, within the bounds of Earthly sustainability, seeking to meet human needs directly.

That noted, there are a number of assumptions, myths and confusions that have arisen over time that are worth addressing upfront. The first is the idea that this model is "centrally planned". What this assumes, based on historical precedent, is that an elite group of people will make the economic decisions for the society.

A NLRBE is not centrally planned. It is a Collaborative Design System (CDS). It is based entirely upon public interaction, facilitated by programmed, open-access systems, that enable a constant, dynamic feedback exchange that can literally allow for the input of the public on any given industrial matter, whether personal or social.

Given this, another outcry is "but who programs the system?", which once again assumes that an elitist interest could exist behind the mediating software programs themselves (as will be expanded upon more so in this essay). The answer, as odd as it may sound, is everyone and no one. The tangible rules of the laws of nature, as they apply to environmental sustainability and engineering efficiency, are an objective frame of reference. The nuances may change to some degree over time, but the general principles of efficiency and sustainability remain, as they have been deduced by basic physics, along with several thousand years of recorded history by which we have been able to recognize basic, yet critical patterns in nature.

Moreover, the actual programming utilized by this interactive system would be available in an open source platform for public input and review. In fact, the system is predicated entirely upon the intelligence of the "group mind" and the open source/open access sharing virtue will help bring all viable interests to the surface for public consideration, in an absolutely transparent manner.

Another confusion surrounds a concept that has, to many, become, the defining difference between capitalism and most all other historically proposed social models. That has to do with whether the "means of production" is privately owned or not. In short, the means of production refers to the non-human assets that create goods, such as machinery, tools, factories, offices and the like. In capitalism, the *capitalist* owns the means of production, by historical definition.

There has been an ongoing argument for a century that any system that does not have its means of production owned as a form of private property, using currency as the information mechanism, is not going to be as economically efficient as one that does. This, as the argument goes, is because of the use of the price mechanism.[792]

Price, to its credit, has the ability to create exchange value amongst virtually any set of goods due to its divisibility. This creates a feedback mechanism that connects the entire market system in a certain, narrow way. Price, property and money work together to translate subjective demand preferences into semi-objective exchange values. The notion of "semi" is employed here because it is a culturally relative measure only, absent almost every factor that gives true technical quality to a given material, good or process.

Arguably, the only tangible technical data price that embodies, crudely, relates to a resource's 'scarcity' and the 'labor energy/complexity' put into the creation of a given good. Keep this in mind, as these two value variables will also be addressed again later in this essay with respect to non-price oriented calculation.

That all noted, the reasonable question becomes: is it possible to create a system that can more efficiently facilitate feedback with respect to consumer preference, demand, labor value and resource or component scarcity, without the price system, subjective property values or market exchange? The answer is yes. The modern solution is to completely eliminate exchange and create a direct control and feedback link between the consumer and the means of production itself. The consumer actually becomes part of the means of production and the industrial complex as a whole becomes a tool that is accessed by the public, at will, to generate goods.

To illustrate this, most today likely own a simple paper printer connected to a home computer. When a file is sent to print from the computer, the user is in control of a miniature version of a means of production. Likewise, in some cities today, there are now 3D printing labs, where people in the community can send their 3D design and use these machines to print what they need in physical form. The model being presented here is a similar idea. The next step in this scaling process is the creation of a strategically automated industrial complex, localized as much as possible, which is designed to produce, through automated means, the average of everything any given region has found demand for. As will be described, this is very feasible given the current state of technology and the ephemeralization trends at hand.

Imagine, for example, a clothing store except that is not organized like a "store" as is currently understood. It is a multi-purpose textile-printing house. You find the design you are interested

---

792 This objection is common to the Austrian school of economics. Reference: http://mises.org/econcalc.asp

in online, along with the materials you prefer and other customizations, and you print that article of clothing "on-demand" at that facility. Consider for a moment how much storage space, transport energy, and overrun waste is eliminated by this approach if virtually everything could be created on-demand, done by automated systems which can continually produce a greater variety of goods, from increasingly smaller manufacturing configurations.

In truth, the real fallacy of this "private ownership of the means of production" objection is its culture lag. Today, industry is witnessing a merger of capital goods, consumer goods and labor power. Machines are taking over human labor power, becoming capital goods, while also ever reducing in size to become consumer goods. The result is an increasingly smaller and more optimized industrial complex that can do more and more with less and less.

It is also worth mentioning that labor automation is now making the historically notable 'labor theory of value'[793] increasingly moot as well. Today, the labor energy that goes into a given good, while still a factor for process recognition, does not have much of a quantifiable correlation anymore. Today, machines now make and design machines. While the initial creation of a machine might require a good deal of human planning and initial construction at this time, once set in motion, there is a constant decrease in that labor value transference over time.

---

793 Reference: investopedia.com (http://www.investopedia.com/terms/l/labor-theory-of-value.asp)

Structure and Processes

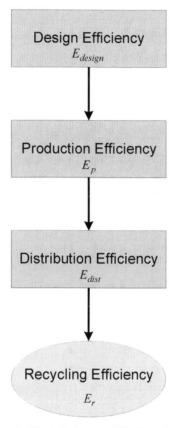

Figure 1. Block-Scheme of System Process

$$f_P(E_{design}, E_p, E_{dist}, E_r) \to \max$$

Figure 2. System process as Expression

Logical symbol	Description
E_{design}	Design efficiency
E_p	Production efficiency
E_{dist}	Distribution efficiency
E_r	Recycling efficiency
f_p	Production functional
E_{design}^i	Design efficiency standards
t_d	Durability
A_{design}	Adaptivity
$g_c^1, g_c^2, \ldots g_c^i, \ldots g_c^{Nc}$	Genre components
Nc	Minimum number of genre components
H_L	Human labor
A_L	Automated labor
f_{design}	Design efficiency functional
D_S	Demand splitting value
$\widetilde{A}$	Flexible automation process
$\overline{A}$	Fixed automation process
C_i	Consumer with index i
D_i	Distributor with index i
d_p	Distance to the production facilities
d_{dist}	Distance to the distribution facilities
P_{reg}	Regenerative protocol

Figure 3. Logic Symbols and Description

As will be described in detail by section, figure 1 shows the linear schematic of the industrial process, moving from design to production to distribution and recycling. Figure 2 shows how an optimization of such efficiency can be considered from a mathematical point of view, as a minimization or maximization of some functional.

Because we are talking about efficiency, we can consider the problem as a maximization of the production function f_P. Figure 3 is a table of symbols and descriptions, as will be used in the following explanations. It is important to note that not all attributes will be covered in this text. The purpose of this essay and the formulas suggested are done so to give a starting point for calculation, highlighting the most relevant, overarching attributes for consideration.

A full algorithmic calculation of this nature, taking into account all related sub-processes in real life terms would require an enormous text/programming treatment and will likely occur in a future edition of this text's appendix, as an ongoing project development.

Collaborative Design Interface

The starting point for interaction in a NLRBE is the CDI, or collaborative design interface. The CDI could abstractly be considered the "new "market" or the market of ideas or designs. Design is the first step in any production interest and this interface can be engaged by a single person; it can be engaged by a team; it can be engaged by everyone. It is open source and open access and it would come in the form of an online web interface.

The notion of "market" is expressed here not to conflate the notion of trade, but rather the notion of sharing and group decision-making. As with the traditional sales market, there is a swarm type of behavior which makes decisions over time as a group whole with respect to what goods will develop (demand) and what goods will perish (lack of demand). In a certain sense, this democratic process is embraced in a NLRBE, but by different means.

Moreover, all submitted designs, in creation or deemed complete, are stored in an open access, searchable database. This database makes all designs available for others to use or build upon. In this way, it is similar to a traditional goods catalog commonly found today, except it contains digital designs that can be sent into production at any time, on demand.

This design creation and proposal system is how demand itself is assessed. Instead of traditional advertising and the unidirectional consumer good proposal system - where companies work to persuade the consumer as to what they should buy, with the public mostly going with the flow, favoring or not favoring a company's pitched good, component or feature by purchase or not - this system works in an opposite, more involved and democratic manner.

In this new, open source type design approach, the entire global community has the option of presenting ideas for everyone to see, weighing in on and building upon designs, harnessing the power of collective experience and global knowledge.

The mechanism of the CDI would come in the form of an interactive interface, such as we see commonly today with computer-aided design (CAD) or computer-aided engineering (CAE) software. In short, these programs are able to digitally create and represent any given product design, containing all information as to how it should be made in final, physical manufacturing.

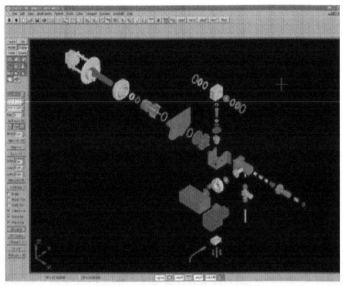

Above: CAD Interface Design Example

As an aside, many considering the educational requirements to engage such an interface, might be concerned about use-complexity. Naturally, the more dedicated designer will develop the skills needed to whatever degree interested while, for the more casual user, different degrees of interface complexity and skill orientation can be utilized.

This more user-friendly interfacing can develop in a similar fashion to how personal computers transitioned from complex proprietary coding interfaces with manually input instructions, to the now ubiquitous, simple graphic interface icon system, which allows users to operate more intuitively. Future CAD/CAE type programs will likely evolve in the same way, making the interactive process more accessible.

In many cases, as the database is always populated with current, already existing designs, the practice will be to build upon other's work. For example, if an engineer is interested in the optimization of a cell phone, they have the option of building upon any existing phone product design in the database, rather than starting from scratch.

The benefit of this cannot be emphasized enough as a collaborative platform. Rather than limit the design input to, say, a boardroom of engineers and marketers, as is common practice today, literally millions of minds can be brought together to accelerate any given idea in this approach. This new incentive system also ensures everyone interested in the good will receive exactly what everyone else is likely to receive in its advanced optimization states, where *personal interest becomes directly tied to societal interest.*

Also, given the patterns today, likely not everyone would want or need to be a designer. Many people would be satisfied enough by what had been set in motion already by others, with perhaps minor customization along the way. Today, a very small percentage of the population actually create and engineer the dominant technology and goods we use; and this specialization may naturally continue in the future to some degree, even though it is to the advantage of everyone if more minds came together. If the educational system is orientated away from rote learning and its antiquated basis that originated in the 19th century social order, we could see an explosion of input and creativity.

All that understood, an incredibly important component of these design and engineering programs today is how they can now incorporate advanced physics and other real world, natural law properties with the proposed design for testing. In other words, the good isn't just viewable in a static visual model with noted properties, it can actually be tested right there, virtually, to a relevant degree.

For instance, all new automobile designs today, long before they are physically built, are run through complex digital testing processes that assist in design integrity greatly.[794] Over time, there is no reason to believe that we will not be able to digitally represent, and set in motion for testing, most all known laws of nature, applying them in different contexts, virtually.

Optimized Efficiency Standards:

Efficiency standards are standards by which a given design must conform. This evaluation will be calculated automatically, or algorithmically, by the CDS's programming. This can also be thought of as a *filtering* process.

In short, any proposed design will be digitally filtered through a series of *sustainability* and *efficiency* protocols which relate not only to the state of existing resources, but also to the current performance of the total industrial system.

These would include the following "efficiency standards".[795]
a) Strategically Maximized Durability
b) Strategically Maximized Adaptability
c) Strategic Standardization of Genre Components
d) Strategically Integrated Recycling Conduciveness
e) Strategic Conduciveness for Labor Automation

---

794 Reference: *Engineering revolution: CAD/CAE advancements changing vehicle development.* (http://wardsauto.com/news-amp-analysis/engineering-revolution-cadcae-advancements-changing-vehicle-development)

795 Please note these protocols were also addressed in the essay *True Economic Factors*, in the context of "microeconomic components", with mild variation in the language.

$$E_{design} = f_{design}\left(t_d, A_{design}, c_r, Nc, H_L\right)$$

Figure 4. Symbolic Logic for the "Optimized Design Efficiency" function

As per figure 4, design efficiency E_{design} is one of the main factors that can affect the overall efficiency of the manufacturing and distribution process. This design efficiency depends on several key factors, which can be called *current efficiency standards* E^i_{design}. Here the index i corresponds to some particular standard.

Each standard will be generally explored as follows, expanding in certain cases with respect to the symbolic logic associated, for the sake of clarity.

a) 'Strategically Maximized Durability' means to make the good as strong and lasting as relevant. The materials utilized, comparatively assuming possible substitutions due to levels of scarcity or other factors, would be dynamically calculated, likely automatically by the design system, to be most conducive to an optimized durability standard.

Durability t_d maximization. This *durability* $t_d(d_1, d_2, ..., d_i)$ maximization can be considered as a local optimization issue. It can be analyzed by introducing the factors d_i which affect it where

$d_1^o, d_2^o, ..., d_i^o$ are some optimal values of the factors.

$$t_d(d_1, d_2, ..., d_i) \rightarrow \max, t_d = t_{\max}(d_1^o, d_2^o, ..., d_i^o)$$

b) 'Strategically Maximized Adaptability' A_{design} means the highest state of flexibility for replacing component parts is made. In the event a component part of a good becomes defective or out of date, the design facilitates that such components are easily replaced to maximize full product life span, always avoiding the interest to replace the good as a whole.

c) 'Strategic Standardization of Genre Components'

$$g_c^1, g_c^2, \ldots g_c^i, \ldots g_c^{Nc}$$

means all new designs either conform to or replace existing components which are either already in existence or outdated due a lack of comparative efficiency. This logic should not only apply to a given product, it should apply to the entire good genre, however possible.

$$Nc-> \min$$

The aim is to minimize the total number of genre components Nc. In other words, the standardization of the process will enable the possibility of lowering the number Nc to a possible minimum.

d) 'Recycling Conduciveness' c_r means every design must conform to the current state of regenerative possibility. The breakdown of any good must be anticipated in the initial design and allowed for in the most optimized way.

e) 'Strategic Conduciveness for Labor Automation' means that the current state of optimized, automated production is also taken into account, seeking to refine the design to be most conducive to production with the least amount of complexity, human labor or monitoring. Again, we seek to simplify the way materials and production means are used so that the maximum number of goods can be produced with the least variation of materials and production equipment.

This is denoted by human labor H_L and automated labor A_L. The aim is to minimize the human interaction with the production process.

This can be written as:

$$H_L / (H_L + A_L) \to \min$$

Using this equation, we could also write a simpler condition:

$$H_L(l_1,...,l_i) / A_L(l_1,...,l_i) \to \min$$

where l_i are factors that influence human and automatic labor.

So, returning to Figure 4, this "Optimized Design Efficiency" function can be described by a function f_{design} where t_d is durability,

A_{design} is adaptability, c_r is recycling conduciveness, Nc is the minimum number of genre components and H_L is a human labor.

The Industrial Network
The industrial network refers to the basic network of physical facilities that are directly connected to the design and database system just described. The system connects servers, production facilities, distribution facilities and recycling facilities. (Figure 5)

Industrial Network

Design servers

Production facilities

Distribution facilities

Recycling facilities

Global Resource Management Network

Figure 5. Industrial Network visual aid

Design Servers:
These computer servers connect the design database to the designers/consumers, while constantly being updated with relevant physical data to guide the process of product creation in the most optimized and sustainable way.

As noted, the engaged CDI (or collaborative design interface) is an open source program that facilitates collective, computer-aided design, running each step through the set of efficiency and sustainability filters (I.e. Figure 4) which assure optimized design. These designs are tested in real time, digitally, and in most cases, the good will exist in whatever state online for others to obtain, on demand, or for use as a preliminary model by which new ideas can be built upon.

Production Facilities:
These structures facilitate the actual manufacturing of a given design. These would evolve as automated factories that increasingly are able to produce more with fewer material inputs and fewer machine configurations. Again, if the interest existed to consciously overcome unnecessary design complexities, we can further this efficiency trend with an ever-lower environmental impact and ever lower resource use per task, while maximizing our abundance producing potential.

The number of production facilities, whether homogeneous or heterogeneous, would be strategically distributed topographically based on population statistics, no different than how grocery stores today try to average distances between pockets of people around neighborhoods. This is the "proximity strategy", which will be revisited in this essay.

Distribution Facilities:
Distribution can either occur directly from the production facility, usually in the case of an on-demand, one-off production for custom use, or sent to a distribution *library* for public access in masse, based on regional demand interest.

Some goods will be conducive to low demand, custom production and some will not. Food is the easiest example of a mass production necessity, while a personally tailored piece of furniture would come directly from the manufacturing facility once created.

It is worth reiterating that regardless of whether the good is classified to go to a library or directly to a user, this is still an 'access system'. In other words, at any time, the user of the custom or mass produced good can return the item for reprocessing or restocking.

Recycling Facilities:
Recycling Facilities would likely exist as part of the production facility, allowing access to returned parts for updating and reprocessing. As noted in the design protocol, all goods have been pre-optimized for 'conducive recycling'. The goal here is a zero-waste economy. Whether it is a phone, a couch, a computer, a jacket, or a book, everything

goes back to a recycling facility, likely the point of origin, which will directly reprocess any item as best it can.

Of course, an item may be returned elsewhere if needed; the integrated and standardized production and recycling centers, having been conceived of as a complete, compatible and holistic system, would be able to handle returned goods optimally, as is not the case today.

Global Resource and System Management:
These four facilities are also connected, to one degree or another, to a *Global Resource Management* (GRM) network, which is a sensor and measurement system that provides feedback and information about the current state of raw materials and the environment.

Resource Management, Feedback & Value
As noted, this computer-aided design and engineering process does not exist in a vacuum; it does not process designs with no input as to the current state of the planet and its resources. Connected to the design process, literally built into the noted "Optimize Design Efficiency" function, is dynamic feedback from an Earth-wide accounting system that gives data about all relevant resources which pertain to all productions.

To whatever degree technically possible, all raw materials and related resources are tracked and monitored, in as close to real time as possible. This is mainly because maintaining equilibrium with the Earth's regenerative processes, while also working strategically to maximize the use of the most abundant materials, while minimizing anything with emerging scarcity, is a critical efficiency calculation. Again, this is, in part, the purpose of the Global Resource Management system mentioned prior.

As far as "value" calculation, perhaps the two most important measures, which will undergo constant dynamic recalculation through feedback as industry unfolds, is the level of (a) 'scarcity' and the degree of (b) 'labor complexity'.

(a) 'Scarcity value' can be assigned a numerical value, from 1-100. 1 would denote the most severe scarcity with respect to the current rate of use and 100 the least severe. 50 would be the steady-state dividing line. The scarcity value of any given resource would exist at some value along this line, dynamically updated by the Global Resource Management network.

Scarcity Assessment

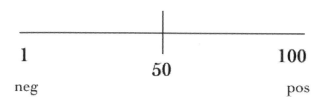

Figure 6. Scarcity Rank visual aid

For example, if the use of wood passes the steady state level of 50, which would mean consumption is currently surpassing the Earth's natural regeneration rate, this would trigger a counter move of some kind, such as the process of 'material substitution' or finding a replacement for wood in any future productions.

As far as a comparative evaluation, in a market system the price mechanism is used to decide which material is more cost efficient, assuming a given price will have already accounted for relevant technical information or, in this case, the issue of scarcity.

This new approach, rather than use price to compare or assess value, accounts for a given technical quality directly by a comparative quantification. In the case of scarcity concerns, it is best to organize genres or groups of similar use materials and quantify, to the highest degree possible, their related properties and degrees of efficiency for any given purpose. Then, a general numerical value spectrum is applied to those relationships.

For example, there is a spectrum of metals that have different efficiencies for electrical conductivity. These efficiencies can be physically quantified and then compared by value. So, if copper, a conductive metal, goes below the 50 value of equilibrium regarding its scarcity, calculations are triggered by the management program to compare the state of other conducive materials, their *scarcity level* and their *efficiency level*, preparing for substitution.

This is just one example and naturally this type of reasoning would get extremely complicated depending on the material and purpose problems posed. However, that is exactly why it is calculated by machine, not people. The human mind, either singly or organized into large groups, simply cannot process such data effectively. Also, it is worth pointing out that this type of direct value calculation, based around purpose, conduciveness and sustainability, dramatically eclipses the price mechanism when it comes to true resource awareness and intelligent resource management in calculation.

(b) Likewise, "labor complexity" and its assessment simply means estimating the complexity of a given production and drawing a numerical value based on the degree of process complexity. Complexity, in the context of an automation-oriented industry, can be quantified by defining and comparing the number of 'process stages.' Any given good production can be foreshadowed as to how many 'stages' of production processing it will take. It can then be compared to other good productions, ideally in the same purpose genre, for a quantifiable assessment. In other words, the units of measurement are these 'stages'.

For example, a chair that can be molded in three minutes, from simple polymers in one process, will have a lower 'labor complexity' value than a chair which requires automated assembly down a more tedious production chain, with mixed materials. In the event a given process value is too complex or hence comparatively inefficient in terms of what is currently possible (by comparison to an already existing design of a similar nature), the design would be flagged and would hence need to be re-evaluated.

Such adjustments and flagging would come in the form of feedback from the design interface, during the design stage. There is also no reason not to assume that with ongoing advancement in AI, the system could actually feed back with actual suggestions or even direct solutions to a given efficiency or sustainability problem, in real time.

Design Calculation
Those generalizations noted, a walkthrough of this overall, linear process is expressed below. There will be some repetition here for the sake of clarity. If we were to look at good design in the broadest possible way with respect to industrial unfolding, we end up with about four functions or processes, each relating to the four dominant, linear stages, including design, production, distribution and recycling. Again, each of these processes is directly tied to the Global Resource Management system that provides value feedback that assists in the regulatory apparatus to ensure efficiency and sustainability.

The following propositions apply (Figure 1):

All Product Designs must adapt to:
1) Optimized Design Efficiency
2) Optimized Production Efficiency
3) Optimized Distribution Efficiency
4) Optimized Recycling Efficiency

$$f_P(E_{design}, E_p, E_{dist}, E_r) \rightarrow \max.$$

Figure 1. (repeated)

1) Optimized Design Efficiency:
A product design must meet or adapt to criteria set by
[Current Efficiency Standards] E_{design}^{i}.

[Current Efficiency Standards] have five evaluative sub-processes, as expressed before:

[Durability] = t_d

[Adaptability] = A_{design}

[Standardization] = Nc

[Recycling Conduciveness] = c_r

[Automation Conduciveness] = H_L

Please note that further breakdown of each of these sub-processes and logical associations can be figuratively made as well to ever-reducing minutiae. However, as noted, this expression is the "top" tier by which all other sub-processes are oriented. It is, again, not the scope of this text to provide all attributes of a working algorithm. It is also not implied here that the parameters expressed are total or absolutely complete.

2) Optimized Production Efficiency
This filter's parameters can change based on the nature of the facilities and how much machine variation in production (fixed automation vs. flexible automation)[796] is required at a given time. For the purpose of expression, two facility types will be distinguished: one for high demand or mass production and one for low demand or short-run, custom goods.

---

796 "Fixed automation", also known as "hard automation," refers to an automated production facility in which the sequence of processing operations is fixed by the equipment configuration. It is fast but has less variation in output design capacity. Flexible automation can create more variation but the disadvantage is the time required to reprogram and change over the production equipment. These terms are common to the manufacturing and robotics industry when it comes to plant design.

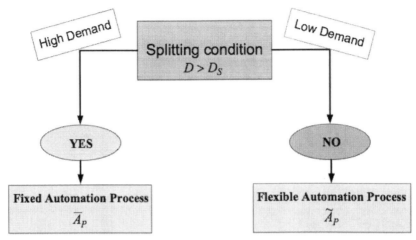

Figure 7. Dividing by low and high. Application of the class determination process

Very simply, a class determination is made which splits D_S the destination facilities based upon the nature of production requirements. The 'high demand' target assumes fixed automation $\overline{A}(a_i)$, meaning unvaried production methods ideal for high demand/mass production. The 'low demand' target uses flexible automation $\widetilde{A}(t, D_c(t), a_i)$, which can do a variety of things but usually in shorter runs.

Again, this schematic assumes only two types of facilities are needed. There could be more facility types based upon production factors, generating more splitting conditions. However, if the design rules are respected, there shouldn't be too much variation over time as the intent is always to reduce and simplify.

To state the process in linear form (Figure 7):

All product designs are filtered by a [Demand Class Determination] process. The [Demand Class Determination] process filters based on the standards set for [Low Demand] or [High Demand]. All [Low Consumer Demand] product designs are to be manufactured by the [Flexible Automation] process. All [High Consumer Demand] product designs are to be manufactured by the [Fixed Automation] process. Also, both the manufacturing of [Low Consumer Demand] and [High Consumer Demand] product designs will be regionally allocated as per the [Proximity Strategy] d_p of the manufacturing facilities.

3) Optimized Distribution Efficiency

Once process 2 is finished, the product design becomes a 'product' and moves to the [Optimized Distribution Efficiency] filter. In short, all products are allocated based on its prior [Demand Class Determination]. [Low Consumer Demand] products follow the [Direct Distribution] process. [High Consumer Demand] productions follow the [Mass Distribution] process, which would likely be the libraries, mentioned prior. Both the [Low Consumer Demand] and [High Consumer Demand] product will be regionally allocated as per the [Proximity Strategy], as before.

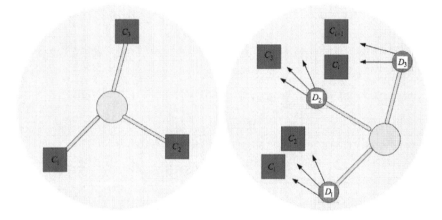

Figure 8. Illustration of the distribution schemes
A (left) – Direct Distribution – low demand case,
B (right) – Mass Distribution – high demand case

In the case of [Low Consumer Demand]

$$D_c < D_S$$

the distribution scheme is direct (Figure 8a). In this case the product goes directly to the consumer without the help of network intermediaries.

In the case of [High Consumer Demand]

$$D_c > D_S$$

the distribution scheme is mass (Figure 8b). In this case the product

goes to intermediary facilities, such as libraries D_i to engage the

potential consumers C_i .

Similar to the production efficiency considerations, in the case of

'Distribution Efficiency' E_{dist} , for the low and high demand, the

distribution process will be optimized in terms of the distance d_{dist}

to the existing facilities. In this case the facilities are places in regional

distribution (libraries), based on the level of demand in the given

region. (i.e. Proximity Strategy d_p).

4) Optimized Recycling Efficiency

After distribution, the product then goes through its life-cycle. Once its life-cycle ends, the product becomes "void" and moves to process #4, or the [Optimized Recycling Efficiency] filter. In short, all voided

products will follow the current [Regenerative Protocol] P_{reg} . This

protocol embraces the standards employed at that time to ensure the optimized reuse or reincorporation of any given good or component. Naturally, the sub-processes of this are vast and complex and it is the role of engineers, embracing natural law physics, to best understand exactly what parameters will be set.

The Domestic Economy
The prior schematic regarding sustainable and technically efficient processes, optimized dynamically to gain the most stability and maximize the potential of any given economic operation, is both extremely complex in detail and deceptively simple in theory.
The tedium of creating a complete, industry-orienting

algorithm that serves as the natural law regulatory filter, by which humanity can assure the most optimized technical practices, is certainly a major intellectual project to undertake, once again. The sub-processes inherent to such a multidimensional calculation would run into the thousands, for sure.

Yet, at the same time, the unfolding of the overall process is quite elegant in form. The idea of placing each human, if interested, at the helm of industrial creation, facilitating the "group mind" interaction for problem solving and creation, contains a deeply unifying community gesture, coupled with a kind of personal freedom of expression in the creative process which has not been seen before.

The very notion of extremely versatile, on-demand production systems which can produce a good for a single person or goods for an entire cultural demographic, is profound in its implications, not to mention the vast positive outcomes inherent when it comes to creating a more peaceful, humane society.

Given the technological trends, it is not far-fetched to imagine a small town which, just as it may today have an electrical grid which unifies that town in its central source of power, now has a production plant network designed to literally create most everything that town may need, on demand. Raw resources are brought into the plant as per conditions and allocation algorithms surrounding the "global resource management system", which connects all such economic facilities both regionally and globally.

Yet, within this scenario, the role of the human being is often confused. While the pursuit of post-scarcity in this way will create a sustainable and abundance generating paradigm where people can live without the burden of "working for a living", the debate over "what will people do?" is a question that often arises, along with another inevitable question: "Who is running the machines for no pay!?"

The first question gets to the heart of human values. People have always found interesting things to do and explore, and it is severely doubted that an era of boredom would arise given that people would no longer need to fight just to live a high quality life. Rather, people might very well be elevated to a new type of existence and engage in higher order interests that were simply unattainable in the prior model.

The second question is more interesting. In an automated economy, which strategically works to remove humans from any kind of monotonous, difficult or unsafe labor, there will still be some basic need for oversight and management. For many who shun post-scarcity rhetoric, this fallback is common, arguing that only in a 100% automated utopia, where people literally have no obligation, would the society be possible. Otherwise, some sub-culture will be required to do the remaining labor and hence some kind of stratified oppression would be inherent.

The problem with this assumption is that it is deeply locked into a market-oriented worldview where time is equated to money. People today have a knee-jerk reaction to assume that in order for anything to actually get done, money must be in play as an incentive.

Yet, statistically, this is simply untrue. In a 1992 Gallup Poll, more than 50% of American adults (94 million Americans) volunteered time for social causes, at an average of 4.2 hours a week, for a total of 20.5 billion hours a year.[797] A more recent poll in December 2013 showed a steady increase in volunteering from 2001 until 2013.[798] Figures from 2008 in the US also showed an increase in non-religious volunteering, underlining the point that social contributions can exist for their own sake, as well as for religious reasons, and during great economic difficulties.[799] The truth of the matter is that human beings, even in the highly competitive and materialistic orientation of the United States, still decide to do a great deal without an interest in monetary reward.

Open source programming is another example. Linux, which started in 1991 as a simple experiment, was able to complete its community-driven, almost moneyless programming development in just three years. Linux has over 10,000 lines of code and the vast amount of its creation was done for free by a global community. Wikipedia is yet another example of a non-profit, community generated creation, research and expression. It has been estimated that Wikipedia took 100 million hours of volunteer time to create, and features a technically advanced and complex backend, demonstrating that well-engineered interrelating systems, when leveraged with large volunteer efforts, can create world-first systems previously considered unrealistic or unfeasible.

So, while money still rules the overall motivation in the current society, given some free time, people have proven they will contribute greatly to projects which have no monetary return and the real issue underlying the motivation of such labor is the satisfaction and the *feeling of contribution.* Today, most jobs do not generate this feeling. Most people walk into a private dictatorship five days a week and are under the control of superiors, knowing they can be fired at any moment.

The contribution they make rarely has a direct return to them and the feeling of accomplishment is diminished. Some jobs might even make one wonder what the point of the occupation even is in the context of social contribution or personal development. Many jobs exist today simply for the sake of generating or moving money and nothing more. Advertising and Wall Street occupations, for example, are examples of high value occupations which, in truth, do very little to improve society.

---

797 *Source: Giving and Volunteering in the United States: Findings from a National Survey,* Hodgkinson & Weitzman, 1992, p2

798 Source: *Most Americans Practice Charitable Giving, Volunteerism* (http://www.gallup.com/poll/166250/americans-practice-charitable-giving-volunteerism.aspx)

799 Reference: *Despite Economy, Charitable Donors, Volunteers Keep Giving* (http://www.gallup.com/poll/113497/despite-economy-charitable-donors-volunteers-keep-giving.aspx)

This perhaps might explain the "lazy" tendency many feel once off their job at the end of the day, returning home feeling defeated and tired. Over time, many lose spirit and motivation overall and find that their job becomes the only thing that is supposed to have meaning in their life, forgetting the enjoyable passions once inherent to their development.

That considered, in a fully realized NLRBE, it is estimated that perhaps 5% of a region's population (5% of the global population as well), on average, would be needed to assist the fluid operation of this industrial system and this figure would likely continually diminish in the future as technology advances. This participation might best be expressed in the form of what has been termed the "domestic" economy. The domestic economy embodies the helpful actions of people in a non-paid environment. Household work, family and community interests are traditional examples.

In a NLRBE, such labor would be relegated in the same gesture and the delegation of such labor roles could be distributed amongst a large-scale population making the actual time commitment miniscule overall. Even by current standards, if one were to ask the average worker if they would be willing to live, say, the equivalence of a $100,000 a year lifestyle, but having to volunteer 5% of their time for maintenance of the system that supports their standard of living, there is little doubt agreement would be met by most. The amount of time saved alone in this type of socioeconomic model, coupled again with the vast problem alleviation of the environmental problems and social conflicts inherent to the market, leave little room for rational objection.

Likewise, once set free, the creative, collaborative contribution propensity itself, which is the true driver of progress, will no longer be inhibited by the monotony of labor or the income system. It is very difficult to predict the incredible level of productivity and focus a society may achieve once such oppressive factors are removed.

The Decentralization Paradox

While the rhetoric of a *global society* with *global values* underscores this socioeconomic model, it is important to understand the nature of its redundancy and its decentralized layout. John Dalberg-Acton, 1st Baron Acton, once stated "Power tends to corrupt, and absolute power corrupts absolutely".[800] This power-fearing perspective is certainly well justified in history and many who hear about a NLRBE often assume this global society is "ruled" by one mainframe, one machine, an elite group of technocrats or something similar.

It is important to remind ourselves that almost all prior societies have lived within great scarcity and hence great conflict. This, coupled with the fact that money and resources have been a means to gain power - usually after a good deal of battle, reinforcing a status and dominance hierarchy - illustrates that we should not be surprised

---

800 John Emerich Edward Dalberg Acton, first Baron Acton (1834–1902). The historian and moralist, who was otherwise known simply as Lord Acton, expressed this opinion in a letter to Bishop Mandell Creighton in 1887

at these reactions. However, this statement is also deeply counter-productive on the whole as it gives the paranoid sense that no one can ever be trusted, if they are given any type of control over others.

A NLRBE is, indeed, a global structure in how it processes economic information and assesses output possibilities. Once a good is designed, it runs through the aforementioned efficiency and sustainability filters, which invariably tie back to the status of global resources, along with a global network for design contribution. At the same time, larger order societal decisions, meaning those decisions once made by elected representatives, are also achieved by consensus by the population, directly.

The only real centralization inherent is this digital network connecting the world itself. Given that, we could consider a few possible problems in this circumstance in the same way we think about the Internet today, which is essentially the same infrastructure. "Hacking", for example, which is the act of disturbing, stealing or corrupting a program or digital information by invading the source code, might be a concern.

However, we have to first ask *why* anyone would perform such an act in the new model. Since the entire system is designed to provide for everyone, where is the incentive to disturb it? Anyone shutting down such a system is also shutting down their means to contribute and develop. An analogy would be a person today living in an apartment building, where everyone shares the utility infrastructure, deciding to destroy the fuse or electrical breaker box which divides the incoming electricity to power the whole apartment building. Why would they do it if it shuts down their own electricity as well?

It is important to review why people can be so vicious today. Anger is bred by deprivation and some external act is often interpreted as the source of this abuse. So, in retribution, people today "hack" and violate websites and the like to either make a protest point or to get revenge.[801] In a NLRBE, it is hard to fathom where the source of such angst and outrage would materialize. If a person doesn't like the way the system is working in a specific way, they have the capacity to change it by assessing consensus with others. The system is emergent.

However, in the event that this did happen, there is a simple solution: active redundancy. In a monetary-driven society, based around cost efficiency, we see little fail-safe redundancy in place as it is unaffordable. For example, we see an airplane with two engines and both are needed to fly. Why not create an airplane with two main engines and two back-up engines, which are not running when the full plane is in working order, but in the event an engine fails, another engine is able to take over.

The main server network which facilitates social connectivity

---

801 An example would the group known as "Anonymous", which is a loosely associated international network of "hacktivist" entities that disrupt websites and computer databases as a form of protest.

and unification could have 5,6,7...20 levels of redundancy and automatic backup in the event anything went down. It might not be perfect. Some data may be lost. However, again, this isn't a utopia. With respect to who has the "power" to notice the problem and implement this redundancy, technical teams exist to monitor the network, just like any other existing vocation.

Of course, the question then arises: what if someone on the technical team is corrupted and purposefully messes up the system? Once again, the counter question is: why would they do it? What is the incentive? In the event this did happen, it would not take long for others to notice and the system could be corrected in the same semblance of redundancy, with the person removed. That person would then be questioned by his or her peers and society overall to better understand why this act occurred.[802]

Overall, we trustfully give ourselves over to "authority" all the time. Doctors, mechanics, and any other specialization always involve a level of trust by those seeking such help, and most of the time, even in a monetary society which generates dishonesty, people are mostly honest, or as honest as they *can be,* the majority of the time. It is simply too cynical to assume that any allocation of control is dangerous. At no time in human history have we not shared some level of delegated power responsibility to each other, and in almost all cases, as with dentistry or mechanics, the nature of the "power" delegated in question is characterized by its technical merit; precisely the kind of oversight advocated within the present context.

In a NLRBE, the reinforcement is to help oneself, which means to help society, not to exploit or abuse. There is literally no reward reinforcement for such negative behavior, as opposed to the natural state of general corruption we endure today.

As far as the physical network itself, it is decentralized in its orientation in many ways, often more so than we see today. The topographic layout of Earth makes many things logically obvious as far as structure placement. People, being social, naturally have an interest to have some kind of community centralization; the existence of certain energy providing areas, such as for solar/wind/geothermal/hydro, carve out their own locations logically; extraction, production and distribution networks also have a topographical logic inherent as efficiency mandates we keep such facilitates as close to each other as possible, reducing energy waste and transport; etc.

Cities themselves will change in two major ways. For one, the construction and networking of the internal city system will seek to meet the highest state of technical efficiency possible, including sustainable infrastructure, homes, production/distribution networks and the like, taking the systems basis into direct account.[803] Secondly,

---

802 The subject of "enforcement" and how such an act is dealt with, will be talked about in the essay *Lifestyle, Freedom and The Humanity Factor*
803 The design work of Jacque Fresco, specifically his city system concepts, is a good example of this reasoning.

it is expected that due to the evolution of ephemeralization, a given city will produce all regional goods *locally*. Management of the city on the level of broad infrastructure, such as where to put a bridge, will also be a regional decision making process, set in motion by the direct democracy, CDS system. Land allocation works the same way, even though that is a larger subject, which is addressed in the essay "Post-Scarcity Trends, Capacity and Efficiency".

Of course, each city naturally connects to other cities, ideally with advanced transport systems, which can cleanly and fluidly move people. Maglev type trains systems are on pace to be the next stage of fast, safe and efficient transport with little to no environmental footprint, as compared to oil-powered planes, buses and cars.[804]

As for as the "engine" of a city, which is its industry, digital networks and sensor systems work to gather important regional and non-regional data. This relates to the "global resource management" network as described before and both regional and global networks of measurements allow all cities/citizens to have a holistic sense of what is going on, affecting production and other important environmental factors.[805]

So, this network might very well be "centralized" in its data and raw resource flow to a city's internal production facilities, but it is *decentralized* in that a city imports nothing else. It is mostly self-contained. All productions occur internally, importing and exporting no produced goods, only resources. This idea of "self-containment per scale degree"[806] is important and even applies towards structures, such as houses. The ideal house would be off-the-grid and self-contained in its energy sourcing and with redundant backup energy sources in place should anything become compromised.

Put another way, there is no central "off switch" in such a natural redundancy based system. For example, if a base-load providing power grid is being used and that grid goes down, it would have little effect on houses if those houses are also designed to harvest local energy sources (i.e. solar) and hence be self-contained.

Ref: Jacque Fresco, *The Best That Money Can't Buy,* Global Cybervisions, 2002, Chapter 15

804 "Maglev" transport uses less energy and moves substantially faster than commercial airlines and can also be used as local transport systems within a city. ET3 is a company currently working on this technology. http://www.et3.com/ Otherwise, the use of extremely safe, driverless cars would serve other transportation needs. http://www.nytimes.com/2010/10/10/science/10google.html?pagewanted=all&_r=0

805 Such sensor technology and system networks have already been hypothesized and are slowly making their way into certain facets of society. The task is simply to scale it out. HP has introduced an idea for what it calls a "A Central Nervous System for the Earth". http://hbr.org/web/2009/hbr-list/central-nervous-system-for-earth

806 To clarify "per scale degree" - this simply means smaller and larger order systems, with the smaller inside the larger. For example, a *house* is one degree, while the *city* that contains the house is a larger degree.

Likewise, no one thing can upset the international system. Unlike modern monetary finance and currency structures, which are highly centralized and can wreak havoc globally if things go wrong, a problem in one city has little effect on any other city in a NLRBE.

So, in truth, a properly organized NLRBE is not centralized in any real sense. It is more accurate to say that it is a global decentralized system, with various degrees of inherent redundancy, which, degree by degree, connects itself by information flow and physical channels to acquire proper resources, to be used for each region's local economy.

-LIFESTYLE, FREEDOM AND THE HUMANITY FACTOR-

Is freedom anything else than the right to live as we wish? Nothing else.[807]
-Epictetus

What is happiness?
It is difficult for most in the world today to imagine a society without the duress and daily strife endured by the act of simply trying to survive and keep a healthy mental and physical state. So much of our lives today is centered around staying financially ahead and making sure we have enough money for today, tomorrow, our family and even perhaps for the next familial generation, we often lose sight of what it is that actually creates well-being and happiness.

In fact, this fear and often predatory motivation has created a social climate that has even generated a positive value association toward narrow, self-interested behavior. While the line is always subjective as to what behaviors are to be considered "ethical" or not, the competitive, scarcity-driven orientation toward gaining an acceptable quality of life continually reinforces our lower brain, "fight-or-flight" propensities, perpetuating a constant sense of social detachment and general loss of empathy for others. In many ways, money itself has even become the reward and status standard, not what it can do with its potential to move the world.

Therefore, given these values, it is always a challenge to discuss a NLRBE's non-market premise with the vast majority of those in modern culture, as certain knee-jerk contradictory assumptions almost always prevail. It is not the purpose of this essay to address these in detail but to denote how communication of a future lifestyle not based on these now long-sustained values is difficult, as the idea of existence without such strife is almost impossible for many, due to our history.

Merging Society and Individuality
Ayn Rand and other famous authors and theorists in the 20th century spent a great deal of time talking about a duality between self-interest and social interest, or individualism and collectivism.[808] In these works, whether in fiction-based literary form or in actual economic treatment, rarely is consideration given to a possible balance between the two.

Martin Luther King Jr. once said: "Communism forgets that life is individual. Capitalism forgets that life is social, and the kingdom of brotherhood is found neither in the thesis of communism nor the

---

807 Source: quote-wise.com (http://www.quote-wise.com/quotes/epictetus/is-freedom-anything-else-than-the-right-to-li)
808 Ayn Rand's famous novel "Anthem" is a notable, influential example of this artistic culmination of values. It takes place in a dystopian future where mankind has entered another dark age characterized by irrationality, collectivism, and socialistic thinking and economics. The concept of individuality has been eliminated. For example, the use of the word "I" is punishable by death.

antithesis of capitalism but in a higher synthesis. It is found in a higher synthesis that combines the truths of both."[809]

There is no denying that human beings have evolved with a deeply social nature. It could be argued that what really defines us are the relationships we have created in our lives, not to mention the vast influence of cultural development itself, which is the main source of most value orientations at any given time in any given society.

Yet, at the same time, we cannot deny the personal development needs, freedom of expression sought and general independence most all humans tend to need to feel in their day-to-day lives. While the notion of "free will" might be highly complex in analysis, there appears to always be a part of us that navigates based on what we consider to be "choice" and if we feel oppression of that choice, it tends to upset us and destabilize.

So, while it is true that when the synergy of the total life experience is brought into focus we can well argue that all of our choices exist under some level of duress, influence or impulse and hence are actually not entirely "free", we cannot ignore the emotional interest we tend to have in perceiving ourselves as separate, independent and individual in some way. True or not, the very idea of *free determination* appears critical to personal development, confidence and wellbeing.

This is brought up, as perhaps the most important sociological outcome of a NLRBE is something historically unprecedented on a large scale in the history of human society. Today, we have the technological means to not only bring all human beings into a high standard of living due to the rapid advancement of technology and basic understandings in science, we also have the ability to structurally rationalize ourselves as being *actually responsible to each other* and *the Earth itself.*

The market system has been unable to reinforce this sense of community or harmony with the habitat because its very foundation works against both as a value or virtue. The Earth, in the market model, is viewed as an inventory of resources waiting for financial exploitation and the more goods in service, the more money is made and hence more jobs are created. Likewise, perpetual human oppression has been a natural byproduct of the underlying Malthusian, scarcity-based orientation, since the dawn of existence.

This old system, which is a natural consequence of this scarcity-driven order, worked well during primitive periods where our impact on the Earth and how much damage we could do to each other had "acceptable" limits, if you will. The larger structural problems inherent simply could not be understood at that time. However, today the market has revealed itself as no longer a method towards sustainability or a means for intelligent resource management and it

---

809 From "Where Do We Go From Here?," Delivered at the *11th Annual SCLC Convention Atlanta*, Ga., 1967 (http://mlk-kpp01.stanford.edu/index.php/encyclopedia/documentsentry/where_do_we_go_from_here_delivered_at_the_11th_annual_sclc_convention/)

also creates a constant propensity to view other human beings as threats to one's own survival.

On the social level, the entire edifice justifies a zero-sum game. Two people going into a coveted job interview for the same job may be respectful to each other, but they both know only one of them will get the job. This fear-based competitive nuance runs the gamut of societal affairs from justifying massive wealth gaps and class imbalance in the developed world to the overall ignoring of mass poverty and the genocide it is in the developing world.

A NLRBE, on the other hand, structurally combines societal interest with personal interest and environmental interest. Its functioning is directly tied to the resources and environment, actually *rewarding* sustainability and efficiency. Likewise, there is no gain to be had by the exploitation of others or behaving in the dishonest and corrupt ways we tend to accept as normality. Theft, crime, fraud and all structural outcomes common to the scarcity-based market, will no longer have any real incentive as the entire society is oriented to *serve itself,* and *harming others only harms one's self.*

For example, an enormous number of laws exist today that protect one's private property. People might be motivated to steal for a number of reasons, but statistically a lack of means, general deprivation and hence relative or absolute poverty, is the common precondition. When people steal physical goods, they are usually stealing exchange value in most cases. In a NLRBE there is no exchange value and hence to "steal" an item that cannot be sold is mostly pointless.

Likewise, a common objection is that if goods were available without price, there is no restriction on taking vastly more than one needs. Once again, we need to consider the reason for such an action. Since the same goods cannot be sold, they would simply exist in another place, perhaps even inconveniencing the person who took them. What is one to do with, say, 200 televisions? Why would someone take five times the amount of food needed if they cannot eat it all and it will go to waste?

From an ethical standpoint, which is often seen as culturally subjective, we see a great number of customs in society today based upon what is considered "appropriate". When a person walks down the street and litters on the ground, anyone watching would likely not applaud such behavior. In regions where water or electricity is paid for with a flat rate, people do not just let the water run all day long or keep lights on constantly, simply because they don't need to care, financially. There has always been a general social and environmental sense of responsibility under the surface of the current zeitgeist and a NLRBE will finally *amplify* these same responsible propensities to a vast degree, rather than incentivize their suppression, which is what the current system does.

Humanity Factor & Access Rights

Still, while a NLRBE will set in motion, for the first time in history, a kind of economic and social premise that reinforces sustainability, human solidarity, empathy and sharing on a global scale, working to literally unite the human family with common concern, there will always be problems of some kind, including behavioral.

There is an unpredictable element to human development. The great many and complex environmental and biological influences, which create our personalized form, comprehension and propensities, can be difficult to understand in causality to any degree of absolutism. We simply cannot account for all relevant factors. While a great deal has been learned about human influences and how certain things *should* and *should not* happen to a person during development, as they have statistically predictable consequences with respect to behavior, there is always a possibility of things going wrong that are out of a family or society's control.[810] We can call this the "humanity factor".

The current social order, which is, again, literally built out of the market-oriented, scarcity-driven, competitive premise of economy, has an enormous legal apparatus to control human behavior. In the new approach, we could likely expect a 90-95% decrease in such "criminal" acts since the vast majority of "crime" has to do with money, trade and property. These very ideas are no longer relevant in this post-scarcity model for there is no basis for those problems in general. They have been *designed out*.

However, this "humanity factor" can still generate unexpected circumstances and problems that require a socially accepted course of action. A simple example is mental illness, which can develop slowly over time and unexpectedly. It is a medical problem and must be treated as such. A volunteer group working to help those sick in the behavioral context would need to be in place, no different than those who work in any other facet of societal maintenance. However, this team would be a vast departure from the crude idea of "police" and "security" we see today. Likewise, there are certainly no prisons existing to incur inhumane treatment and punishment.[811]

Even in the case of "crimes of passion" or the like, the worst scenario is containment if the individual is unable to control destructive actions. Just as we might quarantine a person with a highly contagious, infectious disease if it were a serious threat, the logic to

---

810 The essays *The Final Argument: Human Nature* and *Defining Public Health* are suggested for review.

811 This may sound like a utopian step for a society in the current climate, but this trend can actually be observed embryonically in some societies today, such as in the Netherlands and Sweden, where prisons are being closed down due to exceptionally low crime rates. Reference: http://www.theguardian.com/society/2013/dec/01/why-sweden-closing-prisons & The Netherlands: http://jcjusticecenter.com/2013/09/14/netherlands-closing-19-prisons-due-to-lack-of-criminals/

contain people who pose behavioral threats to others would suggest a similar scenario - only this containment would be humane and for the sake of research. Whether biological or developmental, all aberrant behaviors have a source of some kind and as complex as they may be, only further study can work to source solutions.

On a more moderate level, such as the case of adolescent kids who, in the common discovery and rebellious stage of development, act in socially offensive ways in experimentation, a different kind of understanding is culminated where the community can come together to assess the nature of the problem and work to deter the behavior as a community. Just as minors are treated in the Western world today, given non-criminal condemnation in most cases, the same type of community assessment can be provided, which will likely come natural to any family or local region.

However, in some cases, there might be a need for a type of rights system when dealing with accessed goods. In other words, a simple rule system of some kind might be useful, centered not on *property rights* but *access rights.*

Imagine a scenario where an individual parks his or her bike on a street, without a lock, entering a house. This bike was checked out of a local distribution library for the person's use. Then, a bystander, who is in a hurry, not close to a distribution library, sees this bike and makes an inappropriate decision to take the bike to get where he needs to go. This is a dishonest and rude act.

In a property system, this would be called "theft". In an access system it might take a different term, such as an "access violation". The severity of the action is very different and it is more of an annoyance than a crime. In a property system the bike would likely be sold for money or kept. In an access system, the original user would simply obtain a new bike and move on, inconvenienced, while the person who took the bike would likely just drop it off after use, as there is no resale value and hence no real reason to keep it.

Yet, it doesn't mean the act should be ignored and go unnoticed in its access violation, as such behavior, as rare as it likely would be, would need acknowledgment to serve as a form of operant education. It is no different than how people today learn basic decency, respect and etiquette. Therefore, rather than property rights, a simple access rights rule could be installed to deter such behavior. In other words, any person obtaining items through the system would have *access rights* to those items for the duration of use and if another comes and takes those items, it is an offense. Reinforcement to deter such future acts would first be warnings. If persisted over time, it could mean a temporary limitation of future access in some genre for that offending person.

In reality, it could be considered a "slap on the wrist" for essentially being annoying and rude. However, if a person were to repeat this over and over, it might take on the role of *mental illness*, as something of an impulsive behavior disorder and that medical context might come into play at that time. But once again, this type of behavior would be extremely rare and if far from a serious concern. However, such possible measures should be understood, as this isn't a utopia. It should also be noted that technical resolutions are always sought after as the primary prevention strategy to design out any such problems.

Crisis management is another issue. Just as we have a volunteer fire department in most cities in America, who live their normal lives until they get the call for an emergency, this same approach can work for natural disasters or acts of extreme behavior, such as behavioral violence. In the case of an earthquake, flood, tornado or the like, each case would naturally have a plan in place by the society to assure proper handling. This preparation can cross regional lines as well, with contingency plans agreed upon on the global level to know how the rest of the world may help if a given region has a severe problem. This is actually similar to how the international community works to help in crises even today, when such problems occur.

Overall, we can speculate on all these ideas and problem-solving measures to a vast degree, but the underlying precondition set in motion by the NLRBE, will dramatically reduce the commonality and severity of each issue and that is important to remember. For example, buildings constructed in regions susceptible to earthquakes will be made to withstand them as best they can. This is very difficult in the current world due to the associated financial costs as the revisions deeply needed are great. Such impediments will no longer exist and proper, technically accurate construction and infrastructure can be made to assure the least amount of damage in the event of such a natural disaster.

Lifestyle
As technology unfolds and scientific understanding evolves, culture changes. This has been the trend of history. With the exponential development of information-based technologies and hence the applied technology that then emerges, each generation develops new values, associations, means and expressions. Let's imagine waking up one morning in a NLRBE - a day in the life:

You rise to a generally quiet hum of mild traffic, with maglev trains whisking about the city. Having a love for high views, you get out of bed on the 20th storey of a simple yet elegant, mold- extruded apartment complex that converts all sunlight into energy through photovoltaic paints on its outer shell. You have a fleeting moment of marveling at this reality as the sun bursts through the windows, forcing increased alertness out of your early morning stupor.

As you emerge, you are also reminded of your cousin having taken part in that global, university driven initiative about two decades ago, which sought to perfect this paint technology to a degree of efficiency never before seen. In just a few years of collaboration, this PV paint achieved 90% energy efficiency, making it workable in almost any structure. You remember the joy and satisfaction your cousin felt when his team was on the front lines when this breakthrough for humanity was achieved. It was like the elation felt amongst soccer teammates after a goal has been scored.

Slowly gaining focus as your pupils find balance with the invading light, you glance out of the window and notice an enormous machine, suspended from a crane of sorts, slowly adding a new section to the very building structure you are a part of. Almost like magic, the machine is able to form, from what first appears like a kind of liquid plastic, a new apartment configuration and appends that form onto the existing structure. Quietly, safely and oddly with very few parts, there is no technician in sight, even though likely someone is monitoring the process from somewhere. Blinking and scanning sensor lights on the huge machine appear to suggest that it understands everything about the surrounding area and what it needs to do.

Glancing further around the city's skyline, there is an immediate sense of synergy with nature. The city has no awkward concentrations or imbalance. The slick transport systems that zoom by, which are high-tech indeed, seem to merge seamlessly with the greenery, lakes and canals. Suddenly, a picture on the wall next to the window catches your eye. It is an old archival shot of almost the same perspective, but taken many, many decades before, during what modern folk now call the "last dark age".

In this shot a sense of tension, congestion and strife is felt. A long stream of automobiles is seen on a strip of crude concrete highway backing up all the way out of frame. You remember from your history education years ago that back then a monetary practice created great duress and discord, with people piling into cities to gain employment and hence to gain the money, in order buy things and survive. You then think of how things have changed indeed, feeling rather sorry for that primitive culture and happy you were born when you were. Of course, realizing that you too live in a fleeting era as time marches on, you further try to imagine what aspects of your life today will one day be considered outdated in the future.

Feeling hungry, you enter into the apartment's kitchen. It is a fairly new design you hadn't seen before. While the systems concept and the interest to combine and unify industrial design was mentioned prolifically in your educational materials as an engineering student, you notice the advanced degree of efficiency now achieved. The kitchen is one unit. The dishes and ware are designed for the washing and placement process, which is directly built in. Once a plate is dirty, it is set into a compartment that already understands the nature of the pre-designed plate and processes the plate with a kind of cleansing steam and a UV configuration that also sterilizes it. Automatically, the plate is then returned to the proper disperser location in the shelf for the next use. It was as though the kitchen was one big, unified machine.

However, checking the refrigerator, you realize you have forgotten to pick up provisions for your short stay. You ponder whether to do go down to the lower level to pick up such provisions and come back, but you decide it is time to get going and you will grab something at a café on the way. As you exit the apartment, you swipe the access key into the control panel to confirm your final exit and then glance at the control panel to find the "clean" button. After a bit of frustration, you finally realize the apartment has been designed with a time-based motion sensor system to clean itself automatically when no motion is detected.

You then notice the CF6 robot in the corner and take pause as to the amazing technical feat it is to have this robot understand the exact nature of the space, where things belong and where they do not, all programmed with absolute 3D spatial awareness of the apartment to clean and arrange. It is hard for you to imagine what it must have been like to maintain such daily drudgery generations prior.

Exiting the apartment, which is actually a temporary access location you "rented" through an online service, you then enter the hallways and almost collide with a fast moving older man who drops a small laptop. You realize he is one of the managers of the apartment complex. You help him pick it up and he apologizes profusely. "Very sorry!" he exclaims. "We have a problem with the CF6 on level 12 and I need to reboot him!" "Good thing we always have a few backups for each room!"

You thank him kindly for his well-kept place and continue on your way, with a brief reflection back to that historical photo in the room you just left. Long ago, people's sense of contribution was always associated to money. They had jobs, as they were called. Today, people's vocation is a matter of choice, facilitated also by a basic sense of social responsibility. Our society is designed to take care of us as one, so why should we not take care of society itself in return? The man who passed you maintains that building because he enjoys helping others and since he, himself, only needs to work a few hours a week at this role, he views his volunteer time as valuable and without burden, happily assisting others who very much appreciate the contribution. It makes him feel like he is more a part of the community.

Exiting the building, the street is bustling with motion. You notice an artsy looking, retro French café on the corner and laugh to yourself at the pointless, yet cute nostalgia. You enter and sit at a small corner table, smiling politely at the family across the way. Realizing you are running out of time since you have to catch a train to attend a conference a couple hundred miles away, you tap a simple order into the kiosk menu in the center of the table. Tea and waffles. Once submitted you can't help but notice a mild vibration occurring behind your head.

Since your grandfather was an engineer who helped design the original automated kitchen system, this is curious to you as the usual tradition was to put the processing facility above and center in the space. It appears there was some restriction in this narrow area so they hid it to the side. About two minutes later, a red light appears on the table to alert you that your order is ready. A glass door opens that is perpendicular to the table-top and a conveyor extends to reveal your tea and waffles. You grab the tray and rush to finish in the hope not to miss your train. Once done, you slide the tray back into the opening and it closes for cleaning.

As you exit the café, you can't help but notice a decal with the silhouette of a female form with a tray, bending over what looks like a table. At first the image confuses you and then you remember that at one time in history people were slaves to others in this very way. Before the automated restaurant, people actually wasted their potential by waiting on each other and manually bringing food and taking orders. Once again, you are happy you were born when you were.

Emerging back outside you realize you have a fairly long walk. Pondering jumping on the maglev trolley, which constantly circles about the city like a giant worm, you decide it is probably going to be too slow. So, you make your way to the street parallel, which is where the automated cars zoom around in their custom paths. Pulling out your cell phone, which has a special application linked to the region's transport system, a white cab quickly notices your call and stops on the corner. You enter the front of the cab and verbally describe the address. A voice confirms your request and you are off.

Arriving at the train station, you exit the cab and begin to make your way. Gliding along you notice a person with a very large bag next to you, strolling it along. This perplexes you. It appears so arduous and unnecessary. You ask yourself why anyone would need such a large bag when the basic things everyone needs can be found in any city in the world, on demand. The idea of luggage seemed awkward and strange. Yet, before you have a moment to ponder this any further, the man in front of you suddenly collapses to the ground.

Instantly a large crowd begins to form to see if they can assist. Being the closest to him, you notice the characteristics appear to be of a heart attack. While extremely rare in the world at that time, they still occasionally occur. Pulling out your phone you text emergency number 331 with the word 'medical'. This sends instant notification of an emergency to a local team of volunteers trained in medical practice, along with the location via GPS. Within minutes a team arrives and works to save the man's life. With the man still breathing, he is placed into an automated emergency vehicle, which zooms off to the local hospital. Concerned about the fate of the poor man, you collect yourself and continue on, even more late than before.

Finally making it to your train, you enter and sit. Within moments the doors close and you breathe a sigh of relief. In your seat is an entertainment center with has on demand media. As the train begins to accelerate, you suddenly remember that your nephew produced a feature film about whale migration recently, but you can't remember the name. Given this media center has a link to literally all media ever produced in human history, digitized and contained in one accessible database, you balk at the idea of searching for it amongst the millions of films.

Then, it comes to you! So, you enter the title and there it is. However, your remember your trip is only about 275 miles so you know you won't get far as this maglev train goes about 3000 mph. You will be lucky if you get 8 minutes into the film. So, rather than spoil the experience, you decide to go over some notes you brought for the conference. The subject of the conference is terraformation. Great interest is being shown by humanity to further explore the idea of inhabiting space, and this conference will address the potentials currently available.

However, before too much thought can be done, you arrive at your destination. You exit the train and enter the station. You realize you need some equipment for some program work that will be addressed at the conference, so you make your way to the local technology library. You need a versatile laptop and a series of storage cards to bring your notes and work with you after it is done. You enter the library and feel a buzz on your phone. You pull it out and a curious notification welcomes you to that region's technology center and asks if you need search assistance.

This perplexes you at first but then you remember that the library network in that region has recently been updated to allow for a universal recognition system, facilitated by a phone application you had installed prior, while using another library in the same region years ago. You had forgotten about this. "How convenient!", you think. You describe the laptop and memory cards and it returns the product profiles. You find that it is correct. Once confirmed, a visual map of the library appears that shows your location and the location of the area with the goods you need. You navigate to that area and check out the items. Then, you exit the library, retrieve an automated cab, and you are off to the conference.

A number of hours later the conference ends. You are inspired, exhausted and hungry, having forgotten to eat most of the day. You decide an Italian style meal sounds good. Luckily, you notice just such a restaurant a few blocks down and start walking. Your phone rings. It is an associate from your hometown. He states there is a problem with one of the food production manifolds and he is unable to respond due to his own personal emergency. You state you will go online and check the system status and get back to him.

You quickly enter the Italian restaurant and take a seat at a small table. It is a pretty busy night so it is noisier than you would prefer. You whip out the laptop, which has a satellite-based Internet connection at all times, and navigate to your region's technical mainframe to check for status errors. Sure enough, there is a power problem in sector five of the automated vertical farm structure in the northeast region. You bring up a digital image of the physical layout, which, by a kind of color-coding, reveals a severed cable line to a power converter. Having seen this problem before, since you have been overseeing your region's food production for about eight years, you gain a sense of relief, as the problem is very simple to fix.

With a few keystrokes, a CR9 modular robot is now under your control in the farm. Through this remote control ability you are able to guide the machine to the problem area and explain the issue. This robot, like the one in the apartment rental you had prior, has a complete understanding of all physical and technical systems in the operation. A 3D model of the plant and its infrastructural design is literally programmed into these CR9s and all it needs is a little orientation from the management team and it quickly goes into action to fix a problem. Once in place, the CR9 quickly understands the problem clearly and moves to replace the bad power cable. In a few minutes, the problem is solved. You call your associate back and he thanks you kindly for the assistance.

Now extremely hungry, you whip around the menu kiosk and find the largest plate of pasta you can! You enter your order, along with a strong cocktail and some water, and wait. About ten minutes later a mechanism in the table opens from the side, elevating your now ever-enticing looking meal to the surface in front of you. You dive in! Eating away, you can't help but notice a gentle faced woman staring at you from the corner. You smile and she comes over.

She asks, "How is everything?" You state "Quite good. Are you the manager here?" She nods. You then go on to describe how your grandfather helped design the kitchen system she is using. She lights up and says, "My family has been feeding people for nine generations. Sometimes I go back and cook the food myself, just for fun!" You both laugh at the nostalgia, comparing the idea to those who still manually fix up old cars just for fun.

After the meal and conversation, you decide it is time to retire for the evening. Pulling out your phone you locate an available room a few doors down. You enter the building, obtain a keycard from an automated key wall, and ascend to your room and sleep. Life moves forward.

PART IV: THE ZEITGEIST MOVEMENT

-SOCIAL DESTABILIZATION AND TRANSITION-

I am convinced that if we are to get on the right side of the world revolution, we...must undergo a radical revolution of values...we must rapidly begin the shift from a thing-oriented society to a person-oriented society. When machines and computers, profit motives and property rights are considered more important than people, the giant triplets of racism, extreme materialism and militarism are incapable of being conquered.[812]
Dr. Martin Luther King Jr.

Trends
The early 21st century marks an extremely interesting period of time. On one side we see many clear and present problems that, as this essay will discuss, show an accelerating gravitation toward further negative consequences, both environmental and social. Yet, on the other side, an ever present and accelerating solution orientation, technically, reveals so much potential to change course for the better, positive future possibilities appear profound and limitless.

To the casual observer, the idea that "the worst is over" regarding the evolution of human culture may appear intuitively accurate, depending on where one resides on the planet. We have seen an overall increase in life expectancy, an overall decline in behavioral violence,[813] a rising standard of living on the whole in the Western world, along with a generally maturing global culture which has been inching its way out of vast periods of bigotry, sexism, racism, and nationalism, further promoting a much needed global consciousness.

Yet, the truth of the matter is that any such social "progress", specifically the overall *standard of living* elevation occurring due to our technological ingenuity, is actually amalgamating *within* a highly detrimental framework that has just started to really reveal itself as such. These surfacing problems are of a *scientific* nature, not an ideological one. The fact is, market capitalism, no matter how you wish to regulate it or not regulate it, contains severe structural flaws, which will always, to one degree or another, perpetuate *environmental abuse and destabilization,* along with *human disregard and caustic inequality.*

As expressed at length in other essays, this market/trade concept manifested out of an environmental condition which viewed all material things in the world as universally scarce. This has forged a competitive and invariably exploitative value system that generates certain behavioral propensities and loyalties that are *misaligned* with the natural order of reality, as per our modern environmental and

---

812 Source: Speech by Dr. King, 1967
  (http://www.democracynow.org/2013/1/21/dr_martin_luther_king_in_1967
)
813 Reference: *Violence Vanquished*
  (http://online.wsj.com/news/articles/SB10001424053111190410670457658
  3203589408180)

sociological understandings.[814]

The difference between capitalism's effect today and in the 16th century is that our technical ability to rapidly *accelerate* and *amplify* this competitive and exploitative process has brought to the surface consequences that simply couldn't be recognized or even anticipated during those earlier periods. Today, we are seeing the surfacing of these previously hidden tendencies in full force, and the end result is that what we see as progress now will likely be overcome, in time, by the larger order force of capitalism's misaligned detrimental principles. It is like a massive tidal wave which has been on pace to crashing on a ship for a very long time and no matter how well developed and organized that ship is, it is no match for this larger order force of nature.

Perhaps the most notable example of this is the fact that virtually *all life support systems are in decline.*[815] [816] It really doesn't matter how many people have achieved a coveted, ideal, upper-class lifestyle if it is occurring on the back of unsustainable methods. It is simply a matter of time before the effects of resource depletion; biodiversity loss and pollution evolve to destroy this *illusion* of success. Likewise, while it may be true that we have seen a decline in violence, mass genocide and the once enormous fatalities common to global warfare, we need to step back even further and remember the *causality* itself, not the mere trend of reduction. If resource scarcity and geo-economic strategy have been the cause of most national conflicts in the world in the past (which it has), then all it takes is that precondition to re-materialize. The rapid decline of human-environment relations in the past few decades is setting the stage for this once again.

The 2003 Iraq war, by some analysts, was a *resource war* for oil, and this is rather difficult to deny when the evidence is weighed.[817] There is little doubt that if the world was faced with real energy, water, food and mineral scarcity, to the extent that it would deeply affect the economies of larger national powers, we would regress rapidly back to mass global warfare and mass casualties, not to mention massive civil unrest as well. Today, all major superpowers continue to increase armaments and weapon power clearly in preparation for such events.[818]

---

814 As an aside, it is important to qualify that market capitalism is not deemed the sole root of the problem. Capitalism is a symptom as well, birthed out of the fear-oriented psychology inherent to the historical condition of a scarcity-saturated society.

815 Reference: *Data shows Earth's systems in decline* (http://www.bt.com.bn/science-technology/2011/08/01/data-shows-earths-systems-decline)

816 Reference: *Study highlights global decline* (http://news.bbc.co.uk/2/hi/science/nature/4391835.stm)

817 Reference: *Top REPUBLICAN Leaders Say Iraq War Was Really about Oil* (http://www.washingtonsblog.com/2013/03/top-republican-leaders-say-iraq-war-was-really-for-oil.html)

818 Reference: *Water scarcity to drive conflict, hit food and energy, experts say*

On a different level, almost paradoxically, the very things that have been helping society increase its standard of living, *science and technology*, is also driving its increased vulnerability towards destruction. While science can, on one side, illuminate the natural alignments we as a species need to adhere to in order to find balance with the habitat and each other, it can also be used *locally* and *narrowly,* within the context of the distorted incentive structure the market perpetuates, to create and accelerate destructive and inhumane consequences. The atomic bomb is one extreme of this reality. Our increased, high-tech capacity to more efficiently destroy biodiversity, over use our resources and pollute, is another.

In some ways, the rapid development of science and technology is pushing humanity into a corner. It is as though the species is marching farther back into the apex of a three-dimensional triangle, laid on its back, with its edges sloping quickly down, once passed over. One side is a negative acceleration into social and ecological decline and the other a positive acceleration into an age of abundance, balance, peace and progress. As time moves forward, the farther we move back into this apex, the less space we have. At some point, we are going to succumb to one side or the other.

Population & Resources

Statistics suggest that well over nine billion people will inhabit Earth by 2050,[819] sourced mainly in the developing world. Along with this come dramatic increases in demand for (a) food, (b) water, (c) energy, and (d) minerals/material resources. Each one of these will be discussed.

(http://www.trust.org/item/?map=water-scarcity-to-drive-conflict-hit-food-and-energy-experts)

819 Source: *World population projected to reach 9.6 billion by 2050 – UN report* (http://www.un.org/apps/news/story.asp?NewsID=45165#.UtyMb2TTm2w)

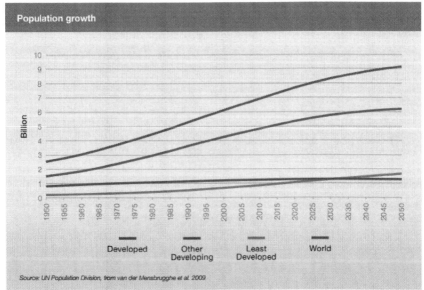

Reproduced from the Food and Agriculture Organization's *Expert Forum*, 2009[820]

(a) As far as food, there is no shortage of studies that project that our traditional food production methods are not going to come close to meeting demand by 2050.[821] [822] Estimates put production needs at a 60 to 110% increase[823] and given the current industrial climate which also has an extremely wasteful and inefficient supply chain, wasting 30-50% of all food created,[824] the only logical expectation is a worsening of the global poverty and starvation levels in terms of population percentage. This doesn't even bring into consideration the ongoing plea for more sustainable agricultural practices to stop pollution/soil erosion, which would not be a convenience if this pressure accelerates, assuming traditional land-based methods are still

---

820 Source: *Global agriculture towards 2050*
(http://www.fao.org/fileadmin/templates/wsfs/docs/Issues_papers/HLEF205 0_Global_Agriculture.pdf)

821 Source: *Food Security Raises the Obvious: Can We Feed 9.6 Billion by 2050?* (http://www.huffingtonpost.com/michael-zacka/food-security-raises-the-_b_3948986.html)

822 Source: *Yield Trends Are Insufficient to Double Global Crop Production by 2050*
(http://www.plosone.org/article/info:doi/10.1371/journal.pone.0066428)

823 Reference: *Current Global Food Production Trajectory Won't Meet 2050 Needs*
(http://www.sciencedaily.com/releases/2013/06/130619195135.htm), *UN: farmers must produce 70% more food by 2050 to feed population* (http://www.theguardian.com/environment/2011/nov/28/un-farmers-produce-food-population)

824 Source: *Feeding the 9 Billion: The tragedy of waste*
(http://www.imeche.org/knowledge/themes/environment/global-food)

in use.

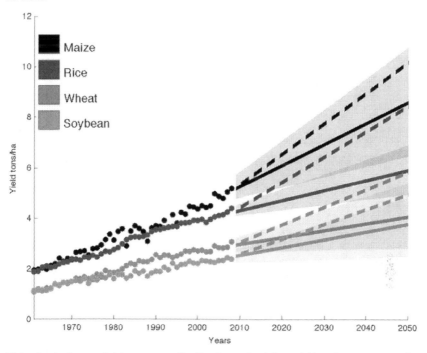

This chart shows yields per acre for the important foundational crops corn, rice, wheat and soybeans. The solid lines show what would happen if this growth continued. The dashed lines, however, show what is really needed to satisfy expected demand by 2050.[825]

(b) Potable water statistics are equally if not more dramatic, and needless to say, water scarcity means even more problems for traditional agriculture. According to the United Nations, by 2025, an estimated 1.8 billion people will live in areas plagued by water scarcity, with two-thirds of the world's population living in water-stressed regions.[826] The OECD projects that fresh water demand will rise by 55% by 2050, corroborating the U.N. water stress statistic, extending it to 3.9 billion by 2050, or nearly half the world's population.[827]

---

825 Source: *Yield Trends Are Insufficient to Double Global Crop Production by 2050* (http://www.plosone.org/article/info%3Adoi %2F10.1371%2Fjournal.pone.0066428)
826 Source: *A Clean Water Crisis* (http://environment.nationalgeographic.com/environment/freshwater/fresh water-crisis/)
827 Source: *Water: The Environmental Outlook to 2050* (http://www.oecd.org/env/resources/49006778.pdf)

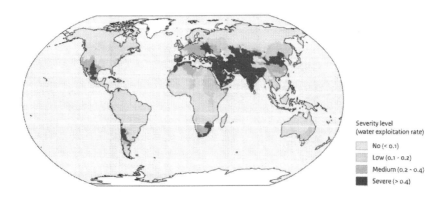

Severity level
(water exploitation rate)

☐ No (< 0.1)

▨ Low (0.1 - 0.2)

▨ Medium (0.2 - 0.4)

■ Severe (> 0.4)

Source: The Environmental Outlook Baseline projections; output from the IMAGE suite of models (PBL)

2050 projection of water stressed areas.
Reproduced from the OCED *Water, The Outlook to 2050*, 2011[828]

Likewise, water *pollution*, which further compounds the problem, is on pace to continue as developing countries increase industry and agriculture in their interest to raise their overall standard of living.[829] Sadly, this interest to increase industry will only further the pollution problem as the methods used are often much more primitive and environmentally dangerous than what the developed nations are slowly emerging out of. China is a case in point. While considered a developed industrial nation, its internal policies are excessively relaxed when it comes to environmental standards and regulation. This is a natural capitalist outgrowth as the intention is to free up commerce and further economic growth. Today, China contains 16 out of 20 of the world's most polluted cities[830] and only further development, population growth and hence pollution is to be expected.

As far as water pollution, globally, nitrogen and phosphorous contamination, mostly from agriculture, is now a major problem, creating both "dead zones"[831] in certain surface bodies, along with making people sick who drink it via ground water.[832] Likewise, many other pollution sources are ubiquitous. For example, air pollution from coal plants enters the atmosphere and then find its way into the

---

828 Source: *Water:The Environmental Outlook to 2050*
   (http://www.oecd.org/env/resources/49006778.pdf)
829 Reference: *Water Pollution Rises From Farms, Costing Billions*
   (http://www.bloomberg.com/news/2012-03-13/water-pollution-tied-to-
   agriculture-increasing-costing-billions.html)
830 Source: *The Most Polluted Places On Earth*
   (http://www.cbsnews.com/news/the-most-polluted-places-on-earth/)
831 Reference: *Too Much Nitrogen and Phosphorus Are Bad for the Bay*
   (http://www.cbf.org/how-we-save-the-bay/issues/dead-zones/nitrogen-
   phosphorus)
832 Reference: *Nitrates in Drinking Water*
   (http://www.ext.colostate.edu/pubs/crops/00517.html)

ocean. The mercury released by the burning of coal then pollutes the fish and those fish are then caught as a food source, containing this deadly toxin, hurting human health. Given current trends, mercury pollution is expected to rise as well.[833]

In short, if all patterns stay the same, water, both in the context of its symbiotic relationship to biodiversity and its direct relationship to human survival, given that humans can only go a few days before dying without it, is on pace for severe shortages and extremely detrimental environmental outcomes overall. This again assumes we conduct ourselves in the same basic ways we have for the past 50 years, embracing market logic, which is life-blind and decoupled from environmental awareness.

(c) As far as energy, as alluded to in the prior note about coal, there is literally nothing positive about any fossil fuel combustion process when it comes to environmental sustainability.[834] These means will always have a detrimental footprint and it can only get worse as population and industry increases.[835] Compounding this is also the fact that such resources are *non-renewable* and ensuing scarcity is simply a matter of time.

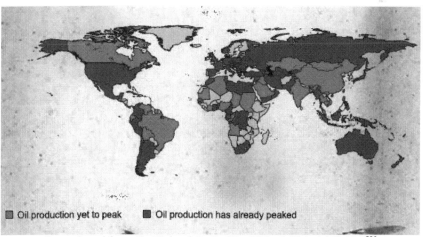

Reproduced from Dr Michael R. Smith, CEO of Globalshift Ltd.[836]

833 Source: *Mercury contamination in fish expected to rise in coming decades*
(http://www.cbsnews.com/news/mercury-contamination-in-fish-expected-to-rise-in-coming-decades/)
834 Reference: *The Hidden Cost of Fossil Fuels*
(http://www.ucsusa.org/clean_energy/our-energy-choices/coal-and-other-fossil-fuels/the-hidden-cost-of-fossil.html)
835 Reference: *Leaked UN Report: If We Don't Stop Polluting Now, We May Never Have The Technology To Save Ourselves*
(http://www.businessinsider.com/leaked-un-draft-report-on-climate-change-2014-1)
836 See globalshift.co.uk for more country details.

The issue of *peak oil* has been looming for many decades.[837] While controversial, what we know today is that *convention* oil production, meaning the usual raw crude which used to occur in large vast pockets under the Earth's surface, is in decline on the global scale, with an estimated 37 countries already past their peak of production.[838]

According to Dr. Richard G. Miller, who worked for British Petroleum from 1985 to 2008, "We need new production equal to a new Saudi Arabia every 3 to 4 years to maintain and grow supply... New discoveries have not matched consumption since 1986. We are drawing down on our reserves, even though reserves are apparently climbing every year. Reserves are growing due to better technology in old fields, raising the amount we can recover – but production is still falling at 4.1% p.a. [per annum]."[839]

Of course, many others today speculate that the world is still "awash in oil", with grand speculations of future capacity. However, these projections are centered on *non-conventional* source that are often extremely difficult to extract and process. Oil shale and tar sands, along with "fracking" for natural gas, are currently accelerating methods and, on paper, they can give the sense of abundance. However, there is a great deal of dispute about just how viable these means are to meet growing demand,[840] while the environmental costs of these complex and often destructive practices are vast and counterproductive.

According to the Center for Biological Diversity, "The development of 'oil shale' and 'tar sands' has been shown to be environmentally destructive, and water and energy intensive. Extracting oil from U.S. public lands through oil shale or tar sands would deal a disastrous blow to any hope of reducing atmospheric CO_2 levels to below 350 parts per million — the level we need to reach soon to stabilize Earth's climate. Besides helping push us toward global warming catastrophe, oil shale and tar sands development destroys species habitat, wastes enormous volumes of water, pollutes air and water, and degrades and defiles vast swaths of land."[841]

Likewise, hydraulic fracturing or "fracking" has been found to be exceptionally polluting and dangerous with even recorded instances of ground water being so polluted that home water supplies have become literally *flammable*.[842] Regardless of such contaminated water

837 Reference: Peakoil.net (http://www.peakoil.net/)
838 Reference: *Former BP geologist: peak oil is here and it will 'break economies'* (http://www.theguardian.com/environment/earth-insight/2013/dec/23/british-petroleum-geologist-peak-oil-break-economy-recession)
839 Ibid.
840 Ibid.
841 Source: *Oil Shale and Tar Sands* (http://www.biologicaldiversity.org/programs/public_lands/energy/dirty_energy_development/oil_shale_and_tar_sands/)
842 Reference: *Fracking hot: N. Dakota man 'sets tap water on fire'* (http://rt.com/usa/flammable-water-dakota-fracking-023/)

supplies, given the dangerous air pollution, destroyed streams, and devastated landscapes, fracking continues to accelerate globally.[843]

The bottom line is that the fossil fuel economy is unsustainable. The economic manner by which this will become apparent in the current model will be through extreme price. The visceral problem is how supply and demand will set up a condition where scarcity will raise prices so high that industry and public simply can't afford it. This would severely limit the entire facet of industry itself since fossil fuels and hence energy are what move agriculture, production, distribution and the like. At the same time, these practices could bring human society in a pollution nightmare that could take generations to overcome.

(d) General resource scarcity, embracing both biotic and abiotic resources, is rapidly increasing globally, coupled with a parallel loss of biodiversity. In 2002, 192 countries, in association with the United Nations, got together over something called the Convention on Biological Diversity, making a public commitment to significantly reduce the losses by 2010. However, when 2010 arrived, no progress has been made. In their official 2010 publication, they stated:

"None of the twenty-one sub-targets accompanying the overall target of significantly reducing the rate of biodiversity loss by 2010 can be said definitively to have been achieved globally...Actions to promote...biodiversity receive a tiny fraction of 'funding' compared to... infrastructure and industrial developments...Moreover, biodiversity considerations are often ignored when such developments are designed...Most future scenarios project continuing high levels of extinctions and loss of habitats throughout this century."[844]

In a 2011 study published, which was in part a response to an ongoing general call to isolate and protect certain regions of Earth to ensure the security of biodiversity, it was found that even with millions of square kilometers of land and ocean currently under legal protection, it has done very little to slow the trends of decline.[845]

They also made the following, highly troubling conclusion with respect to resource consumption: "[The] 'excess' use of the Earth's resources or 'overshoot' is possible because resources can be harvested faster than they can be replaced...the cumulative overshoot from the mid-1980s to 2002 resulted in an 'ecological debt' that would require 2.5 planet Earths to pay. In a business-as-usual scenario, our demands on planet Earth could mount to the productivity of 27 planets

---

843 Reference: *The rapid expansion of natural gas drilling across the nation endangers human health and the environment.*
   (http://www.nrdc.org/energy/gasdrilling/)
844 Source: *Global Biodiversity Outlook 3* (http://www.cbd.int/gbo3/)
845 Reference: *Ongoing global biodiversity loss and the need to move beyond protected areas: a review of the technical and practical shortcomings of protectedareas on land and sea* (http://www.int-res.com/articles/theme/m434p251.pdf)

by 2050."[846]

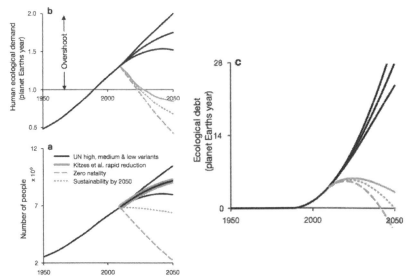

Projections for (a) human population size, (b) human ecological demand and (c) ecological debt under different scenarios of human population growth and use of natural resources. Ecological demand is calculated by multiplying the size of the world's human population by the average yearly demands of a person and dividing this amount by the Earth's biocapacity; this yields the number of planet Earths required to meet the whole human demand. Reproduced from Marine Ecology Progress Series, Vol. 434[847]

Today, one could search through all peer reviewed scientific documents in the world and likely not find one review of humanity's resource and biodiversity relationships that are neutral or positive. While estimates may vary, one thing is clear: the species is growing rapidly and expanding its industrial activity in a climate of absolute deficiency with respect to the unsustainable methods and values being put forward. It is important to remind the reader, however, that this problem is a system issue, not an immutably empirical one, once again.[848]

The problem is not our mere existence or a growing population. The problem is that we have a global economic tradition in place rooted in 16th century, pre-industrial, handicraft oriented thought, that places the act of consuming (buying and selling) at the core of all social unfolding. A good analogy is to consider the gas pedal on a car. The more consumption of fuel, the faster it goes; buying

846 *Marine Ecology Progress Series*, Vol. 434: p.261, 2011
847 *Ongoing global biodiversity loss and the need to move beyond protected areas: a review of the technical and practical shortcomings of protectedareas on land and sea* (http://www.int-res.com/articles/theme/m434p251.pdf)
848 See the essay *Post-Scarcity, Trends and Capacity* for why this is so.

things in our world is the fuel. If you slow down consumption, economic growth slows, people lose jobs, purchasing power declines and social conditions destabilize. This is an artificial reality generated by misaligned economic principles, not the physical reality itself.

The Perfect Storm

While the preceding sections have addressed specific, major issues in some detail, we cannot overlook the economic synergy which links them all in the financial and technical systems related. Energy, water, food and material accessibility interlock into one societal mechanism, which can have dramatic effects on employment, social stability, and many other issues if any one of them is disturbed.

There are numerous scenarios that could materialize that compound this overall sustainability problem. For example, global GDP has a powerful connection to water. The IFPRI states "current 'business as usual' water management practices and levels of water productivity will put at risk approximately $63 trillion, or 45 percent of the projected 2050 global GDP (at 2000 prices), equivalent to 1.5 times the size of today's entire global economy."[849]

Likewise, from a mere production standpoint, 70% of all freshwater is used for agriculture.[850] Any large-scale water scarcity would then also mean reduced yields, assuming the same traditional practices are used for cultivation. The same goes for energy, especially hydrocarbons. The effect of a substantial reduction of these resources on traditional agriculture alone is staggering, while the effect it would have on industry as a whole as far as the vast amount of petroleum-based products and power needs would be nearly apocalyptic in the current model.

We also cannot overlook the social stability issue and how the decline of such resources will change human, social and national behavior, inciting indifference and a loss of empathy as fear and narrow self-preservation is triggered and exacerbated. We can imagine, for instance, a steep price increase in gasoline where it becomes unprofitable for those transporting critical, life- supporting materials. The result might very well be a union strike that stops the flow of goods, compounding the problem. Imagine for a moment if the dominant food transport unions on the west coast of America went on-strike, stopping the flow of basic commodities. This could spark a highly detrimental chain reaction.

Scarcity breeds crime, conflict and anti-social behaviors. On the micro scale, it is not difficult to see the increase in gangs; theft and prohibitive underground economies flourish in this climate, as they have statistically proven to do so in regions still enmeshed in great poverty and a lack of job opportunities. Disease, and other issues arising out of such poor conditions, is another viable concern. On a

---

849 Source: *Water in 2050: The Future of Water Requires a Sustainable, Blue Path* (http://growingblue.com/water-in-2050/)
850 Source: *Water* Uses
(http://www.fao.org/nr/water/aquastat/water_use/index.stm)

macro level, as noted prior, national war has historically mostly been driven by resource scarcity and national/business self-preservation.

It should be no surprise that America and many other nations have been beefing up nuclear arsenals and delivery systems for some time,[851] [852] with the world currently capable of destroying itself many, many times over with its existing arsenal of over 26,000 nuclear warheads.[853] Thousands of these weapons remain on high alert today, ready to be fired at any time and the reaction of the global outcry to stop proliferation has literally been met with more proliferation, behind the scenes.[854]

At the same time, the mechanics of the global financial system are also in play. Since all money is created out of debt and loaned with interest attached – interest that actually *doesn't exist* in the money supply outright – there is always more global debt in existence than money to pay for it. This has culminated into vast personal, business and government defaults, both real and pending. A 2010 report from the Standard & Poor's rating agency estimates that the United States will have a debt of 415% of GDP by 2050, while by 2060, 60% of *all the countries in the world* will be bankrupt.[855]

A cursory glance at the financial status of most countries in the world today reveals a spectrum of medium debt to extreme debt. Amazingly, there appears to be no country on Earth with a balanced budget, and as of early 2014, the public debt of the planet is equivalent to about 52 trillion dollars.[856] However, that is just public or government debt. The real figure, combining both public and *private* debt is a staggering 223.3 trillion dollars.[857] Dividing that number by the 7.1 billion people on the planet as of early 2015, we find that each human owes about $31.5 thousand dollars.

So, we have to ask ourselves: how possible is it that we are going to be able to financially facilitate the vast technological reforms

851 Reference: *U.S. nuclear weapon plans to cost $355 billion over a decade: CBO report* (http://www.reuters.com/article/2013/12/20/us-usa-nuclear-arms-idUSBRE9BJ1FH20131220)
852 Reference: *2200 nuclear weapons in state of high operational alert: Report* (http://www.presstv.com/detail/2012/06/05/244720/2200-nuclear-warheads-ready-to-fire/)
853 Reference: ctbto.org (http://www.ctbto.org/faqs/?uid=16&cHash=aa30bc1b1be1d08f3a48d4cff1b8a0db)
854 Reference: *How a Massive Nuclear Nonproliferation Effort Led to More Proliferation* (http://www.theatlantic.com/international/archive/2013/06/how-a-massive-nuclear-nonproliferation-effort-led-to-more-proliferation/277140/)
855 Source: *S&P: 60% of countries will be bankrupt within 50 years* (http://www.rawstory.com/rs/2010/10/09/sp-60-countries-bankrupt-50-years/)
856 Source: *The global debt* clock (http://www.economist.com/content/global_debt_clock)
857 Source: *Number of the Week: Total World Debt Load at 313% of GDP* (http://blogs.wsj.com/economics/2013/05/11/number-of-the-week-total-world-debt-load-at-313-of-gdp/)

needed to generate some degree of sustainability when it is clear that massive overhauls of our agricultural system, water processes, pollution control, energy sources, infrastructure and industrial methods are desperately needed? We know we have the technical means to do it, but do we have the money?

The more one thinks about this latter question, the more incredible and outright idiotic the financial mechanisms in play become. It isn't that some progress will not be made, as the major powers in the world pretty much don't take debt seriously to begin with. The difference between a 1 trillion dollar deficit and a 100 trillion dollar deficit is only as important as the ability to service it. In truth, the major powers *know* the full amounts will never be paid back and the process of alleviation will likely take a political form rather than financial, likely in the context of market incentive negotiations, geo-political negotiation and resource acquisition negotiations.

However, those deals are usually behind the scenes and the growing pressure to cut social programs and spending on what are more often than not the very programs that help keep some order, continues for the sake of public perception and other levels of differential advantage. Likewise, while the larger powers have great advantage in this predicament, the smaller developing countries are the ones who really suffer, as they have no economic or military power to gain clout in international appeal. Given this, it is easy to see that the developing countries will be the ones firmly underwater, continuing to be vulnerable to austerity, exploitation and the basic ignoring of its internal social strife.

In 2011, the United Nations noted a statistic that 1.5 billion people were living in "absolute poverty", with a representative from Nepal at a pertaining conference adding that "at the rate of decline observed from 1990 to 2005, it would take another 88 years to eradicate extreme poverty".[858] If we reflect on the rapid economic growth that occurred from 1990 to 2005, which was considered by many a "boom" period for much of the world,[859] we see that the existing negative pressures were not even close to what we are seeing two decades later. Hence, it is logical to speculate that what progress (growth) was achieved in the 1990s with respect to the rather minimal percentage reduction of extreme poverty is likely to be reversed as exponential population growth amidst an ever-deteriorating financial and environmental situation accelerates.

Likewise, and as a final topic of this section with respect to emerging negative pressures, we have the issue of *technological unemployment.* As partly expressed in the essay *Market Efficiency vs. Technical Efficiency,* machine automation is rapidly evolving to mirror or exceed the vast majority of industrial activities common to human

---

858 Source: *1.5 Billion People Living in Absolute Poverty Makes Its Eradication Humankind'sMost Significant Challenge, Second Committee Told* (http://www.un.org/News/Press/docs/2011/gaef3313.doc.htm)
859 Reference: *1990s boom 'stunting world growth'* (http://news.bbc.co.uk/2/hi/business/3160052.stm)

laborers. A 2013 study out of the University of Oxford states "45 percent of America's occupations will be automated within the next 20 years."[860] Given America's advancement, this naturally also implies that *half the world's occupations* could be automated as well.

More specifically, a detailed examination of automation technology by sector at the present time, both in the fields of manual labor and the service industry, show that there is really no tangible occupation in existence that isn't on pace to being replaced by machine and/or artificial intelligence. It is simply a matter of time and intention. Unfortunately, the market economy is *predicated* on people "earning a living" and cycling money through the society to maintain economic stability and growth. This, of course, means such a trend is actually economically detrimental in the context of the market system.

Likewise, since such automation technology is subject to Moore's law, or more accurately ephemeralization, such machines are getting cheaper and eventually they will become more cost effective than hiring human beings, who require insurance, vacations, a limited number of hours to work a week, and so forth. The productivity now possible is exponentially more effective with machines than with people, and this reality will only increase as time moves forward. Yet, this creates a *system contradiction,* for if machines displace people, how do they get income to cycle money into the economy by purchase?

In traditional market principles, there is no solution, other than the false assumption that humans will constantly shift in exact accord with such labor displacement. This might have worked in the mid 20th century, but it will no longer work given the rapid, exponential advancement of modern technology today. Even more, it could be well-argued that it is *socially irresponsible* not to pursue this new attribute of our means of production for it removes humans from unsafe and monotonous, life-wasting roles, possibly freeing them also to do more sensitive, creative, high-order things. Such a transition, however, would require the entire edifice of market capitalism to be uprooted and replaced by a new social approach that does not require labor-for-income.

The Fatal Incentive: Business Acumen
"Business acumen" can be defined as "keenness and quickness in understanding and dealing with a business situation in a manner that is likely to lead to a good outcome."[861] Put another way, it is about gauging each situation to best maximize profits, in the most strategic way. This is brought up to convey two related propensities that have a great relevance in the way most people, particularly the wealthy, will likely cope with increasing scarcity and/or social destabilization.

The first is the rather simple observation that the pursuit of

---

860 Source: *Report Suggests Nearly Half of U.S. Jobs Are Vulnerable to Computerization* (http://www.technologyreview.com/view/519241/report-suggests-nearly-half-of-us-jobs-are-vulnerable-to-computerization/)
861 Source: *Business acumen* (http://en.wikipedia.org/wiki/Business_acumen)

business is really nothing more than the pursuit of money. While the business mindset will often romanticize about "helping the world" and "pleasing consumers", the only real measure is *profit*. It is simply assumed that gaining profit means helping the world, which is clearly not the case given the vast declines in our habitat integrity and the fact that there are now *more slaves in the world than ever before.*[862]

The second is subtler and it has to do with the psychology of fear and greed. Research done in the Department of Psychology at the University of California, Berkeley found that increased wealth actually creates *reduced empathy and compassion* towards others, along with elevating one's sense of entitlement.[863] In short, increased wealth tends to make one "mean" and there is no shortage of corroborating studies that have confirmed this very propensity. A study done by the University of Michigan titled "Higher social class predicts increased unethical behavior" states:

"Seven studies using experimental and naturalistic methods reveal that upper-class individuals behave more unethically than lower-class individuals. In studies 1 and 2, upper-class individuals were more likely to break the law while driving, relative to lower-class individuals. In follow-up laboratory studies, upper-class individuals were more likely to exhibit unethical decision-making tendencies (study 3), take valued goods from others (study 4), lie in a negotiation (study 5), cheat to increase their chances of winning a prize (study 6), and endorse unethical behavior at work (study 7) than were lower-class individuals. Mediator and moderator data demonstrated that upper-class individuals' unethical tendencies are accounted for, in part, by their more favorable attitudes toward greed."[864]

A study titled "Class and compassion: socioeconomic factors predict responses to suffering" revealed that lower-class individuals respond with greater compassion to viewing human suffering than upper class individuals.[865] In a related study titled "Social Class, Contextualism, and Empathic Accuracy" it was found that individuals of a lower social class are more empathically accurate in judging the emotions of other people. In its three studies, lower-class individuals received higher scores than upper class individuals on a test of empathic accuracy; judging the emotions of an interaction partner; and made more accurate inferences about emotion from static images of muscle movements in the eyes.[866]

---

862 Reference: *There Are More Slaves Today Than at Any Time in Human History*
(http://www.alternet.org/story/142171/there_are_more_slaves_today_than_at_any_time_in_human_history)

863 Reference: *Does money make you mean? (TED lecture by Paul Piff)*
(http://www.examined-life.info/2013/12/does-money-make-you-mean-ted-lecture-by-paul-piff/)

864 Source: *Higher social class predicts increased unethical behavior*
(http://www.pnas.org/content/early/2012/02/21/1118373109)

865 Source: *Class and compassion: socioeconomic factors predict responses to suffering.* (http://www.ncbi.nlm.nih.gov/pubmed/22148992)

866 Source: *Social Class, Contextualism, and Empathic Accuracy*

In a report titled "Having Less, Giving More: The Influence of Social Class on Prosocial Behavior" it was found that across four studies, lower class individuals proved to be more generous, charitable, trusting, and helpful, as compared with their upper class counterparts.[867] A 2012 article in the The Chronicle of Philanthropy reports that low-income people give a far bigger share of their discretionary income to charities. People who make $50,000 to $75,000 give an average of 7.6 percent of their discretionary income to charity, compared with an average of 4.2 percent for people who make $100,000 or more.[868]

Now, such reports are not noted to suggest this is a universal phenomenon. However, there is clearly something going on in the psychology of those who become wealthy and a heightened sense of protection, indifference and entitlement seems consistent. With this in mind, let's return to our consideration of how different classes would respond to threatening social circumstances. Given the fact that the world now has almost 2,200 billionaires worth about 6.5 trillion in total[869] (that's an average of 2.9 billion each), with the top 100 capable of *ending global poverty four times over,*[870] a great deal of attention has been placed on these figures in the hope for social help.

Given the anger that has risen due to the reality of tremendous and growing inequality in the world, one can imagine the general sense of unease of those who are super-rich. Yet, apart from what could be argued as a public relations move, combined with both honest intentions and the specter of philanthropy, such as the so-called billionaire's "Giving Pledge",[871] one can't help but feel deep animosity for such figures and the system that enabled their extreme and clearly unnecessary wealth.

This, again, isn't to say anyone is "bad", but rather to note that any system which has the *capacity* to even create such extreme wealth imbalance, in and of itself, needs to be addressed as the root problem it is – not the supposed charity of those who have been able to play the market game to such an extent as to accrue such irrational and wasteful sums. It is not a cynical view in this light to consider such things as the "Giving Pledge" as more of an insult than a solution.

(http://pss.sagepub.com/content/21/11/1716.abstract)

867 Source: *Having less, giving more: the influence of social class on prosocial behavior.* (http://www.ncbi.nlm.nih.gov/pubmed/20649364)

868 Source: *Wealthiest Don't Rate High on Giving Measure* (http://philanthropy.com/article/America-s-Geographic-Giving/133591/)

869 Source: *Number of world's billionaires hits record; U.S. Leads* (http://ca.finance.yahoo.com/blogs/insight/number-world-billionaires-hits-record-u-leads-152954753.html)

870 Source: *Annual income of richest 100 people enough to end global poverty four times over* (http://www.oxfam.org/en/pressroom/pressrelease/2013-01-19/annual-income-richest-100-people-enough-end-global-poverty-four-times)

871 Reference: *Forty U.S. billionaires pledge to give half their money to charity* (http://news.xinhuanet.com/english2010/world/2010-08/05/c_13430367.htm)

So given the noted psychological studies put forward and the current state of extreme and growing wealth imbalance and destabilization (good intentions by the wealthy aside), there is no evidence that the rich will save us. If current trends remain, as they likely will, the rich will simply isolate themselves more and more in fear and protection as problems continue to emerge. This propensity also applies to the entire chain of social stratification in general as narrow, short-term self-preservation will always be a knee-jerk tendency when one finds his or herself susceptible to financial loss and as the studies show, the higher a given person is in class status, the more indifferent they tend to become.

This is the signature of "class war", and as these trends persist, we can hence expect increased uprisings and anger at the state of affairs and gross imbalance in society. While this may seem like an elusive kind of phenomenon, it should be thought about in the same context of other negative factors, such as resource depletion, unemployment and the like. An angry population can become a divisive and violent population, and the emergence of large-scale social insurrection can have very negative social consequences if root causes are not clearly understood.

Transition

The idea of *transitioning* fluidly out of the current model into a NLRBE can be a daunting and difficult speculation. Perhaps the first consideration is to think more deeply about what it is we are transitioning into exactly. In many ways, this move from a scarcity-preserving economy to a system of direct resource management and scientific application in the pursuit of a post-scarcity or abundance economy to meet the needs of the human species, while securing the integrity of the habitat, is really *a transition of values.*

At the same time, it is also a transition of *operant reinforcement,* which simply means the new structure actually works to *reward* conservation, balance, social contribution and ecological respect, rather than what we reinforce today, which is essentially selfishness, competition, consumption and exploitation. In fact, the market system could gesturally be viewed as not a "social system", per se, but an *anti-social system.*

As far as physical transition itself, it is naturally naive to assume we can predict the future regarding such a vast societal shift, especially given how forceful and present the pressures are that keep the current system in place. All of us are coerced on a daily basis into this market psychology in order to maintain survival, and hence our values are deeply associated to these methods, practices and general worldview whether we like it or not.

It could even be said that these pressures generate a "syntax" of thought, if you will. Our brains seem to wire themselves as we engage the environment, constantly reinforced by existing pressures and our responsive actions. Just as a person can learn a skill and have that skill become "second nature", without much direct conscious thought to execute once learned, we humans perform actions constantly with the same kind of learned, subconscious patterning. For example, we often *don't even know* we are behaving in so-called "narrow selfish" ways at times, since everyone around us appears to be working in the exact same manner, creating perceived normality.

Therefore, TZM naturally views the shifting of people's values as the most important necessity for transition. How this is done is deeply related, of course, to education, while also attempting to actively create conditions that, again, hopefully reinforce these new, sustainable values, inching out larger order change.

That stated, there are perhaps two broad ways to think about transition, with the first giving something of a logical framework for the second. This first scenario assumes that there is the basic sanction of the political/economic power structure and the community overall. It assumes that the human species has definitively decided to make this move in a step-by-step manner on the global scale. Of course, the sad truth is that it would likely never happen this way.

Yet, this hypothetical is expressed because the reasoning inherent is relevant with respect to how we think about transition as a general process and certain attributes noted would likely still come into play in the second scenario. This second scenario is the more realistic scenario as it assumes there is no large-scale public sanction and the transition must originate from activism and influence. This essentially looks at exactly where we are today, taking into account the vast range of divisive opinions, political polarization, national hatred, commercial warfare, etc.

So, to conclude this introduction to *transition*, it is also worth noting, as an aside, that many who criticize The Zeitgeist Movement do so not because they disagree with the direction but because they do not understand how to get there. A relevant analogy to counter this argument is the idea of a very sick person seeking to get well. This person might not even know the cure or the medical path to get there, but given his or her life is at stake, the task to learn and try to realize the proper means toward resolution does not end because of mere ambiguity.

Likewise, the difficulty or confusion in transitioning into a NLRBE does not remove the necessity for it. The fact is, we are all humans on this planet and we can change the world quite easily if we can find unified, shared common ground to relate. Furthermore, it's also important to note that *we are always in transition* to one degree or another. There are no utopias and even if we accomplish only 50% of such a move, as we may define it in theory, it would still be well worth it.[872]

---

872 The idea of partially achieving a NLRBE might be confusing to some. This statement is made to express how certain management practices and half-measures, constituting a "hybrid-economy" are not out of the question toward some degree of sustainable, abundance generating progress. This will not be explored in this essay but the possibility is worth personal consideration.

Scenario One: Systematic Dismantling

A systematic move from the market economy to a NLRBE could theoretically occur through a step-by-step "socialization" of the core attributes of the societal infrastructure. Essentially, we dismantle one layer while implementing a new one in the most fluid way we can. This term "socialization", which is of course a stigmatized notion in the West given the hyper-glorification of the market economy and the demonization of anything otherwise, is still technically appropriate to use in this context, bias aside. This simply means that the necessity of money and the market mechanism would no longer apply to the given social attribute (not that a traditionally "socialist", in the political and economic sense of the word, structure would replace it). Direct, advanced technical means would produce and distribute without a price tag, meeting these needs directly.

As noted in detail in prior essays, a critical component that enables the new social model to produce a high standard of living is the liberal application of modern technology and a systems approach to social organization based on strategic technical efficiency. Since the current model is literally based on a technical *inefficiency* to keep it going, the more technically efficient the system becomes, the less traditional labor is required. Therefore, in a transition starting from within the market economy, measures to compensate for this financial loss are required. These can consist, in part, of the *adjustment of wages* to compensate for job losses, along with the *shortening and sharing of the workweek* to also compensate.

The core societal attributes to be discussed for this exercise consist of (a) food production, (b) utilities, (c) basic good production and (d) transportation. Obviously, these fragments have a synergistic relationship, which require other types of technical evaluation. However, since these core attributes of our day-to-day lives are essentially what maintain our general health and basic standard of living, these abstractions should suffice for the sake of simple reasoning exemplification. It is also worth noting that the post-scarcity relationships denoted in each subject can be explored more so in the essay *Post-Scarcity Trends, Capacity and Efficiency.*

(a) Food Production:
The technology for high efficiency, automated food production is now a reality today, with vertical farm technology and low energy/low impact cultivation methods such as hydroponics, aquaponics and aeroponics. Desalinization processes, for example, could enable the building of these vertical farm facilities along most major coastlines, producing organic food in quantities to meet and exceed the needs of the regional population.

In short, if such advanced methods were implemented, the strategic abundance possibility reveals that the need to place restrictive monetary value on basic food resources is simply not required. There is no legitimate technical reason, even within an existing monetary economy, grocery stores today cannot provide the same produce resources to a given regional population, without the need for financial exchange. It is simply a matter of getting the advanced automated systems in place.

(b) Utilities:
The hydrocarbon economy today continues to cause a great deal of turmoil, not only on the environmental level but also due to the inevitable scarcity of the resources themselves. While the debate continues regarding "peak oil", there is no legitimate debate as to the fact that fossil fuels are essentially finite and its combustion is detrimental to the environment. Given the advanced state of renewable energy means such as solar, tide, wind, geothermal and the like, coupled with advanced localization means, there is no reason any of us would need to pay for energy if the system was properly designed. Advanced solar systems alone applied to every existing structure, even feeding excess energy back into a community's redundant base-load grid, would eliminate electricity needs immediately based on current statistics.

The same phenomenon also assists with natural gas and water utilities. Since electricity can be used to replace gas for heating and most other utility purposes, its use can simply be *designed out* in this context. Water, which is of a generally nominal financial expense today in the West, can be made dramatically more abundant via further industrial efficiency to recede pollution and maintain a regional surplus by strategic use. Those who do have water shortages in the world have had technical resolutions for years via desalinization and other purification systems, both on the large scale and small scale. It has been, again, the lack of financial resources that have caused the problems, not the lack of technical ability.

(c) Basic Good Production:
The spectrum of basic good production is wide, ranging from core staples such as household items, clothes and communication technology, to specific tools for specialized tasks, such as musical instruments and other increasingly less demanded items. The best way to think about this is as a "spectrum of demand", with daily needs on one side and specialized, or "luxury" type goods on the other.

While the advancement of automation technology will likely facilitate a vast amount of variation in production once the revolution in modular robotics and nanotechnology comes to fruition, for the sake of transition in the immediate future, we can think about industry in the more established context. Overall, each industry or sub-industry could be unified in operations to enable the highest level of production and output efficiency possible as a deliberate whole. In other words, the corporate structures would combine based on genre or sector, using that collaborative capacity to increase efficiency, while reducing waste and competitive multiplicity. This would set the stage for the creation of a fully synergistic industrial system, applying advanced, ideally simplifying automation processes liberally at every turn to remove human labor and inevitably increase efficiency.

In this, primitive versions of the Collaborative Design System, as described at length in the essay *The Industrial Government*, could also gain traction. While certain limitations would occur given the absence of larger order cooperation, the inching in of this process would set the stage for larger incorporation while also increasing sustainability.

Now, returning to the prior point about *compensation* for the loss of paid work hours, the loss of sales naturally means a loss of growth and hence a loss of jobs. In the current model, this is structurally a negative thing, of course. However, in this hypothetical transition proposal, wages would shift in proportion to the resulting job losses and/or with the shifting of workday hours. In other words, assuming an initial average work day need of 8 hours per person, incurring a loss of jobs by 50% due to the application of automation and new levels of technical efficiency, the work day would then be cut by 50% and spread across the existing workforce, keeping everyone employed but for a shorter period.

So, if we had a hypothetical economy with 1000 people and 50% of them were displaced by this deliberate *technological unemployment,* the workday is then divided between them so everyone now works only 4 hours, instead of 8. Again, the fact that these goods and services are becoming free in the economy means that there is less of a need for prior levels of purchasing power. Therefore a 50% cut in wages is calculated to be directly compensated for. Overall, we are phasing the monetary system out in this process. In cases where this isn't feasible, there would be an increase in hourly wage rates in the same basic proportion, compensating for the average losses incurred. In theory, this hourly reduction of the total workforce, assuming 100% employment through these standards, coupled with the compensating increase in now free resources, would fluidly move the society out of the labor market over time. Again, this is the abstract hypothetical.

(d)Transportation:
The next social staple is transportation. The production of vehicles, which is already largely automated today, is one consideration and this isn't much of a problem to perfect. This issue here is access, application and necessity. Of course, this thought exercise could be quite elaborate. If we were to calculate the vast amount of energy and resources used on a daily basis today for all of us to travel to centralized offices, usually participating in occupations with questionable relevance in the broad view, we would be amazed at the inefficiency apparent on the whole. While there are certainly exceptions, there are very few occupations today that really require direct location interaction anymore, given the vast power of the Internet and such communication tools. Even industrial production facilities, once further automated, would only require a small number

of people on location, with most processes administered remotely.

So, with a strategic move to simply stop from wasteful 9-5, 5 day workweek, traditional travel to work and back would create a great alleviation of pressure on many levels. Having everyone equipped by whatever means needed to operate their business function from their homes is a logical and sustainable idea for energy reduction, reduced accidents, reduced pollution, reduced stress and the like.

Beyond that, as far as infrastructure, systems of sharing, such as the currently existing rental street bicycles and the like, should be applied to vehicles (and everything else we can), coupled with the liberal incorporation of mass transit. This, again, is to be a step-by-step process of improvement where different regions are purposefully reorganized to favor the highest level of technical travel efficiency possible.

In short, localizing labor locations/remote access to limit travel needs, coupled with sharing systems for vehicles and liberal mass transit, would profoundly change the nature of transport infrastructure, easing into the foundation of a NLRBE, even if some of those services still need money to pay for them.

Scenario Two: The Real World
Now, with the following truncated yet logically purposeful train of thought towards a hypothetical break down the current system and a systematic implementation of attributes of the new one in mind, let's now take a *realistic* look at what a transition to this new society may hold given the complex and dichotomous reality we endure today.

It's first important to understand that the intention of social and environmental sustainability has been developing under the surface of culture for a long time. For example, the now common notion of the "green" economy, which is being pushed forward by environmentalists, coupled with periodic outbursts by civil rights groups such as Occupy Wall Street, reveals a deep seeded interest to aspire for a world that is more equal, humane and sustainable. While our current social system, as argued, often reinforces the opposite of those values, it still seems that deep down most of our core historical philosophies still suggest an interest in social equality and sustainable balance.

So again, it is important to acknowledge that in order to really create a more sustainable, humane world, a *complete move* out of the current social architecture is required. Otherwise the same basic problems will persist, even if reduced to some degree by half-measures. To do this, global social movement tactics become critical to put *pressure* on the existing system, along with helping change the intents and values of the culture itself by vast education and communication projects.

However, before such ideas are addressed, it is worth revisiting the issue of "societal collapse", this time in the context of what we could term *eco-bio-social pressures.* A backdrop to our cultural evolution are pressures that can take both a positive and negative form. Positive pressures of this nature could include the development and expression of life-advancing technologies where the viewing public is so impressed by the possibilities, the social demand for that feature or implementation becomes unwavering.

On the other side are the negative pressures, such as the dramatic failure of a social edifice that shocks the culture and creates unease, loss of confidence and a dire interest in problem resolution by new methods. Given the prior section on societal problems we can logically expect as the current model grinds along, that these negative pressures are bound to help facilitate new incentives toward change. Of course, this is out of the control of TZM and at no point does TZM promote furthering any harm upon anyone. TZM focuses on positive pressure influence in its activist work, showing the world what can be done through education and think tank projects. Yet, TZM does not deny the existence of these other emerging negative pressures and acknowledges them also as a form of mobilizing incentive.

It is also important to note that so-called "societal collapse" is not an absolute distinction. It is relative. In general day-to-day operations, specifically in the West, one typically does not look around and deem the society as being in a state of "breakdown". This is because most people have simply become accustomed to the pollution, cancer, debt, homelessness, depletion, poverty, wars, uprisings, periodic financial crises, unemployment and other inefficiencies. It isn't as though one day everyone wakes up and finds the whole world suffering or dead in the streets. Societal collapse, or system failure, is a process and the real question is actually how bad are we prepared for it to become before we act to change it.

In truth, all systems change and while such a process of failure is a very negative thing in the short-term, it is also ultimately a natural consequence of cultural evolution. Problems can lead to creativity and creativity leads to new solutions, if we are willing to move on. At any rate, with these eco-bio-social pressures apparent, coupled with a basic understanding of how a step-by-step transition could unfold (scenario one), let's now talk about *transitional activism.* The goal here is to not only facilitate a move to the new model, but to also work to *help* those suffering in the current model, basically bringing them in first in this process of transition. This is done by creating *parallel systems,* which do not use money but still provide helpful services to people.

With growing technological unemployment and most governments and corporations still looking the other way for as long as they can, creating solutions to ease this stress on the population, coupled with removing support for the current system, is a win-win goal. For example, the use of mutual credit systems[873] or "time banks", facilitate a kind of non-currency transactions, often based upon labor only. While taxation of these transactions apply in some countries, this

---

873 Reference: *New Money for Healthy Communities*
(http://www.ratical.org/many_worlds/cc/NMfHC/chp12.html)

system is able to bypass money overall (i.e. for those who have skills but are poor), along with reducing overall financial circulation (as a means of protest and transition).

A mutual credit system is a form of barter for services or goods, which allow non-monetary exchange values to be applied to other goods and services, removing the 1:1 good to good correlation common to simple barter. LETS[874] is an example. It assists an interest free, non-inflationary form of exchange where value cannot float or fluctuate, as it does today, among many other positives. In the case of the "time bank", it is based on the prior work of the person, in effect. There are a number of variations of these kinds of systems and they are becoming ever more sophisticated in their programming and malleability.

Another tactic, which has a similar effect, is the use of *community sharing systems*. TZM Toronto, for example, has a tool sharing network where basic tools exist in a facility, like a library, and one can check out these tools in rotation, as needed.[875] As minor as this may seem, it is easy to see how this library concept could extend greatly in a community, such as with automobiles and other items used more sparsely. Again, this would help those who didn't have a means of access, along with removing growth pressure for the economic system. It would also be more environmentally friendly and sustainable, needless to say.

Likewise, more traditional social policy influencing methods, such as mass online petitions and other such acts are to be viewed as minor in effect but still relevant for awareness. TZM does not endorse physical protest in the sense of piling into a parking lot and yelling at buildings as an effective means of social change, but it does not dismiss them either as such activities can draw attention toward a given issue to some degree. Likewise, petitions have been ubiquitous in the world today, along with working to influence political officials by also publicly challenging them in the purview of news media. These are other such expressions that come down to one's creativity, courage and personal interests.

However, there is one specific political lobbying proposal worth mentioning that has been around for a long time. While not a long-term solution in and of itself, its implementation would at least generate improved public health and eliminate general poverty. It is called a "guaranteed" or "unconditional income" system. This simply means people are given basic life-supporting funds each year to meet basic needs, with no one left behind. In late 2013, activist groups in Switzerland were pushing very hard to implement this idea.[876]

---

874 Reference: *The LETSystem Design Manual* (http://www.gmlets.u-net.com/design/home.html)

875 Reference: *Toronto's first Tool Library gears up to open in Parkdale* (http://www.thestar.com/news/gta/2013/02/05/torontos_first_tool_library_gears_up_to_open_in_parkdale.html)

876 Reference: *Switzerland's Proposal to Pay People for Being Alive* (http://www.nytimes.com/2013/11/17/magazine/switzerlands-proposal-to-

Now, all that aside, TZM's most important activist initiatives are the ever emerging think tank style projects, which literally can work to show a better way. R. Buckminster Fuller once stated "You never change things by fighting the existing reality. To change something, build a new model that makes the existing model obsolete". This is the transitional motto of TZM as well.

As will be expressed in the essay "Becoming The Zeitgeist Movement", apart from general awareness events, think tank projects that can literally start to *build* the new social model, both physically and in its programming for sustainably and efficiency, is perhaps by far the most profound method of activism. The digital revolution has taken the complexity and arduous development process of industrial design and provided the option to virtually represent most any physical idea for the sake of communication. Likewise, while the *Collaborative Design System* noted prior may not be in existence today, there is no reason programming for it cannot be created now, even if it is to merely exist as an over simplified "mock-up".

Likewise, the Global Redesign Institute, which is a macro-industrial design interface designed to enable anyone to think about the logic of redesigning the topographical layout of Earth, is another idea. In the end, the range of possibilities to *virtually create* almost exactly what TZM speaks of is becoming more possible and this has powerful communication potential. We can imagine, after these developments occur, large-scale conferences that can be conducted in any given region, showing how much more efficient that region would be, if such technical system or designs were implemented.

The Lone Country Transition

Building on the prior paragraph, imagine a fairly small country with a vast range of natural resources (a possible realistic location could be a lush country in Latin America). It is some time in the future and technical progress has been continuing its phenomenon of doing "more with less". The result is such that known methods of industrial production now require fewer raw materials – to such an extent that if a well-organized, resource-rich country adapted strategically - there would be no need for imports or exports in that region. The country could be "off-the-grid", so to speak, in the context of globalization and international influence.

However, the leaders of this country really were not aware of this technical reality. So, one day a relative of one of the leaders finds his or herself at a TZM conference talking about those very design initiatives and advancements in production methods. This person notifies the leaders of the country and the government takes notice. This hypothetical government is perhaps impoverished, as many Latin American countries are, mostly due to international trade dealings, corruption, debt problems, unemployment problems and the like. This government, enlightened by what they have learned, decides to take

---

pay-people-for-being-alive.html?_r=0)

the initiative to incorporate a *localized* NLRBE, as best they can.

They understand that a true NLRBE is global, with a total Earthly resource management system. However, knowing this will not occur anytime soon in the current global climate, they calculate that with a number of adjustments, they can still utilize the model to a limited but powerful degree, solving most all of its country's material/financial woes. So, the country then adjusts its industrial methods in accord, creates a domestic sensor system and management network to understand its resources and keep equilibrium, fully digests the new industrial capacity to do more with less, also installing the sustainability and efficiency protocol algorithms inherent to the CDS - and they proceed with the new model in full force, literally *stopping all trade* with foreign nations, being self-contained and 100% sustainable in their region, once established.

After a period of this success, the world slowly begins to see the incredible result of their moneyless economy. The population, which had a very low standard of living prior, is elevated to an economic abundance they have never seen. It helps greatly that the people's values in that country consist of conservation and modest living, furthering balanced progress of the nation.

So, given this evidence of feasibility and fruitfulness, other adjacent nations begin to understand the vast merit of the new model and decide to take part. This process of *joining* expands the resource network greatly and the more it expands, the more other country's people also see the merit and the more they demand it, and so on. In time, the world unites.

Now, while this example might be over simplified, also clearly ignoring the international political pressures that most certainly would cause conflict, the reader should be able to understand that it is still a possibility. In truth, we don't really know what exactly will start such a move, but we do know that planting as many "seeds" of possibility as possible is the key, coupled with the increasingly negative eco-bio-social pressures that will appear to have no end in sight.

-BECOMING THE ZEITGEIST MOVEMENT-

Sometimes the slightest things change the directions of our lives, the merest breath of a circumstance, a random moment that connects like a meteorite striking the earth. Lives have swiveled and changed direction on the strength of a chance remark.[877]
-Bryce Courtenay

Responsibility
While on the surface the following proposition may seem like a mere poetic gesture, the truth of the matter is that it is absolutely true and inescapable. *We are all in The Zeitgeist Movement whether we like it or not.*

Everyday of our lives we make decisions in social and environmental contexts that create influence on the *wellbeing* and *perception* of others. It doesn't matter what one's political, religious or overall ideological disposition may be specifically; if you live on this planet you are influencing it and the cultures spawned from it. What this also means is that you are *responsible*. You are responsible for what you set in motion and hence responsible for state of the habitat and you are response for the balance or imbalance of the human species itself, to one degree or another.

Each act of empathy or indifference resonates with those who received those effects, and due to the basic, evolutionary laws of human adaption we adjust our expectations and propensities as we experience the environment around us. Naturally, early childhood is the most sensitive period to our species, as we try to figure out if this new world we have come into is safe and supportive or if the world is unsafe and indifferent. This type of *programming,* while established in early childhood most dominantly, still continues throughout our lives, and the effect it has on the larger order cultural perception is also profound.

Yet, while our capabilities are truly powerful, particularly when it comes to human society's recent capacity to build technological tools, which can change the societal construct rapidly, it is easy to forget that at the root core of this existence is a kind of *subservience* and acceptance of factors that we will never have control of. After millennia of confusion about the nature of our existence, inventing complex and ultimately false systems of belief as we cope with this confusion, the slow discovery of what are commonly termed the *laws of nature* have provided not only a means to create and invent, but to also understanding that we are actually *not in control* in many profound ways.

We appear to only be in control of how we relate to this existing rule structure and those natural law rules show no sign of changing. Our submission to this reality rests at the heart of the technical proposals made by The Zeitgeist Movement. It is merely a process of adaptation to better optimize human existence and create a

---

877 Source: goodreads.com (http://www.goodreads.com/quotes/tag/change?
page=2)

314

condition that improves our lives and allows for future generations to inhabit this planet without severe deficiency and a loss of sustainability. In truth, the human species today does not just share the world with itself and the habitat. It also shares it with the extended family of the species and the extended family of the other life inherent in the habit, generations into the future.

There has also been an eclipsing tendency for an idealized sense of self-importance. Traditional religions and such notions of being "created in the image of God" and other ideas tend to separate humans from the natural world, as though we are not to be "reduced" to some kind of mere artifact of nature. The great astronomer Carl Sagan perhaps best addressed this problem in his text *Pale Blue Dot:*

"The Earth is a very small stage in a vast cosmic arena. Think of the endless cruelties visited by the inhabitants of one corner of this pixel on the scarcely distinguishable inhabitants of some other corner, how frequent their misunderstandings, how eager they are to kill one another, how fervent their hatreds. Think of the rivers of blood spilled by all those generals and emperors so that, in glory and triumph, they could become the momentary masters of a fraction of a dot.

Our posturings, our imagined self-importance, the delusion that we have some privileged position in the Universe, are challenged by this point of pale light. Our planet is a lonely speck in the great enveloping cosmic dark. In our obscurity, in all this vastness, there is no hint that help will come from elsewhere to save us from ourselves."[878]

Of course, there is no denying that our capacity to think, create, problem solve and alter our world places us in a very unique rank with respect to the other species we share this habitat with. The human organism is so incredible in so many functional and adaptive ways, yet modern science has not even begun to understand how this ever-complex array of organs and chemistry is able to do what it does so well. In fact, our creativity is so powerful; we have been able to extend our mental and physical forms to include physical and computational possibilities that would otherwise be impossible. This is the true nature of our technological ingenuity.

A computer, a car, a phone, a table, a pencil or any other tool we may utilize, are not merely detached abstractions we engage in. They are extensions of ourselves in very real and direct ways, improving some type of function we wish to complete. As time moves on, the logic is clear that problem resolution can become ever more powerful, so much so that the social models we may embrace in one generation will be made obsolete in another generation. The desired transition from the competitive, market model of economics to a NLRBE is just such a move.

---

878 *Pale Blue Dot: A Vision of the Human Future in Space*, Carl Sagan, 1994

Roles & Projects

The Zeitgeist Movement is a global organization that has no papers to fill out or any formal acceptance process. One's interest in the proposals of TZM, coupled with some type of action to promote such change, is the only defining feature of a "member" and the degree of participation comes down to the comfort zone and ingenuity of the individual and/or groups they choose to be a part of. It is also important to point out that simply being a part of this community is, in many ways, a contribution to *transition* itself, as a changing of social values is critical to such a move, and this starts by generating a growing sub-culture that simply finds alignment with those values, even though the old, caustic social model is still in place.

More specifically, getting involved invariably means trying to raise awareness in the community, while ideally contributing to development projects. The range of activist possibilities can be as simple as an isolated person online working to post relevant data to target audiences in places such as forums, media sites, social networks and the like, while the others may take a more detailed approach and contribute to design and programming projects that can serve to facilitate the actual mechanics of the system proposed.

Three such developing projects are the (a) Global Redesign Institute or GRI; (b) the Localized Solutions Project or LSP; (c) and the Collaborative Design System or CDS.

(a) GRI is an online collaborative interface that functions in a similar manner of public contribution as Wikipedia does, except with a much higher degree of logical assessment and minus much of the semantic problems that arise with an encyclopedia. The purpose is to redesign the surface of Earth, graphically and mathematically, region by region, based upon the most advanced principles of sustainability and efficiency. This *systems theory* oriented approach does not observe human contrivances and artificial limitations such as countries, property rights and other inhibiting factors existing today.

The best way to think about it is as a *macro-industrial* design initiative, which removes all topographical and infrastructural attributes of modern society, working to replace them with more optimized means. The goal is to virtually implement a NLRBE in the largest scale theoretical way. Of course, many hear such a proposal, coupled with the understanding that this is an open access project and anyone on the planet can contribute, might conclude that the vastness of subjective human opinion on such a matter would make settling on such a design impossible.

This is actually not the case when the scientific method is brought into play. While the *localized* technology (more on this in the LSP section) will always change over time, since that is the nature of it as things technically improve, the basic topographical reasoning will change far less. More specifically, the manner by which these "macro" decisions are arrived at would have a direct relationship to the *characteristics* of any given area, coupled with the logical reasoning inherent to the networks that emerge to synergistically connect social functionality.

For example, different terrains have different propensities for settlement, while the location of renewable energy sources demands that harvesting exist in certain places. If production of a particular genre of goods requires certain materials and those materials happen to be local, it is logical to construct production facilities as close as possible to the extraction source. Likewise, any other attributes of the supply chain are best allocated using the same logic, including the means of distribution. Distribution centers, would naturally be close to large city centers where the population has easy access within short distances. Furthermore, the creation of parks, recreation and the like becomes self-evident as well, finding conducive placement in areas that fit such a given profile, such as large flat expanses for games and the like.

In short, this process of logically deducing topographical placement to maximize efficiency and sustainability is a technical process overall. This isn't to say one can "push a button" and the entirety of a given region can be deduced automatically with no human consensus or interfering values. Rather, it is to say that what we have in the world today, with the wasteful, market-derived practices of international markets, globalization and other inefficiencies, is deeply misaligned. Through this basic *natural law reasoning*, we can further create ease, safety, and abundance and hence increase our quality of life, while reducing our environmental footprint dramatically.

As far as communication and education, which are ultimately the points of any such project, in part, the task once a certain area has been "updated" is to then show the world what has been made possible. The statistics that would accompany these end design proposals would likely relay mathematically derived feedback, such as how much less energy and fewer resources are being used; the overall ecological footprint reduction; the ease of transport; the efficient increase in production and distribution; the statistical creation of a material abundance based on population, and so forth.

(b) The Localized Solutions Project or LSP can be thought about as a *micro-industrial* initiative, as compared to the "macro" one just discussed with the GRI. This is simply a good design project where people can think about smaller order systems that could be a part of the larger order, "macro" context.

For example, a house design that is lightweight, off-the-grid and easily constructed or prefabricated out of Earth friendly and abundant materials, could be one such project. Once such a design is found to be most versatile, sustainable and optimized by the community through the online collaborative system, it can then go into a database for both general reference and even incorporation in the

GRI as a *sub-system*.[879]

(c) Likewise related to the LSP, the CDS or Collaborative Design System, is a programming project that would seek to produce the actual regulatory and network aware source code that facilitates the process discussed in the essay "The Industrial Government". This system could be coded in the exact same, open source and open access manner by which the prior two projects are, utilizing the group mind and the scientific method to help maximize potential.

As a communication tool, this project would not have to be "complete" to be effective. Even if only a small set of parameters were utilized that relay the calculation of a theoretical design evaluation, the educational value alone has great potential. In time, primitive versions of the CDS could be directly incorporated into the LSP and GRI, since they are connected in purpose. Such expressions could be demonstrated at movement conferences.

Chapters and Events

A TZM activist almost always has a relationship to a regional *chapter*. As of 2014 there are many chapters across dozens of countries. A chapter can be a few people or thousands, and those in regions currently without local chapters are encouraged to start one. It is a very easy process and the time commitment needed comes down to the degree of dedication and one's time availability.[880]

Chapters are organized by local and international tiers. For example, there is national chapter coordination for the entire United States, while each US state has its own chapter (or "sub-chapter"). Likewise, each city in any given state can also have its own chapter. This network creates a multi-dimensional information flow and while it may appear hierarchical, the ethic of the movement is not a top-down power system. Chapters often hold *meetings* about their work in each tier and the ideas talked about are brought up the chain as much and they are brought down the chain.

As far as *events,* since the inception of TZM in 2008, certain periodic events have emerged as staples of the movement, with two occurring annually. These two are called "Zeitgeist Day" (or "ZDay") and the Zeitgeist Media Festival. 2013, for example, marked the fifth annual ZDay and the third annual Media Festival. ZDay is the movement's flagship public awareness event, which is intellectually driven, describing progress in the movement and expanding relevant research. It is also a public media activism event, always trying to entice media outlets to cover it in order to further spread awareness of TZM's mission.

---

879 In many ways, this process of design and evaluation is a crude, manual version of the algorithmic system proposed in the essay *The Industrial Government*

880 Those interested in *chapters* or are new to TZM participation are encouraged to review the "Chapters Guide" and "Quickstart Guide" on the global website, www.thezeitgeistmovement.com

In contrast, the Zeitgeist Media Festival is a multi-media arts event, which works to bypass the intellectual side and use art for the sake of personal transformation. The arts have an emotional and experimental capacity to inspire change and generate new ideas and TZM views the arts as an underpinning of scientific development itself. This event is also a means to express the creative and exciting capacity and potential of the human condition and to remind ourselves that we should also *celebrate* humanity, as we work to improve it.

Each of these events has the same basic format. There is a *main event* and there are *sympathetic* chapter events. In the case of ZDay, the "global main event" tends to focus on the most dominant global issues and projects for the movement each year, usually featuring well-known speakers and contributors to the movement. Mirrored sympathetic events, which are regionally targeted, occur the same day or weekend around the world via the chapters. In 2009, for example, there were over 400 sympathetic events, along with the main event in New York City.[881] Likewise, very often chapters conduct food and resource charity drives for the suffering in their community.[882]

Other events, such a *townhalls*, which can be monthly or bi-monthly, are also common. It is up to a given group/chapters to decide the frequency of these public meetings.[883] Beyond these core ideas, many other possibilities are out there and it is, again, up to any chapter to be creative in how it conducts its activism.

Mission Statement
In conclusion, the official mission statement of TZM will be stated in full.

Founded in 2008, The Zeitgeist Movement is a *sustainability advocacy organization,* which conducts community based activism and awareness actions through a network of global/regional chapters, project teams, annual events, media and charity work.

The movement's principle focus includes the recognition that the majority of the social problems that plague the human species at this time are not the sole result of some institutional corruption, absolute scarcity, a political policy, a flaw of "human nature" or other commonly held assumptions of causality. Rather, the movement recognizes that issues such as poverty, corruption, pollution, homelessness, war, starvation and the like appear to be "symptoms" born out of an *outdated social structure.*

While intermediate reform steps and temporal community support are of interest to the movement, the defining goal is the installation of a new socioeconomic model based upon technically responsible resource management, allocation and design through what

---

881 Source: ZDayGlobal.org (http://zdayglobal.org/)
882 The inaugural 2011 Media Festival main event in Los Angeles raised enough food to provide 12,000 meals.
883 Reference: *TZM Events* (http://thezeitgeistmovement.com/tzm-events-townhalls)

would be considered *the scientific method* of reasoning problems and finding optimized solutions.

This "Natural Law/Resource-Based Economy" (NLRBE) is about taking a direct technical approach to social management as opposed to a monetary or even political one. It is about updating the workings of society to the most advanced and proven methods known, leaving behind the damaging consequences and limiting inhibitions that are generated by our current system of monetary exchange, profit, business and other structural and motivational issues.

The movement is loyal to a *train of thought*, not figures or institutions. The view held is that through the use of socially targeted research and tested understandings in science and technology, we are now able to logically arrive at societal applications that could be profoundly more effective in meeting the needs of the human population, increasing public health. There is little reason to assume war, poverty, most crime and many other monetarily-based scarcity effects common in our current model cannot be resolved over time. The range of the movement's activism and awareness campaigns extend from short to long term, with methods based explicitly on non-violent methods of communication.

The Zeitgeist Movement has no allegiance to country or traditional political platforms. It views the world as a single system and the human species as a single family and recognizes that all countries must disarm and learn to share resources and ideas if we expect to survive in the long run. Hence, the solutions arrived at and promoted are in the interest to help *everyone* on Earth, not a select group.[884]

Join us:
www.thezeitgeistmovement.com

---

884 Source: *Mission Statement* (http://thezeitgeistmovement.com/mission-statement)

83589475R00178

Made in the USA
Columbia, SC
11 December 2017